DARRAGH

GW00789964

NEW EXPLORATIONS

COMPLETE LEAVING CERTIFICATE POETRY
FOR EXAMINATION IN **2015 AND ONWARDS**

EDITED BY JOHN G. FAHY
CONTRIBUTORS: JOHN G. FAHY, CAROLE SCULLY,
BERNARD CONNOLLY, MARIE DUNNE, ANN HYLAND, SEAN SCULLY
AND MARTIN WALLACE.

Gill & Macmillan

Gill & Macmillan
Hume Avenue
Park West
Dublin 12

www.gillmacmillan.ie
© John G. Fahy, Carole Scully, Bernard Connolly, Marie Dunne, Ann Hyland, Sean Scully
and Martin Wallace 2013
978 07171 5570 5

Design by Tanya M Ross, Elementinc.ie

The paper used in this book is made from the wood pulp of managed forests.
For every tree felled, at least one tree is planted, thereby renewing natural resources.

For permission to reproduce photographs, the authors and publisher gratefully acknowledge the following:

© Alamy: 1, 13, 16, 35, 42, 44, 47, 49, 51, 66, 79, 92, 107TL, 107TR, 107BL, 107BR, 129, 146, 148, 152, 154, 166,
175, 192, 214, 249, 258, 284, 296, 301, 324R, 331, 353, 356, 380, 394, 407, 409, 415, 422, 436, 451, 199, 510,
515, 534, 540; © Bridgeman Art Library: 89, 115, 189; © Bridgeman Art Library / Staatsgalerie Stuttgart/
© DACS 2013: 179; © Collins: 333, 388; © Corbis: 46, 64, 76, 87, 271; © Crawford Art Gallery, Cork:
519; © Elizabeth Bishop / Alice Helen Methfessel: 205, 210; © Getty Images: 5, 19, 21, 23, 30, 73, 84, 149,
160, 169, 199, 225, 232, 236, 241, 245, 247, 253, 267, 278, 289, 293, 327, 337, 346, 351, 361, 400, 404, 412,
424, 427, 430, 432, 440, 444, 454, 466, 469, 473, 476, 486, 493, 496, 502, 504, 512, 521, 527, 531, 537, 543;
© Imagefile: 116, 221, 317, 324L, 342; © Irish Times: 355, 445; © Keats-Shelley Memorial House, Rome/
Christopher Warde-Jones: 39; © Mary Evans Picture Library: 104; © National Library of Ireland: 140, 419;
© Press Association: 458; © Rex Features: 276; © RTÉ Stills Library: 300; © Topfoto: 196, 223; Courtesy
of Wikimedia: 321.

The authors and publisher have made every effort to trace all copyright holders, but if any has been
inadvertently overlooked we would be pleased to make the necessary arrangement at the first opportunity.

Course Overview

Auden, W.H
Funeral Blues

Bryce, Colette
Self-Portrait in the Dark (with Cigarette)

Delanty, Greg
After Viewing, *The Bowling Match at Castlemary, Cloyne, 1847*

Dickinson, Emily
I felt a Funeral, in my Brain
I Heard a fly buzz – when I died

Donne, John
The Flea
Song: Go, and catch a falling star

Duffy, Carol Ann
Valentine

Frost, Robert
The Tuft of Flowers
Mending Wall
'Out, Out—'

Hardie, Kerry
Daniel's Duck

Hardy, Thomas
The Darkling Thrush
During Wind and Rain

Herbert, George
The Collar

Hughes, Ted
The Stag

Kennelly, Brendan
A Glimpse of Starlings

Levertov, Denise
An Arrival (North Wales, 1897) [xxx]

Explorations

Lochhead, Liz
Revelation

Montague, John
The Cage
The Locket
Like Dolmens Round My Childhood

Morgan, Edwin
Strawberries

Muldoon, Paul
Anseo

Murphy, Richard
Moonshine

Ní Chuilleanáin, Eiléan
Street
The Bend in the Road
To Niall Woods and Xenya Ostrovskaia, married in Dublin on 9 September 2009

O'Callaghan, Julie
The Net

Plath, Sylvia
Poppies in July
Child
The Arrival of the Bee Box

Shuttle, Penelope
Jungian Cows

Wall, William
Ghost Estate

Yeats, William Butler
The Wild Swans at Coole
An Irish Airman Foresees His Death

Bishop, Elizabeth
  The Fish
  The Prodigal
  Filling Sation

Boland, Eavan
  Child of Our Time
  This Moment
  Love

Bryce, Colette
  Self-Portrait in the Dark (with Cigarette)

Donne, John
  The Flea
  Song: Go, and catch a falling star

Durcan, Paul
  Wife Who Smashed Television Gets Jail
  Parents
  Sport

Eliot, Thomas Stearns
  Preludes
  Aunt Helen

Gallagher, Tess
  The Hug

Hardie, Kerry
  Daniel's Duck

Hopkins, Gerard Manley
  Spring
  Inversnaid

Keats, John
  On First Looking into Chapman's Homer
  La Belle Dame Sans Merci

Kennelly, Brendan
  Night Drive

Lochhead, Liz
  Revelation

Longley, Michael
  Badger

Milton, John
  When I consider how my light is spent

Muldoon, Paul
  Anseo

O'Callaghan, Julie
  Problems

O'Reilly, Caitriona
  Interlude

Perry, Paul
  River of Light

Piercy, Marge
  Will we work together?

Plath, Sylvia
  Poppies in July
  Child
  The Arrival of the Bee Box

Sirr, Peter
  Madly Singing in the City

Soto, Gary
  Oranges

Stafford, William
  Travelling Through the Dark

Woods, Joseph
  Letting the Cat out of the Bag

Beer, Patricia
  The Voice

Boland, Eavan
  Child of Our Time
  This Moment
  Love

Coady, Michael
  New World

Duffy, Carol Ann
  Valentine

Durcan, Paul
  Wife Who Smashed Television Gets Jail
  Parents
  Sport

Frost, Robert
  The Tuft of Flowers
  Mending Wall
  'Out, Out —'

Harrison, Tony
  Book Ends I

Herbert, George
  The Collar

Hopkins, Gerard Manley
  Spring
  Inversnaid

Hughes, Ted
  Hawk Roosting

Keats, John
  On First Looking into Chapman's Homer
  La Belle Dame Sans Merci

Kennelly, Brendan
  Night Drive

Larkin, Philip
  Ambulances
  The Explosion

Montague, John
  The Cage
  The Locket
  Like Dolmens Round My Childhood

Morrissey, Sinéad
  Genetics

Nemerov, Howard
  The Vacuum

Ní Chuilleanáin, Eiléan
  Street
  The Bend in the Road
  To Niall Woods and Xenya Ostrovskaia,
  married in Dublin on 9 September 2009

O'Callaghan, Julie
  The Net

Piercy, Marge
  Will we work together?

Shuttle, Penelope
  Zoo Morning

Wheatley, David
  Chronicle

Williams, William Carlos
  This is just to say

Woods, Macdara
  Fire and Snow and Carnevale

Wyley, Enda
  Poems for Breakfast

New Explorations CDs

Critical Notes CD (CD 1)

CD 1 contains detailed Critical Notes on all the prescribed poems for Higher and Ordinary Level English for students sitting the Leaving Certificate examination in 2015 and onwards.

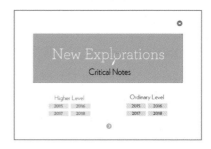

TO ACCESS THE CONTENT ON THE CD-ROM:

Windows

1. When the CD is inserted, you should get a prompt to open the folder and view files.

2. Once you have opened the folder you should see the pdf file for the Critical Notes.

3. Double click the pdf file to open.

Mac OS X

1. Once you insert the CD, open the Finder window.

2. From there click on the CD icon under Devices and view the files.

3. Double click the pdf file to open.

Note: For both Windows and Mac operating systems you may need to install the most recent version of Adobe Reader.

Track listing for audio CD (CD 2)

John Montague: Track 1 Killing the Pig, Track 2 The Locket, Track 3 The Cage, Track 4 Like Dolmens Round My Childhood; **Eiléan Ní Chuilleanáin**: Track 5 The Bend in the Road, Track 6 To Niall Woods and Xenya Ostrovskaia, Track 7 Street, Track 8 On Lacking the Killer Instinct, Track 9 Deaths and Engines, Track 10 Translation, Track 11 Following, Track 12 All for You, Track 13 Lucina Schynning in Silence of the in the Nicht; **Eavan Boland**: Track 14 Child of Our Time, Track 15 Outside History, Track 16 This Moment, Track 17 Love, Track 18 The Pomegranate; **Paul Durcan**: Track 19 Nessa, Track 20 The Difficulty That Is Marriage, Track 21 Wife Who Smashed Television Gets Jail, Track 22 En Famille, 1979, Track 23 'Windfall', 8 Parnell Hill, Cork, Track 24 Six Nuns Die in Convent Inferno, Track 25 Sport, Track 26 The Arnolfini Marriage, Track 27 Rosie Joyce, Track 28 The MacBride Dynasty; **Michael Longley**: Track 29 Badger; **Macdara Woods**: Track 30 Kavanagh in Umbria, Track 31 Fire and Snow and Carnevale; **Peter Sirr**: Track 32 Madly Singing in the City.

CONTENTS

John Donne

(1572–1631)

Prescribed for Higher Level exams in 2015 and 2017

John Donne was born in 1572 in Bread Street, London, into a prosperous Catholic family. However, Catholicism was banned by the Anglican Queen Elizabeth I. Many Catholics, including some of Donne's relatives, were either imprisoned or died for their faith. Up until the age of 12, Donne was educated at home by Catholic tutors. He then attended the University of Oxford. After university, he went to study law at Lincoln's Inn, London, where he discovered the pleasures of London life.

When he inherited a sum of money from his father, he spent some time travelling on the Continent, probably in Spain and France. Subsequently, he joined two expeditions, one to attack the Spanish port of Cadiz and the other to the Azores. On his return to England, he became personal secretary to a powerful courtier, Sir Thomas Egerton. At about this time, Donne decided to change to the Anglican religion. At the age of 30, he eloped with Ann More, Sir Thomas's 17-year-old niece, to the intense annoyance of her family. Donne lost his job and was unable to find another. For a long time, he had great difficulty supporting his ever-growing family. Ann had 12 pregnancies and seven of their children survived.

Donne began to write religious works and the king, James I, was so impressed that he persuaded Donne to become an Anglican priest. He became famous for his wonderful sermons, some of which are still read today, and was made a royal chaplain to the king. Donne died on 31 March 1631. He was buried in St Paul's Cathedral.

The Flea

This poem is also prescribed for Ordinary Level exams in 2015 and 2017

Mark but this flea, and mark in this,
How little that which thou deny'st me is;
Me it sucked first, and now sucks thee,
And in this flea, our two bloods mingled be;
Confess it, this cannot be said   5
A sin, or shame, or loss of maidenhead,
   Yet this enjoys before it woo,
    And pampered swells with one blood made of two,
    And this, alas, is more than we would do.

Oh stay, three lives in one flea spare,   10
Where we almost, nay more than married are.
This flea is you and I, and this
Our marriage bed, and marriage temple is;
Though parents grudge, and you, we are met,
And cloistered in these living walls of jet.   15
   Though use make you apt to kill me,
   Let not to this, self-murder added be,
    And sacrilege, three sins in killing three.

Cruel and sudden, hast thou since
Purpled thy nail, in blood of innocence?   20
In what could this flea guilty be,
Except in that drop which it sucked from thee?
Yet thou triumph'st, and say'st that thou
Find'st not thyself, nor me the weaker now;
   'Tis true, then learn how false, fears be;   25
   Just so much honour, when thou yield'st to me,
    Will waste, as this flea's death took life from thee.

Notes

6	**maidenhead:**	virginity
7	**woo:**	courts
11	**nay:**	even
16	**apt:**	have a tendency
17	**self-murder:**	suicide

Explorations

1.

a   Discuss your reaction to a flea appearing in a piece of poetry. Try to explain why you react in the way that you do. Does it have something to do with how you view poetry?

b   Consider what turns a passage of writing into a poem.

2.

a   Describe in your own words what happens to the flea in each of the three stanzas.

b   Are you amused or disgusted by these descriptions? Perhaps you have another reaction.

c   How would you react if you saw a real flea?

3.

a   Examine each stanza and discuss the way in which Donne uses the flea's fate to express his feelings.

b   How do you feel about this approach? Does it help you to understand more about Donne or is it simply confusing?

4.   Describe the situation in which Donne finds himself.

SECOND READING

5.   Can you suggest the tone of voice that should be used to read this poem? Which words in the poem indicate this tone to you?

6.   Choose two phrases from the poem that you found surprising, and discuss how Donne's use of language and imagery make them surprising.

7.   Look at Donne's attitude to love in this poem. In particular, consider lines 1–4, lines 12–13 and lines 25–7. What is your reaction to his view?

THIRD READING

8.

a   Do you think this poem succeeded in persuading Donne's beloved of his point of view?

b   Do you find it a persuasive piece of writing? Why or why not?

9.   During the 16th century, many bawdy love poems were written about the activities of fleas on the female body. Do you feel that Donne simply repeated this formula or did he take a more individual approach?

10.   One famous critic, Sir Arthur Quiller-Couch, described 'The Flea' as 'about the most merely disgusting in our language'. Would you agree or disagree with this statement? Refer closely to the text of the poem to support your answer.

Song: Go, and catch a falling star

This poem is also prescribed for Ordinary Level exams in 2015 and 2017

Go, and catch a falling star,
    Get with child a mandrake root,
Tell me, where all past years are,
    Or who cleft the Devil's foot,
Teach me to hear mermaids singing,   5
Or to keep off envy's stinging,
    And find
    What wind
Serves to advance an honest mind.

If thou be'est born to strange sights,   10
    Things invisible to see,
Ride ten thousand days and nights,
    Till age snow white hairs on thee,
Thou, when thou return'st, wilt tell me
All strange wonders that befell thee,   15
    And swear
    No where
Lives a woman true, and fair.

If thou find'st one, let me know,
    Such a pilgrimage were sweet,   20
Yet do not, I would not go,
    Though at next door we might meet,
Though she were true, when you met her,
And last, till you write your letter,
    Yet she   25
    Will be
False, ere I come, to two, or three.

Notes

2	**mandrake root:**	a poisonous plant believed to have human qualities
4	**cleft:**	split
15	**befell:**	happened to

Explorations

1.

a   List the tasks Donne describes in the three stanzas. Do they have anything in common?

b   Could you suggest a similar list of present-day tasks?

2.   What language does Donne use to give a magical or supernatural feeling to the poem? Why do you think he does this?

3.

a   In each stanza, Donne uses two very short lines (lines 7–8, 16–17 and 25–6). What effect does this have on the rhythm of the poem? You may find it helpful to read the poem aloud.

b   Discuss why Donne chose to use this structure.

4.

a   Each of the three stanzas seem to build up to the final line. Do the three final lines help you to understand the theme of this poem?

b   Can you explain the theme in your own words?

SECOND READING

5.   Examine two images from the poem that you feel are particularly effective. Explain how they achieve their effectiveness.

6.   Consider the feelings that Donne reveals in the following lines: 'And swear | No where | Lives a woman true, and fair.' What is your reaction to these lines?

7.   How would you describe the tone of this poem? Would you consider it to be the same throughout? Pay particular attention to lines 19–20.

THIRD READING

8.

a   In some manuscripts this poem appears in a group entitled 'Songs which were made to certain airs that were made before'. Would the effect of this poem be changed if it were sung?

b   Try making up a piece of music for the poem.

9.

a   Examine Donne's attitude to women in this poem and compare it to the one expressed in 'The Flea'. Discuss your findings.

John Donne

b   Based on this, how would you describe Donne as a person?

c   Try reading 'The Sun Rising', where Donne expresses another view about women.

10.

a   In the 16th century, listing impossible tasks in a poem was a popular device used for emphasis or hyperbole. Do you feel that this device is used successfully in 'Song: Go, and catch a falling star'?

b   What was Donne trying to emphasise?

The Sun Rising

Busy old fool, unruly sun, Why dost thou thus,
    Through windows, and through curtains call on us?
Must to thy motions lovers' seasons run?
Saucy pedantic wretch, go chide   5
    Late schoolboys, and sour prentices,
    Go tell court-huntsmen, that the King will ride,
    Call country ants to harvest offices;
    Love, all alike, no season knows, nor clime,
Nor hours, days, months, which are the rags of time.   10

Thy beams, so reverend, and strong
    Why shouldst thou think?
I could eclipse and cloud them with a wink,
But that I would not lose her sight so long:
    If her eyes have not blinded thine,   15
    Look, and tomorrow late, tell me,
    Whether both th'Indias of spice and mine
    Be where thou left'st them, or lie here with me.
Ask for those kings whom thou saw'st yesterday,
And thou shalt hear, All here in one bed lay.   20

She is all states, and all princes, I,
    Nothing else is.
Princes do but play us; compared to this,
All honour's mimic; all wealth alchemy.
    Thou sun art half as happy as we,   25
    In that the world's contracted thus;
    Thine age asks ease, and since thy duties be
    To warm the world, that's done in warming us.
Shine here to us, and thou art everywhere;
This bed thy centre is, these walls, thy sphere.   30

Notes

5	**pedantic:**	strictly adhering to formal rules
8	**offices:**	duties
9	**clime:**	climate
17	**mine:**	gold mines
24	**mimic:**	imitation
24	**alchemy:**	the science seeking to turn base metal into gold

Explorations

FIRST READING

1. Consider the various reactions you might feel on being awakened by the sunrise. Are any of these reactions echoed by Donne in the way he addresses the sun in the first eight lines of the poem?

2.

a Donne indicates the reason for his outburst in the first and second stanzas. Can you explain what it is?

b Do you have a certain sympathy for his feelings?

3.

a In the third stanza, Donne compares his situation to that of the sun. Is there a change in the tone he uses?

b Can you explain why this happens?

4. Discuss two images from the poem that you find particularly effective.

SECOND READING

5. Consider the various emotions that Donne expresses in the poem. Is there a dominant one?

6. Examine the language and imagery Donne uses to communicate the intensity of the love he feels. Does he persuade you of his sincerity?

7. Contrast the rhythm and sounds of lines 1–4 with those used in lines 27–30. How do they help to convey Donne's emotions?

THIRD READING

8.

a Discuss the way in which Donne uses concepts of time and space within the poem. Do you find them confusing or do they help you to understand Donne's mood?

b Would you agree with him that emotions can transcend the confines of time and space?

9. This poem is centred on the conceit of love and royalty. Trace the development of this conceit in the poem. Do you find it a successful connection of ideas or irritatingly clever?

10. Read 'The Flea' again. Which poem would you consider to be more realistic and vivid?

The Anniversarie

All kings, and all their favourites,
   All glory of honours, beauties, wits,
The sun itself, which makes times, as they pass,
Is elder by a year, now, than it was
When thou and I first one another saw: 5
All other things, to their destruction draw,
   Only our love hath no decay;
This, no tomorrow hath, nor yesterday,
Running it never runs from us away,
But truly keeps his first, last, everlasting day.   10

   Two graves must hide thine and my corse,
     If one might, death were no divorce,
Alas, as well as other princes, we,
(Who prince enough in one another be,)
Must leave at last in death, these eyes, and ears,   15
Oft fed with true oaths, and with sweet salt tears;
   But souls where nothing dwells but love
(All other thoughts being inmates) then shall prove
This, or a love increased there above,
When bodies to their graves, souls from their graves remove.   20

   And then we shall be thoroughly blessed,
     But we no more, than all the rest.
Here upon earth, we are kings, and none but we
Can be such kings, nor of such subjects be;
Who is so safe as we? where none can do   25
Treason to us, except one of us two.
   True and false fears let us refrain,
Let us love nobly, and live, and add again
Years and years unto years, till we attain
To write threescore, this is the second of our reign.   30

Notes

11	**corse:**	corpse
27	**refrain:**	avoid
30	**threescore:**	sixty

Explorations

1.

a   Do you find this poem immediately understandable or rather confusing?

b   Did you feel drawn into the poem on the first reading?

c   Is there any aspect of the poem that would encourage you to explore it further?

2.   The poem is entitled 'The Anniversarie'. Can you explain what type of anniversary Donne is writing about?

3.   Consider the way in which Donne conveys a sense of time passing in the poem. Do you find the images depressing?

4.   How does Donne describe the love he is celebrating in the poem?

5.   Can you express the theme of this poem in a few sentences?

SECOND READING

6.   How would you feel if you received this poem as a gift?

7.   Examine Donne's use of images connected with the royal court. Do you find them effective in helping you to understand Donne's feelings?

8.   Can you describe Donne's mood in the poem? Is it constant or can you detect changes as the poem progresses?

THIRD READING

9.   'True and false fears let us refrain, | Let us love nobly, and live, and add again | Years and years unto years, till we attain | To write threescore, this is the second of our reign.'

Do you find these lines convincing, coming as they do at the end of the poem? Does the poem successfully support this ending?

10.   Imagine that John Donne has asked you to read this poem and give him some advice on how, if necessary, it could be improved. Outline what you would say to him.

John Donne

Sweetest love, I do not go

Sweetest love, I do not go,
    For weariness of thee,
Nor in hope the world can show
    A fitter love for me;
     But since that I   5
Must die at last, 'tis best,
To use my self in jest
    Thus by feigned deaths to die.

Yesternight the sun went hence,
And yet is here today,   10

He hath no desire nor sense,
    Nor half so short a way:
     Then fear not me,
But believe that I shall make
Speedier journeys, since I take   15
    More wings and spurs than he.

O how feeble is man's power,
    That if good fortune fall,
Cannot add another hour,
    Nor a lost hour recall!   20
     But come bad chance,
And we join to it our strength,
And we teach it art and length,
    Itself o'er us to advance.

When thou sigh'st, thou sigh'st not wind,   25
    But sigh'st my soul away,
When thou weep'st, unkindly kind,
    My life's blood doth decay.
     It cannot be
That thou lov'st me, as thou say'st,   30
If in thine my life thou waste,
    Thou art the best of me.

Let not thy divining heart
    Forethink me any ill,
Destiny may take thy part,   35
    And may thy fears fulfil;

But think that we
Are but turned aside to sleep;
They who one another keep
Alive, ne'er parted be.   40

Notes

8	**feigned:**	pretended, simulated
33	**divining:**	intuitive

Explorations

FIRST READING

1. Describe the setting in which Donne places himself. Does the poem make it easy for you to imagine? Discuss the clues that helped you.

2. What tone of voice should be used to speak this poem? Can you choose some words or phrases that you feel indicate this tone?

3. Trace the ways that Donne attempts to reassure his beloved. Would you feel reassured by this poem?

4. What view does Donne convey of death? Why do you think he approaches it in this way?

SECOND READING

5. Consider the third stanza. Do you find it different in any way from the other stanzas of the poem? Discuss the part that it plays in the overall structure of the poem.

6. What age do you think Donne was when he wrote this poem? Do you learn anything about his personality? What evidence is there in the poem to support your views?

7. This poem is addressed to Donne's beloved. Do you feel that the emphasis is on Donne's own feelings or on those of his beloved? What does this tell you about their relationship?

THIRD READING

8. Discuss the rhythm and rhyme used in this poem. Do they add to the overall effect of the piece? Were you aware of them in your reading of the poem?

9. There are some indications that Donne intended this piece to be sung. What aspects of the poem support this? Could you suggest the type of music that might have been used? Would you react differently to the poem if it were a song?

10. Compare Donne's view of death in this poem with the one he communicates in 'The Anniversarie'. Consider the images and language used in each case. Do you think Donne was trying to achieve different effects? If so, why?

John Donne

A Valediction: Forbidding Mourning

As virtuous men pass mildly away,
   And whisper to their souls, to go,
Whilst some of their sad friends do say,
    The breath goes now, and some say, no:

So let us melt, and make no noise,   5
   No tear-floods, nor sigh-tempests move,
'Twere profanation of our joys
    To tell the laity our love.

Moving of th'earth brings harms and fears,
   Men reckon what it did and meant,   10
But trepidation of the spheres,
    Though greater far, is innocent.

Dull sublunary lovers' love
   (Whose soul is sense) cannot admit
Absence, because it doth remove   15
    Those things which elemented it.

But we by a love, so much refined,
   That our selves know not what it is,
Inter-assured of the mind,
   Care less, eyes, lips, and hands to miss.   20

Our two souls therefore, which are one,
   Though I must go, endure not yet
A breach, but an expansion,
   Like gold to aery thinness beat.

If they be two, they are two so   25
   As stiff twin compasses are two,
Thy soul the fixed foot, makes no show
    To move, but doth, if th'other do.

And though it in the centre sit,
   Yet when the other far doth roam,   30
It leans, and hearkens after it,
    And grows erect, as that comes home.

Such wilt thou be to me, who must
    Like th'other foot, obliquely run;
Thy firmness makes my circle just,
    And makes me end, where I begun.

Notes

	Valediction:	words used to bid farewell
7	**profanation:**	treat a sacred thing with irreverence
8	**laity:**	lay people
11	**trepidation:**	agitation, anxiety
13	**sublunary:**	earthly
16	**elemented:**	physically contributed to
19	**Inter-assured:**	mutually convinced
31	**hearkens:**	listens, yearns
34	**obliquely:**	slanting

John Donne

Explorations

1.

a   Describe the scene that Donne conveys in the first stanza. Do you find it an effective opening to the poem?

b   What are your expectations of the content of the rest of the poem?

2.

a   How does this opening scene lead into the second stanza?

b   What is the quality in the opening scene that Donne uses to illustrate the type of separation he desires?

c   Do you feel that this connection works?

3.   'No tear-floods, nor sigh-tempests move'.
Consider the connection between this line from the second stanza and the images in the third stanza.

4.   There is a similar connection between a line in the third stanza and the content of the fourth stanza; can you explain what it is? Is it now possible to trace Donne's line of thought through the first four stanzas?

SECOND READING

5.   In the fourth to the sixth stanzas, Donne assures his beloved that their love is special. Examine the language and images used to convey this. Do you find them persuasive?

6.   Donne compares himself and his beloved to a pair of compasses in the final three stanzas of the poem. Explain in your own words how this conceit

works. Consider the effectiveness of Donne's description of the compasses.

THIRD READING

7.   Dr Johnson was uncertain 'whether absurdity or ingenuity' underlay Donne's conceit of the lovers and the pair of compasses. Discuss which of the two you feel the conceit represents.

8.   What is your reaction to this poem? Did you find the line of thought confusing or did it lead you further into the poem? Were you irritated or fascinated?

9.

a   Do you feel that Donne became so interested in his intellectualising that he lost track of the emotional content of his poem?

b   On the other hand, does his intellectualising enable him to communicate a depth of emotion?

10. Compare this poem to 'Sweetest love, I do not go'. If you were Donne's beloved, which one would you prefer to receive? Support your decision by close reference to the two poems.

The Dreame

Dear love, for nothing less than thee
Would I have broke this happy dream,
     It was a theme
For reason, much too strong for phantasy,
Therefore thou waked'st me wisely; yet   5
My dream thou brok'st not, but continued'st it;
Thou art so true, that thoughts of thee suffice,
To make dreams truths, and fables histories;
Enter these arms, for since thou thought'st it best,
Not to dream all my dream, let's act the rest.   10

As lightning, or a taper's light,
Thine eyes, and not thy noise waked me;
     Yet I thought thee
(For thou lov'st truth) an angel, at first sight,
But when I saw thou saw'st my heart,   15
And knew'st my thoughts, beyond an angel's art,
When thou knew'st what I dreamed, when thou knew'st when
Excess of joy would wake me, and cam'st then,
I must confess, it could not choose but be
Profane, to think thee anything but thee.   20

Coming and staying showed thee, thee,
But rising makes me doubt, that now,
     Thou art not thou.
That love is weak, where fear's as strong as he;
'Tis not all spirit, pure, and brave,   25
If mixture it of fear, shame, honour, have.
Perchance as torches which must ready be,
Men light and put out, so thou deal'st with me,
Thou cam'st to kindle, goest to come; then I
Will dream that hope again, but else would die.   30

Notes

4	**reason:**	reality
7	**suffice:**	are enough
11	**taper:**	slim candle
20	**Profane:**	irreverent

John Donne

Explorations

FIRST READING

1.

a   How would you describe the tone of this poem?

b   Compare it with 'The Sun Rising', where Donne is also awakened. What factors contribute to the different tone used by Donne in each of the poems?

2.

a   Trace the narrative line of this poem. Do you feel that it is a convincing incident?

b   How does Donne make the situation seem real?

3.   Examine the language and images that Donne uses to describe his beloved. What do they convey about the quality of his love?

SECOND READING

4.   Consider the way in which Donne blends the states of waking and sleeping. Do you find it a successful evocation of a half-waking condition?

5.   Is this a particularly revealing poem? Consider how the language Donne uses contributes to the sense of sincerity.

6. The final four lines of the poem reveal an anxiety that underlies Donne's love poems, a doubt that he is able to attract true love. Would you agree or disagree with this statement?

7. Dryden held the view that Donne 'perplexes the minds of the fair sex with nice speculations of philosophy, when he should engage their hearts'. Discuss this statement with reference to this poem and two of the other love poems on the course.

8. 'Yet I thought thee | (For thou lov'st truth) an angel, at first sight'

   'This flea is you and I, and this | Our marriage bed, and marriage temple is'

   'And swear | No where | Lives a woman true, and fair.'

   'She is all states, and all princes, I, | Nothing else is.'

   Discuss which of these quotations, if any, reveals Donne's true view of love. Which would you like it to be? Why?

Batter my heart

Batter my heart, three-personed God; for, you
As yet but knock, breathe, shine, and seek to mend;
That I may rise, and stand, o'erthrow me, and bend
Your force, to break, blow, burn, and make me new.
I, like an usurped town, to another due,   5
Labour to admit you, but oh, to no end,
Reason your viceroy in me, me should defend,
But is captived, and proves weak or untrue.
Yet dearly I love you, and would be loved fain,
But am betrothed unto your enemy,   10
Divorce me, untie, or break that knot again,
Take me to you, imprison me, for I
Except you enthral me, never shall be free,
Nor ever chaste, except you ravish me.

Notes

5	**usurped:**	wrongfully seized
7	**viceroy:**	a ruler who exercises authority on behalf of a sovereign
9	**fain:**	gladly
13	**enthral:**	captivate, enslave
14	**ravish:**	rope, enrapture

John Donne

Explorations

1. Discuss your initial reaction to this poem. Are you surprised, shocked, overwhelmed? Perhaps you have another reaction?

2.

a Consider the actual appearance of this poem on the page. What are the differences in the visual impact of this poem and that of 'Song: Go, and catch a falling star'?

b Does the visual structure of these poems imply anything about their content?

3.

a Examine the language Donne uses to address God. Choose any words from the poem that you find particularly vivid.

b How does Donne use the actual sounds of the words to emphasise their effect? What tone of voice do they require?

SECOND READING

4. Trace the series of images that Donne uses to communicate his relationship with God. Are they what you would expect in a religious poem? Do they help you to understand Donne's feelings?

5.

a How does Donne convey his inability to commit totally to God? What is the attraction that pulls him away from God?

b Are you made to believe in his indecision?

6. Consider the rhyme scheme in the poem. How does Donne use it to add impact to his writing? Does it dominate or underpin the sense of emotion?

7. Why do you think Donne wrote this poem? What was he trying to do? Do you feel that it would have helped him?

8. 'Take me to you, imprison me, for I | Except you enthral me, never shall be free, | Nor ever chaste, except you ravish me.'

    Discuss the effect of Donne's use of paradox in these lines. Do you think this device helps to communicate the intensity of his feelings or does it simply get in the way?

9. Robert Graves felt that Donne's opening inspirations frequently wear out after two or three lines and that it is only his wit that moves him forward. Does he run out of steam in this poem? Does he move forward?

10. This poem is one of a group entitled *Divine Meditations*. Can you find evidence of either the 'Divine' or the 'Meditation' in it?

At the round earth's imagined corners

At the round earth's imagined corners, blow
Your trumpets, angels, and arise, arise
From death, you numberless infinities
Of souls, and to your scattered bodies go,
All whom the flood did, and fire shall o'erthrow,   5
All whom war, dearth, age, agues, tyrannies,
Despair, law, chance, hath slain, and you whose eyes,
Shall behold God, and never taste death's woe.
But let them sleep, Lord, and me mourn a space,
For, if above all these, my sins abound,   10
'Tis late to ask abundance of thy grace,
When we are there; here on this lowly ground,
Teach me how to repent; for that's as good
As if thou hadst sealed my pardon, with thy blood.

Notes

3	**infinities:**	infinite numbers
5	**o'erthrow:**	overthrow, conquer
6	**dearth:**	scarcity
6	**agues:**	fevers

John Donne

Explorations

1.

a   Do you feel that Donne wanted to lead you through this poem or sweep you along? Who was in charge, you or Donne?

b   What was your reaction when you had finished reading the poem?

2.   Examine the ways in which Donne communicates the drama of the Day of Judgement in the octet (lines 1–8) of this sonnet. Pay particular attention to the senses that he appeals to in his descriptions.

3.   What happens to the focus of the poem in the sestet (lines 9–14)? Is the change gradual or sudden? Were you taken by surprise or did you expect it?

SECOND READING

4.

a   How would you describe Donne's attitude towards the Day of Judgement?

b   Do you feel that this attitude remains constant or alters in the course of the poem?

c   What do you learn about Donne's emotional state from this?

5.

a   Examine the verbs that Donne uses. Do they help to convey the tone of the poem?

b   Are they reminiscent of any of Donne's other poems?

6.   What do you learn about Donne's relationship with (a) God and (b) his fellow men from this poem?

THIRD READING

7.   Consider the way in which Donne uses the sounds of words to add depth and pace to his writing. Do you feel that such attention to detail weakens or strengthens the emotional impact of the piece?

8.   Are you convinced of Donne's emotional sincerity or is this simply an intellectual exercise for him? Support your opinion by close reference to the poem.

9.

a   How do you feel about Donne, the man, as he is revealed in this poem? Would you like him as a friend?

b   Did you prefer the man who wrote the love poems? Are they two separate people or aspects of the same man?

10. The critic Mario Praz felt that Donne was more concerned with 'the whole effect' of his writing rather than a search for truth. Choose any three of Donne's poems and discuss this comment.

Thou hast made me

Thou hast made me, and shall thy work decay?
Repair me now, for now mine end doth haste,
I run to death, and death meets me as fast,
And all my pleasures are like yesterday,
I dare not move my dim eyes any way,   5
Despair behind, and death before doth cast
Such terror, and my feeble flesh doth waste
By sin in it, which it towards hell doth weigh;
Only thou art above, and when towards thee
By thy leave I can look, I rise again;   10
But our old subtle foe so tempteth me,
That not one hour I can myself sustain;
Thy Grace may wing me to prevent his art,
And thou like adamant draw mine iron heart.

Notes

14	**adamant:**	magnet

John Donne

Explorations

1. What age do you think Donne was when he wrote this poem? What words convey a sense of his physical condition?

2. Discuss the tone of voice that would be most suitable for this piece. Is there a connection between the sense of Donne's physical state and the tone of the poem?

3.

a   Psychologically, this poem reveals a great deal about the difficulties Donne faced with his religious faith. Can you trace how he communicates the intensity of his mental struggle?

b   Do you feel that this poem enabled him to arrive at a resolution?

SECOND READING

4. 'And all my pleasures are like yesterday'.
    How do you think the Donne of this poem felt about his earlier love poems?

5.

a   Donne assigns specific roles to God and to himself. Can you describe what these are?

b   Compare Donne's approach here with the one he takes in 'Batter my heart'. Is there a poignancy about Donne's role in this poem?

6. The final couplet (two rhyming lines) can be interpreted in different ways. Discuss what these might be and consider which one seems to be most fitting.

THIRD READING

7. Joan Bennett wrote, 'Metaphysical poetry is written by men for whom the light of day is God's shadow.' Consider Donne's religious poetry in the context of this statement.

8. Donne never intended his poetry for mass publication and during his life most of his works were circulated around a small circle of friends. Do you think that this gave him greater freedom to express himself or would he have felt more self-conscious? Refer to the poems you have explored.

9. 'Donne is adept at keeping the ball in the air.' (Robert Graves)

    'The wheels take fire from the mere rapidity of their motion.' (Coleridge)

    'The spell holds for the duration of the poem.' (Michael Schmidt)

    Was Donne simply a poetic trickster or did he truly create magic?

10. 'But when I saw thou saw'st my heart, | And knew'st my thoughts'.
    In the poems that you have explored, did you see Donne's heart and know his thoughts? Did Donne see your heart and know your thoughts? Discuss.

John Keats

(1795–1821)

Prescribed for Higher Level exams in 2017 and 2018

John Keats was born at Finsbury, near London, on 31 October 1795, the eldest child of Frances Jennings Keats and Thomas Keats, a livery-stable keeper. From 1803 to 1811 he attended Rev. John Clarke's school in an old Georgian country house at Enfield, north London. John Keats was a small boy (fully grown, he was only five feet tall), but he was athletic and liked sports, and though he had a quick temper, he was generally popular.

Clarke's was a liberal, progressive boarding school, which did not allow the flogging or 'fagging' (junior boys acting as servants to the older boys) common at the time. The pupils, who were mostly of middle-class background and destined for the professions, received a well-rounded education. They had their own garden plots to cultivate and interest in music and the visual arts was also encouraged, as well as the usual study of history, geography, arithmetic, grammar, French and Latin. Keats received a particularly good classical Latin education.

Keats left school in 1811 to begin an apprenticeship as a surgeon. This was then the manual side of the medical profession, involving bone-setting, tooth-pulling and amputation, and was considered socially inferior to becoming a physician, which would have entailed expensive university education. After some years as an apprentice, in 1815 Keats registered as a student at Guy's Hospital, London, and attended lectures in anatomy, physiology and chemistry.

In May 1816 the sonnet 'O Solitude' was the first of Keats's poems to be published. In June, Keats wrote 'To One Who Has Been Long in City Pent'. Later that year he composed 'On First Looking into Chapman's Homer'.

He qualified in July 1816 and was licensed to practise as a surgeon and apothecary, but by then he had developed an aversion to surgery (then performed without anaesthetic, in primitive conditions) and he devoted more of his time to writing poetry. His early poems reflect liberal attitudes and a rebellious outlook on life.

Keats began to express his ideas on poetry. He placed great value on the imagination, the importance of feelings and the central place of beauty in poetry.

Sometime in January or February 1818 Keats wrote 'When I have fears that I may cease to be', a sonnet dealing with three major concerns in his life – love, death and his poetry.

In September 1818 Keats met Fanny Brawne. She became the great love of his life and they were engaged in the autumn of 1819, which was an extraordinary year, the most productive of Keats's career. He was writing mature poems, sometimes dashing them off at great speed. In April 'La Belle Dame Sans Merci' was written. Between April and May the five great odes were written, also known as the Spring Odes: 'Ode to Psyche', 'Ode to a Nightingale', 'Ode on a Grecian Urn', 'Ode on Melancholy' and 'Ode on Indolence'. Keats's poetic reputation today chiefly rests on these.

In February 1820 Keats suffered a severe lung haemorrhage, the significance of which was apparent to him, as he wrote, 'I know the colour of blood; – it is arterial blood; – I cannot be deceived in that colour; – that drop of blood is my death-warrant.' Indeed, it was the beginning of the end. He spent that summer being cared for by, and falling out with, various friends, and eventually he ended up in the care of Fanny and her mother, who nursed him in their home.

He was advised to avoid the English winter and arrived in Rome in November to stay with friends. Though ably nursed, Keats deteriorated throughout the winter and he died on 23 February 1821, aged 25. He is buried in the Protestant cemetery in Rome, having requested as an inscription for his tombstone: *HERE LIES ONE WHOSE NAME WAS WRIT IN WATER.*

To One Who Has Been Long in City Pent

To one who has been long in city pent,
'Tis very sweet to look into the fair
And open face of heaven, – to breathe a prayer
Full in the smile of the blue firmament.
Who is more happy, when, with heart's content,   5
Fatigued he sinks into some pleasant lair
Of wavy grass, and reads a debonair
And gentle tale of love and languishment?
Returning home at evening, with an ear
Catching the notes of Philomel, – an eye   10
Watching the sailing cloudlet's bright career,
He mourns that day so soon has glided by:
E'en like the passage of an angel's tear
That falls through the clear ether silently.

[Handwritten annotations: "Trapped or lives in a city"; "See the open sky without building"; "embracing nature with a book"; "Daughter of king of Athens"; "a nightingale"; "area above the clouds"]

Notes

1	To one… :	the opening line echoes a line of Milton's: 'As one who long in populous city pent' (*Paradise Lost*, book IX, line 445)
1	pent:	confined, shut up in a small space
8	gentle tale:	presumed to be Leigh Hunt's *The Story of Rimini*, a retelling of a tragic love story from Dante's *Inferno*, which Keats was reading at that time
10	Philomel:	the nightingale from the classical myth of Philomela, who was turned into a nightingale

Explorations

FIRST READING

Examine the poem in two sections.

1. What do you see in the first section (the octave)? What words create this picture for you?

2. How does the speaker feel? What words or phrases suggest these feelings? Examine the connotations of these words. Is there any alteration in the mood?

3. Examine the speaker's mood in the sestet. What words, phrases or images suggest this mood?

SECOND READING

4. What ideas about nature and the lifestyle of human beings are implicit in this poem?

5. What is your reaction to the philosophy of this sonnet? Do you find it convincing? Do you think it should be read by students today?

THIRD READING

6. Examine this poem as an example of the sonnet form. Do you think it is a good sonnet?

His experience with poetry

On First Looking into Chapman's Homer

This poem is also prescribed for Ordinary Level exams in 2017 and 2018 *metpho-*

Much have I travell'd in the realms of gold, *He travelled compares*
  And many goodly states and kingdoms seen; *reading poem like visiting*
  Round many western islands have I been *a country*
Which bards in fealty to Apollo hold. *swore loyalty to apollo*
Oft of one wide expanse had I been told *often heard of some pla-*
  That deep-brow'd Homer ruled as his demesne; *of work that homer*
  Yet did I never breathe its pure serene *finally greek wrote*
Till I heard Chapman speak out loud and bold: *able to engage with*
Then felt I like some watcher of the skies *Simile*
  When a new planet swims into his ken;   10

John Keats

Or like stout Cortez when with eagle eyes
    He star'd at the Pacific – and all his men
Look'd at each other with a wild surmise –
    Silent, upon a peak in Darien.

men looked at each other amazed what they discovered

Notes

	Chapman:	George Chapman (1559–1634), a contemporary of Shakespeare, who wrote successful plays and translated Homer
	Homer:	Greek epic poet, author of *The Iliad* and *The Odyssey*
1	**realms of gold:**	presumably realms of the poetic imagination; possibly a reference to embossed gold leaf on book covers
3	**western islands:**	Britain and Ireland
4	**Apollo:**	the sun god, also the god of music and poetry, who could foretell the future
6	**demesne:**	dominion
7	**serene:**	air (from the Latin *serenum*, meaning 'clear sky')
9	**watcher of the skies:**	probably a reference to Herschel's discovery in 1781 of the planet Uranus
10	**ken:**	knowledge, range of vision, sight
11–14	**Cortez; Pacific:**	Keats had read about the conquest of America in J.M. Robertson's *History of America*. Balboa was in fact the first European to reach the Pacific; in recollection, Keats has confused Balboa's first sight of the Pacific with the amazement of Cortés's soldiers on seeing Mexico City.
14	**Darien:**	an older name for the Panama isthmus

Explorations

FIRST READING

1. Do you think the poet views his own life as an exploration, a journey? Where? How?

2.

a Do you think he is referring to a purely geographical exploration or has he something else in mind? Discuss this.

b What might 'realms of gold' refer to?

SECOND READING

3.

a The high point of Keats's experience was reading Chapman's translation of Homer. How does he feel?

b Examine the metaphorical comparisons he makes in order to convey his feelings. What is suggested by these?

4.

a How does Keats feel about the reading of poetry in general? Examine in particular the connotations of 'realms of gold', 'goodly states', 'wide expanse', 'deep-brow'd Homer', 'pure serene', 'watcher of the skies', 'wild surmise'.

b How does he communicate the sense of wonder experienced by readers?

5. Briefly explain the theme of this poem.

6. Read the poem aloud to experience its sonorous quality. What phrases or words make the greatest impression on your ear? Discuss the effects of these.

THIRD READING

7. The critic Brian Stone said that this poem demonstrates Keats's 'initial mastery of sonnet form'. Would you agree? Consider the poem as a sonnet and examine the following:

a The sense of unity – trace the development of thought in the poem.

b The volta, or change of tone or thought, in the sestet.

c The rhyming scheme of the Petrarchan sonnet – do you think this is effective or does it limit the choice of vocabulary and so produce a strain on the language? (Consider the bookish literary terms, such as 'demesne', 'serene', 'ken'.) Is this a fault?

d The factual error and the extra syllable in line 12 – would you consider these to be serious blemishes detracting from the perfection of the poem?

8. Do you find that this poem appeals equally to head and heart – in other words, that it has a good balance of thought and feeling, which gives it a sense of completeness? Discuss.

9. The poem celebrates 'not just the private enlightening encounter with Chapman's volume, but rather the human sense of awakening to awe-inspiring beauties and opportunities' (Cedric Watts). Discuss this statement with reference to the text.

When I Have Fears That I May Cease to Be

When I have fears that I may cease to be
   Before my pen has glean'd my teeming brain,
Before high piled books, in charactry,
   Hold like rich garners the full ripen'd grain;
When I behold, upon the night's starr'd face,   5
   Huge cloudy symbols of a high romance,
And think that I may never live to trace
   Their shadows, with the magic hand of chance;
And when I feel, fair creature of an hour,
   That I shall never look upon thee more,   10
Never have relish in the fairy power
   Of unreflecting love; – then on the shore

John Keats

Of the wide world I stand alone and think
Till love and fame to nothingness do sink.

- -

Notes

2	**teeming:**	stocked to overflowing, abundant, prolific
3	**charactry:**	print
4	**garners:**	storehouses for corn, granaries
9	**fair creature of an hour:**	the person referred to has not been identified

Explorations

BEFORE READING

1. Read only the title. What might you expect the poem to feature?

FIRST READING

2. What are the poet's main worries? How do they differ from your own projected fears?

3. What is his greatest fear?

4. What is your first impression of the poet's overall mood? What phrases or images seem to be important in this respect?

SECOND READING

5. Trace the poet's line of thought through each of the quatrains. What exactly is he saying?

6. Examine the images and metaphors that convey these ideas. Do you find them effective? Discuss.

7. What is your considered opinion of the critic Brian Stone's comment that 'its three quatrains are organically separate but logically successive'?

THIRD READING

8. What can we discern of Keats's views on the poetic process and the poet from this sonnet? Examine in particular lines 4, 6, 7–8, 10 and 12–13.

9. Comment on the notion of love featured here.

10. What aspects of this poem, either of theme or presentation, appeal to you? Explain.

La Belle Dame Sans Merci

This poem is also prescribed for Ordinary Level exams in 2017 and 2018

O what can ail thee, knight at arms
Alone and palely loitering?
The sedge has withered from the Lake *grass beside the lake is withered*
And no birds sing!
O what can ail thee knight at arms - *worn out, tired looking*
So haggard and so woe begone?
The squirrel's granary is full → *getting near end of Autumn*
And the harvest's done.

I see a lily on thy brow *Pale face*
With anguish moist and fever dew, - *sweating* 10
And on thy cheeks a fading rose *red cheeks fading*
Fast withereth too –

I met a Lady in the Meads - *meet a fairy lady*
Full beautiful, a faery's child - *elegant moving*
Her hair was long, her foot was light 15
And her eyes were wild –

I made a Garland for her head, *ring of her head*
And bracelets too, and fragrant Zone:
She look'd at me as she did love
And made sweet moan – *sigh of happiness* 20

I set her on my pacing steed *He saw nothing but her*
And nothing else saw all day long *all day*
For sidelong would she bend and sing *she sang songs to him*
A faery's song –

She found me roots of relish sweet *She fed him* 25
And honey wild and manna dew
And sure in language strange she said *fairy told him I love you*
'I love thee true' – *? strange*

She took me to her elfin grot *elf grotto*
And there she wept and sigh'd full sore - *She cried* 30
And there I shut her wild wild eyes *He kissed her*
With kisses four. *to stop her crying*

John Keats

And there she lulled me asleep
And there I dream'd – Ah Woe betide!   *He falls asleep*
The latest dream I ever dreamt   *He dreamt*   35   *Dream Suffering*
On the cold hill side.

I saw pale kings and Princes too   *She had total control*
Pale warriors, death pale were they all;
They cried 'La belle dame sans merci
Thee hath in thrall.'   40

I saw their starv'd lips in the gloam
With horrid warning gaped wide   *Mouths were Starving*
And I awoke and found me here
On the cold hill's side

And this is why I sojourn here   *this is why he is*   45
Alone and palely loitering;
Though the sedge is wither'd from the Lake
And no birds sing –

Background note

This poem was composed on 21 April 1819, in Keats's journal letter to George and
Georgina. It was published in Hunt's new journal, the *Indicator*, on 10 May 1820.
The text used here is the draft in that letter rather than the slightly altered (edited)
published version.

Notes

	La Belle Dame Sans Merci:	the beautiful lady without mercy. The title is taken from a mediaeval ballad composed by Aloin Chartier in 1424 and comes from the terminology of courtly love in mediaeval literature. This 'mercy' has been described as 'the sort of gracious kindness which prompts a woman to accept a lover's pleas' (Brian Stone).
3	**sedge:**	coarse grass
9	**lily:**	of a white or pale colour
13	**Meads:**	meadows
18	**Zone:**	girdle or ornate belt
29	**elfin:**	fairy (originally referred to diminutive supernatural beings in Arthurian legend)
29	**grot:**	grotto, cave
40	**in thrall:**	enslaved, in her power

Explorations

FIRST READING

1. What is your first impression of the atmosphere in this poem? What do you see, hear and feel? Reread and jot down significant phrases and images.

SECOND READING

2. Is there a change of speaker in the fourth stanza? Who is speaking from then onwards? Who asked the questions in the first three stanzas?

3.
a Describe the knight's present condition.

b What happened to him?

4. What are the indications, as the tale progresses, that the woman is an enchantress?

5. How is the otherworldly atmosphere created in this tale of enchantment?

Consider:

- The lady
- The landscape details and imagery
- The dream
- The archaic language
- The metre

THIRD READING

6. What view of love is behind this poem? Read the critical commentary and discuss it.

7.
a How do you understand the theme of this poem?

b Do you think the ballad is an appropriate form of poem for this theme?

8. Do you think the poem is meant to instruct us? If so, comment on the moral.

9. 'The poem has a very simple view of good and evil.'
   Would you agree with this statement? Explain your views.

10. Which elements of the poem did you consider most effective? Explain.

FOURTH READING

11. Consider the following statement: 'If the essence of romantic poetry is to rely on sources of inspiration other than the rational intellect can supply, this poem may be justly considered its quintessence' (Graham Hough).

Ode to a Nightingale

I

My heart aches, and a drowsy numbness pains
    My sense, as though of hemlock I had drunk,
Or emptied some dull opiate to the drains
    One minute past, and Lethe-wards had sunk:
'Tis not through envy of thy happy lot,   5
    But being too happy in thine happiness, –
        That thou, light-winged Dryad of the trees,
           In some melodious plot
Of beechen green, and shadows numberless,
    Singest of summer in full-throated ease.   10

II

O, for a draught of vintage! that hath been
    Cool'd a long age in the deep-delved earth,
Tasting of Flora and the country green,
    Dance, and Provençal song, and sunburnt mirth!
O for a beaker full of the warm South,   15
    Full of the true, the blushful Hippocrene,
        With beaded bubbles winking at the brim,
           And purple-stained mouth;
That I might drink, and leave the world unseen,
    And with thee fade away into the forest dim: 20

III

Fade far away, dissolve, and quite forget
    What thou among the leaves hast never known,
The weariness, the fever, and the fret
    Here, where men sit and hear each other groan;
Where palsy shakes a few, sad, last gray hairs,   25
    Where youth grows pale, and spectre-thin, and dies;
        Where but to think is to be full of sorrow
          And leaden-eyed despairs,

Where Beauty cannot keep her lustrous eyes,
    Or new Love pine at them beyond to-morrow.   30

IV

Away! away! for I will fly to thee,
    Not charioted by Bacchus and his pards,
But on the viewless wings of Poesy,
    Though the dull brain perplexes and retards:
Already with thee! tender is the night,   35
    And haply the Queen-Moon is on her throne,
        Cluster'd around by all her starry Fays;
            But here there is no light,
Save what from heaven is with the breezes blown
        Through verdurous glooms and winding mossy ways.   40

V

I cannot see what flowers are at my feet,
    Nor what soft incense hangs upon the boughs,
But, in embalmed darkness, guess each sweet
    Wherewith the seasonable month endows
The grass, the thicket, and the fruit-tree wild;   45
    White hawthorn, and the pastoral eglantine;
        Fast fading violets cover'd up in leaves;
            And mid-May's eldest child,
The coming musk-rose, full of dewy wine,
        The murmurous haunt of flies on summer eves.   50

VI

Darkling I listen; and, for many a time
    I have been half in love with easeful Death,
Call'd him soft names in many a mused rhyme,
    To take into the air my quiet breath;
        Now more than ever seems it rich to die,   55
To cease upon the midnight with no pain,
        While thou art pouring forth thy soul abroad
            In such an ecstasy!
Still wouldst thou sing, and I have ears in vain –
        To thy high requiem become a sod.   60

John Keats

VII

Thou wast not born for death, immortal Bird!
　　No hungry generations tread thee down;
The voice I hear this passing night was heard
　　In ancient days by emperor and clown:
Perhaps the self-same song that found a path　　　　　　65
　　Through the sad heart of Ruth, when, sick for home,
　　　　She stood in tears amid the alien corn;
　　　　　　The same that oft-times hath
Charm'd magic casements, opening on the foam
　　Of perilous seas, in faery lands forlorn.　　　　　　70

VIII

Forlorn! the very word is like a bell
　　To toll me back from thee to my sole self!
Adieu! the fancy cannot cheat so well
　　As she is fam'd to do, deceiving elf.
Adieu! adieu! thy plaintive anthem fades　　　　　　75
　　Past the near meadows, over the still stream,
　　　　Up the hill-side; and now 'tis buried deep
　　　　　　In the next valley-glades:
Was it a vision, or a waking dream?
　　Fled is that music: – Do I wake or sleep?　　　　　　80

Notes

2	hemlock:	a poison or sedative
3	opiate:	a sedative drug
4	Lethe-wards had sunk:	sunk into forgetfulness. In Greek mythology, Lethe was one of the rivers that flowed through Hades and whose waters had the power of making the souls of the dead forget their life on earth.
7	That:	read as 'because'
7	Dryad:	wood nymph or spirit of the tree, a poetic reference to the nightingale
13	Flora:	in Latin mythology, the goddess of flowers
14	Provençal song:	in the Middle Ages, travelling singers from Provence, a region in southern France, were famous for their music
15	warm South:	southern wine
16	Hippocrene:	a fountain on Mount Helicon, sacred to the Muses, usually referred to in connection with poetic inspiration; here Keats uses the term to describe wine, but it also carries connotations of poetic inspiration

26	Where youth…:	carries echoes of his brother Tom's death the previous December, at the age of 19, from tuberculosis
32	Bacchus:	Roman god of wine
32	pards:	leopards
33	viewless:	invisible
36	Queen-Moon:	Diana, the moon-goddess
37	Fays:	fairies
43	embalmed:	fragrant
43	sweet:	sweetness of taste and smell
46	eglantine:	the sweetbriar, a wild rose
51	Darkling:	in darkness
60	become a sod:	the poet, when dead and buried, will no longer be able to hear the nightingale's music
66	Ruth:	after the death of her husband, Ruth was driven from her native Moab by famine and went to her mother-in-law, a Jew, to Bethlehem, where she worked in the fields (Ruth 2: 1–3); see also Wordsworth's poem 'The Solitary Reaper' (1807)
69	casements:	a type of window
73	fancy:	imagination

John Keats

Explorations

Read the poem aloud or close your eyes and listen to a reading of it.

1. What is your first impression of the general atmosphere in this poem? Think of the poet's repeated wishes, the predominant colours and the general sounds of the words.

2. What stanza or image made the greatest impression on you? Why?

3. What aspect of the nightingale is chiefly celebrated here?

SECOND READING

Stanzas 1–2

4. Do any words or phrases used here surprise or perplex you?

5.

a What is the poet's mood in the first four lines? Examine it in detail.

b Why does his heart ache?

6. How do you picture the nightingale and its environment from the detail of stanza 1?

7. What does the poet yearn for in stanza 2? Why?

8. What atmosphere is conjured up by stanza 2? Explain how the effect is created by an appeal to the senses.

9. Do you notice any similarities and contrasts between stanzas 1 and 2? Discuss.

THIRD READING

Stanzas 3–5

10.

a Explain in detail the poet's view of life that emerges from stanza 3. What is your reaction to this view?

b What do you think prompts this meditation at this particular point in the poem?

11. What exactly is the poet rejecting and proposing in the first three lines of stanza 4?

12. From midway in stanza 4 ('Already with thee …') to the end of stanza 5, Keats is describing the environment of the nightingale, which he is now sharing. What is your general impression of this world? How did the poet get there? How does he convey its appeal to us?

FOURTH READING

Stanzas 1–5

13. What do we learn about the nightingale? Try to picture it. What do we *not* learn?

14. What do you think the nightingale means to the poet? Can you explain its attraction?

15.

a In this encounter with a nightingale, what is the poet attempting to achieve?

b Why does he turn to a 'draught of vintage' (stanza 2) and to the 'viewless wings of Poesy' (stanza 4)? Explain his motivation.

Stanzas 6–8

16. Why does the poet find death attractive in stanza 6? Does he really have a death wish or is his motivation more complex? Explain.

17. In what ways does stanza 6 follow an established pattern?

18. Is the introduction of death completely surprising or has it been prepared for earlier in the poem?

19. What is the poet suggesting about art, as represented by the song of the nightingale, in stanza 7?

20. Why do you think the poet is forlorn in the final stanza? Comment on his philosophical conclusions about art and life and the general mood in that stanza.

SIXTH READING

21. What is the poet writing about in this poem? Consider:

- His attitude to everyday life

- The place of art in life

- The value of imagination

- Immortality

- Death

  Read 'Sailing to Byzantium' by W.B. Yeats for similarity of theme.

22. Rereading the poem as an imaginative attempt to share in the artistic life of the nightingale, where do you consider the highs and lows of the experience to be? Examine the changing moods.

23. Trace the argument of the poem.

24. What is your reaction to Keats's claims for the significance of the imagination?

25. This is a very intimate poem in which the reader is allowed to share in the poet's suffering and joy. Examine how this is achieved in the ode.

26. What is the effect of the sensuous imagery?

27. Explore the part played by contrasts and contradictions in this poem.

28. 'In this ode, song is the predominant sound and journey the predominant metaphor.'
    Discuss.

29. ' "Ode to a Nightingale" is a work of pervasive darkness and mystery' (Brian Stone).
    Discuss this statement.

Ode on a Grecian Urn

I

Thou still unravish'd bride of quietness,
    Thou foster-child of silence and slow time,
Sylvan historian, who canst thus express
    A flowery tale more sweetly than our rhyme:
What leaf-fring'd legend haunts about thy shape   5
    Of deities or mortals, or of both,
        In Tempe or the dales of Arcady?
    What men or gods are these? What maidens loth?
What mad pursuit? What struggle to escape?
    What pipes and timbrels? What wild ecstasy?   10

II

Heard melodies are sweet, but those unheard
    Are sweeter; therefore, ye soft pipes, play on;
Not to the sensual ear, but, more endear'd,
    Pipe to the spirit ditties of no tone:
Fair youth, beneath the trees, thou canst not leave   15
    Thy song, nor ever can those trees be bare;
        Bold lover, never, never canst thou kiss,
Though winning near the goal – yet, do not grieve;
    She cannot fade, though thou hast not thy bliss,
        For ever wilt thou love, and she be fair!   20

III

Ah, happy, happy boughs! that cannot shed
    Your leaves, nor ever bid the spring adieu;
And, happy melodist, unwearied,
    For ever piping songs for ever new;
More happy love! more happy, happy love!   25
    For ever warm and still to be enjoy'd,
        For ever panting, and for ever young;
All breathing human passion far above,
    That leaves a heart high-sorrowful and cloy'd,
        A burning forehead, and a parching tongue.   30

IV

Who are these coming to the sacrifice?
    To what green altar, O mysterious priest,
Lead'st thou that heifer lowing at the skies,
    And all her silken flanks with garlands drest?

What little town by river or sea shore,   35
    Or mountain-built with peaceful citadel,
        Is emptied of this folk, this pious morn?
And, little town, thy streets for evermore
    Will silent be; and not a soul to tell
        Why thou art desolate, can e'er return.   40

                        V

O Attic shape! Fair attitude! with brede
    Of marble men and maidens overwrought,
With forest branches and the trodden weed;
    Thou, silent form, dost tease us out of thought
As doth eternity: Cold Pastoral!   45
    When old age shall this generation waste,
        Thou shalt remain, in midst of other woe
Than ours, a friend to man, to whom thou say'st,
    'Beauty is truth, truth beauty,' – that is all
        Ye know on earth, and all ye need to know.   50

Background note

This ode was composed in May 1819 and published in *Annals of the Fine Arts*
in January 1820 and in the collection *Poems*, 1820. It was probably inspired by
more than a single Greek artefact, but there is in existence, in the Keats-Shelley
Memorial House in Rome, a drawing made by Keats of the Sosibios Vase (above),
taken from the Musée Napoléon, which may have partly been an inspiration for
the poem. The 'heifer lowing at the skies' was probably inspired by the heifer being
led to sacrifice in the south frieze of the Parthenon Marbles.

John Keats

Explorations

1. What do you see? How many scenes are depicted? What is your first impression of the mood or moods?

SECOND READING

2. What qualities of the urn appeal to the poet in the first quatrain? Examine the metaphors used to describe it and discuss the meaning and connotations of each.

3. What do you understand of the first scene from the urn that is described by the poet? Is this unexpected after Keats's initial description of the urn? Comment.

4.

a   In the second stanza the poet suggests that art is superior to reality ('Heard melodies are sweet, but those unheard | Are sweeter'). How does he develop this idea in stanzas 2–3?

b   What reservations does he have about the superiority of art in these stanzas?

THIRD READING

5.

a   In the fourth stanza the poet describes a very different scene. What is the atmosphere here?

b   Why do you think he considers this scene at this particular point and what is the effect on the direction of the poem?

6. Do you think stanza 5 restates some of the misgivings of stanzas 2–3? Explain.

7. In what sense is the urn a 'Cold Pastoral'?

8. Discuss a number of possible interpretations of the aphorism 'beauty is truth, truth beauty'.

FOURTH READING

9. What do you think the poem is about?

10. What values or philosophical attitudes do you think underlie this poem?

11. What conclusion does the poet reach about the value of art?

12. Examine the section 'A reading of the poem' in the Critical Commentary on the CD. Which elements are in accordance with your reading? Which elements differ?

13. Re-examine the critical image of the urn. Consider:

•   How it is described

•   The contradictory qualities

•   Its symbolic value

•   Its particular character

14. Would you consider this ode to be a significant and coherent statement on the value of the arts to society or a mess of confused thinking?

15. Where do you find the beauty in this poem?

FIFTH READING

16. 'Both "Ode to a Nightingale" and "Ode on a Grecian Urn" deal with the problems of the artist.'
    Discuss this statement, with appropriate references to the text.

To Autumn

1

Season of mists and mellow fruitfulness,
  Close bosom-friend of the maturing sun;
Conspiring with him how to load and bless
  With fruit the vines that round the thatch-eves run;
To bend with apples the moss'd cottage-trees,
  And fill all fruit with ripeness to the core;   5
  To swell the gourd, and plump the hazel shells
  With a sweet kernel; to set budding more,
And still more, later flowers for the bees,
  Until they think warm days will never cease,   10
    For summer has o'er-brimm'd their clammy cells.

2

Who hath not seen thee oft amid thy store?
  Sometimes whoever seeks abroad may find
Thee sitting careless on a granary floor,
  Thy hair soft-lifted by the winnowing wind;   15
Or on a half-reap'd furrow sound asleep,
  Drows'd with the fume of poppies, while thy hook
  Spares the next swath and all its twined flowers:
And sometimes like a gleaner thou dost keep
  Steady thy laden head across a brook;   20
  Or by a cyder-press, with patient look,
    Thou watchest the last oozings hours by hours.

3

Where are the songs of spring? Ay, where are they?
  Think not of them, thou hast thy music too, –
While barred clouds bloom the soft-dying day,   25
  And touch the stubble-plains with rosy hue;
Then in a wailful choir the small gnats mourn
  Among the river sallows, borne aloft
    Or sinking as the light wind lives or dies;
And full-grown lambs loud bleat from hilly bourn;   30
  Hedge-crickets sing; and now with treble soft
  The red-breast whistles from a garden-croft;
    And gathering swallows twitter in the skies.

John Keats

Background note

The ode was written on 19 September 1819. The circumstances of its composition were alluded to briefly in a letter Keats wrote to John Reynolds on 21 September:

'How beautiful the season is now – How fine the air. A temperate sharpness about it. Really, without joking, chaste weather – Dian skies – I never lik'd stubble fields so much as now – Aye better than the chilly green of the spring. Somehow a stubble plain looks warm – in the same way that some pictures look warm – this struck me so much in my Sunday's walk that I composed verses upon it ...'

Notes

7	gourd:	large fleshy fruit
15	winnowing:	the process of separating the grain from the chaff (or covering) at harvest time; the beaten corn was thrown in the air and the wind blew off the lighter chaff
18	swath:	a row of corn as it falls when reaped
19	gleaner:	person gathering ears of corn left by the reapers
25	barred clouds:	clouds patterned in bars
25	bloom:	used as a transitive verb and meaning 'to give a glow to'
28	sallows:	low-growing willow trees
30	bourn:	small stream
32	croft:	small agricultural holding

Explorations

10. Overall, what aspects of the season appeal to the poet?

11. Comment on the sensuousness of the language used by Keats in this ode.

12. Keats's poetry is preoccupied with the quest for beauty. Explain how this poem can be seen as part of that search. Refer to specific examples.

13. Keats's other great poetic battle was with change and decay. Is there any evidence of that here?

14. Do you find the poet's attitude to life any different here from that displayed in the other odes?

15. Would you consider this a successful nature poem? Comment.

FIRST READING

1. Decide to concentrate either on what you see or on what you hear as you listen to this poem or read it aloud yourself. What elements of either sights or sounds make an impression on you?

2. On a first reading, what particular qualities of the season are being celebrated?

SECOND READING

3. What do you think is a key statement in the first stanza? Why?

4. What particular aspect of autumn is depicted in the first stanza?

5. Which of our senses is engaged primarily when we read this first stanza?

THIRD READING

6. Comment on the mood of the second stanza.

7. What are your impressions of the personifications of autumn in the second stanza? What is suggested about the season, about humankind's relationship with nature, etc.?

8. Why do you think the poet enquires about the songs of spring in the third stanza?

9. Would you describe the mood of this final stanza as nostalgic, depressed, perfect contentment or something else? Examine the mood in detail.

Bright star, would I were stedfast as thou art –
   Not in lone splendor hung aloft the night,
And watching, with eternal lids apart,
   Like nature's patient, sleepless Eremite, – *lonely*
The moving waters at their priestlike task   5
   Of pure ablution round earth's human shores,
Or gazing on the new soft-fallen mask
   Of snow upon the mountains and the moors;
No – yet still stedfast, still unchangeable,
   Pillow'd upon my fair love's ripening breast,   10
To feel for ever its soft swell and fall,
   Awake for ever in a sweet unrest,
Still, still to hear her tender-taken breath,
And so live ever – or else swoon to death.

Notes

1	**stedfast:**	steadfast, constant
4	**eremite:**	a hermit, recluse
7	**mask:**	as in cover, lace mask, or perhaps death mask
10	**ripening:**	maturing

Explorations

1. What qualities of the star does the poet particularly admire? What quality or characteristic is he less comfortable with?

2.

a How is the star presented in the octave? What do you think of this presentation?

b What do you think the star might symbolise for the poet?

3. How would you describe the particular atmosphere of the octave? Does this change in the sestet? Explain.

4. What is the central problem the poet is trying to resolve? Discuss this.

5. How do you understand the last line? Do you think it is an effective solution?

6. What impression of the author do we get from this poem? Consider:

- The poet's personality

- His view of life

- His ideal of happiness

7. The octave deals with the process of watching, contemplating. If this is a metaphor for poetic vision, what is the poet saying about the mode of poetic contemplation?

8. What particularly attracts the watcher? What is Keats thinking about the subject viewed (the world of nature)? Examine the relationship between nature and mankind as suggested in the poem.

9. One of the characteristics of a Petrarchan sonnet is the contrast between the octave and the sestet. Examine and discuss any contrasts you notice.

10. Do you think the imagery is effective? Discuss.

11. Outline your personal reaction to the poem.

Emily Dickinson

(1830–86)

Prescribed for Higher Level exams in 2015 and 2016

Emily Dickinson was born and lived all her life in Amherst, Massachusetts, in the US. Her family members were prominent in the community as lawyers and public representatives. Emily's early years seemed ordinary enough: education at Amherst Academy and Mount Holyoke Female Seminary; trips to Boston, Washington and Philadelphia; and running the family household when her mother became seriously ill. But she seems to have suffered some kind of psychological crisis in her early thirties, which resulted in her withdrawal from society.

She became somewhat eccentric, the 'myth' of Amherst, who didn't meet strangers or visitors and who spoke to friends from behind a half-closed door or shrouded in shadow at the head of the stairs. She produced a great number of rather cryptic poems of a most unusual form. When she died she was found to have left almost two thousand poems and fragments, in which she explored a number of themes, including love, pain, absence and loss, doubt, despair and mental anguish, and hope. Hardly any were published in her lifetime, and their true worth and originality were not appreciated for many years.

Background note

In 1955 an authoritative collection of Dickinson's work, *The Poems of Emily Dickinson*, was prepared by Thomas Johnson. The poems are dated, but as Johnson himself admitted, this is the result of educated guesswork. It is very difficult to be definite, since Dickinson never prepared the poems for publication and did not title them. Each poem below is headed with Johnson's number.

I taste a liquor never brewed –
From Tankards scooped in Pearl –
Not all the Vats upon the Rhine
Yield such an Alcohol!

Inebriate of Air – am I –   5
And Debauchee of Dew –
Reeling – thro endless summer days –
From inns of Molten Blue –

When 'Landlords' turn the drunken Bee
Out of the Foxglove's door –   10
When Butterflies – renounce their 'drams' –
I shall but drink the more!

Till Seraphs swing their snowy Hats –
And Saints – to windows run –
To see the little Tippler   15
Leaning against the – Sun –

Emily Dickinson

Explorations

1.

a   If you first approach the poem as a riddle, does this help you to decipher stanzas 1–2? For example, can you suggest an answer to any of the following enigmas?

• How could there be a liquor that wasn't brewed?

• How are tankards, or beer mugs, the colour of pearl?

• 'Inebriate of Air', 'Debauchee of Dew' – who or what might she be? Who or what gets drunk on dew?

• She is seen staggering from 'inns of Molten Blue' – an unusual colour for an inn as we know it. What or where are the inns?

b   Is all revealed in the third stanza? Examine the first two lines. Explain your reading of stanzas 1–2.

2.   Now explain the central metaphor of the poem.

3.   Would you agree that the poet's train of thought becomes more whimsical as the poem progresses?

4.   What do the first two stanzas suggest about the speaker's attitude to nature?

SECOND READING

5.   What self-image does the poet attempt to project in this poem? Do you think she sees herself as dissolute, rebellious, assertive or something else? Explain, with reference to phrases or images.

6.   It is generally agreed that this is a humorous poem. Comment on some of the methods by which the humour is achieved.

7.   Do you think there is a substantial theme beneath the whimsical and humorous surface? Make suggestions.

8.   How would you describe the tone of the poem? Refer to words and phrases in the text.

THIRD READING

9.   The literary critic David Porter spoke of a 'tone of ecstatic assurance', reflecting the attitude of the speaker as victor over the pains of life. Would you agree with this?

10. What is your own evaluation of this poem?

'Hope' is the thing with feathers –
That perches in the soul –
And sings the tune without the words –
And never stops – at all –

And sweetest – in the Gale – is heard –   5
And sore must be the storm –
That could abash the little Bird
That kept so many warm –

I've heard it in the chillest land –
And on the strangest Sea –   10
Yet, never, in Extremity,
It asked a crumb – of Me.

Explorations

BEFORE READING

1. Consider briefly what part 'hope' plays in your own day-to-day life.

2. If you had to represent hope figuratively in a painting or an image, how would you describe it?

FIRST READING

3. How does the poet visualise hope?

4.

a Examine the analogy in detail. List the qualities or characteristics of hope suggested by each of the images in the first stanza. Pry beneath the obvious. For example, what does 'sings the tune without the words' suggest?

b What is the effect of the description of hope as the 'thing with feathers'?

5.

a What aspects of hope are suggested in the second stanza?

Emily Dickinson

b	What does the sound effect of the word 'abash' contribute to this picture?

c	What is the effect of the adjective 'little'?

6.	In the third stanza, which qualities of hope are a repetition of suggestions already encountered and which are new?

7.	How do you interpret the last two lines? Do they indicate the strength or a weakness in the virtue of hope? It depends on whether you read the third line as part of the meaning of the previous two or read it with the last line. Experiment with both readings. Is there some ambiguity and does this show a weakness in the virtue of hope?

SECOND READING

8.	Do you think the bird analogy is successful? Explain your views. What other metaphors for hope could you advance?

9.	What insights into the nature of hope did you get from reading this poem?

10.	How would you describe the mood of the poem? Suggest ways in which this mood is created in the text.

THIRD READING

11.	What do you notice about the technical features of the poem: punctuation, sentences, capital letters, etc.? What is the effect of these?

12.	Would you agree that the extraordinary imagery is one of the best features of this poem? Develop your answer with specific references.

13.	Do you find this poem hopeful? Explain your views.

258

There's a certain Slant of light,
Winter Afternoons –
That oppresses, like the Heft
Of Cathedral Tunes –

Heavenly Hurt, it gives us –							5
We can find no scar,
But internal difference,
Where the Meanings, are –

None may teach it – Any –
'Tis the Seal Despair –							10
An imperial affliction
Sent us of the Air –

When it comes, the Landscape listens –
Shadows – hold their breath –
When it goes, 'tis like the Distance						15
On the look of Death –

Explorations

BEFORE READING

1. Try to recall the image of any wintry sunlit afternoon you have experienced. Describe the quality of the sunlight as best you remember it.

FIRST READING

2. On a first reading, what do you notice about the quality of the sunlight described by the poet?

3. Attempt to describe this light. What can we say about it from the descriptive details in the poem? Is it possible to say very much? Explain.

4. Do you notice how we are made aware of the light? Is it described objectively or filtered through the speaker's feelings? Give an example.

SECOND READING

5. Explore in detail the speaker's attitude to this light. Pay particular attention to the images for what they reveal about the speaker's view and examine the connotations of similes and metaphors ('like the Heft | Of Cathedral Tunes', 'the Seal Despair', 'like the Distance | On the look of Death').

6. What do you think is meant by 'We can find no scar, | But internal difference, | Where the Meanings, are'?

7. What religious view or philosophy seems to lie behind this poem?

8.

a How would you describe the tone of the poem? Refer to particular words and phrases.

b What do you think the sounds of words contribute to the tone? Explain.

THIRD READING

9. Briefly set down your understanding of the theme of this poem.

10. Outline your general reaction to the poem. What is your evaluation of it as a nature poem?

11. Can you appreciate that the poem might be seen to reflect the poet's deep despair? In your own words, explain the nature of the despair felt by the speaker.

12. Explore the sound effects – echoes, rhymes, alliteration, etc. – used by the poet. Do you think these musical effects might serve to disguise the deep negative feelings in the poem?

13. What questions do you still have about the poem?

Emily Dickinson

This poem is also prescribed for Ordinary Level exams in 2015 and 2016

I felt a Funeral, in my Brain,
And Mourners to and fro
Kept treading — treading — till it seemed
That Sense was breaking through —

And when they all were seated,   5
A Service, like a Drum —
Kept beating — beating — till I thought
My Mind was going numb —

And then I heard them lift a Box
And creak across my Soul   10
With those same Boots of Lead, again,
Then Space — began to toll,

As all the Heavens were a Bell,
And Being, but an Ear,
And I, and Silence, some strange Race   15
Wrecked, solitary, here —

And then a Plank in Reason, broke,
And I dropped down, and down —
And hit a World, at every plunge,
And Finished knowing — then —   20

Explorations

FIRST READING

1. On a first reading, what images in
   particular hold your attention? What
   do these images suggest about the
   subject matter of the poem?

2. List the images suggestive of funerals
   as they occur throughout the poem.
   Do these conjure up for you the usual
   picture of a conventional funeral or is it
   somehow different? Comment on any
   unusual connotations.

3. Where is the speaker in this poem?
   What suggests this?

SECOND READING

4. If we read this poem as primarily about
   the process of dying, what insights
   about death does it convey?

5. Try a metaphorical reading of the
   poem. Examine the metaphor in the
   first line and then explore the poem
   as a psychological experience of
   breakdown. What insights does this
   reading bring to you?

6. Which view of the poem do you prefer to take? Could we hold both simultaneously?

THIRD READING

7.

a Explore the speaker's feelings in the first stanza. What is suggested by the imagery and the repetitions?

b How do you understand the fourth line?

8. Explore the connotations of the simile 'a Service, like a Drum' in the second stanza. What do the sounds of the words suggest about the speaker's state of mind in this stanza?

9. Explain the speaker's feelings in stanzas 2–3.

10. 'As all the Heavens were a Bell, | And Being, but an Ear'.
What image does this conjure up for you and what does it suggest about the speaker's perception of her relationship with the heavens?

11.

a Is the relationship between the speaker and the universe developed further in the following two lines?

'And I, and Silence, some strange Race | Wrecked, solitary, here –'

Explain your understanding of this.

b How does the speaker feel about her life, her position here?

c Read the last line aloud. What does the rhythm, or lack of it, convey?

12.

a Were you surprised by the actions of the last stanza or was it predictable? Explain.

b Do you think it is an effective ending?

13. Experiment with different oral readings of the last line. What implications for meaning do the different readings have?

FOURTH READING

14. Briefly list the principal themes and issues you found in the poem.

15. Decide on your own interpretation of the poem, grounding your views in the text.

16. Comment on the effectiveness of the imagery used to convey the ideas.

17.

a How would you describe the tone of this poem: anguished, oppressed, lonely, helpless, coldly factual or something else?

b What words, phrases or images do you think best indicate the poet's tone of voice?

18. Explore the writing technique, especially the repetitions, the sound effect of words, the truncated phrases, the use of single, isolated words, the effect of capitalisation and the punctuation.

• What is the effect of 'treading – treading', 'beating – beating' and other repetitions?

• What is the effect of the poet's continuous use of 'and'? Examine its use in the last stanza in particular.

• What is the effect when the dash is used for punctuation? Examine 'Kept beating – beating – till I thought'. What is the effect of the dash at the end of stanzas 4 and 5 in particular?

Emily Dickinson

Look at the poet's use of conventional punctuation – what is the effect in line 16? Read it aloud.

- List the capitalised words. Do they provide a guide through the poem? Trace it.

- What is the effect of the repeated sounds of words ('drum', 'numb'; 'Soul', 'toll')? Explore the suggestions of the onomatopoeic 'creak'. What do these effects contribute to the creation of the atmosphere in the poem?

19. 'Dickinson treats the most tormented situations with great calm' (Helen McNeil). Would you agree with this statement on the evidence of this poem?

328

A Bird came down the Walk –
He did not know I saw –
He bit an Angleworm in halves
And ate the fellow, raw,

And then he drank a Dew   5
From a convenient Grass –
And then hopped sidewise to the Wall
To let a Beetle pass –

He glanced with rapid eyes
That hurried all around –   10
They looked like frightened Beads, I thought –
He stirred his Velvet Head

Like one in danger, Cautious,
I offered him a Crumb
And he unrolled his feathers   15
And rowed him softer home –

Than Oars divide the Ocean,
Too silver for a seam –
Or Butterflies, off Banks of Noon
Leap, plashless as they swim.   20

Explorations

FIRST READING

1. What do you notice about the nature drama unfolding on the walk?

2. Examine the bird's movements. What do they suggest about the creature?

3. Where is the speaker in this picture? When does she enter the 'camera shot'? What does she do and what is the bird's reaction?

SECOND READING

4. What does the speaker actually see and what does she create?

5. Examine how Dickinson creates the sense of the bird's flight in the last five lines of the poem. There is no actual description of the flight; rather, she proceeds by way of negative comparisons ('then', 'or'). What sense of the experience does she give us? What qualities of bird flight are evoked in this way? Refer to words or phrases in the text.

6. Step back or 'zoom out' from this picture and see the poet watching. What do you think is her attitude to this drama? What does she feel about the scene she is viewing? What words or phrases suggest this?

THIRD READING

7. What particular insights into the natural world does this poem offer you? Explain, with reference to the text.

8. Do you think Dickinson is being serious or humorous, or a combination of both here? Examine the tone of this poem.

9. 'Dickinson wickedly disturbs a clichéd vision of nature through her ornithological caricature' (Juhasz, Miller and Smith).

   Comment on this view in light of your own reading of the poem.

Emily Dickinson

After great pain, a formal feeling comes –
The Nerves sit ceremonious, like Tombs –
The stiff Heart questions was it He, that bore,
And Yesterday, or Centuries before?

The Feet, mechanical, go round –   5
Of Ground, or Air, or Ought –
A Wooden way
Regardless grown,
A Quartz contentment, like a stone –

This is the Hour of Lead –   10
Remembered, if outlived,
As Freezing persons, recollect the Snow –
First – Chill – then Stupor – then the letting go –

Explorations

BEFORE READING

1. Have you ever experienced severe pain, such as from a broken bone or appendicitis, or a severe toothache or headache? Try to recollect how you felt as the pain ebbed away and you were free of it for the first moment in a long while. Were you elated or just exhausted, tired, numbed, etc.? Recapture how you felt in short phrases or images.

FIRST READING

2. Explore the images in the poem for some indication of the speaker's feeling 'After great pain'.

- What are the connotations of 'The Nerves sit ceremonious, like Tombs'?

- What might 'The stiff Heart' indicate?

- What does the heart's disorientation in lines 3–4 suggest about the strength of the pain?

- What do the images of the second stanza intimate about the speaker's present mood and condition?

- What does the image 'Hour of Lead' conjure up for you?

- Are the references to snow comforting or threatening? Explain.

SECOND READING

3.

a Is there a common thread running through any of these images that might give an overview of the speaker's condition? Consider, for instance, 'The Nerves sit ceremonious', 'The stiff Heart', 'The Feet, mechanical'.

b	Taken together, what do these external physical manifestations reveal about the speaker's inner feelings?

c	What do the natural references to wood, quartz and lead suggest about the speaker's condition?

4.	Comment on the poet's own description of this condition as 'a formal feeling'. Is this unusual definition supported by any other evidence from the poem? Explain.

5.	Can you express the central concern of this poem in one sentence?

6.	Do you find the conclusion of this poem in any way hopeful or just totally bleak? Explain your reading of it.

THIRD READING

7.	Do you think this poem is an effective evocation of the particular feeling? Comment.

8.	What do you find most unusual or striking about it?

465

This poem is also prescribed for Ordinary Level exams in 2015 and 2016

I heard a Fly buzz — when I died —
The Stillness in the Room
Was like the Stillness in the Air —
Between the Heaves of Storm —

The Eyes around — had wrung them dry —   5
And Breaths were gathering firm
For that last Onset — when the King
Be witnessed — in the Room —

I willed my Keepsakes — Signed away
What portion of me be   10
Assignable — and then it was
There interposed a Fly —

With Blue — uncertain stumbling Buzz —
Between the light — and me —
And then the Windows failed — and then   15
I could not see to see —

Emily Dickinson

Explorations

1. Have you ever been present at a death, read about a deathbed scene or visited someone who was seriously ill and not expected to live? What did you notice and what were your thoughts?

FIRST READING

2. What do you notice about the deathbed scene here? What elements do you think might be ordinary or common to any such scene? What would you consider unusual about the scene?

3. Who is the speaker in the poem?

SECOND READING

4. Comment on the atmosphere in the room. Would you consider it to be emotional or controlled, expectant, frightened, indifferent or something else? What words and phrases suggest this?

5. What is your impression of the onlookers?

6. How does the poet suggest that this is a dramatic moment?

THIRD READING

7. How is the prospect of death viewed (a) by the onlookers and (b) by the speaker?

8. 'There interposed a Fly'.

   What is your reaction to the fly and what do you think might be its significance in the poem? Refer to words or phrases.

9. In general, what understanding of death is conveyed by this poem? Explore the connotations of phrases such as 'Heaves of Storm', 'that last Onset', 'the King | Be witnessed', 'With Blue – uncertain stumbling Buzz', 'And then the Windows failed'.

10. Do you find the speaking voice effective? Comment on the tone and the style of speech. What part do the phrasing and punctuation play in this?

FOURTH READING

11. 'Few poets have dealt with this all-engrossing subject with such intense feeling under such perfect control' (Richard Sewall).
    Do you find intense feeling and perfect control here?

The Soul has Bandaged moments –
When too appalled to stir –
She feels some ghastly Fright come up
And stop to look at her –

Salute her – with long fingers –   5
Caress her freezing hair –
Sip, Goblin, from the very lips
The Lover – hovered – o'er –
Unworthy, that a thought so mean
Accost a Theme – so – fair –   10

The soul has moments of Escape –
When bursting all the doors –
She dances like a Bomb, abroad,
And swings upon the Hours,

As do the Bee – delirious borne –   15
Long Dungeoned from his Rose –
Touch Liberty – then know no more,
But Noon, and Paradise –

The Soul's retaken moments –
When, Felon led along,   20
With shackles on the plumed feet,
And staples, in the Song,

The Horror welcomes her, again,
These, are not brayed of Tongue –

Notes

1	**Soul:**	psyche or spirit
3	**Fright:**	a personification of fear or horror
7	**Goblin:**	a small malevolent spirit
10	**Accost:**	speak to, question
14	**swings upon the Hours:**	an image of childlike play, lasting through all the hours of the day
16	**his Rose:**	the flower with its nectar, source of the bee's energy

Emily Dickinson

18	**Noon:**	the term is used with different connotations in various Dickinson poems; here it probably symbolises the paradise of earthly love. The bee soul escapes from his dungeon, finds fulfilment in the rose and is transported into an ecstasy of love ('Noon, and Paradise').
20	**Felon:**	a criminal
21	**the plumed feet:**	could suggest freedom of flight, which is in this case curtailed with shackles. In Greek mythology the messenger of the gods, Mercury, had plumed feet. Perhaps poetic inspiration is the theme in question here.
22	**staples:**	metal fastenings, in this case restricting the song
24	**These:**	refers to the soul's 'retaken moments', the capturing horror

Explorations

FIRST READING

1. What images, phrases or sounds made the most impression on you on a first reading?

2. What is your first impression of the mood or moods of the speaker? What leads you to say this?

3. Is there a narrative line in this poem? Can you trace the sequence of events?

SECOND READING

4. Explore the following 'thinking points'. Make notes to yourself to clarify your thinking on them.

a 'The Soul has Bandaged moments'. How do you visualise this? What does it suggest about the condition of the soul?

b What does the second line add to our picture of the soul?

c The soul is named as feminine. How do you perceive the scene in lines 3–4?

d The situation becomes more threatening in lines 5–6. Explain the nature of that threat. What is the impact of the adjective 'freezing'?

e Do you think there is a change of attitude by the speaker in line 7 ('Sip, Goblin')? Explain.

f 'lips | The Lover – hovered – o'er'. What does 'hovered' mean? What does it suggest about the lover and the nature of the relationship? Is the use of the past tense significant?

g Do you think lines 9–10 refer to the thoughts of the lover or the speaker's present feelings? Could they refer to both? What implications does each interpretation have?

h What is suggested about the speaker's state of mind by the first and second stanzas?

i How would you describe the different mood of the third stanza? Do the verbs help create it?

j Is there any suggestion that this mood is also perilous? Explain.

k In the fourth stanza, this new mood is compared to the activities of a bee escaped from captivity. What does this simile convey about the nature of the mood? (Refer to the Notes for the significance of 'Noon'.) Explore the effect of the many long vowel sounds in this stanza.

l   In the fifth stanza, how does the poet visualise the soul? Do you think this image is effective? Explain the mood in this stanza.

m   In the fifth stanza, do you think the true horror of captivity is hidden somewhat by the simple repetitive hymn metre and the musical rhyme of lines 20 and 22?

n   Is there any community support for the speaker's predicament? What is suggested in the last line about how this mental suffering must be borne? (Note: 'These' refers back to the 'retaken moments'.)

THIRD READING

5.   What are your impressions of the mental state of the speaker? Refer to the text.

6.   Explore the appropriateness of the different images and similes Dickinson uses to symbolise the soul.

7.   What do you consider to be the main issues and themes explored in this poem? Refer to the text.

8.   After some critical thinking, outline a reading you yourself find satisfactory and can substantiate with references to the poem.

FOURTH READING

9.   What insights into the human condition does this poem offer?

10. 'This poem deals with the intimate aspects of pain and loss.' Comment on the poem in light of this statement.

11. What part does the music of words – sound effects, metre, rhyme, etc. – play in creating the atmosphere of this poem?

I could bring You Jewels – had I a mind to –
But You have enough – of those –
I could bring You Odors from St. Domingo –
Colors – from Vera Cruz –

Berries of the Bahamas – have I –   5
But this little Blaze
Flickering to itself – in the Meadow –
Suits Me – more than those –

Never a Fellow matched this Topaz –
And his Emerald Swing –   10
Dower itself – for Bobadilo –
Better – Could I bring?

Notes

3	**St. Domingo:**	Santo Domingo, capital city of the Dominican Republic, on the Caribbean island of Hispaniola (so named by Columbus)
4	**Vera Cruz:**	a city and the main seaport of Mexico. The original settlement was founded in 1519 by Cortés and became the main link between the colony of Mexico and Spain.
5	**the Bahamas:**	islands in the West Indies, the first land touched by Columbus in 1492
9	**Topaz:**	a yellow sapphire (precious stone)
10	**Emerald:**	a precious stone of bright green colour
11	**Bobadilo:**	probably an allusion to Francisco Bobadilla, a tyrannical Spaniard and Columbus's enemy, who replaced Columbus as governor of the Indies and sent him back to Spain in chains. He 'seized the admiral's gold, plate, jewels and other valuables, plus an enormous treasure in gold wrested from the islanders'. Thus, jewels equal to a dower for Bobadilla would be priceless. We can assume that Dickinson had read Washington Irving's *Life of Columbus*, which contains the information about Bobadilla.

Explorations

986

A narrow Fellow in the Grass
Occasionally rides –
You may have met Him – did you not
His notice sudden is –

The Grass divides as with a Comb –   5
A spotted shaft is seen –
And then it closes at your feet
And opens further on –

He likes a Boggy Acre
A Floor too cool for Corn –   10
Yet when a Boy, and Barefoot –
I more than once at Noon

Emily Dickinson

Have passed, I thought, a Whip lash
Unbraiding in the Sun
When stooping to secure it   15
It wrinkled, and was gone –

Several of Nature's People
I know, and they know me –
I feel for them a transport
Of cordiality –   20

But never met this Fellow
Attended, or alone
Without a tighter breathing
And Zero at the Bone –

Background note

On the other side of the street where Emily lived was the 'Dickinson Meadow', where she might have encountered the 'narrow Fellow' in a 'Boggy Acre'.

Explorations

You might approach this poem as a sort of literary riddle and explore the clues carried by the connotations and sounds of words and images.

1.

a Consider the 'narrow Fellow'. What is actually seen of him? Is this enough to identify the creature with any certainty?

b What does the title lead you to expect?

2. There are incidental indications of his presence. Where are they and what do they add to our understanding of the 'narrow Fellow'?

3. How do you imagine the speaker? What persona or character does the speaker adopt for this narrative? (See the third stanza.) Do you think this is in any way significant?

SECOND READING

4. Consider the metaphorical descriptions of the creature. Perhaps the most exciting is 'Whip lash'. What are the connotations of the words? What does the term suggest about the creature? Do these connotations clash with the image of it 'Unbraiding in the Sun'?

5. How did it move when the speaker bent to pick it up?

6. In general, what is your impression of the qualities and nature of this creature?

7. Are there any attempts to make the creature seem less threatening? Refer to the text.

8. What does 'Barefoot' add to the atmosphere of the scene? Who is barefoot? When did this happen?

9.

a Was the speaker less troubled by this when in her youth? What is the speaker's present or adult reaction to an encounter with the 'narrow Fellow'? Refer to the text.

b What does 'Zero at the Bone' suggest about her feelings?

THIRD READING

10. What does the poem convey to us about the writer's attitude or attitudes to nature? Support your ideas with references to the text.

11. Do you think this is an effective evocation of a snake? Support your answer with references to the text.

12. Would you agree that there is real fear beneath the apparent casualness of this poem?

FOURTH READING

13. 'When she opened her eyes to the real hidden beneath the daily, it was to the peculiarity, awesomeness, and mystery of it' (John Robinson). Would you agree with this interpretation of the poem?

Thomas Hardy

(1840–1928)

Prescribed for the Higher Level exam in 2015

Thomas Hardy, a major poet and novelist, was born in Dorset on 2 June 1840. A sickly child, he did not attend school until he was eight years old. He made rapid progress and learned Latin, French and German. The Bible was his main focus of attention; he taught in Sunday school and considered taking holy orders. After leaving school he went to work for an ecclesiastical architect in Dorchester in 1859, and three years later he left for London to further his career. He was influenced by Darwin, Mill and Huxley and became an agnostic, in contrast with his earlier religious enthusiasm. Hardy pursued his interest in writing as a career and in 1871 published his first novel, *Desperate Remedies*. In 1872 *Under the Greenwood Tree* was published, followed by *A Pair of Blue Eyes* in 1873. His first major success, *Far from the Madding Crowd* (1874), allowed him to become a full-time writer and to contemplate marriage.

He met Emma Gifford on a working visit to Cornwall in 1870 and they married four years later. The marriage was initially happy but came under increasing strain. Emma considered Hardy to be her social inferior and resented his literary success. Her conventional attitudes were offended by the subject matter of *Tess of the D'Urbervilles* (1891), and especially *Jude the Obscure* (1896), which she tried to have suppressed. This final novel received so much adverse critical reaction on moral grounds that Hardy gave up the novel as a form and concentrated on his first love, poetry. Hardy's first volume of poetry, *Wessex Poems*, was published in 1898, when he was 58 years old. He went on to publish over 900 poems. When Emma died in 1912 Hardy was stricken by intense remorse. He was moved to write a remarkable series of love poems based on the early days of their relationship and the places associated with Emma. Nevertheless, he married Florence Dugdale in 1914, with whom he had had a relationship since 1905. When Thomas Hardy died in 1928 his cremated ashes were buried under a spade full of Dorset earth at Westminster Abbey. His heart was, according to his wishes, buried in Stinford with his first wife, Emma. Hardy published eight volumes of poetry and 14 novels. He is remarkable for the variety of his themes and his range of poetic styles.

I

They throw in Drummer Hodge, to rest
  Uncoffined – just as found:
His landmark is a kopje-crest
  That breaks the veldt around;
And foreign constellations west   5
  Each night above his mound.

II

Young Hodge the Drummer never knew –
  Fresh from his Wessex home –
The meaning of the broad Karoo,
  The Bush, the dusty loam,   10
And why uprose to nightly view
  Strange stars amid the gloam.

III

Yet portion of that unknown plain
  Will Hodge for ever be;
His homely Northern breast and brain   15
  Grow to some Southern tree,
And strange-eyed constellations reign
  His stars eternally.

Notes

3	**kopje:**	a small hill on the African veld (veldt)
4	**veldt:**	grassland of South Africa
9	**Karoo:**	dry tableland of southern Africa
10	**loam:**	a soil consisting of a friable mixture of clay, silt and sand
12	**gloam:**	archaic word for twilight

Thomas Hardy

Explorations

FIRST READING

1. 'They throw in Drummer Hodge, to rest | Uncoffined – just as found'. What is your reaction to the burial afforded to Drummer Hodge?

2. What do we learn about Drummer Hodge in the poem? What kind of person do you think he was, based on the evidence of the text?

3. How does the speaker feel about the dead drummer? What words or images suggest his attitude?

4. Compose a brief diary extract about or a letter to the young soldier suggesting how he feels about South Africa.

5. How do you visualise the scene in stanza 3? How does the poet suggest its foreignness? What impression are you left with?

SECOND READING

6. Compose an epitaph for Drummer Hodge that is true to the poem.

7. Why do you think Hardy uses the Afrikaans vocabulary, 'kopje-crest', 'veldt' and 'Karoo'? Does it help to visualise South Africa's landscape and how alien the country was for Drummer Hodge?

8. What effect is achieved by the mention of 'foreign constellations', 'Strange stars' and 'strange-eyed constellations'?

9. 'His homely Northern breast and brain | Grow to some Southern tree'. Is there an element of hope or consolation in these lines?

10. What is the mood of this poem? Look at the descriptions, choice of words and style of speech.

THIRD READING

11. Briefly outline the themes of this poem as you understand them.

12. Comment on the appropriateness of the imagery. Do you find any images particularly effective?

13. Do you find this poem moving? Explore your personal reaction to the text.

FOURTH READING

14. 'Nature and the heavens provide the background and foreground to the poem; for they are permanent, whereas man's life is transitory.' Discuss the setting of the poem and the imagery associated with it.

15. 'Drummer Hodge' has been described as 'a kind of poetic equivalent of the grave of the Unknown Warrior', because it shows how quiet lives are disrupted and destroyed by war. Comment on how the poem has universal relevance while at the same time retaining individuality and a particular sense of place.

16. 'Hardy combines simplicity of language and form with strikingly individual vocabulary.' Discuss. Base your answer on a close reading of 'Drummer Hodge'.

The Darkling Thrush

This poem is also prescribed for the Ordinary Level exam in 2015

I leant upon a coppice gate
   When Frost was spectre-gray,
And Winter's dregs made desolate
   The weakening eye of day.
The tangled bine-stems scored the sky   5
   Like strings of broken lyres,
And all mankind that haunted nigh
   Had sought their household fires.

The land's sharp features seemed to be
   The Century's corpse outleant,   10
His crypt the cloudy canopy,
   The wind his death-lament.
The ancient pulse of germ and birth
   Was shrunken hard and dry,
And every spirit upon earth   15
   Seemed fervourless as I.

At once a voice arose among
   The bleak twigs overhead
In a full-hearted evensong
   Of joy illimited;   20
An aged thrush, frail, gaunt, and small,
   In blast-beruffled plume,
Had chosen thus to fling his soul
   Upon the growing gloom.

So little cause for carolings   25
   Of such ecstatic sound
Was written on terrestrial things
   Afar or nigh around,
That I could think there trembled through
   His happy good-night air   30
Some blessed Hope, whereof he knew
   And I was unaware.

Thomas Hardy

Notes

1	**coppice:**	a thicket; grove or growth of trees
7	**haunted:**	frequented
7	**nigh:**	near or nearby
10	**outleant:**	laid out or outlined
13	**pulse:**	edible seed of leguminous crops such as peas, beans or lentils
22	**beruffle:**	to roughen; trouble or erect in a ruff

Explorations

FIRST READING

1. 'I leant upon a coppice gate'.
   What did the poet see in stanza 1?

2.

a Examine the funeral arrangements for the 'Century' in stanza 2. What represents the laid-out corpse?

b Other elements in the description represent the tomb and funeral music. Explain.

3.

a What details do you consider to be significant in the description of the thrush in the third stanza?

b How do you think the poet feels about the thrush?

4. Why is the poet so surprised by the bird's song in the final stanza?

SECOND READING

5. What details make the first two stanzas 'desolate'?

6. Is there a contrast between the bird's physical appearance and the 'joy illimited' of its song?

7. 'Some blessed Hope': does the poet share this feeling?

THIRD READING

8. The poem was originally published under the title 'By the Century's Deathbed'. Do you think this title helps you understand the poet's purpose in writing the poem? Explain your answer.

9. 'At once a voice arose among'. Comment on Hardy's use of sound as the birdsong is described.

10. Describe the central mood of the poem. How is it created? Is the mood modified at any stage? Comment on the words or images that help to achieve such a change.

11. What images in the poem appeal to you particularly? Explain why you find them effective.

FOURTH READING

12. ' "The Darkling Thrush" is not just a poem about a bird, but a profound and wide-ranging meditation on time, history and faith.' Discuss.

13. Philip Larkin wrote that 'the dominant emotion in Hardy is sadness'. Based on the evidence of this poem, do you agree?

14. ' "The Darkling Thrush" is rich in imagery, personification and contrasts.' Discuss.

The Self-Unseeing

Here is the ancient floor,
Footworn and hollowed and thin,
Here was the former door
Where the dead feet walked in.

She sat here in her chair,   5
Smiling into the fire;
He who played stood there,
Bowing it higher and higher.

Childlike, I danced in a dream;
Blessings emblazoned that day;   10
Everything glowed with a gleam;
Yet we were looking away!

Explorations

BEFORE READING

1. What is your favourite piece of dance
    music? How does the music make
    you feel? Make a list of words that
    help describe how the music affects
    you. Do you associate the music with
    a particular person, place or time?

FIRST READING

2. How do you visualise the setting in
    the first stanza? What do you think
    is left of 'the ancient floor' and 'the
    former door'?

3. As a young man, Hardy played the
    violin at parties and dances. Can
    you imagine the scene described
    in the second stanza? What kind of
    atmosphere was there? Hardy had
    been known to burst into tears while
    playing. Do you get any sense of that
    kind of intensity from the text? A
    short paragraph will suffice for your
    answer.

4. How did the speaker feel as the third
    stanza opens? Did the feeling last?
    How does she or he feel now?

5. How do you imagine the speaker as a
    young person? How do you see him/
    her as the poem was written?

SECOND READING

6. 'Where the dead feet walked in.'
    Describe your reaction to this line.

7. 'She sat here in her chair, | Smiling
    into the fire'.
    Visualise the girl. How do you
    imagine her? Why do you think she
    is mentioned in a poem that is so
    economical in its use of detail?

8. 'Blessings emblazoned that day'.
    What does Hardy mean by this
    phrase?

9. 'Yet we were looking away!'
    Read stanza 3 aloud. What tone of
    voice would you use for this line?

Thomas Hardy

10. State briefly the theme of this poem as you understand it.

11. What is the mood of this poem? How is the mood created? What details contribute to the poem's atmosphere?

12. Comment on Hardy's use of alliteration in the poem. What effects does he achieve?

13. Write a diary entry for any of the characters mentioned in the poem. Imagine their feelings and impressions.

14. 'Hardy has succeeded in conveying both the musical delight of the past and the evanescent (transient) quality of that past, though perhaps with the compensation that it can be recalled.' Discuss, with reference to the text.

15. 'A craftsman with words.' Evaluate Hardy's use of language in 'The Self-Unseeing'.
    Does the ballad format suit the subject matter? Comment on the verbal music.

Channel Firing

That night your great guns, unawares,
Shook all our coffins as we lay,
And broke the chancel window-squares,
We thought it was the Judgment-day

And sat upright. While drearisome   5
Arose the howl of wakened hounds:
The mouse let fall the altar-crumb,
The worms drew back into the mounds,

The glebe cow drooled. Till God called, 'No;
It's gunnery practice out at sea   10
Just as before you went below;
The world is as it used to be:

'All nations striving strong to make
Red war yet redder. Mad as hatters
They do no more for Christés sake   15
Than you who are helpless in such matters.

'That this is not the judgment-hour
For some of them's a blessed thing,
For if it were they'd have to scour
Hell's floor for so much threatening ...   20

'Ha, ha. It will be warmer when
I blow the trumpet (if indeed
I ever do; for you are men,
And rest eternal sorely need).'

So down we lay again. 'I wonder,   25
Will the world ever saner be,'
Said one, 'than when He sent us under
In our indifferent century!'

And many a skeleton shook his head.
'Instead of preaching forty year,'   30
My neighbour Parson Thirdly said,
'I wish I had stuck to pipes and beer.'

Again the guns disturbed the hour,
Roaring their readiness to avenge,
As far inland as Stourton Tower,   35
And Camelot, and starlit Stonehenge.

April 1914

Thomas Hardy

Notes

3	**chancel:**	part of the church containing the altar and seats for the clergy or choir
7	**altar-crumb:**	referring to the mouse stealing pieces of the consecrated bread
9	**glebe:**	a plot of land belonging or yielding profit to a parish church

Explorations

BEFORE READING

1. What do you associate with the dates 1914 or 1939? Describe the thoughts, feelings and pictures that come to your attention. What enduring impression are you left with?

FIRST READING

2. How do you imagine the scene described in the first two stanzas? What details strike you on a first reading?

3. Who is speaking in the opening stanza? What kind of character is she or he? How do you see the person?

4. What does God have to say? What is His attitude to events in the world? How do you react to His sense of humour ('Ha, ha')?

5. Why did 'many a skeleton [shake] his head'? What is meant by this gesture?

6. What point do you think the parson is making when he says, 'I wish I had stuck to pipes and beer'? Does he think his life was spent productively?

SECOND READING

7. What details dramatise the effects of the guns being fired? Look at the various reactions and the words and images used.

8. 'The world is as it used to be'. What do you understand by this line? What view of the world is apparent in this poem?

9. Read the poem aloud. What tone(s) of voice would you use? How should the poem sound? Do you notice anything on reading the poem aloud that you might have missed in a silent reading?

10. What is Hardy suggesting by his references to 'Camelot, and starlit Stonehenge' in the final stanza?

THIRD READING

11. Outline the main themes of this poem as you understand them.

12. What is the effect of Hardy's use of direct speech? Examine the poem's language.

13. 'I wonder, | Will the world ever saner be'. How do you think Hardy would have answered this question?

14. Comment on the imagery used in the poem. Do you find it effective?

FOURTH READING

15. This poem is dated April 1914, but it has a timeless relevance. Do you agree? What view of the world and humanity is presented in the text?

The Convergence of the Twain

(Lines on the loss of the Titanic*)*

I

In a solitude of the sea
Deep from human vanity,
And the Pride of Life that planned her, stilly couches she.

II

Steel chambers, late the pyres
Of her salamandrine fires,   5
Cold currents thrid, and turn to rhythmic tidal lyres.

III

Over the mirrors meant
To glass the opulent
The sea-worm crawls – grotesque, slimed, dumb, indifferent.

IV

Jewels in joy designed   10
To ravish the sensuous mind
Lie lightless, all their sparkles bleared and black and blind.

V

Dim moon-eyed fishes near
Gaze at the gilded gear
And query: 'What does this vaingloriousness down here?'   15

VI

Well: while was fashioning
This creature of cleaving wing,
The Immanent Will that stirs and urges everything

VII

Prepared a sinister mate
For her – so gaily great –   20
A Shape of Ice, for the time far and dissociate.

VIII

And as the smart ship grew
In stature, grace, and hue,
In shadowy silent distance grew the Iceberg too.

Thomas Hardy

IX

Alien they seemed to be:
No mortal eye could see
The intimate welding of their later history,

25

X

Or sign that they were bent
By paths coincident
On being anon twin halves of one august event,

30

XI

Till the Spinner of the Years
Said 'Now!' And each one hears,
And consummation comes, and jars two hemispheres.

- -

Notes

	Twain:	archaic word for two
5	salamandrine:	refers to a mythical creature who lived in fire; also a mass of solidified material, largely metallic, left in a blast furnace hearth
6	thrid:	a vibrating noise produced by engines
6	lyre:	an ancient stringed musical instrument
12	bleared:	blurred

Explorations

1. Brainstorm what the *Titanic* suggests to you. Jot down the words and phrases that come to mind. Visualise the ship: how do you see it? Do any details stand out?

FIRST READING

2. 'Deep from human vanity'.
   What aspect of human vanity is referred to in the opening stanza?

3. What point is made about the liner's opulent decoration in stanzas 3–5?

4. 'The Immanent Will that stirs and urges everything'.
   What role is played in stanzas 6–8 by the 'Immanent Will'?

5. How is a sense of drama built up in the final three stanzas?

6. How do you visualise 'the Spinner of the Years'? Does this 'Spinner' care about people or the consequences of actions? Is this a conventional Christian picture of God?

SECOND READING

7. Read the poem aloud. What do you notice about the sounds and rhythms? Do some phrases strike you as particularly effective? Does the sound echo the sense anywhere? Make a brief note of your observations.

8. What is the poet's attitude to the ship? Does he admire it or is he critical of some aspects of its construction?

9. How does Hardy suggest the iceberg's sinister potential? What words and images are employed?

THIRD READING

10. Analyse how contrast is employed to dramatic effect in this poem. Choose one example to comment on in detail.

11. What is the mood of the poem? Describe how Hardy's choice of words and images establish the atmosphere.

12. 'This is a more public poem in terms of content and style than the others by Hardy on your course.'
    Discuss.

13. Do you think the stanza form is effective in this poem? What effects does Hardy achieve with the long third lines? Do you find the rhyme scheme off-putting or does it work well for you?

FOURTH READING

14. What do you think of the absence of people in the poem? Does the operation of fate and the depiction of 'human vanity' overshadow the human tragedy of lives lost and separation?

15. Does Hardy display a pessimistic vision of life in 'Convergence of the Twain'? Comment.

Thomas Hardy

77

Under the Waterfall

'Whenever I plunge my arm, like this,
In a basin of water, I never miss
The sweet sharp sense of a fugitive day
Fetched back from its thickening shroud of gray.
   Hence the only prime   5
   And real love-rhyme
   That I know by heart,
   And that leaves no smart,
Is the purl of a little valley fall
About three spans wide and two spans tall   10
Over a table of solid rock,
And into a scoop of the self-same block;
The purl of a runlet that never ceases
In stir of kingdoms, in wars, in peaces;
With a hollow boiling voice it speaks   15
And has spoken since hills were turfless peaks.'

'And why gives this the only prime
Idea to you of a real love-rhyme?
And why does plunging your arm in a bowl
Full of spring water, bring throbs to your soul?'   20

'Well, under the fall, in a crease of the stone,
Though where precisely none ever has known,
Jammed darkly, nothing to show how prized,
And by now with its smoothness opalized,
   Is a drinking-glass: 25
   For, down that pass
   My lover and I
   Walked under a sky
Of blue with a leaf-wove awning of green,
In the burn of August, to paint the scene,   30
And we placed our basket of fruit and wine
By the runlet's rim, where we sat to dine;
And when we had drunk from the glass together,
Arched by the oak-copse from the weather,
I held the vessel to rinse in the fall,   35
Where it slipped, and sank, and was past recall,
Though we stooped and plumbed the little abyss
With long bared arms. There the glass still is.
And, as said, if I thrust my arm below

Cold water in basin or bowl, a throe   40
From the past awakens a sense of that time,
And the glass we used, and the cascade's rhyme.
The basin seems the pool, and its edge
The hard smooth face of the brook-side ledge,
And the leafy pattern of china-ware   45
The hanging plants that were bathing there.

'By night, by day, when it shines or lours,
There lies intact that chalice of ours,
And its presence adds to the rhyme of love
Persistently sung by the fall above.   50
No lip has touched it since his and mine
In turns therefrom sipped lovers' wine.'

Notes

9	**purl:**	a swirling stream or rill; a gentle murmur of water
40	**throe:**	a pang or spasm
47	**lours:**	darken or threaten

Explorations

1. Imagine your favourite place. Briefly describe the colours, sounds, sights and smells that come to mind. Do you associate the place with any special memory or person? How do you feel when you think of this place?

FIRST READING

2. 'Hardy could always tell a good story.' What story is told in this poem?

3. What impression do you have of the narrator in this poem?

4. Describe the setting of the waterfall as you visualise it. What details strike you? Is it a romantic location?

5. The narrator speaks of the only love-rhyme 'that leaves no smart'. What do you understand this to mean?

6. What is it about the waterfall that most impresses the narrator? Is it something other than its physical beauty?

SECOND READING

7. How would you describe the mood of the poem? Select words and images that convey the mood.

8. 'And why does plunging your arm in a bowl | Full of spring water, bring throbs to your soul?'
   What gives this incident such significance for the narrator?

9. Imagine the scene as the lovers are about to start their picnic 'In the burn of August'. What details stand out?

10. Write a diary entry that one of the lovers would have written on returning from the picnic. Explore thoughts and feelings.

THIRD READING

11. Read the poem aloud and explore its rhythms, cadences and musical sound effects.

12. 'From the past awakens a sense of that time'.
    What role does nostalgia play in this poem?

13. Explore Hardy's descriptions of nature. Which do you consider to be most memorable? Does nature reflect the lovers' feelings?

14. 'There lies intact that chalice of ours'. Comment on how symbolism is used in the poem.

FOURTH READING

15. Based on the evidence of this poem, what is your assessment of Thomas Hardy as a love poet?

16. 'Hardy has the ability to make poetry from slight incidents.'
    Discuss this statement, taking 'Under the Waterfall' as the basis for your answer.

The Oxen

Christmas Eve, and twelve of the clock.
 'Now they are all on their knees,'
An elder said as we sat in a flock
 By the embers in hearthside ease.

We pictured the meek mild creatures where   5
 They dwelt in their strawy pen,
Nor did it occur to one of us there
 To doubt they were kneeling then.

So fair a fancy few would weave
 In these years! Yet, I feel,   10
If someone said on Christmas Eve,
 'Come; see the oxen kneel

'In the lonely barton by yonder coomb
 Our childhood used to know,'
I should go with him in the gloom,   15
 Hoping it might be so.

1915

Notes

| 13 | barton: | the domain land of a manse (country estate) or a farmyard |
| 13 | coomb: | a hollow in a hillside; a shelter |

Explorations

BEFORE READING

1. Think back to what Christmas meant to you as a child. Contrast that attitude with what Christmas means as a young adult. Do you have any sense of regret or nostalgia for the childhood experience?

FIRST READING

2. How do you visualise the scene described in the first stanza? Who is present? Where is the scene located? When is it set?

3. 'We pictured the meek mild creatures'.
Comment on how the animals are presented. What is the significance of them 'kneeling'?

4. What do you think the poet means by 'So fair a fancy'? Does he suggest that attitudes have changed 'In these years'?

5. How does the speaker feel in the final stanza?

Thomas Hardy

6. Describe how you imagine the speaker to be. Is it an old or a young person? Does the speaker feel that the world is a good and happy place?

7. 'Nor did it occur to one of us there | To doubt they were kneeling then.' What do you think Hardy means by this?

8. How does the poet feel about 'So fair a fancy'? Are his feelings a little mixed?

9. Use headings, a flow chart or a spider diagram to trace the development of thought in the poem.

10. How would you describe the tone in this poem? Which words and images contribute to the tone?

11. What do you notice about the style of language used in the poem? Why is direct speech used?

12. Would you agree that the poem displays a sense of nostalgia?

13. Comment on 'as we sat in a flock'. What does the image suggest to you? Did you find the imagery used in the poem effective?

14. What effect did reading this poem have on you? Could you identify with the poet's feelings?

15. 'In Hardy there is a tension between the man who loved the simple things in life and the intellectual sceptic who thought there was no benevolent God guiding the universe.' Discuss this statement and its relevance to 'The Oxen'.

During Wind and Rain

This poem is also prescribed for Ordinary Level exams in 2015

They sing their dearest songs –
He, she, all of them – yea,
Treble and tenor and bass,
    And one to play;
With the candles mooning each face ...   5
    Ah, no; the years O!
How the sick leaves reel down in throngs!

They clear the creeping moss –
Elders and juniors – aye,
Making the pathways neat   10
    And the garden gay;
And they build a shady seat ...
    Ah, no; the years, the years;
See, the white storm-birds wing across!

They are blithely breakfasting all – 15
Men and maidens – yea,
Under the summer tree,
    With a glimpse of the bay,
While pet fowl come to the knee ...
      Ah, no; the years O! 20
And the rotten rose is ript from the wall.

They change to a high new house,
He, she, all of them – aye,
Clocks and carpets and chairs
    On the lawn all day, 25
And brightest things that are theirs ...
     Ah, no; the years, the years;
Down their carved names the rain-drop ploughs.

Notes

15	blithely:	in a joyous manner

Explorations

FIRST READING

1. Describe what is happening in the first stanza. Who do you think the people are?

2. What does the image of 'sick leaves' suggest to you? How significant is Hardy's choice of the word 'sick'?

3. Explain how you view the people in stanza 3. Is their life comfortable? Is their home important to them?

4. 'Blithely breakfasting all'. What makes the breakfast scene so pleasant? Examine the scene in detail.

5. Is stanza 4 a good description of the organised chaos involved in moving house? Is this family moving up in the world? What is the poet saying about the 'brightest things that are theirs'?

Does the inclusion of the clock subtly suggest something?

SECOND READING

6. What do the images of 'storm-birds' and 'rotten rose' mean to you? What are they saying about human happiness?

7. 'Down their carved names the rain-drop ploughs.' How do you feel about the ending? Do you think the final line is prepared for earlier in the poem?

8. Who do you think the speaker in the poem is? What connection does she or he have with the people? How does she or he feel about them? Are the events described in the poem recent or are they set long in the past? Refer to the text in your answer.

Thomas Hardy

9. Is the title 'During Wind and Rain' appropriate? What do you think Hardy is drawing attention to?

THIRD READING

10. Briefly describe the four scenes of family life sketched by Hardy. What do the scenes have in common?

11. What does the reader learn about the people? Are the characters individuals or are they meant to represent humanity in general?

12. Contrast is used effectively in this poem. Examine the images that occur in the final lines of the four stanzas and explain what you understand by each of them. Do the images increase in power?

13. Music played an important role in Hardy's life. Comment on the verbal music in this poem. What techniques does the poet use to achieve musical effects in language?

14. In what ways can the poem be considered dramatic? Bear in mind Hardy's use of language and imagery.

FOURTH READING

15. Does this poem display Hardy's gifts as a novelist? Pay particular attention to his narrative abilities and his powers of observation and description.

16. Hardy has been accused of being overly pessimistic in his view of life. On the evidence of this poem, what do you think?

17. Compare and contrast Hardy's treatment of death in this poem with 'Afterwards'.

18. Hardy wrote, 'The business of the poet ... is to show the sorriness [sic] underlying the grandest things and the grandeur underlying the sorriest of things.' Is this statement applicable to 'During Wind and Rain'? Explain your answer.

Afterwards

When the Present has latched its postern behind my tremulous stay,
   And the May month flaps its glad green leaves like wings,
Delicate-filmed as new-spun silk, will the neighbours say,
   'He was a man who used to notice such things'?

If it be in the dusk when, like an eyelid's soundless blink,   5
   The dewfall-hawk comes crossing the shades to alight
Upon the wind-warped upland thorn, a gazer may think,
   'To him this must have been a familiar sight.'

If I pass during some nocturnal blackness, mothy and warm,
   When the hedgehog travels furtively over the lawn,   10
One may say, 'He strove that such innocent creatures should come no harm,
   But he could do little for them; and now he is gone.'

If, when hearing that I have been stilled at last, they stand at the door,
   Watching the full-starred heavens that winter sees,
Will this thought rise on those who will meet my face no more,   15
   'He was one who had an eye for such mysteries'?

And will any say when my bell of quittance is heard in the gloom,
   And a crossing breeze cuts a pause in its outrollings,
Till they rise again, as they were a new bell's boom,
   'He hears it not now, but used to notice such things'?   20

Notes

1	postern:	a back door or gate; also a private entrance
1	tremulous:	characterised by trembling; exceedingly sensitive
10	furtively:	done by stealth

Explorations

BEFORE READING

1. What does the title suggest to you? Jot down the ideas that come to mind. Share them with your classmates.

2. Imagine you had to deliver a funeral eulogy for someone you admired. What would you have to say about how the person would be remembered? What memories of the person would you refer to? Write the speaking notes you would use.

Thomas Hardy

3. ' "He was a man who used to notice such things".'
   What does the poet notice in the first stanza? How do you visualise the scene?

4. What impression do you get of the hawk in stanza 2? Do you detect a sense of menace?

5. On the evidence of the third stanza, what is the poet's attitude to 'such innocent creatures'? What does it tell us about him?

6. What 'mysteries' are present in the sky? Do you think Hardy is referring to his passion for astronomy, his lifelong interest in philosophy or both?

7. How do you think the poet feels about his death in the final stanza? Does he believe in any sort of afterlife?

SECOND READING

8. On the evidence of the poem, what kind of a man was Thomas Hardy? Describe how you see him and the things he cared about. Was he a self-important person?

9. List the five expressions (euphemisms: a mild word or phrase instead of a frank one) for death in each of the five stanzas. Are these images intimidating? How would you describe them?

10. This poem deals with death, but it is not at all bleak. Would you agree? How would you describe the tone of the poem? Comment on the choice of words and images that convey the tone.

11. Read the poem aloud. What do you notice about the sounds and movement of the poem? Does the use of language reflect the mood and the sense?

THIRD READING

12. Notice how Hardy appeals to the different senses in the poem. Find examples that you feel are particularly effective. Comment, for instance, on his choice of 'mothy' in stanza 3.

13. Hardy was an accomplished musician. Examine how he uses verbal music in the poem. It might be useful to bear in mind the following technical terms: sibilant ('s') sounds, assonance, alliteration and rhyme.

14. What does the imagery contribute to the effectiveness of the poem? Refer to specific examples.

15. Briefly express the theme.

FOURTH READING

16. Is Hardy's attitude to death different in this poem from that displayed in the other poems on your course? Sum up your conclusions on Hardy's treatment of death.

17. Do you like this poem? Explain your reaction.

When I set out for Lyonnesse

When I set out for Lyonnesse,
A hundred miles away,
The rime was on the spray,
And starlight lit my lonesomeness
When I set out for Lyonnesse   5
A hundred miles away.

What would bechance at Lyonnesse
While I should sojourn there
No prophet durst declare,
Nor did the wisest wizard guess   10
What would bechance at Lyonnesse
While I should sojourn there.

When I came back from Lyonnesse
With magic in my eyes,
All marked with mute surmise   15
My radiance rare and fathomless,
When I came back from Lyonnesse
With magic in my eyes!

Notes

	Lyonnesse:	this was the name of his first wife Emma Gifford's house. In legend, it is the home of King Arthur and Merlin the magician.
3	**rime:**	frost; an accumulation of ice
7	**bechance:**	happen
8	**sojourn:**	stay for a time
9	**durst:**	dared

Thomas Hardy
87

Explorations

FIRST READING

1. Briefly tell the story in the poem.

2. 'With magic in my eyes'.
   How is the sense of magic built up in the poem?

3. What do we know about the speaker? How do you visualise him? Is information deliberately kept from the reader to enhance the sense of mystery?

4. In medieval romance poems, the hero is frequently on a quest where he must overcome hardship. What is the hero of this poem on a quest for? Explain your answer.

SECOND READING

5. What details help to convey the poet's 'lonesomeness' in stanza 1?

6. What is the effect of the archaic language, such as 'bechance' and 'durst', in stanza 2? What does such diction contribute to the poem?

7. How do you think the final stanza relates to the rest of the poem? Has it been prepared for in the earlier stanzas?

8. How does the speaker's state of mind alter as he travels? Refer to the text in your answer.

THIRD READING

9. Does the knowledge that this poem was written against the background of a marriage that later failed affect how you view the poem?

10. Hardy wrote of Cornwall, 'The place is pre-eminently the region of dream and mystery.' What does 'Lyonnesse' suggest to you? Do you think of it as a place or a state of mind?

11. The poem has many features of the traditional ballad. Comment on the subject matter and Hardy's use of simple diction, archaic words, repetition, rhyme and musical sound effects.

FOURTH READING

12. Does this poem fit in with the view of Thomas Hardy's work you have gained from reading the other poems on your course? Explain your answer.

13. What does this poem say to you about love? How would you rate 'When I set out for Lyonnesse' as a love poem?

14. 'When I set out for Lyonnesse' is remarkable for the way in which the poet has been able to transmute autobiographical details into that of a medieval romance. Discuss.

Gerard Manley Hopkins

(1844–89)

Prescribed for Higher Level exams in 2017 and 2018

On Saturday, 8 June 1889, at 85 St Stephen's Green, Dublin, a Jesuit priest died of typhoid. None of the other priests who shared the rat-infested building with the odd little man from England could have guessed that he would be commemorated a hundred years later as one of the most important poets in the English language.

Gerard Manley Hopkins was born into a prosperous Anglican family on 28 July 1844 at Stratford in Essex. He was the oldest of nine children. The Hopkins household had a great interest in poetry, drawing, music and architecture. In 1854, Gerard was sent to Highgate School as a boarder. One of his teachers described him as 'a pale young boy, very light and active, with a very meditative and intellectual face'. He was fiercely independent and an outstanding student, winning prizes for poetry and a scholarship to study Classics at Balliol College, Oxford. At Oxford, Hopkins converted to Catholicism and in 1868 he joined the Jesuit Order. He decided to destroy the poems that he had written because he wished to devote his life totally to the service of God (an act which he described as 'the slaughter of the innocents').

'In my salad days, in my Welsh days': St Beuno's College, North Wales, 1874–77

Hopkins was sent to St Beuno's College in North Wales to study theology. In 1875, he was encouraged by one of his superiors to write a poem to commemorate the death of five German nuns in a shipwreck. The result was 'The Wreck of the Deutschland', a poem of extraordinary brilliance and originality; in fact, it was so innovative in its use of language and rhythm that no editor would publish it. Undeterred by the unfavourable reaction, Hopkins continued to write poetry. He corresponded regularly with a friend from his days at Oxford, Robert Bridges. Despite Bridges's dislike for his technical experimentation, Hopkins sensed the importance of his own work. It was Bridges who first published Hopkins's work in 1918, almost 30 years after the poet's death.

The first five poems by Hopkins in this anthology were written in St Beuno's in 1877, between the months of March and August. This was one of the happiest times in the poet's adult life – he called them 'my salad days'. These poems are often referred to as the 'bright sonnets' because of the poet's optimistic mood and obvious delight in the beautiful Clwyd Valley and distant Snowdonia. They contrast starkly with the 'terrible sonnets' he wrote later.

'The encircling gloom': Liverpool and Glasgow, 1878–81

After his ordination, Hopkins spent time teaching Classics and doing some parish work. Towards the end of 1879, he was sent to work in a parish in Bedford Leigh, near Manchester, and then to St Francis Xavier's in the heart of industrial Liverpool. The poet who had such a love of nature was shocked to see the full impact of England's Industrial Revolution. The population of the city had increased dramatically as a result of immigration from famine-stricken Ireland and pollution from the factories was unregulated. He found some comfort in the warmth of the local people who made him feel welcome.

One of these local people, a 31-year-old farrier, died from consumption on 21 April 1880. His name was Felix Spencer. A week later, Hopkins wrote the poem 'Felix Randal', which is included in this anthology.

In 1881, Hopkins spent a few months working in St Joseph's Parish in Glasgow. Before he left Scotland, on 28 September, he paid a visit to Inversnaid, on the eastern shore of Loch Lomond. William Wordsworth's poem 'To a Highland Girl (At Inversnayde, upon Loch Lomond)' may well have prompted this visit. He wasn't very happy with the poem that he composed, 'Inversnaid'. It remained unseen until after his death.

'To seem the stranger lies my lot, my life': Dublin, 1884–89

Hopkins's appointment as Fellow of the Royal University of Ireland and Professor of Greek and Latin Literature at the Catholic University of Ireland was not the accolade one might think. The English Provincial of the Jesuits did not know where to employ the eccentric priest and the President of the University wanted a fellow Jesuit so that he could spend the annual salary of £400 on the upkeep of the college. Thus began the most miserable period in the poet's short life.

'Gerard Hopkins was at an opposite pole to everything around him: literary, political, social, etc. (a thorough John Bull incapable of understanding Rebel Ireland). No one took him seriously.' (Fr Joe Darlington, a colleague of Hopkins in the university)

To make matters worse, the poet's primary responsibility for the five years he lived in Dublin was correcting examination papers. Alienation and physical exhaustion took its toll on his spiritual wellbeing and he began to suffer from deep depression. The so-called 'terrible sonnets' – 'No Worst, There Is None' and 'I Wake and Feel the Fell of Dark' – were written in 1885 and mark the nadir of his life.

Even though there is evidence of a spiritual recovery, his physical deterioration was hastened by the unsanitary conditions in which he lived. One of his last poems, 'Thou Art Indeed Just, Lord', was written on St Patrick's Day 1889, a few months before he died at the relatively young age of 44. His final words were, 'I am so happy, I am so happy.' He is buried in Glasnevin Cemetery in Dublin.

God's Grandeur

The world is charged with the grandeur of God.
  It will flame out, like shining from shook foil;
  It gathers to a greatness, like the ooze of oil
Crushed. Why do men then now not reck his rod?
Generations have trod, have trod, have trod;   5
  And all is seared with trade; bleared, smeared with toil;
  And wears man's smudge and shares man's smell: the soil
Is bare now, nor can foot feel, being shod.

And for all this, nature is never spent;
  There lives the dearest freshness deep down things;   10
And though the last lights off the black West went
  Oh, morning, at the brown brink eastward, springs –
Because the Holy Ghost over the bent
  World broods with warm breast and with ah! bright wings.

Notes

		This poem was written while Hopkins was studying in St Beuno's (pronounced 'Bíno') College in North Wales. The poet sent it as a birthday present to his mother on 3 March 1877.
1	charged:	as in electrically charged, suggesting a force rather than a substance: 'All things therefore are charged with love, are charged with God, and if we know how to touch them, give off sparks and take fire, yield drops and flow, ring and tell of him.' *Hopkins*
2	foil:	as in tin foil, a leaf of metal often used to set something off by contrast
3	ooze of oil:	a reference to the harvesting of fruit, compared with: 'Or by a cyder-press, with patient look, Thou watchest the last oozings hours by hours.' *Keats, 'Ode to Autumn'*
4	reck:	heed
4	rod:	authority
6	seared:	withered, scorched
9	spent:	used up, exhausted
12	brink:	brink of daylight

Explorations

BEFORE READING

1. Have you ever been startled by the beauty of a natural scene? Do you ever feel that development, 'progress', the work of mankind is destroying the beauty of the natural world? Discuss these ideas before reading the poem.

FIRST READING

2. All poetry should be experienced 'through the ears' at first. This is especially true of Hopkins's poetry. Read the poem aloud several times. Experiment with the placing of stresses until you find a version that is satisfactory.

3. Pick out a phrase, image or even a word that appeals to you and say why you chose it. (Imagine that you are thinking up a name for a band, e.g. Crushed!)

4. This is the first of Hopkins's so-called 'bright sonnets'. Can you suggest a reason why the poem is considered 'bright'?

SECOND READING

5. What qualities of the natural world does the poet admire?

6. How does the poet contrast the different manifestations of God's grandeur?

7. At what point does the poet move from admiration to reflection?

8. What, according to the poet, has been the impact of mankind on the natural world?

9. Identify the ways in which mankind is perceived to have affected the physical world.

10. What is the effect of the last word of the image in line 8, 'nor can foot feel, being shod'? What does it suggest about the poet's attitude to human development?

11. How does the mood of the poem change in the sestet?

12. Consider the possible meanings of the line, 'There lives the dearest freshness deep down things'. What word is missing from this statement? The omission of a word from a line is a stylistic device called ellipsis. Hopkins used it frequently. When you have encountered more examples of it, consider its effect.

13. Lines 11–12 state in an unusual way that the sun sets and rises again. How does the poet's manner of expressing this idea add greater significance to this mundane event? Does this image have any religious resonance?

14. What is the effect of the 'ah!' in the final line?

THIRD READING

15. Identify the changes of tone in the poem. Which one is predominant?

16. There is a great sense of energy in the first quatrain. How does the poet generate this energy? Pay close attention to rhythm and sound.

17. How does the second quatrain differ from the first in terms of sound and rhythm?

18. Carefully consider the implications of the final image of the poem. How is the Holy Ghost represented?

FOURTH READING

19. How does the poet perceive the relationship between man, God and the natural world?

20. What words or phrases appeal to your senses?

21. How does this poem vary from the standard Petrarchan sonnet?

22. Carefully consider the meaning, the sound and the position of the word 'Crushed'. Would you agree that the poet draws attention to the word? Watch out for other words in later poems that are highlighted by their position in a similar way.

23. What peculiarities of style can you identify in this poem? Pay particular attention to the sound effects.

24. Is there a tension in the poem between the poet who loves beauty and the priest who feels a duty to moralise? Consider the manner in which the poet moves from joy in the contemplation of the natural world to dismay at the way mankind has abused the world, and finally to the assertion that the Holy Ghost will continue to nurture the world. Do you find this movement satisfying?

25. In what way are the poet's concerns relevant to today's world?

26. If you had to recommend this poem to a friend, what aspect or aspects of the poem would you choose to highlight?

Gerard Manley Hopkins

As Kingfishers Catch Fire, Dragonflies Draw Flame

As kingfishers catch fire, dragonflies draw flame;
   As tumbled over rim in roundy wells
   Stones ring; like each tucked string tells, each hung bell's
Bow swung finds tongue to fling out broad its name;
Each mortal thing does one thing and the same: 5
   Deals out that being indoors each one dwells;
   Selves – goes itself; *myself* it speaks and spells,
Crying *What I do is me: for that I came.*

Í say more: the just man justices;
   Keeps gráce: thát keeps all his goings graces;   10
Acts in God's eye what in God's eye he is –
   Chríst. For Christ plays in ten thousand places,
Lovely in limbs, and lovely in eyes not his
   To the Father through the features of men's faces.

Background note

'All things therefore are charged with love, are charged with God, and if we know how to touch them give off sparks and take fire, yield drops and flow, ring and tell of him.' *Notebooks and papers of Hopkins*

Notes

1	**kingfisher:**	a bird with brilliant plumage
1	**dragonfly:**	an insect
3	**tucked:**	plucked
6	**indoors:**	within
7	**Selves:**	(verb) asserts its own nature, individuality
9	**justices:**	(verb) acts in a way that promotes justice: 'acts in a godly manner, lives fully energised by grace, justness, sanctity' (R.V. Schoder SJ).

Explorations

BEFORE READING

1. 'I am what I am,' a politician once said in self-defence. What do you think he meant? Was it a declaration of apology or defiance? How many of us have the courage to be what we are? Do we express our individuality

or hide it behind a veneer of conformity? Is there any other creature or object in existence that possesses such individuality as we do?

2. Read the poem aloud several times. What sounds dominate?

3. Pick out a phrase or image that you find appealing, intriguing or strange. Explain your choice.

4. This poem can be quite difficult to grasp on a first reading. The language itself is not difficult; however, the poet has concentrated his meaning through the use of ellipsis and unusual syntax. It becomes easier to understand when one realises that the same idea is expressed in different ways throughout the octet. Consider the statement, 'What I do is me: for that I came.' It asserts not only the individuality of all things, but also the notion that everything and everyone has its role in God's creation. With this in mind, attempt an explanation of the first line of the poem.

5. Identify the images in lines 2, 3 and 4. What do they have in common?

6. What are all these creatures and things doing?

7. The poet seems to give a sense of destiny or purpose to animate and inanimate objects alike. Identify examples of each. Consider the significance of this idea.

8. Do you agree that there is an extraordinary intensity and sense of conviction to the octet? How is this intensity conveyed?

9. How does the sestet develop the thought in the octet? Would you agree that there is a change of emphasis from the philosophical to the religious?

10.

a What is your reaction to a statement such as 'the just man justices'? Does it read well? Is it poetic? Can you think of a reason why the poet should express himself in such a way?

b Are there any other expressions in the poem that strike you as odd or unusual?

11. In the last three lines, the poet suggests that the 'imprint' of Christ's love is evident in all aspects of God's creation. Everything in existence is unique and has its own essence, but each individual person and thing shares in God's design. The poet sees Christ in 'ten thousand places' and in 'men's faces'. This is the unifying and moral principle that governs the universe. This is how Hopkins sees the incarnation of Christ. Find out what you can about the word 'incarnation'. It is a very important word if you want to understand the way Hopkins relates to the world.

12. How does this poem differ from 'God's Grandeur'? Would you agree that the nature imagery is employed in a different way in this poem?

13. This poem is believed to have been written as a defence of Scotism against Thomism. The teachings

Gerard Manley Hopkins

of Duns Scotus advocated the uniqueness of all things and the ability of the senses to perceive what is good and beautiful. In this philosophy there is a moral value to what is beautiful. This point of view has great significance for a priest who was made to doubt the value of poetry by his superiors. Thomas Aquinas, on the other hand, was suspicious of the senses and stressed the importance of reason. Try to relate these ideas to the poem. What is your own view on this debate, which is sometimes characterised as a debate between the emotions and reason, romance and pragmatism, the heart and the head?

Spring

This poem is also prescribed for Ordinary Level exams in 2017 and 2018

Bad definite statment

Nothing is so beautiful as Spring —
   When weeds, in wheels, shoot long and lovely and lush;
   Thrush's eggs look little low heavens, and thrush
Through the echoing timber does so rinse and wring
The ear, it strikes like lightnings to hear him sing;   5
   The glassy peartree leaves and blooms, they brush
   The descending blue; that blue is all in a rush
With richness; the racing lambs too have fair their fling.

What is all this juice and all this joy?
   A strain of the earth's sweet being in the beginning   10
In Eden garden. — Have, get, before it cloy,
   Before it cloud, Christ, lord, and sour with sinning,
Innocent mind and Mayday in girl and boy,
   Most, O maid's child, thy choice and worthy the winning.

Notes

2	**wheels:**	an architectural term that describes a design similar to the wheel of a bicycle with spokes radiating from the centre
3	**low heavens:**	the eggs mirror the pattern of the clouds against the sky (a dappled effect)
4	**timber:**	tree or wood
4	**rinse and wring:**	the effect of the bird's song on the ear
6	**leaves and blooms:**	these nouns are used as verbs here
8	**fair:**	abundant

9	juice:	possibly meaning the essence or spirit of a thing
10	strain:	a musical term meaning a remembered melody and/or an inherited quality
11	cloy:	satiate, fill to the limit, lose its appeal (verb having 'innocent mind' and 'Mayday' as object)
12	cloud:	verb having 'innocent mind' and 'Mayday' as object
12	sour:	verb having 'innocent mind' and 'Mayday' as object
13	Mayday:	Hopkins associates May with the purity of Mary, the Blessed Virgin and Mother
14	maid's child:	Jesus

Explorations

1. Read the poem aloud several times. Listen carefully to the rhythm or movement of the lines in order to pick up the mood of the poem. Is this a happy or sad poem? Pick out phrases or images that capture the mood of the first verse.

2. Does this poem remind you of 'God's Grandeur' in any way? Discuss the similarities briefly.

SECOND READING

3. The opening line of the poem is very simple. What is the effect of such a simple beginning? Does it draw you into the poem?

4. Does it surprise you that the poet enthuses about weeds in the second line? What qualities do weeds have that might appeal to the poet? Does his admiration for weeds tell us anything about his personality? How has your attitude to weeds been developed?

5. What does the poet mean by the phrase 'rinse and wring | The ear'?

Consider carefully the meanings and associations attached to these two words. Do you think they are unusual words to describe the effect of the bird's song? Suggest a reason for the poet's choice of image.

6. In 'God's Grandeur', the poet described how God's grandeur 'will flame out'. Here, he describes the song of the bird striking him 'like lightning'. What effect is the poet creating with these images?

7. Would you agree that there is a great sense of startled delight in the octet? How does the poet achieve this?

8.

a In the octet, the poet provides us with a rich array of movement, sounds, shapes, textures and colours. Identify each one of them.

b How does the poet move from weeds to thrush's eggs, to the 'glassy peartree' and finally to the 'descending blue'? Would you agree that the movement follows the eye naturally?

c How does the poet return from the sky to the lambs?

v₁·6,9 ,16,17

Gerard Manley Hopkins

9. What is the tone of the sestet? How does it differ from the octet? Consider the effect of the question in line 9.

10. The poet seems to associate springtime with paradise, but it is only a strain that will soon disappear. Does the poet suggest any reason for this?

11.

a Do you find the reflection in the sestet satisfying or an intrusion on the wonderful description of spring?

b Does the complicated syntax (sentence structure) jar the ear after the vibrant octet?

THIRD READING

12. Look for examples of the following features: alliteration, assonance, rhyme, ellipsis. Explain how they contribute to the poem.

FOURTH READING

13. Do you consider this an optimistic or pessimistic poem? Give reasons for your answer.

14. What is the theme of this poem?

15. Do you note any variations in the use of the Petrarchan sonnet?

16. What similarities have you discovered between this poem and 'God's Grandeur' in terms of theme and poetic technique?

17. Which poem do you prefer and why? Do you prefer the poet's descriptions of nature or his meditations on its significance? Or do you find the combination of description and reflection most satisfying?

The Windhover

To Christ our Lord

I caught this morning morning's minion, kingdom
  of daylight's dauphin, dapple-dawn-drawn Falcon, in his riding
  Of the rolling level underneath him steady air, and striding
High there, how he rung upon the rein of a wimpling wing
In his ecstasy! then off, off forth on swing,   5
  As a skate's heel sweeps smooth on a bow-bend: the hurl and gliding
  Rebuffed the big wind. My heart in hiding
Stirred for a bird, – the achieve of, the mastery of the thing!

Brute beauty and valour and act, oh, air, pride, plume, here
  Buckle! And the fire that breaks from thee then, a billion   10
Times told lovelier, more dangerous, O my chevalier!

  No wonder of it: shéer plód makes plough down sillion
Shine, and blue-bleak embers, ah my dear,
  Fall, gall themselves, and gash gold-vermilion.

Notes

		Hopkins described this poem as 'the best thing I ever wrote'.
	Windhover:	a kestrel, common in the Clwyd area of Wales. At St Beuno's College there was a glass case of stuffed birds on which the following inscription was written: 'The Kestrel or Windhover: The commonest and most conspicuous of British falcons remarkable for its habit of remaining suspended in the air without changing position while it scans the ground for its prey.'
1	**caught:**	caught sight of (an example of ellipsis)
1	**minion:**	favourite
2	**dauphin:**	prince, heir apparent to the French throne (to the kingdom of daylight)
2	**dapple-dawn-drawn:**	a coined adjective meaning 'dappled and drawn out in front of the dawn' or 'dappled and attracted by the dawn'
4	**rung upon the rein:**	(i) a technical term of the riding school – 'to ring on the rein' is said of a horse that circles at the end of a long rein held by its trainer; (ii) 'to ring' in falconry means to rise in spirals
4	**wimpling:**	pleated
6	**bow-bend:**	as the skater forms the figure 8
6	**hurl:**	normally a verb, but here it is a noun meaning the vigorous forward motion
8	**achieve:**	verb used as noun meaning 'achievement'
10	**Buckle:**	this complex word is crucial to the meaning of the poem. There are several possible interpretations: (i) prepare for action, come to grips, engage the enemy; (ii) clasp, enclose, bring together as one; (iii) give way, bend, collapse under stress or pressure. Interpretations (i) and (ii) can be combined in the image of the chivalric knight putting on his armour in order to do battle. Perhaps the poet is pleading for the qualities mentioned to be united 'here' in his heart.
10	**fire:**	characteristic energy
11	**chevalier:**	a knight (French), a reference to Christ
12	**shéer plód:**	sheer hard work
12	**sillion:**	a strip of arable land
14	**gall:**	hurt
14	**gold-vermilion:**	a mixture of gold and red colour

Explorations

1. Some people erroneously regard poetry as a kind of cryptic puzzle to be solved, a sort of verbal Rubik's Cube. If the primary purpose in reading a poem is to 'find the meaning', then surely the poet would have been better employed writing his or her ideas in understandable prose. Clearly, there is more to a poem than 'meaning'. The way in which the 'meaning' is expressed provides the 'beauty' or aesthetic value of a poem. It is possible to enjoy the beauty of a poem without understanding the meaning. Discuss your attitude to poetry in general and how your view of it has been formed.

FIRST READING

2. In a letter to Robert Bridges about this poem, Hopkins invited him to 'Take breath and read it with the ears, as I always wish to be read, and my verse becomes all right.' Read the first eight lines several times and try to get a sense of the rhythm. Pay particular attention to the changes of pace. Do you agree that the rhythm seems to capture the flight of the bird and that there is a sense of awe and breathlessness as one reaches the end of the octet? How is this achieved?

3. The poet gives a procession of titles to the kestrel, 'as in some royal proclamation of medieval pageantry' (Peter Milward SJ). What is the effect of this? How does it lead into the imagery of horse-riding?

4. How does the poet convey the sense that the bird is in complete control of its environment?

5.

a   The poet uses imagery from the worlds of horse-riding and skating to describe the movement of the bird. Look closely at these images and describe the movements of the bird in your own words.

b   Do you think the poet's use of imagery is effective in communicating the grace, elegance and energy of the bird?

6. Is there a paradox in the combination of 'hurl' and 'gliding'? Explain.

7.

a   Why is the poet's heart 'in hiding'? Is he afraid, ashamed, humbled, envious?

b   Why might a student priest feel envious of this magnificent bird in flight?

c   Why does he write 'for a bird' rather than 'for the bird'?

8. The first tercet begins with a list of qualities the bird embodies. Describe these qualities in your own words.

9.

a   Look at the possible meanings of 'Buckle' and arrive at your own conclusions on its meaning.

b   Does the capitalisation of the word 'and' imply a consequence of 'Buckle'?

c   What does 'thee' refer to? His heart? The bird? Christ? Consider the possibilities.

10. The second part of the tercet is addressed to 'my chevalier'. What connection does the poet see between the windhover and Christ our Lord? Is there a physical similarity between the bird with its outstretched wings and Christ on the Cross? Does the poet see the bird battling against the wind as a symbol of Christ battling against evil? Consider these possibilities.

SECOND READING

11. The poet uses quite a varied diction in this poem. At the start, the language is regal – 'minion', 'kingdom', 'dauphin'. What other categories of words are used in the poem? Note the contrast between words like 'Buckle', 'plód' and 'minion', 'sillion', 'billion', 'vermilion'. Describe the texture of these words.

12. The second tercet presents the reader with two images of beauty evolving out of what appears to be unpleasant. The drudgery of ploughing the land brings forth a radiant surface.

    The embers of a dying fire fall from the grate, breaking open to reveal the glowing interior. What resonances do these images create in the context of the whole poem? Do they connect with the image of Christ on the Cross in any way?

13.

a Would you agree that there is a passionate intensity to this poem? How is this effect created?

b Is there a mystical quality to this poem? Discuss your understanding of mysticism.

THIRD READING

14.

a Compare this poem with the previous three poems under the following headings: theme, mood, development of thought, style and use of the sonnet form.

b Would you agree that it is quite different in terms of development of thought and use of the sonnet form?

15. Find out what you can about the Spiritual Exercises of St Ignatius Loyola, in particular his 'Meditation on the Kingdom'.

16. Find out what you can about sprung rhythm, inscape and instress.

17. This poem is written in a remarkably original style. Consider the elements of that style, such as the use of alliteration, assonance, exclamation, ellipsis, inversion, compound adjectives, the use of verbs as nouns, sprung rhythm and rhyme. What is the primary purpose of all these poetic devices? It might be useful to consider their effect.

18. Do the difficulties of interpretation make 'The Windhover' a richer or more frustrating poem? Is it possible to enjoy the parts of the poem without a clear understanding of the whole? Consider this question in relation to poetry in general.

Pied Beauty

Glory be to God for dappled things –
  For skies of couple-colour as a brinded cow;
    For rose-moles all in stipple upon trout that swim;
Fresh-firecoal chestnut-falls; finches' wings;
  Landscape plotted and pieced – fold, fallow, and plough;   5
    And áll trádes, their gear and tackle and trim.

All things counter, original, spare, strange;
  Whatever is fickle, freckled (who knows how?)
    With swift, slow; sweet, sour; adazzle, dim;
He fathers-forth whose beauty is past change: 10
  Praise him.

Notes

	Pied:	of different colours
1	**dappled:**	irregular patches of different colours. Hopkins was particularly fond of 'dappled' things. It is a word that he used frequently in his writings.
2	**brinded:**	brindled, brownish with streaks of another colour
3	**rose-mole:**	rose-like spots
3	**stipple:**	dotted
4	**Fresh-firecoal:**	In his journal (17 September 1868), Hopkins refers to 'Chestnuts as bright as coals or spots of vermilion'. (Vermilion is a brilliant red pigment.)
4	**chestnut-falls:**	see 'Fresh-firecoal' above
5	**fold:**	pasture for sheep to graze
5	**fallow**	unused
5	**and plough:**	planted with crops
6	**áll trádes ... tackle:**	the variety of trades with their different implements
7	**counter:**	all things that stand in contrast with other things
7	**spare:**	rare

Explorations

1.

a   Make a class list of 'beautiful things' to see if there is any consensus on what constitutes beauty. Consider the view that 'beauty is in the eye of the beholder'.

b   Is there a social pressure to conform to or agree on a single type of physical beauty? If so, where does this pressure come from? Have you ever considered as beautiful someone or something no one else admires?

FIRST READING

2.   This poem seems to be very simple in its message. It is a celebration of 'pied beauty' or the beauty that comes from a variety of colour and/or contrast. List all the examples of such beauty to be found in the poem.

3.

a   Are all the poet's illustrations of beauty taken from the natural world?

b   What does the poet mean in line 6 by 'áll trádes, their gear and tackle and trim'?

4.

a   Does his appreciation of variety and contrast extend beyond the mere physical in the last four lines?

b   Do you find it unusual that a priest in the 19th century should celebrate 'All things counter, original, spare, strange'?

c   Have you noticed any other aspects of Hopkins's poetry that suggest his unconventionality? Take another look at the descriptive adjectives used in lines 7–8.

SECOND READING

5.   How would you describe the tone of this poem?

6.   Do you notice a difference between this poem and 'As Kingfishers Catch Fire' on the one hand and 'God's Grandeur' and 'Spring' on the other?

7.   Consider the significance of line 10. Who is 'He'? How is his beauty 'past change'?

8.   What is the effect of the brief last line?

THIRD READING

9.   The poem supports the views of the painter John Ruskin, for whom Hopkins had great admiration. Find out what you can about Ruskin's aesthetic theory.

10. The simple opening and conclusion echo the Ignatian mottoes *Ad Maiorem Dei Gloriam* (AMDG) and *Laus Deo Semper* (LDS). The poem thus becomes a kind of prayer of praise and a meditation on the glory of God. Consider the efficacy of the poem as a prayer.

11. This is a curtal sonnet, i.e. a sonnet that has been cut short. How has the sonnet been shortened? Why do you think the poet chose to write such a sonnet?

12. This is the last of the five poems on your course that were written during a seven-month period in North Wales. Write a summary of the poet's central concerns in these poems. Make a list of stylistic features that are characteristic of Hopkins's poetry.

Felix Randal

[handwritten: heard news of death]

Felix Randal the farrier, O is he dead then? my duty all ended,
Who have watched his mould of man, big-boned and hardy-handsome
Pining, pining, till time when reason rambled in it and some *[handwritten: lost his mind]*
Fatal four disorders, fleshed there, all contended?

[handwritten left margin: wasting away]

Sickness broke him. Impatient, he cursed at first, but mended
Being anointed and all; though a heavenlier heart began some *[handwritten: focused on heaven]*
Months earlier, since I had our sweet reprieve and ransom
Tendered to him. Ah well, God rest him all road ever he offended!

[handwritten: priest anyway]

This seeing the sick endears them to us, us too it endears.
My tongue had taught thee comfort, touch had quenched thy tears,
Thy tears that touched my heart, child, Felix, poor Felix Randal;

[handwritten: Brought him comfort before death]

How far from then forethought of, all thy more boisterous years,
When thou at the random grim forge, powerful amidst peers,
Didst fettle for the great grey drayhorse his bright and battering sandal!

*[handwritten: Death was far from his mind that young
Died age (32)]*

[handwritten compass diagram: NW N NE W E SW S SE]

[handwritten: 10]

Notes

1	**farrier:**	a blacksmith or horse doctor
4	**fleshed:**	took hold of the flesh
4	**contended:**	competed
6	**heavenlier:**	more focused on the next world
7	**sweet reprieve and ransom:**	Holy Communion
8	**all road:**	in any way (colloquial Lancashire phrase)
12	**How far from then forethought of:**	how far away were the thoughts of death when you were in your prime
13	**random:**	an architectural term, meaning built with rough irregular stones; or it could refer to the untidiness of the forge
14	**drayhorse:**	a horse suitable for pulling heavy loads or dray carts

Explorations

BEFORE READING

1. One of the most challenging roles for a priest is to provide comfort to the sick and the dying. He must reconcile the existence of suffering with faith in a loving God. What must it be like to minister to the terminally ill? Does one become indifferent? Does it become a job? How important is faith in the afterlife? Imagine for a moment how you would cope in that role.

FIRST READING

2.

a Read the poem through several times. Would you agree that the meaning of the poem is relatively easy to grasp?

b Write a summary of the thoughts in the poem.

3.

a The poet provides the reader with a vivid picture of the farrier. What do we learn about his physical appearance and the changes that took place as a result of illness?

b What do we learn about his personality? Does it undergo any change?

4.

a How would you describe the relationship between the poet/priest and the farrier? Look at the opening statement and lines 9–11 in particular.

b Do you see any change or development in the poet's attitude to the farrier?

5. What is the effect of the questions in the first quatrain?

6. The first eight lines of the poem are primarily descriptive. How do the next six lines differ in mood?

7. In the first tercet (lines 9–11), how does the poet convey the idea that his relationship with the farrier was mutually rewarding?

8. In 'The Windhover', the student priest seemed to envy the bird's ability to 'achieve' something. Is there any hint in this poem to suggest that the poet finds satisfaction in his parish work?

9.

a The second tercet reflects another change of mood. The poet seems to be looking back to a time when the blacksmith was at his physical peak. What is the poet trying to achieve in these lines?

b How does the ending affect the overall mood of the poem?

10. Suggest reasons why the sandal is described as 'bright and battering'.

SECOND READING

11. The image of Holy Communion in line 7 ('our sweet reprieve and ransom') is a very rich one. Explore its connotations.

12. What is the effect created by the use of ellipsis (omission of words) in phrases such as 'my duty [is] all ended'?

13.

a Hopkins tended to use complex syntax in his poetry. The final sentence is a good example. What is the effect of such an unusual arrangement of words?

b Can you suggest a reason for this arrangement? Try arranging the sentence in a more normal manner and consider the merits of each arrangement.

14. Show how rhythm and imagery combine to create a powerful and triumphant conclusion to the poem.

15. Are there dramatic elements in this poem? Identify them.

THIRD READING

16. What elements of the sonnet form are recognisable in this poem? How does it differ from a conventional sonnet? How do the innovations contribute to the impact of the poem?

17. Is this a poem about death or a poem about religious faith? Explain your answer.

18. What significance is there in the phrase 'child, Felix, poor Felix Randal'? Does this phrase have a biblical resonance?

19. Return to your original summary. Would you agree that there is much more to this poem than you thought at first? Elaborate.

20. There is no record of a man named Felix Randal dying in Liverpool around this time, but there is a record for a man called Felix Spencer, who was a farrier. Look up the words 'felix' and 'rand' in the dictionary. Can you suggest a reason why the poet would have changed the man's name in this way?

21. Hopkins writes poetry that appeals to the senses. Discuss.

Inversnaid

This poem is also prescribed for Ordinary Level exams in 2017 and 2018

This darksome burn, horseback brown,
His rollrock highroad roaring down,
In coop and in comb the fleece of his foam
Flutes and low to the lake falls home.

A windpuff-bonnet of fáwn-fróth   5
Turns and twindles over the broth
Of a pool so pitchblack, féll-frówning,
It rounds and rounds Despair to drowning.

Degged with dew, dappled with dew
Are the groins of the braes that the brook treads through,   10
Wiry heathpacks, flitches of fern,
And the beadbonny ash that sits over the burn.

What would the world be, once bereft
Of wet and wildness? Let them be left,
O let them be left, wildness and wet;   15
Long live the weeds and the wilderness yet.

Gerard Manley Hopkins

Notes

1	burn:	a term frequently used by Scottish poets for a small stream. Arklet Water flows from Loch Arklet among the Trossachs and enters Loch Lomond near Inversnaid.
3	coop:	an enclosed space; suggests the idea of water trapped in pockets
3	comb:	the water combs over the rocks, in contrast to 'coop'
4	Flutes:	could describe the flute-like shape (an architectural term) of the water falling and/or the sound made by the waterfall
5	fáwn-fróth:	the froth is a fawn colour
6	twindles:	a verb coined from an obscure noun, 'twindle', meaning 'twin'. It is a combination of 'dwindle' and 'twitch' and describes the movement of the water.
6	broth:	one of the poet's favourite words to describe the seething water, suggestive of a witch's brew
7	féll-frówning:	'frowning' suggests the gloomy appearance of the scene. 'Fell' can mean a mountain, an animal's hide or ruthless. It could also come from the verb 'to fall' (with theological implications).
9	Degged:	sprinkled (Lancashire dialect)
9	dappled:	one of the poet's favourite words to describe patches of different (contrasting) colours
10	groins:	folds, another architectural term to describe the joints of vaulting in an arched roof or possibly a bodily metaphor
10	braes:	steep banks (Scottish term)
11	heathpacks:	patches of densely packed heather
11	flitches:	strips cut from a tree, i.e. ragged tufts
12	beadbonny ash:	refers to the beautiful (bonny) orange/red berries of the rowan tree or mountain ash

Explorations

BEFORE READING

1. Look carefully at the pictures of Inversnaid. Does the place appeal to you? Give reasons for your answer.

2. 'Long live the weeds and the wilderness yet.'
   Do you know any place that remains untouched by human development? Write a brief description of it.

FIRST READING

3. Read the poem aloud several times in the classroom. What sounds are dominant?

4. Choose an image or phrase that appeals because of its sound or association. Explain your choice.

5. In general terms, what sort of scene is evoked by the words in the poem?

6. With the aid of the glossary and in your own words, describe the actions and appearance of the water in the first two verses. Does the poet make it easy for you to visualise the scene? How does he do it? Comment on the effect of words such as 'horseback', 'rollrock', 'pitchblack' and 'féll-frówning'.

7. Would you agree that there is a great sense of energy in the first verse? How does the poet achieve this effect? Is the downward movement of the water echoed in the rhythm of the lines?

8. Is there a darkening of mood in the second verse? What words convey the change?

9. In the third verse, the poet describes the terrain the stream runs through. Describe the scene in your own words. How do the poet's words ('degged', 'groins', 'braes', 'beadbonny') flavour the description?

10. How is the fourth verse different from the previous three? In your own words, explain what aspect of Inversnaid appeals most to Hopkins.

11. Now that your understanding of the poem has deepened, read it aloud again. Would you agree that this is a very simple poem once the difficulties of language are overcome?

12. Would it surprise you to learn that Hopkins once thought of being a landscape painter? Pick out examples of his attention to detail. Use the accompanying photographs to get a sense of the accuracy of his descriptions.

No Worst, There Is None

[handwritten: going through greif]

No worst, there is none. Pitched past pitch of grief,
More pangs will, schooled at forepangs, wilder wring. *[handwritten: — more violent]*
Comforter, where, where is your comforting? *[handwritten: calls for comfort]*
Mary, mother of us, where is your relief? *[handwritten: wheres your reilif — sadness]*
My cries heave, herds-long; huddle in a main, a chief- *[handwritten: complete sadness 5]*
Woe, world-sorrow; on an age-old anvil wince and sing
Then lull, then leave off. Fury had shrieked 'No ling- *[handwritten: not happy in coils]*
ering! Let me be fell: force I must be brief.' *[handwritten: personife to fury]*

[handwritten: rain]
[handwritten: man hanging off a mountain]
O the mind, mind has mountains; cliffs of fall
Frightful, sheer, no-man-fathomed. Hold them cheap *[handwritten: — no I can relate — depression 10]*
May who ne'er hung there. Nor does long our small
Durance deal with that steep or deep. Here! creep, *[handwritten: cant hang on for long]*
Wretch, under a comfort serves in a whirlwind: all
Life death does end and each day dies with sleep.

[handwritten: He will die and it will be all over]

Gerard Manley Hopkins

Notes

1	**Pitched past pitch:**	to pitch (verb) could mean 'to throw' and 'pitch' (noun) could either mean pitch-black, as in tar, or it could be used in a musical sense. There are other possible combinations of meaning. The sense of the line seems to be that the poet has been cast beyond what are considered to be the normal limits of human suffering.
2	**forepangs:**	previously experienced agonies
3	**Comforter:**	the Holy Spirit
5	**herds-long:**	a long line of cries, like a herd of cattle, huddled together
6	**wince and sing:**	words chosen as much for their sound as their meaning; they suggest the beating of a hammer against an anvil
7	**Fury:**	an avenging spirit sent to punish crime, or possibly the personification of a guilty conscience
8	**fell:**	cruel
8	**force:**	perforce, of necessity
10	**no-man-fathomed:**	(coinage) no man has fathomed or explored the depths of this mental abyss
10-11	**Hold them cheap ... hung there:**	those who ... anguish it causes
12	**Durance:**	endurance

Explorations

BEFORE READING

1. This is a poem about mental suffering and a struggle with despair. If you have ever experienced such feelings, try to describe them.

FIRST READING

2. When you have read the poem several times, pick out the images or impressions that are most vivid. Discuss these with the rest of the class.

3. Does this poem come as something of a shock after the previous poems? Explain your answer.

SECOND READING

4. The opening sentence is short and dramatic. Note carefully that the poet uses the superlative 'worst', not the comparative 'worse'. How does this change the meaning?

5. The second sentence seems to suggest that the agonies that are about to torment him have been 'schooled' by previous agonies and will therefore be even more skilled at inflicting pain. How does the poet's expression of this idea surpass this paraphrase? Would you agree that there is an extraordinary intensity in the line?

6.

a   In his address to the Holy Ghost, Hopkins repeats the word 'where'. What is the effect of this repetition?

b Are there any other examples of this in the poem?

c What is the cumulative effect of this technique?

7.

a How does the second quatrain differ from the first? Is it easier or more difficult to comprehend? Give reasons for your answer.

b Despite the obscurity of the lines, certain impressions are communicated. What are they?

8. How does the poet engage our senses in the octet?

9. In the sestet, the poet suggests that mental torment can feel like hanging onto the edge of a cliff. Is it a good image? Give reasons for your answer.

10. At the end of the poem, Hopkins seems to find some scrap of comfort in the idea that sleep brings the day to a close just as death brings life to a close. What does this 'comfort' say about his state of mind?

THIRD READING

11. Are we told at any stage in the poem what it is that is causing such anguish? Is the poet concerned more with the experience of suffering than the cause?

12. Do you ever get the feeling that the poet is just feeling sorry for himself? Or is his documentation of suffering a testament to his courage?

13. What variations in the use of the sonnet form are evident in this poem?

14. Consider the overall impact of such poetic devices as alliteration, assonance, ellipsis, repetition, compound words and onomatopoeia.

I Wake and Feel the Fell of Dark

I wake and feel the fell of dark, not day.
What hours, O what black hoürs we have spent
This night! what sights you, heart, saw; ways you went!
And more must, in yet longer light's delay.

With witness I speak this. But where I say   5
Hours I mean years, mean life. And my lament
Is cries countless, cries like dead letters sent
To dearest him that lives alas! away.

I am gall, I am heartburn. God's most deep decree
Bitter would have me taste: my taste was me;   10
Bones built in me, flesh filled, blood brimmed the curse.

Selfyeast of spirit a dull dough sours. I see
The lost are like this, and their scourge to be
As I am mine, their sweating selves; but worse.

Notes

1	fell:	an adjective meaning 'cruel'; or a noun meaning 'a stretch of moorland' or 'the skin of an animal'; or a verb meaning 'to strike down'; it could also be a play on the word 'fall'. Here, the word is used as a noun.
9	gall:	a bitter substance secreted in the liver
9	heartburn:	burning sensation in the lower part of the chest
9	decree:	judgement
12	Selfyeast:	yeast is a fungus substance used in baking bread; thus, it 'sours' a 'dull dough'. Originally, Hopkins used the phrase 'my selfstuff', i.e. the very stuff of my being or self.
13	The lost:	those in Hell

Explorations

BEFORE READING

1. Darkness, nightmares and terror, a sense of abandonment, self-disgust – these are the powerful forces at work in this poem. Which of these images do you find most terrifying? Give reasons for your answer.

FIRST READING

2. To what extent is this poem a sequel or continuation to 'No Worst, There Is None'?

3. How is the sense of darkness emphasised in the first quatrain?

4. What effect is created by the poet's address to his 'heart'?

5. Does Hopkins use any of the poetic devices found in 'No Worst, There Is None'?

6. How does the poet create a sense of spiritual desolation? Is it described in abstract terms or does he create a sense in which it is physical as well as spiritual?

7. To whom are his 'dead letters' sent? Why does he describe them as 'dead'?

8. In the sestet, there is a powerful impression of self-disgust. Identify the images used by the poet to create this effect.

9.
a Hopkins changed the phrase 'God's most deep decree' to 'God's most just decree' and then changed it back to the original. How do the two phrases differ?

b What do we learn about the poet's state of mind from this information?

10. Lines 11–12 are a kind of definition of self. His physical body is described in gruesome terms; his spirit, instead of lifting the dough, sours it and makes it worse. What is your reaction to this self-definition? Does it inspire shock or pity?

11. Does the poem end with despair or consolation? Who is 'worse'?

SECOND READING

12. Are we told why the poet feels such desolation? Does it matter?

13. Pick out examples of the poet's use of inversion (of normal word order). How does this device contribute to the sense of anguish in the poem?

14. Compare this poem with 'No Worst, There Is None'. (They are usually referred to as 'the terrible sonnets'.) Which of the two is more effective in communicating the poet's suffering? Give reasons for your answer.

Thou Art Indeed Just, Lord, If I Contend

Justus quidem tu es, Domine, si disputem tecum; verumtamen justa loquar ad te: Quare via impiorum prosperatur? etc.

Thou art indeed just, Lord, if I contend
With thee; but, sir, so what I plead is just.
Why do sinners' ways prosper? and why must
Disappointment all I endeavour end?

Wert thou my enemy, O thou my friend,   5
How wouldst thou worse, I wonder, than thou dost
Defeat, thwart me? Oh, the sots and thralls of lust
Do in spare hours more thrive than I that spend,

Sir, life upon thy cause. See, banks and brakes
Now, leavèd how thick! lacèd they are again   10
With fretty chervil, look, and fresh wind shakes

Them; birds build – but not I build; no, but strain,
Time's eunuch, and not breed one work that wakes.
Mine, O thou lord of life, send my roots rain.

Background note

The Latin quotation is taken from Jeremiah 12: 1. The full text is: 'Thou indeed, O Lord, art just, if I plead with thee, but yet I will speak what is just to thee: why doth the way of the wicked prosper: why is it well with all of them that transgress and do wickedly? Thou hast planted them, and they have taken root: they prosper and bring forth fruit. Thou art near in their mouth and far from their reins. And thou, O Lord, hast known me, thou hast seen me, and proved my heart with thee.'

It was customary for a Jesuit priest to repeat the phrase, '*Justus es, Domine, et rectum iudiciumtuum*' (You are just, O Lord, and your judgement is right), like a mantra. It signifies an acceptance of God's will, however unpalatable it may seem.

Gerard Manley Hopkins

Notes

7	**sots:**	drunkards
7	**thralls:**	slaves
9	**brakes:**	thickets
11	**fretty:**	fretted or interlaced
11	**chervil:**	cow parsley
13	**eunuch:**	castrated male employed in a harem
13	**wakes:**	comes to life

Explorations

BEFORE READING

1. Have you ever felt that life is unfair and that there seems to be no connection between effort and reward? Describe the circumstances and the feeling.

FIRST READING

2. Read the poem aloud. Can you hear the sense of hurt, anger and frustration? Identify where you think the feelings are at their most intense.

SECOND READING

3. The first quatrain takes the words from Jeremiah and arranges them to suit the constraints of the sonnet form. Is there any tension in these lines or is the poet simply repeating the formula from the Bible?

4. Is there a tone of humility or anger in the first quatrain?

5. Is there any evidence in the second quatrain to suggest that the poet's feelings are becoming unmanageable? Look carefully at the metre and syntax.

6. What is the effect of the apostrophes, 'Lord', 'sir', 'O thou my friend', 'O thou lord of life'?

7. It is difficult to separate the third stanza from the second. Is this deliberate? What does the poet intend to convey by this arrangement?

THIRD READING

8. What is the poet's complaint?

9. Is there a sense of growing anger as the poem progresses? Does it continue to build until the end of the poem?

10. To what extent does the syntax contribute to the expression of tortured innocence?

11. How does the imagery change in the sestet?

12. What sort of relationship exists between the poet and God?

13. What kind of 'work' does the poet want? Does he write as a poet or as a priest? Or both?

14. Hopkins included this poem in a letter to Robert Bridges. He suggested that it be read 'adagio molto' (a musical term meaning very slowly) 'and with great stress'. How would such a reading enhance the impact of the poem?

William Butler Yeats

(1865–1939)

Prescribed for Higher Level exams in 2015 and 2016

In 1865 William Butler Yeats was born in Dublin to a County Sligo family. His grandfather had been rector of the Church of Ireland at Drumcliff. His father, the portrait painter John Butler Yeats, had married Susan Pollexfen, who belonged to a family of substantial traders and ship-owners from County Sligo. His brother, Jack B. Yeats, was to become one of Ireland's best-known painters. William Yeats was educated intermittently at the Godolphin School in London, the High School in Dublin and the Dublin Metropolitan School of Art.

He was interested in mysticism and the supernatural and developed a great curiosity about Irish mythology, history and folklore. It became one of his life's great passions to develop a distinctive, distinguished Irish literature in English. His first long poem, 'The Wanderings of Oisin' (1889), established the tone of what became known as the Celtic Twilight. His early volumes of poetry reflect his interest in mysticism, theosophy and mythology but also deal with his hopeless love affairs, most notably that with Maude Gonne. In 1889 he had met and fallen in love with her, and though she would not marry him, he remained obsessed with her for most of his life. With Lady Gregory of Coole Park, Gort, County Galway and John Millington Synge he founded the Irish Literary Theatre Society in 1899 and later the Abbey Theatre in 1904.

By the end of the century Yeats had changed his decorative, symbolist style of poetry and began to write in a more direct style. From *The Green Helmet* (1910) onwards he shows a more realistic attitude to love and also begins to write about everyday cultural and political affairs. *Responsibilities* (1914) contains satires on the materialism of Dublin's middle class. Among the major themes of his mature years are the need for harmony in life, the search for perfection in life and art, and the mysteries of time and eternity. These are to be found particularly in the poems of the later volumes, *The Tower* (1928), *The Winding Stair* (1933) and *Last Poems* (1936–39).

Yeats was made a senator in 1922 and was very active in public life; he supervised the design of the new coinage in 1926. He was awarded the Nobel Prize for Literature in 1923. He died in Rome in 1939 and his body was not brought back to Ireland until after the war, when it was buried in Drumcliff.

The Lake Isle of Innisfree

I will arise and go now, and go to Innisfree,
And a small cabin build there, of clay and wattles made:
Nine bean-rows will I have there, a hive for the honey-bee,
And live alone in the bee-loud glade.

And I shall have some peace there, for peace comes dropping slow,   5
Dropping from the veils of the morning to where the cricket sings;
There midnight's all a glimmer, and noon a purple glow,
And evening full of the linnet's wings.

I will arise and go now, for always night and day
I hear lake water lapping with low sounds by the shore;   10
While I stand on the roadway, or on the pavements grey,
I hear it in the deep heart's core.

Notes

1	**I will arise ...:**	this has echoes of the return of the Prodigal Son in Luke 15: 18 – 'I will arise and go to my father' – so they were the words of another returning emigrant
1	**Innisfree:**	(in Irish, *Inisfraoich*: Heather Island) – a rocky island on Lough Gill, County Sligo
2	**wattles:**	rods interlaced with twigs or branches to make a fence

Explorations

BEFORE READING

1. Read only the title. What comes into your mind when you read the title?

FIRST READING

2. What do you notice about Yeats's island?

3. What sights and sounds will the poet see and hear? List them.

4. Contrast this island with the poet's present surroundings.

SECOND READING

5. Do you think that the features of the island mentioned by the poet are the usual sights and sounds of everyday life in the country or will this place be special? Explain your thinking on this.

6. What kind of space or place is the poet attempting to create? What does that indicate about his needs and philosophy of life or values? Refer to the poem to support your theories.

7. What is the poet's attitude to nature as suggested in the poem? Refer to specific lines and phrases.

THIRD READING

8. The poet seems almost impelled or driven to go and create this ideal place. Where is the sense of compulsion in the poem and how is it created? Explore the style of language he uses, the syntax, the rhythms of his language and the repeated phrases in order to help you with this.

9. What do you think is the meaning and significance of the last line?

FOURTH READING

10. State succinctly what you think the poem is about.

11. What mood do you think the poet creates here and how do the images and the sounds of words contribute to this?

12. Does anything about the poet's vision here appeal to you? Discuss this.

September 1913

What need you, being come to sense,
But fumble in a greasy till
And add the halfpence to the pence
And prayer to shivering prayer, until
You have dried the marrow from the bone;   5
For men were born to pray and save:
Romantic Ireland's dead and gone,
It's with O'Leary in the grave.

Yet they were of a different kind,
The names that stilled your childish play,   10
They have gone about the world like wind,
But little time had they to pray
For whom the hangman's rope was spun,
And what, God help us, could they save?
Romantic Ireland's dead and gone,   15
It's with O'Leary in the grave.

Was it for this the wild geese spread
The grey wing upon every tide;
For this that all that blood was shed,
For this Edward Fitzgerald died,   20
And Robert Emmet and Wolfe Tone,
All that delirium of the brave?
Romantic Ireland's dead and gone,
It's with O'Leary in the grave.

Yet could we turn the years again,   25
And call those exiles as they were
In all their loneliness and pain,
You'd cry, 'Some woman's yellow hair
Has maddened every mother's son':
They weighed so lightly what they gave.   30
But let them be, they're dead and gone,
They're with O'Leary in the grave.

Background note

During 1913 Yeats spent a great deal of energy in support of Lady Gregory's nephew, Sir Hugh Lane, a wealthy art collector, who made a gift to the city of Dublin of an extraordinary collection of modern painting on condition that the city build a suitable gallery. There was a great deal of dispute about the structure, the location and the cost. Yeats was furious at what seemed a mean-spirited, penny-pinching, anti-cultural response to the project.

Notes

8	O'Leary:	John O'Leary (1830–1907), a Fenian who was arrested in 1865 and sentenced to 20 years' imprisonment. After a number of years he was released on condition that he went into exile. Returning to Dublin in 1885 he was greatly influential in Yeats's developing views on Irish nationalism.
17	the wild geese:	Irish soldiers who were forced into exile after the Williamite victory of the 1690s. They served in the armies of France, Spain and Austria.
20	Edward Fitzgerald:	Lord Edward Fitzgerald (1763–98), one of the leaders of the United Irishmen, who died of wounds received while being arrested
21	Robert Emmet:	leader of the rebellion of 1803
21	Wolfe Tone:	Theobald Wolfe Tone (1763–98), leader of the United Irishmen. Captured and sentenced to death, he committed suicide in prison.

Explorations

FIRST READING

Stanza 1

1. 'What need you' – the 'you' here refers to the new Irish, relatively prosperous and Catholic middle classes, whom Yeats is addressing. What does he suggest are their main concerns or needs in life?

2. Explore the connotations of the images used in the first five lines, i.e. what is suggested by each of the pictures? List all the suggestions carried by each of the following and discuss them in groups: 'fumble', 'greasy till', 'add the halfpence to the pence', 'add ... prayer to shivering prayer', 'dried the marrow from the bone'.

3. As a consequence of your explorations, what do you think is Yeats's attitude to these people? What words do you think best convey the tone?

4. 'For men were born to pray and save'. Does the poet really mean this? If not, what does he mean? How should it be read? Try reading it aloud.

5.

a Read aloud the last two lines of the stanza as you think the poet would wish it to be read.

b How is this refrain different from the earlier lines of the stanza?

c What do you understand by 'Romantic Ireland' and how does Yeats feel about it?

6. Now read the entire stanza aloud, differentiating between the sections that are sarcastic, bitter or condemnatory and the lines that are wistful, nostalgic or plaintive.

SECOND READING

Stanza 2

7. 'They' – the romantic generations of heroes – had great power and influence in society. How is this suggested? Explore all the possible suggestions carried by lines 10–11.

8. How were they different from the present generation?

9. Is there a suggestion that they were fated to act as they did? Examine line 13.

10. In groups, discuss the best possible way of reading this stanza aloud, then do it.

THIRD READING

Stanza 3

11. 'for this ... For this ... For this'. Through this repetition, Yeats punches out the contrast between past and present. His attitude to the present generation is quite clear by now. But what does this stanza say about his attitude to the heroes of Ireland's past? Explore in detail the suggestions carried by the images.

12. 'All that delirium of the brave'. Discuss what this implies about heroism.

Stanza 4

13. 'All Yeats's sympathy and admiration is with the past generations of heroes.'
Discuss this and refer to the text in support of your ideas.

14. 'You'd cry, "Some woman's yellow hair | Has maddened every mother's son".'
What do you think is meant by this?

FOURTH READING

15. 'In this poem we find a quite grotesque portrayal of the middle classes in contrast to an unreal and highly romanticised portrayal of past patriots.'
Discuss this as an interpretation of the poem.

16. What do you think is the effect of the refrain?

17. Do you think this was a politically risky, even dangerous, poem to publish? Explain.

18. Are you surprised by the passion and strength of feeling here? Outline your reactions.

The Wild Swans at Coole

This poem is also prescribed for Ordinary Level exams in 2015 and 2016

The trees are in their autumn beauty,
The woodland paths are dry,
Under the October twilight the water
Mirrors a still sky;
Upon the brimming water among the stones   5
Are nine-and-fifty swans.

The nineteenth autumn has come upon me
Since I first made my count;
I saw, before I had well finished,
All suddenly mount   10
And scatter wheeling in great broken rings
Upon their clamorous wings.

I have looked upon those brilliant creatures,
And now my heart is sore.
All's changed since I, hearing at twilight,   15
The first time on this shore,
The bell-beat of their wings above my head,
Trod with a lighter tread.

Unwearied still, lover by lover,
They paddle in the cold   20
Companionable streams or climb the air;
Their hearts have not grown old;
Passion or conquest, wander where they will,
Attend upon them still.

But now they drift on the still water,   25
Mysterious, beautiful;
Among what rushes will they build,
By what lake's edge or pool
Delight men's eyes when I awake some day
To find they have flown away?   30

Notes

	Coole:	Coole Park, outside Gort, County Galway, and home of Lady Augusta Gregory. She was a friend and benefactor to the poet and collaborated on many of his projects. Yeats regarded Coole Park as a second home and a welcoming refuge and retreat.
6	**nine-and-fifty swans:**	there actually were 59 swans on the lake at Coole Park
7	**The nineteenth autumn:**	Yeats is referring to the summer and autumn of 1897, which was the first time he stayed for a lengthy period at Coole. At that time he was passionately involved with Maude Gonne and in a state of acute nervous exhaustion.
18	**Trod with a lighter tread:**	it is interesting that the poet chooses to recast 1897 as a hopeful and even carefree period, when this was not the case

Explorations

FIRST READING

Stanza 1

1. Notice all the details that draw Yeats's eyes and ears to the scene. Visualise them intently, with your eyes closed if you can. If you came upon this scene, what would your thoughts be?

2. How would you describe the atmosphere of this scene? What particular images or sounds contribute to this atmosphere? Explain.

Stanza 2

3. Read the second stanza with energy, aloud if possible, and see if you can make the swans come alive.

4.

a Examine the description of the swans here. What attributes or qualities of these creatures does the poet wish to convey?

b How are these qualities carried by the language? Look at images, verbs, adverbs, the sounds of words and the structure of the long single sentence.

SECOND READING

5. In the third stanza the poet introduces a personal note. What does he reveal about himself?

6. In stanzas 3–4 the poet explores the contrasts between the life and condition of the swans and his own life and condition. In your own words, explain the detail of these contrasts.

7. Do you think the poet envies the swans? If so, what exactly does he envy? Refer to phrases and lines to support your thinking.

8. Is this a logical or a poetic argument? Explain.

THIRD READING

9. If we read the first four stanzas as lamenting the loss of youth, passion and love, what particular loss frightens the poet in the final stanza? Explain.

10. What general issues or themes does Yeats deal with in this poem?

11. Do you think there is any sense of resolution of the personal issues raised by Yeats in this poem? Does he come to any definite conclusion? Explain your thinking.

12. Examine how the poem is structured stanza by stanza, moving from the very particular local beginning to the general speculation about love in stanza 4, then opening up into the rather mysterious ending that seeks to look into the future. What is the effect of this?

13. The poem is built upon a series of antitheses: the swans and the poet, the poet then and the poet now, and contrasting moods. Show how these are developed.

14. What do you think the symbolism adds to the poem? Explore the elements of sky and water, trees and paths, great broken rings and of course the swans themselves.

FOURTH READING

15. Would you agree that the poem creates a 'hauntingly evocative description of the swans'? Discuss or write about this.

16. 'Ageing and the diminution of visionary power are bitterly regretted' (Terence Brown).
    Discuss this view of the poem, referring in detail to the text to substantiate your argument.

An Irish Airman Foresees His Death

This poem is also prescribed for Ordinary Level exams in 2015 and 2016

I know that I shall meet my fate
Somewhere among the clouds above;
Those that I fight I do not hate,
Those that I guard I do not love;
My country is Kiltartan Cross,   5
My countrymen Kiltartan's poor,
No likely end could bring them loss
Or leave them happier than before.
Nor law, nor duty bade me fight,
Nor public men, nor cheering crowds,   10
A lonely impulse of delight
Drove to this tumult in the clouds;
I balanced all, brought all to mind,
The years to come seemed waste of breath,
A waste of breath the years behind   15
In balance with this life, this death.

William Butler Yeats

Notes

	An Irish Airman:	the speaker in the poem is Major Robert Gregory, the only son of Yeats's friend and mentor, Lady Augusta Gregory of Coole Park, near Gort, County Galway. He was a pilot in the Royal Flying Corps in the First World War and at the time of his death, on 23 January 1918, was on service in Italy. It emerged later that he had been accidentally shot down by the Italian allies.
3	Those that I fight:	the Germans
4	Those that I guard:	the English or possibly the Italians
5	Kiltartan Cross:	a crossroads near Robert Gregory's home at Coole Park, Gort, County Galway

Explorations

BEFORE READING

1.

a   Read only the title. What do you expect to find in this poem?

b   Imagine what this man's thoughts might be. How might he visualise his death? How might he feel about it? Jot down briefly the thoughts, pictures and feelings you imagine might go through his mind.

FIRST READING

2.   Who is the speaker in this poem? If in doubt, consult the note ('An Irish Airman') above.

3.   Focus on lines 1–2. Are you surprised by how definite he is? Can you suggest any reasons why he might be so definite about his coming death? How would you describe his mood?

4.   How do you think the speaker would say these first two lines? Experiment with various readings aloud.

5.   Taking the first four lines as a unit, are you surprised that they are spoken by a military man, a pilot? In your own words, describe how he views his situation.

SECOND READING

6.   In lines 5–8 the speaker talks about the people of his home area. How does he feel about them? Does he identify with them in any way? Have the people and the speaker anything in common? How does he think his death will affect their lives? Does he feel they will miss him? Do you think his attitude to them is uncaring or that he feels unable to affect their lives in any way? Discuss these questions and write down the conclusions you come to, together with evidence from the text.

7.   What do you think is the purpose of mentioning his Kiltartan countrymen in the context of his explanation? How does it fit in with his reasoning?

8.   In your own words, explain the further reasons in lines 9–10 that the speaker discounts as having had any influence on his decision to volunteer.

9. What is revealed about the character of the speaker in the lines you have explored so far?

THIRD READING

10. We get to the kernel of his motivation in lines 11–12. Examine the language very carefully.

a 'A lonely impulse of delight': can you understand why he might feel this sense of delight? Explain how you see it.

b 'Impulse': what does this tell us about the decision? 'A lonely impulse': what does this suggest about the decision and the man?

c 'Drove': what does this add to our understanding of how he felt and of his decision?

d 'Tumult in the clouds': in what other context might the words 'tumult' or 'tumultuous' be used? Suggest a few. What does the sound of the word suggest? What does it suggest about the speaker's view of flying?

11. In light of what you have discovered so far, and in the voice of the speaker, write a letter home explaining your decision to volunteer as a pilot. Try to remain true to the speaker's feelings as outlined in the poem.

12. 'In spite of his hint of excitement earlier, the speaker did not make a rash and emotional decision.'
On the evidence of lines 13–16, would you agree with this statement? Write a paragraph.

13. 'The years to come seemed waste of breath ... In balance with this life, this death.'

Yet the speaker seemed to want this kind of life very much. Explore how the use of 'breath' and 'death' as rhyming words help to emphasise this.

FOURTH READING

14. Having read this poem, what do you find most interesting about the speaker?

15. What appeals to you about the poem? Do you find anything disturbing about it?

16. Thousands of Irishmen fought and died in the British army during the First World War; others could not bring themselves to join that army while Ireland was governed by England. How does the speaker deal with this issue? Is the title significant?

17. As well as being a rhetorical device, the repetition of words and phrases emphasises certain ideas and issues. List the main ideas thus emphasised.

18. What are the principal themes or issues the poem deals with? Write a number of short paragraphs on this.

19. 'The pictures and images are sparsely used but very effective.'
Comment on any two images.

20. To whom is this poem being spoken? Read it aloud. Is the tone more appropriate to a letter or to a public statement or speech? Explain your view with reference to phrases or lines in the text.

Easter 1916

I have met them at close of day
Coming with vivid faces
From counter or desk among grey
Eighteenth-century houses.
I have passed with a nod of the head   5
Or polite meaningless words,
Or have lingered awhile and said
Polite meaningless words,
And thought before I had done
Of a mocking tale or a gibe   10
To please a companion
Around the fire at the club,
Being certain they and I
But lived where motley is worn:
All changed, changed utterly: 15
A terrible beauty is born.

That woman's days were spent
In ignorant good-will,
Her nights in argument
Until her voice grew shrill.   20
What voice more sweet than hers
When, young and beautiful,
She rode to harriers?
This man had kept a school
And rode our wingèd horse;   25
This other his helper and friend
Was coming into his force;
He might have won fame in the end,
So sensitive his nature seemed,
So daring and sweet his thought.   30
This other man I had dreamed
A drunken, vainglorious lout.
He had done most bitter wrong
To some who are near my heart,
Yet I number him in the song;   35
He, too, has resigned his part
In the casual comedy;
He, too, has been changed in his turn,
Transformed utterly:
A terrible beauty is born.   40

Hearts with one purpose alone
Through summer and winter seem
Enchanted to a stone
To trouble the living stream.
The horse that comes from the road,   45
The rider, the birds that range
From cloud to tumbling cloud,
Minute by minute they change;
A shadow of cloud on the stream
Changes minute by minute;   50
A horse-hoof slides on the brim,
And a horse plashes within it;
The long-legged moor-hens dive,
And hens to moor-cocks call;
Minute by minute they live: 55
The stone's in the midst of all.

Too long a sacrifice
Can make a stone of the heart.
O when may it suffice?
That is Heaven's part, our part   60
To murmur name upon name,
As a mother names her child
When sleep at last has come
On limbs that had run wild.
What is it but nightfall?   65
No, no, not night but death;
Was it needless death after all?
For England may keep faith
For all that is done and said.
We know their dream; enough   70
To know they dreamed and are dead;
And what if excess of love
Bewildered them till they died?
I write it out in a verse –
MacDonagh and MacBride   75
And Connolly and Pearse
Now and in time to be,
Wherever green is worn,
Are changed, changed utterly:
A terrible beauty is born.   80

William Butler Yeats

Notes

	Easter 1916:	on Monday, 24 April 1916, a force of about 700 republicans who were members of the Irish Volunteers and the Irish Citizen Army took over the centre of Dublin in a military revolution and held out for six days against the British army. This was known as the Easter Rising.
1	**them:**	those republicans, in the pre-1916 days
3	**grey:**	built of granite or limestone
12	**the club:**	probably the Arts Club, where Yeats was a founder member in 1907
17	**That woman:**	Constance Gore-Booth (1868–1927) of Lissadell, County Sligo, who married the Polish Count Markiewicz. She became a fervent Irish nationalist and was actively involved in the Fianna and the Citizen Army. She was sentenced to death for her part in the Rising but the sentence was later commuted to penal servitude for life. She was released in 1917 under the general amnesty.
24	**This man:**	Padraig Pearse (1879–1916). Barrister, teacher and poet, he was the founder of St Enda's School and editor of *An Claidheamh Soluis*. He believed that a blood sacrifice was necessary to revolutionise Ireland. A member of the revolutionary IRB and the Irish Volunteers, he was the Commandant General and President of the Provisional Government during Easter week.
25	**wingèd horse:**	Pegasus, the winged horse, was a symbol of poetic vision
26	**This other:**	Thomas MacDonagh (1878–1916), poet and academic who taught at University College Dublin
31	**This other man:**	Major John MacBride, who had fought with the Boers against the British in South Africa and in 1903 married Maude Gonne, the woman Yeats loved. He too was executed for his part in the Rising.
33	**He had done most bitter wrong:**	reference to rumours of family violence and debauchery
34	**To some who are near my heart:**	Maude Gonne and her daughter
41–3	**Hearts ... stone:**	'stone' at its simplest is usually taken to be a symbol for the fanatical heart, i.e. those who devote themselves fanatically to a cause, become hardened and lose their humanness as a result
67–8	**needless death ... England may keep faith:**	the Bill for Irish Home Rule had been passed in the Westminster Parliament. In 1914, however, it was suspended on the outbreak of World War I, but with the promise that it would be put into effect after the war.

| 76 | **Connolly:** | James Connolly (1870–1916). Trade union organiser and founder of the Citizen Army, he was military commander of the insurgents in Dublin, Easter 1916. |

Explorations

BEFORE READING

1. First reread 'September 1913' and remind yourself how Yeats felt about the Irish middle class of his time.

FIRST READING

Stanza 1

2. Concentrate on the first 14 lines. These are the same people who feature in 'September 1913'. Yeats is no longer savagely angry, but he certainly has no respect for them. Visualise the encounter he describes – time of day, atmosphere, what the poet does, what he says, how he behaves. Share these ideas.

3.

a What 'polite meaningless words' might he have said? Invent some dialogue for him.

b As he speaks these 'polite meaningless words', what is he actually thinking? Script his thoughts and the 'tale' or 'gibe' he might tell later.

4. 'Where motley is worn': what does this tell us about how Yeats regarded Ireland at this time?

5. How would you describe the poet's feelings and mood in this first section?

6. The first 14 lines are transformed by lines 15–16 and given a new context. Framed by use of the perfect tense – 'I have met them', 'I have passed' – the impression is given that that was then, this is now.

a Reread the first section from this perspective.

b Do you think Yeats is ashamed of his earlier treatment of these people? Discuss this with reference to lines or phrases in the poem.

7. 'A terrible beauty is born.' Explore all the implications of this phrase.

SECOND READING

Stanza 2

8. According to the poet, what are the effects on Constance Markiewicz of fanatical dedication to a political cause?

9. 'This other his helper'.
   In contrast to the portrait of Constance Markiewicz, which is somewhat masculine, this portrait of Thomas MacDonagh is quite feminised. Would you agree? Explain your thinking with reference to words and phrases in the poem.

10. There is great emphasis on change in this section. List all the instances and comment on them.

11. There is a sense that this change or transformation was not something actually effected by these people, but rather something that happened to them: 'He, too, has been changed in his turn, | Transformed utterly'. They were changed by death and by executions. Do you think Yeats is exploring how ordinary people are changed into heroes? What is he suggesting? Discuss this.

THIRD READING

Stanza 3

12. Here Yeats is fascinated by flux and the process of change.

a   List all the examples he uses.

b   Comment on the atmosphere created here. Is it an appealing picture?

13. In this section he is exploring the paradox that only a stone (the fanatical heart) can alter the flow of a stream, i.e. the course of life. But it can do this only at the expense of losing humanness. What does this indicate about Yeats's thinking on revolutionary politics?

FOURTH READING

Stanza 4

14. What is your initial impression of the tone of this section? Is the poet weary, worried, confused, giving up? Refer in detail to the text.

15. 'our part | To murmur name upon name'.
    How does he see the poet's role here?

16. 'sleep ... not night but death ... needless death ... excess of love | Bewildered them'.
    The poet is attempting to think through his confusions and uncertainties here. Trace his thoughts in your own words.

17. Finally, at the end of the poem, Yeats lists out the dead, almost as a sacred act. What is the effect of this for the poet, the reader and those who died?

FIFTH READING

18. Yeats had been severely disillusioned by the new Irish Catholic middle class, but he had to rethink this view after 1916. Explain the process of his rethinking as it happens in the poem.

19. 'Despite his sense of awe and admiration for the change brought about, this poem does not represent a totally unqualified approval of revolutionary politics.'
    Discuss this view of the poem, supporting your answer with references to the text.

20. Though written in 1916, Yeats did not have this poem published until October 1920. Speculate on his possible reasons. Do you think they were justified?

The Second Coming

Turning and turning in the widening gyre
The falcon cannot hear the falconer;
Things fall apart; the centre cannot hold;
Mere anarchy is loosed upon the world,
The blood-dimmed tide is loosed, and everywhere   5
The ceremony of innocence is drowned;
The best lack all conviction, while the worst
Are full of passionate intensity.

Surely some revelation is at hand;
Surely the Second Coming is at hand.   10
The Second Coming! Hardly are those words out
When a vast image out of *Spiritus Mundi*
Troubles my sight: somewhere in sands of the desert
A shape with lion body and the head of a man,
A gaze blank and pitiless as the sun,   15
Is moving its slow thighs, while all about it
Reel shadows of the indignant desert birds.
The darkness drops again; but now I know
That twenty centuries of stony sleep
Were vexed to nightmare by a rocking cradle,   20
And what rough beast, its hour come round at last,
Slouches towards Bethlehem to be born?

Notes

	The Second Coming:	in its Christian interpretation, this refers to the prediction of the second coming of Christ (see Matthew 24). In Yeats's occult and magical philosophy, it might also refer to the second birth of the Avatar, or great antithetical spirit, which Yeats and his wife felt certain would be reincarnated as their baby son, whose birth was imminent. In fact, the child turned out to be a girl, dashing that theory.
1–2	**Turning ... falconer:**	the bird is rising in ever-widening circles and so making the pattern of an inverted cone, or gyre. These lines could be read as the trained bird of prey reverting to its wild state or, in a more religious sense, taken to represent Christian civilisation growing further away from Christ (the falconer).
12	***Spiritus Mundi:***	'the spirit of the world', which Yeats describes as 'a general storehouse of images which have ceased to be a property of any personality or spirit'

14	**A shape with lion body and the head of a man:**	instead of the second coming of Christ, Yeats imagines this horrific creature, a sort of Antichrist
20	**rocking cradle:**	the birth of Christ in Bethlehem began the then two-thousand-year period of Christian history

Explorations

BEFORE READING

1. Read Matthew 24: 1–31 and some of the Book of Revelations, particularly chapters 12, 13, 20 and 21. Discuss these.

FIRST READING

2. The trained falcon is released and it circles, looking for prey. What do you think might happen if the falcon cannot hear the falconer?

3. What do you see and imagine when you read (a) line 3 and (b) line 4?

4. 'The blood-dimmed tide is loosed'. What does this picture conjure up for you? Do you find it sinister, frightening or something else?

5. Lines 7–8 focus on people. What types of people do you think the poet has in mind? Discuss this.

SECOND READING

6. Taking the first stanza as a whole, what does it communicate about Yeats's view of civilisation as he saw it at that time?

7. 'The first stanza or section is full of the tension of opposites.'
   Discuss or write about this.

8. In the second section of the poem Yeats is looking for some sufficiently weighty reason which would explain this collapse of civilisation. What occurs to him first?

9. His first short-lived thought is replaced by this 'vast image' that 'troubles' his sight. Read Yeats's description carefully.

   a Describe what you imagine.

   b What particular qualities are exhibited by this 'rough beast'?

   c What particular images or phrases help create the sense of revulsion?

10. Are you shocked by the association with Bethlehem? What is suggested here? Discuss this.

THIRD READING

11. Yeats is talking about the end of the Christian era, the end of innocence. This is encapsulated in particular in the horrific image of one of the holiest places in Christianity, Bethlehem, being defiled by this beast. What typically nightmarish elements do you notice in the second section of the poem?

12. In your own words, set out briefly what you think the poem is about.

13. Comment on the power of the imagery.

14. Though this was written primarily as a reaction to events in Europe, can you understand how it might be read as a commentary on the Irish situation of that time? Explain your views.

15. Could the poem be seen as prophetic in any way?

16. What did this poem make you think about? Describe the effect it had on you.

Sailing to Byzantium

I

That is no country for old men. The young
In one another's arms, birds in the trees
– Those dying generations – at their song,
The salmon-falls, the mackerel-crowded seas,
Fish, flesh, or fowl, commend all summer long   5
Whatever is begotten, born, and dies.
Caught in that sensual music all neglect
Monuments of unageing intellect.

II

An aged man is but a paltry thing,
A tattered coat upon a stick, unless   10
Soul clap its hands and sing, and louder sing
For every tatter in its mortal dress,
Nor is there singing school but studying
Monuments of its own magnificence;
And therefore I have sailed the seas and come   15
To the holy city of Byzantium.

III

O sages standing in God's holy fire
As in the gold mosaic of a wall,
Come from the holy fire, perne in a gyre,
And be the singing-masters of my soul.   20
Consume my heart away; sick with desire
And fastened to a dying animal
It knows not what it is; and gather me
Into the artifice of eternity.

IV

Once out of nature I shall never take   25
My bodily form from any natural thing,
But such a form as Grecian goldsmiths make
Of hammered gold and gold enamelling
To keep a drowsy Emperor awake;
Or set upon a golden bough to sing   30
To lords and ladies of Byzantium
Of what is past, or passing, or to come.

William Butler Yeats

Notes

	Byzantium:	the Roman emperor Constantine, who became a Christian in 312 AD, chose Byzantium as his capital city, renaming it Constantinople in 330. Yeats idealised Byzantium, in particular at the end of the fifth century, as the centre of European civilisation – a place where all life was in harmony.
1	**That:**	Ireland
4	**The salmon-falls, the mackerel-crowded seas:**	all images of regeneration, new life, energy and plenty
5	**commend:**	praise, celebrate
17	**O sages:**	probably refers to the depiction of the martyrs being burned in a fire in a mosaic at the church of San Apollinare Nuovo in Ravenna, which Yeats saw in 1907
19	**perne in a gyre:**	when Yeats was a child in Sligo he was told that 'pern' was another name for the spool or bobbin on which thread was wound. So the idea of circular movement is carried in the word 'perne', which Yeats constructs here as a verb. A gyre is a revolving cone of time in Yeats's cosmology. Here, Yeats is asking the sages to journey through the cone of time to come to him and teach him perfection and teach his soul to sing.
24	**artifice of eternity:**	artifice is something constructed, created – here, a work of art. The word can also have connotations of trickery or sleight of hand. In a certain sense art is outside time and has a sort of eternal quality about it. Yeats asks the sages to gather him into the eternity of art.
27	**such a form:**	Yeats wrote that he had read somewhere that there existed in the Emperors' Palace in Byzantium 'a tree made of gold and silver, and artificial birds that sang'. Here the golden bird is used as a metaphor for art, which is beautiful, perfect and unchanging.
32	**Of what is past, or passing, or to come:**	though Yeats wished to escape out of the stream of time into the eternity of art, ironically, the golden bird's song is about time

Explorations

FIRST READING

Stanza 1

1. Read the first stanza carefully for yourself, as many times as you feel necessary. In groups, try out different ways of reading the first sentence aloud. Why do you think it should be read in that way?

2. Notice the perspective. The poet has already left Ireland, either in reality or imagination, and is looking back.

a   What does he remember about the country?

b   Why is it 'no country for old men'?

3. The first stanza vividly portrays the sensuality of life. Explore how the poet does this. Consider the imagery, the sounds of words, repeated letters, the crowded syntax, the repetitions and rhythms of the sentence, etc.

4. How do you think the poet feels about this teeming fertility? Ostensibly he is renouncing the world of the senses, but do you think he dwells on these scenes a little too much if he dislikes or hates them? Consider phrases such as 'The young | In one another's arms, birds in the trees'; 'commend all summer long'; 'Caught in that sensual music'. Do you think there might be a hint of nostalgia and a sense of loss here? Discuss the tone of the stanza.

5. In the midst of all this energy and life, there are the seeds of death. Explain the paradox and word punning in 'dying generations'. Where else in the first stanza is there an awareness of time?

6. What does the poet value that he feels is neglected in Ireland?

7. Reread the stanza and list all the reasons you can find for Yeats's departure or withdrawal.

8. Now read the first sentence aloud as you think the poet intended it.

SECOND READING

Stanza 2

9. In this stanza Yeats asserts that only the soul gives meaning to the human being.

a   Explore the contrast between body and soul here.

b   Do you think that the imagery used is effective? Explain.

10. 'Nor is there ... own magnificence'.

a   Tease out the possible meanings of these two lines. Explore the following reading: the only way the spirit learns to sing (achieves perfection) is by studying monuments created by and for itself, i.e. works of art. In other words, art enriches the soul.

b   Explain why the poet has come to Byzantium.

THIRD READING

Stanza 3

11. In the third stanza Yeats entreats the sages of the timeless city to teach his soul to sing, i.e. perfect his spirit. But perfection cannot be achieved without pain and sacrifice. Where in the stanza is this notion dealt with?

12. What is the poet's ultimate goal as expressed in the stanza?

13. Byzantium was renowned as the city of religion, philosophy and a highly formalised art. Where are these elements reflected in the second and third stanzas?

FOURTH READING

Stanza 4

14. In the fourth stanza the poet wishes that his spirit would be transformed into the perfect work of art and so live on, ageless and incorruptible. What do you notice about this piece of art?

15. Do you think Yeats achieves the yearned-for escape from the flux of time into the 'immortality' of art? Carefully consider the irony of the final line.

16. Essentially, what is Yeats writing about in this poem?

17. 'This poem is built around essential contrasts and polarities.' Discuss this with reference to relevant phrases and lines.

18. Can you appreciate Yeats's dilemma as experienced here as well as his deep yearning?

from Meditations in Time of Civil War: VI. The Stare's Nest by My Window

The bees build in the crevices
Of loosening masonry, and there
The mother birds bring grubs and flies.
My wall is loosening; honey-bees,
Come build in the empty house of the stare.   5

We are closed in, and the key is turned
On our uncertainty; somewhere
A man is killed, or a house burned,
Yet no clear fact to be discerned:
Come build in the empty house of the stare.   10

A barricade of stone or of wood;
Some fourteen days of civil war;
Last night they trundled down the road
That dead young soldier in his blood:
Come build in the empty house of the stare.   15

We had fed the heart on fantasies,
The heart's grown brutal from the fare;
More substance in our enmities
Than in our love; O honey-bees,
Come build in the empty house of the stare.   20

Notes

	Stare's Nest:	'stare' is a term sometimes used in the West of Ireland for a starling
	Meditations in Time of Civil War:	this is quite a lengthy poem structured in seven sections. The first was composed in England in 1921; the other sections were written in Ireland during the Civil War of 1922–23.
1	**The bees:**	there is a possible echo of the bees that were sent by the gods to perform certain tasks in Porphyry's mystical writing. At any rate, they may symbolise patient creative endeavour, as distinct from the destructive forces all around.
14	**That dead young soldier:**	this is based on an event that reputedly took place beside Yeats's Galway house, Thoor Ballylee, when a young soldier was dragged down a road, his body so badly battered and mutilated that his mother could only recover his head.

Explorations

BEFORE READING

1. Read only the title. What might you expect to find in this poem?

FIRST READING

Stanzas 1–3

2. Examine the detail of the first three lines of stanza 1. Write about what you see: the details, the sounds, the atmosphere.

3. In the actual historical context, many Big Houses of the establishment class were abandoned or evacuated for fear of reprisals. What do you imagine might have been the poet's thoughts when he first came upon this scene by the window?

4. There are two references to 'loosening' masonry or walls in the first stanza. Do you think these might be significant? Explain.

5. Read the second stanza carefully. What is the atmosphere in the house and what details contribute to this?

6. What single word do you find most powerful in the third stanza? Write about it.

SECOND READING

Stanza 4

7. Tease out the meaning of the fourth stanza in your own words.

8. Comment on the tones you find in the final stanza and suggest how these are created.

9. How do you think the repeated refrain should be read? Try it.

THIRD READING

10. Would you agree that Yeats is torn between a bitter disappointment and a desperate hope here? Discuss this.

11. 'The poem captures the atmosphere of war with vivid realism.'
Discuss this statement with reference to the text.

12. Explore the music of this piece: the onomatopoeia, the effect of the rhyming, the haunting refrain, etc.

FOURTH READING

In Memory of Eva Gore-Booth and Con Markiewicz

The light of evening, Lissadell,
Great windows open to the south,
Two girls in silk kimonos, both
Beautiful, one a gazelle.
But a raving autumn shears   5
Blossom from the summer's wreath;
The older is condemned to death,
Pardoned, drags out lonely years
Conspiring among the ignorant.
I know not what the younger dreams –   10
Some vague Utopia – and she seems,
When withered old and skeleton-gaunt,
An image of such politics.
Many a time I think to seek
One or the other out and speak   15
Of that old Georgian mansion, mix
Pictures of the mind, recall
That table and the talk of youth,
Two girls in silk kimonos, both
Beautiful, one a gazelle.   20

Dear shadows, now you know it all,
All the folly of a fight
With a common wrong or right.
The innocent and the beautiful
Have no enemy but time;   25
Arise and bid me strike a match
And strike another till time catch;
Should the conflagration climb,
Run till all the sages know.
We the great gazebo built,   30
They convicted us of guilt;
Bid me strike a match and blow.

Eva Gore-Booth (1870–1926) was a poet and a reader of Eastern philosophy. She became involved in social work for the poor and was a member of the women's suffrage movement.

Constance Gore-Booth (1868–1927) married a Polish poet and landowner, Count Casimir Markiewicz. A committed socialist republican, she became involved in Irish revolutionary movements and joined the Citizen Army. She was sentenced to death for her part in the Easter Rising, but the sentence was commuted to life imprisonment and she was released in the general amnesty of 1917. She was appointed Minister for Labour in the first Dáil Éireann of 1919 and was the first Irish woman government minister. She took the anti-treaty side in the Civil War.

Notes

1	**Lissadell:**	the County Sligo Georgian mansion built in the early part of the 19th century and home of the Gore-Booth family. Yeats visited in 1894–95.
3	**kimonos:**	traditional Japanese long robes
4	**gazelle:**	a small, delicately formed antelope. The reference is to Eva Gore-Booth.
7	**The older:**	Constance
8	**lonely years:**	Constance's husband returned to his lands in the Ukraine and she was separated from her children
16	**old Georgian mansion:**	Lissadell, an image of aristocratic elegance and good taste for Yeats
21	**Dear shadows:**	both women were dead at the time of writing
30	**gazebo:**	the scholar A.N. Jeffares gives three possible meanings: a summer house; a vantage point; and to make a fool of oneself or be conspicuous (in Hibernian English)

Explorations

Lines 1–4

1. Picture the scene in the first four lines – notice all the details. What do you learn about the lifestyle of the people living here?

2. What questions are you prompted to ask by these lines? Formulate at least three. Share your questions.

3.

a Do you think Yeats treasured this memory?

b What do the lines reveal about what Yeats valued or considered important in life?

Lines 5–6

4. Do you think these lines are an effective metaphor for the passage of time or a rather tired one? Discuss this.

Lines 7–13

5. Read these lines, consult the notes and then briefly state in your own words how the life paths or careers of these two women have developed.

6. Do you think Yeats approved of their careers? Explain your view with reference to words and phrases in the text.

SECOND READING

7. 'Two girls in silk kimonos, both |
Beautiful, one a gazelle.'
These lines are repeated at the end of the first section. Do you think the refrain here should be spoken in the same tone as lines 3–4 or have intervening lines coloured the poet's feeling? Explain your opinion on this. Read the first section aloud as you think Yeats would want it read.

8. Lines 21–5 carry the kernel of the poet's insight, which he feels certain the spirits ('Dear shadows') of the two sisters will understand.

a What is this wisdom or insight?

b Is there a certain weariness of tone here? Explain.

9. What do you understand by Yeats's animated wish at the end of the poem to light a bonfire?

10. What are the main issues or themes that Yeats deals with in this poem? Support your view with detailed reference.

11. What could one discern about the poet's philosophy of life from a reading of this poem? Refer to the detail of the text.

12. Yeats felt that the Anglo-Irish Ascendancy class, with their great houses and wealth, had a duty to set an example of graciousness and cultured living.

a Do you think he felt that Eva and Constance had let the side down? Where and how might this be suggested?

b Do you think he may have considered their activities unfeminine?

13. 'The off-rhymes that Yeats employs from time to time give the poem a conversational naturalism and reinforce the theme of imperfection.' Discuss this with reference to the details of the poem.

14. Many of Yeats's poems about time are structured on quite violent contrasts. Do you think this is an effective device here? Comment.

15. Think or talk about your personal reactions to this poem. What did it make you think about? What insights did it give you?

Swift's Epitaph

Swift has sailed into his rest;
Savage indignation there
Cannot lacerate his breast.
Imitate him if you dare,
World-besotted traveller; he   5
Served human liberty.

Background note

Jonathan Swift (1667–1745) was the most famous dean of St Patrick's Cathedral, Dublin. Poet, political pamphleteer and satirist, he was the author of such well-known works as *The Drapier Letters*, *A Modest Proposal*, *A Tale of a Tub* and *Gulliver's Travels*. Politically conservative, Swift voiced the concerns and values of Protestant Ireland with an independence of mind and a courage that Yeats admired.

This poem is a translation, with some alterations, of the Latin epitaph on Swift's burial stone in St Patrick's Cathedral, Dublin. Yeats changed the first line and added the adjective 'World-besotted' in the penultimate line. The original epitaph, which is in Latin, runs as follows:

William Butler Yeats

Here is laid the Body of
JONATHAN SWIFT
Doctor of Divinity,
Dean of this Cathedral Church,
Where savage indignation
can no longer
Rend his heart,
Go traveller, and imitate,
if you can,
This earnest and dedicated
Champion of Liberty.
He died on the 19th day of Oct.,
1745 a.d. aged 78 years.

Explorations

FIRST READING

1. What does the first line suggest about Swift's death?

2. What can we learn about Swift's life from this epitaph?

3. What qualities of Swift's do you think Yeats admired?

4. Comment on the tone of the epitaph. Do you think it is unusual? Refer in detail to words and phrases.

SECOND READING

5. How do Yeats's alterations in lines 1 and 5 (see Question 2) change the epitaph?

6. Contrast Swift's original epitaph with Yeats's own epitaph.

An Acre of Grass

Picture and book remain,
An acre of green grass
For air and exercise,
Now strength of body goes;
Midnight, an old house   5
Where nothing stirs but a mouse.

My temptation is quiet.
Here at life's end
Neither loose imagination,
Nor the mill of the mind   10
Consuming its rag and bone,
Can make the truth known.

Grant me an old man's frenzy,
Myself must I remake
Till I am Timon and Lear   15
Or that William Blake
Who beat upon the wall
Till Truth obeyed his call;

A mind Michael Angelo knew
That can pierce the clouds   20
Or inspired by frenzy
Shake the dead in their shrouds;
Forgotten else by mankind,
An old man's eagle mind.

Notes

2-5	**An acre of green grass … an old house:**	the reference is to Riversdale, a farmhouse with orchards and fruit gardens at the foot of the Dublin Mountains in Rathfarnham which in 1932 Yeats leased for 13 years
9	**loose imagination:**	unstructured imagination
11	**rag and bone:**	the leftover, discarded bric-a-brac of life. Lines 10–11 might refer to the imagination's everyday, casual focus on life's bric-a-brac.
15	**Timon:**	an Athenian who died in 399 BC who was satirised by the comic writers of his time for his marked misanthropy, or strong dislike of humanity. Shakespeare dramatised the story in *Timon of Athens*.
15	**Lear:**	Shakespeare's King Lear, who couldn't accept old age gracefully, lost his reason and lived wild on the heath
16	**William Blake:**	(1757–1827) by profession an engraver, Blake is best known for his more accessible poems 'Songs of Innocence' and 'Songs of Experience'. Lesser known is a great body and range of work which shows him as a mystic, apocalyptic visionary, writer of rude verses and an independent thinker who challenged the accepted philosophies and values of his age. He was considered mad by his contemporaries. Yeats admired him greatly and co-edited his *Prophetic Books* in 1893. He also wrote an interpretation of Blake's mythology.
19	**Michael Angelo:**	Michelangelo Buonarroti (1475–1564) was one of the premier figures of the Italian Renaissance – sculptor, architect, painter and poet. Among his most famous creations are the statue of *David* and the ceiling of the Sistine Chapel in Rome.

Explorations

1. Explore the images and sounds of the first stanza.

a What do we learn about the condition of the poet?

b How would you describe the atmosphere created in this stanza? What words and sounds contribute most to that?

2. In the second stanza, the poet is still thinking of poetry despite his age. In your own words, describe his dilemma.

3. Examine the metaphor for the mind used in lines 10–11. What do you think of it?

4. Comment on the tones found in stanzas 1–2. Do you think there is a sense of emptiness at the end of the second stanza? Explore how the sounds of the words contribute to this.

SECOND READING

5. 'Grant me an old man's frenzy.' This is a very unusual prayer. Does the remainder of stanza 3 help to explain this intercession? Consult the textual notes and try to outline in your own words what Yeats is actually praying for.

6. What is the connection that Yeats is making between poetry, madness and truth?

7. There is evidence of a new energy in both language and imagery in stanzas 3–4. Comment in detail on this.

8. This extraordinary change or metamorphosis culminates in the final image of 'An old man's eagle mind'. Trace how this conceit (or startling comparison) has been prepared for earlier in the fourth stanza.

THIRD READING

9. Would you agree that this poem is a most unusual response to the theme of old age?

10. Yeats's theories of creativity (partly inspired by the works of the German philosopher Nietzsche) included the need for continual transformation of the self. Trace the transformation that occurs here.

Politics

'In our time the destiny of man presents its meanings in political terms.' (Thomas Mann)

How can I, that girl standing there,
My attention fix
On Roman or on Russian
Or on Spanish politics,
Yet here's a travelled man that knows   5
What he talks about,
And there's a politician
That has read and thought,
And maybe what they say is true
Of war and war's alarms,   10
But O that I were young again
And held her in my arms.

Background note

Written in May 1938, this poem was composed as an answer to an article about
Yeats that had praised his public language but suggested that he should use it on
political subjects.

Notes

Thomas Mann:	a German novelist (1875–1955)

Explorations

FIRST READING

1. In your own words, state the dilemma
   or conflict that Yeats is experiencing
   here.

2. 'And maybe what they say is true | Of
   war'.
   From the context of the poem, what
   do you suppose 'they' say? Examine
   Thomas Mann's epigraph for
   suggestions.

3. 'That girl standing there'. To whom or
   to what do you think the poet might be
   referring?

SECOND READING

4. Write about the essential conflicts
   that are set up here: politics versus
   love, public life versus private, public
   devotion versus private satisfaction, etc.

5. 'For all its simplicity of language, this is a
   very well-crafted poem.'
   Discuss this statement with reference
   to the text.

6. State what you think this poem is about.

7. 'The vision in this poem is that of an old
   man.'
   Argue about this.

William Butler Yeats

from Under Ben Bulben

V

Irish poets, learn your trade,
Sing whatever is well made,
Scorn the sort now growing up
All out of shape from toe to top,
Their unremembering hearts and heads   5
Base-born products of base beds.
Sing the peasantry, and then
Hard-riding country gentlemen,
The holiness of monks, and after
Porter-drinkers' randy laughter;   10
Sing the lords and ladies gay
That were beaten into the clay
Through seven heroic centuries;
Cast your mind on other days
That we in coming days may be   15
Still the indomitable Irishry.

VI

Under bare Ben Bulben's head
In Drumcliff churchyard Yeats is laid,
An ancestor was rector there
Long years ago; a church stands near,   20
By the road an ancient Cross.
No marble, no conventional phrase;
On limestone quarried near the spot
By his command these words are cut:
  Cast a cold eye   25
  On life, on death.
  Horseman, pass by!

September 4, 1938

Background note

The final draft of this poem is dated 4 September 1938, about five months before the poet's death. Parts of it were published in 1939. 'Under Ben Bulben' as a whole can be seen as Yeats's poetic testimony, an elegy for himself, defining his convictions and the poetic and social philosophies that motivated his life's work.

Section V: Yeats urges all artists, poets, painters and sculptors to promote the necessary heroic images that nourish civilisation.

Section VI rounds his life to its close and moves from the mythologies associated with the top of Ben Bulben to the real earth at its foot in the Drumcliff churchyard.

Notes

Section V

2	whatever is well made:	comments on the great tradition of art and letters (see also the note for line 14 below)
3-6	Scorn the sort ... products of base beds:	Yeats had joined the Eugenics Society in London in 1936 and became very interested in its literature and in research on intelligence testing. (Eugenics is the science of improving the human race through selective breeding.)
11-12	Sing the lords ... beaten into the clay:	refers to the Cromwellian settlement of 1652, which evicted the majority of Irish landowners to Clare and Connaught to make room for new English settlers
13	centuries:	the centuries since the Norman invasions
14	other days:	a reference to the great tradition in European art and letters valued by Yeats, but it could also be a reference to Ireland's literary tradition, particularly of the 18th century

Section VI

17	Ben Bulben:	a mountain north of Sligo connected with Irish mythology
18	Drumcliff:	at the foot of Ben Bulben, the site of a 6th-century monastery founded by St Colmcille
19	ancestor was rector there:	the Revd John Yeats (1774–1846), Yeats's grandfather, was rector there and is buried in the graveyard
20-1	a church stands near ... ancient Cross:	as well as the remains of a round tower, there is a high cross and part of an older cross in the churchyard
27	Horseman:	has echoes of the fairy horseman of folk belief, but might also have associations with the Irish Ascendancy class

Explorations

Section V

1. Yeats's advice to Irish poets to write about the aesthetically pleasing ('whatever is well made') is quite understandable, but what do you think of his advice on what they should scorn? Consult the textual notes.

a   What exactly is he saying?

b   What is your reaction to this rant?

2. In your own words, what does Yeats consider to be the proper subjects for poetry?

3. What image of 'Irishry' does Yeats wish to celebrate? Do you think he is being elitist and superior?

SECOND READING

4. Would you agree that this section exhibits an abhorrence for the present at the expense of a romanticised past? Explain your opinion with reference to the details of the verse.

5. This reads like an incantation. What features of poetic technique do you think contribute to this? Consider the metre, the rhyming scheme, the choice of diction, etc.

6. Write about the poet's attitude of mind as you detect it from these lines.

7. Professor Terence Brown has written of 'Under Ben Bulben': 'Skill (i.e. poetic) here is complicit with a repulsive politics and a deficient ethical sense.' On the evidence of the extract, would you agree with this?

THIRD READING

Section VI

8. Yeats visualised the details of his last resting place very carefully. Without checking back, what details of the churchyard can you remember?

9. How would you describe the atmosphere of the churchyard? What details in the verse contribute particularly to this?

FOURTH READING

10. What do these lines reveal about the poet, how he sees himself and how he wishes to be remembered?

11. Discuss the epitaph in the last three lines. How does it differ from most epitaphs you have read?

12. The scholar A.N. Jeffares felt that the epitaph embodied Yeats's essential attitude to life and death, 'which he thought must be faced with bravery, with heroic indifference and with the aristocratic disdain of the horseman'. Consider this as a possible reading of the lines and write a response to it.

Robert Frost
(1874–1963)

Prescribed for Higher Level exams in 2015 and 2018

R obert Lee Frost was born in San Francisco on 26 March 1874. Following his father's death in 1885, he moved with his younger sister Jeanie and his mother to Lawrence, Massachusetts, where his grandparents lived. Robert entered Lawrence High School in 1888, where he studied Latin, Greek, ancient and European history and mathematics. From high school he went to Dartmouth College and Harvard, but left the two colleges without graduating. On 19 December 1895 he married Elinor White, a former classmate. For health reasons he took up farming. In later years he recalled that his favourite activities were 'mowing with a scythe, chopping with an axe and writing with a pen'. He supplemented his income by teaching and lecturing.

Frost devoted his free time to reading the major poets in order to perfect his own writing. Shakespeare, the English Romantics (Wordsworth, Keats and Shelley) and the Victorian poets (Hardy, Kipling and Browning) all influenced his work. The many biblical references in his poems reflect his studies of scripture, while his classical education enabled him to write with confidence in traditional forms. He followed the principles laid down in Wordsworth's 'Preface to the Lyrical Ballads', basing his poetry on incidents from common life described in 'language really used by men'.

Frost and his family emigrated to England in 1912, where he published two collections, *A Boy's Will* (1913) and *North of Boston* (1914). The books were well received and he was introduced into the literary circles in London, where he met W.B. Yeats. After the outbreak of World War I, Frost returned to America and wrote his next collection, *Mountain Interval*. This book contains some of his best-known poems, including 'Birches', 'Out, Out—' and 'The Road Not Taken', with their characteristic themes of isolation, fear, violence and death. Frost bought another farm in Franconia, New Hampshire, and supported his family by college teaching, readings, lectures, book royalties and reprint fees. In January 1917 he became Professor of English at Amherst, Massachusetts. By 1920 he could afford to move to Vermont and devote himself to apple-farming and writing poetry. In recognition of his work he won the Pulitzer Prize four times, in 1924, 1931, 1937 and 1943.

In contrast to his public life, Frost's personal life was dogged by tragedy. His sister Jeanie was committed to a mental asylum. His daughter Lesley had an emotionally disturbed life and blamed her father for her problems. His favourite child, Marjorie, had a nervous breakdown, developed tuberculosis and died in 1934 aged 29. Irma, his third daughter, suffered from mental illness throughout her adult life. Elinor, his wife, died of a heart attack on 20 March 1938 and his only son, Carol, committed suicide in 1940. Frost survived the turbulence of these years with the support of his friend, secretary and manager, Kay Morrison.

In his final years, Frost enjoyed public acclaim. He recited 'The Gift Outright' at John F. Kennedy's inauguration, watched on television by over 60 million Americans. He travelled as a celebrated visitor to Brazil, Ireland and Russia. On his 88th birthday he received the Congressional Gold Medal from President Kennedy and in the same year, 1962, published his final volume, *In the Clearing*. On 29 January 1963, two months before his 89th birthday, Robert Frost died peacefully in a Boston hospital.

The Tuft of Flowers

This poem is also prescribed for Ordinary Level exams in 2015 and 2018

I went to turn the grass once after one
Who mowed it in the dew before the sun.

The dew was gone that made his blade so keen
Before I came to view the levelled scene.

I looked for him behind an isle of trees;   5
I listened for his whetstone on the breeze.

But he had gone his way, the grass all mown,
And I must be, as he had been – alone,

'As all must be,' I said within my heart,
'Whether they work together or apart.'   10

But as I said it, swift there passed me by
On noiseless wing a bewildered butterfly,

Seeking with memories grown dim o'er night
Some resting flower of yesterday's delight.

And once I marked his flight go round and round,   15
As where some flower lay withering on the ground.

And then he flew as far as eye could see,
And then on tremulous wing came back to me.

I thought of questions that have no reply,
And would have turned to toss the grass to dry; 20

But he turned first, and led my eye to look
At a tall tuft of flowers beside a brook,

A leaping tongue of bloom the scythe had spared
Beside a reedy brook the scythe had bared.

I left my place to know them by their name, 25
Finding them butterfly weed when I came.

The mower in the dew had loved them thus,
By leaving them to flourish, not for us,

Nor yet to draw one thought of ours to him,
But from sheer morning gladness at the brim. 30

The butterfly and I had lit upon,
Nevertheless, a message from the dawn,

That made me hear the wakening birds around,
And hear his long scythe whispering to the ground,

And feel a spirit kindred to my own; 35
So that henceforth I worked no more alone;

But glad with him, I worked as with his aid,
And weary, sought at noon with him the shade;

And dreaming, as it were, held brotherly speech
With one whose thought I had not hoped to reach. 40

'Men work together,' I told him from the heart,
'Whether they work together or apart.'

Robert Frost

Notes

1	to turn the grass:	to toss the cut grass so that it will dry
3	keen:	sharp-edged, eager
6	whetstone:	a stone used for sharpening edged tools by friction
23	scythe:	a long, curving, sharp-edged blade for mowing grass

Explorations

FIRST READING

1. Describe the scene in the first five couplets. What do you see? Who is present? What is he doing?

2. Explore the mood in these opening lines. How does the speaker feel? Do you think you would feel the same way?

3. How does the speaker feel after he discovers the butterfly weed? What words or phrases suggest a change in his mood?

4. According to the poem, why did the mower not cut these flowers?

5. What images or phrases caught your attention on a first reading? Why?

SECOND READING

6. In your opinion, what is the 'message from the dawn'?

7. What do you think the poet means when he says 'henceforth I worked no more alone'?

THIRD READING

8. Briefly outline the themes of this poem.

9. Shifts of mood and tone are marked by the word 'but'. Trace these changes in the poem.

10. The speaker describes the mower as a 'spirit kindred to my own'. In what sense is this true?

FOURTH READING

11. Frost introduces the concept of 'turning' three times in the poem. Examine the changes that occur with each of them.

12. Follow the development of the main ideas. Examine the images that convey these ideas and state whether or not you find them effective.

13. 'Frost rejects ornate, poetic diction, preferring a language that is conversational and relaxed.' Examine Frost's use of language in the poem.

14. 'Frost's decision to write in conventional forms, using traditional rhythms and rhymes and syntax, reflects his belief that poetry should be accessible to the ordinary man.' Assess this poem in light of the above statement.

Mending Wall

This poem is also prescribed for Ordinary Level exams in 2015 and 2018

Something there is that doesn't love a wall,
That sends the frozen-ground-swell under it
And spills the upper boulders in the sun,
And makes gaps even two can pass abreast.
The work of hunters is another thing: 5
I have come after them and made repair
Where they have left not one stone on a stone,
But they would have the rabbit out of hiding,
To please the yelping dogs. The gaps I mean,
No one has seen them made or heard them made,   10
But at spring mending-time we find them there.
I let my neighbor know beyond the hill;
And on a day we meet to walk the line
And set the wall between us once again.
We keep the wall between us as we go.   15
To each the boulders that have fallen to each.
And some are loaves and some so nearly balls
We have to use a spell to make them balance:
'Stay where you are until our backs are turned!'
We wear our fingers rough with handling them.   20
Oh, just another kind of outdoor game,
One on a side. It comes to little more:
There where it is we do not need the wall:
He is all pine and I am apple orchard.
My apple trees will never get across   25
And eat the cones under his pines, I tell him.
He only says, 'Good fences make good neighbors.'
Spring is the mischief in me, and I wonder
If I could put a notion in his head:
'*Why* do they make good neighbors? Isn't it   30
Where there are cows? But here there are no cows.
Before I built a wall I'd ask to know
What I was walling in or walling out,
And to whom I was like to give offence.
Something there is that doesn't love a wall,   35
That wants it down.' I could say 'Elves' to him,
But it's not elves exactly, and I'd rather
He said it for himself. I see him there,
Bringing a stone grasped firmly by the top
In each hand, like an old-stone savage armed.   40

Robert Frost

He moves in darkness as it seems to me,
Not of woods only and the shade of trees.
He will not go behind his father's saying,
And he likes having thought of it so well
He says again, 'Good fences make good neighbors.'   45

Explorations

1. You have been asked to paint a picture based on this poem. Where would you place the wall and the two men? What are the men doing? Are they looking at each other? Describe their postures and their facial expressions. What other details would you include?

2. How are the gaps in the wall created?

3. What do you think the poet means when he describes wall-building as 'just another kind of outdoor game'?

4. Outline the arguments Frost uses against building walls.

5. In what sense is the neighbour 'all pine and I am apple orchard'?

6. 'He moves in darkness'.
   What forms of darkness overshadow the neighbour?

7. Describe as clearly as possible your image of the neighbour as Frost portrays him.

8. Walls unite and divide. How is this illustrated within the poem?

9. 'Good fences make good neighbors.' Do you think the speaker agrees with this proverb? Explain your answer.

10. The neighbour repeats the proverb because 'he likes having thought of it so well'. Why is this comment ironic?

11. What do we learn about the narrator's personality in the poem?

12. What themes and issues are raised in this poem?

13. How does Frost achieve a sense of mystery in the poem? Are any of the images mysterious or magical? What effect do they have on the poem?

14. Follow the development of the main ideas. Examine the images that convey these ideas and state whether or not you find them effective.

15. This poem is concerned with unity and division, communication and isolation, hope and disappointment. Do you agree? Where are these tensions most obvious? Are they resolved at the end?

16. 'Human nature, not Mother Nature, is the main concern in Frost's poetry.' Would you agree with this statement based on your reading of this poem?

After Apple-Picking

My long two-pointed ladder's sticking through a tree
Toward heaven still,
And there's a barrel that I didn't fill
Beside it, and there may be two or three
Apples I didn't pick upon some bough.   5
But I am done with apple-picking now.
Essence of winter sleep is on the night,
The scent of apples: I am drowsing off.
I cannot rub the strangeness from my sight
I got from looking through a pane of glass   10
I skimmed this morning from the drinking trough
And held against the world of hoary grass.
It melted, and I let it fall and break.
But I was well
Upon my way to sleep before it fell,   15
And I could tell

Robert Frost

What form my dreaming was about to take.
Magnified apples appear and disappear,
Stem end and blossom end,
And every fleck of russet showing clear.   20
My instep arch not only keeps the ache,
It keeps the pressure of a ladder-round.
I feel the ladder sway as the boughs bend.
And I keep hearing from the cellar bin
The rumbling sound   25
Of load on load of apples coming in.
For I have had too much
Of apple-picking: I am overtired
Of the great harvest I myself desired.
There were ten thousand thousand fruit to touch,   30
Cherish in hand, lift down, and not let fall.
For all
That struck the earth,
No matter if not bruised or spiked with stubble,
Went surely to the cider-apple heap   35
As of no worth.
One can see what will trouble
This sleep of mine, whatever sleep it is.
Were he not gone,
The woodchuck could say whether it's like his   40
Long sleep, as I describe its coming on,
Or just some human sleep.

Notes

7	**Essence:**	scent
12	**hoary:**	white with age (hoarfrost: white particles of frozen dew)
40	**woodchuck:**	or groundhog – a burrowing rodent that hibernates for half the year

Explorations

FIRST READING

1. Imagine the orchard as Frost describes it in the opening lines. What details does he include? How would you describe the scene now that the apple-picking is over?

2. Explain in your own words what happened at the drinking trough in the morning.

3. Why did the apple-picker have to be so careful with the apples?

4. What connects the woodchuck and the harvester?

5. The fruit has been harvested. How does the speaker feel now?

6. What is it that will trouble his sleep?

7. Select your favourite image in the poem and explain your choice.

8. Does the poet successfully capture the sensations of picking apples? Examine his use of images and the language used.

THIRD READING

9. There are moments of confusion in the poem. Is this deliberate? Why? Refer closely to the text in your answer.

10. In the poem, autumn is seen as a season of abundance rather than a time of decay. How does the poet recreate the richness of the harvest for the reader?

11. A dream-like quality pervades the poem. How is this achieved? Consider the language used, the imagery, descriptions, metre and rhyme.

FOURTH READING

12. Frost's language is sensuously evocative and rich in imagery. Discuss his use of tactile, visual and auditory imagery in the poem as a whole.

13. What part do sounds and rhythm play in the creation of the mood in the poem?

14. Briefly explain your personal reaction to 'After Apple-Picking'.

Birches

When I see birches bend to left and right
Across the lines of straighter darker trees,
I like to think some boy's been swinging them.
But swinging doesn't bend them down to stay
As ice storms do. Often you must have seen them   5
Loaded with ice a sunny winter morning
After a rain. They click upon themselves
As the breeze rises, and turn many-colored
As the stir cracks and crazes their enamel.
Soon the sun's warmth makes them shed crystal shells   10
Shattering and avalanching on the snow crust –
Such heaps of broken glass to sweep away
You'd think the inner dome of heaven had fallen.
They are dragged to the withered bracken by the load,
And they seem not to break; though once they are bowed   15
So low for long, they never right themselves:
You may see their trunks arching in the woods
Years afterwards, trailing their leaves on the ground
Like girls on hands and knees that throw their hair

Robert Frost

Before them over their heads to dry in the sun.   20
But I was going to say when Truth broke in
With all her matter of fact about the ice storm,
I should prefer to have some boy bend them
As he went out and in to fetch the cows –
Some boy too far from town to learn baseball,   25
Whose only play was what he found himself,
Summer or winter, and could play alone.
One by one he subdued his father's trees
By riding them down over and over again
Until he took the stiffness out of them,   30
And not one but hung limp, not one was left
For him to conquer. He learned all there was
To learn about not launching out too soon
And so not carrying the tree away
Clear to the ground. He always kept his poise   35
To the top branches, climbing carefully
With the same pains you use to fill a cup
Up to the brim, and even above the brim.
Then he flung outward, feet first, with a swish,
Kicking his way down through the air to the ground.   40
So was I once myself a swinger of birches.
And so I dream of going back to be.
It's when I'm weary of considerations,
And life is too much like a pathless wood
Where your face burns and tickles with the cobwebs   45
Broken across it, and one eye is weeping
From a twig's having lashed across it open.
I'd like to get away from earth awhile
And then come back to it and begin over.
May no fate willfully misunderstand me   50
And half grant what I wish and snatch me away
Not to return. Earth's the right place for love:
I don't know where it's likely to go better.
I'd like to go by climbing a birch tree,
And climb black branches up a snow-white trunk   55
Toward heaven, till the tree could bear no more,
But dipped its top and set me down again.
That would be good both going and coming back.
One could do worse than be a swinger of birches.

Explorations

1. Have you ever climbed a tree? Discuss your experience, explaining where you were, how difficult it was and what skills you needed to climb up and down.

FIRST READING

2. On a first reading, what do you see? Visualise the trees, the ice, the sky and the boy. What sounds can you hear? Are there any other details you should include?

3. What images caught your imagination?

4. How would you describe the general mood of the poem?

SECOND READING

5. Based on the details given by Frost, describe the character of the boy.

6. Would you agree that the boy is a skilled climber? What details support this point of view?

7. Do you think the speaker really intends to climb trees again? What makes him long to be a 'swinger of birches' once more?

8. What do you understand by the line 'And life is too much like a pathless wood'?

9. Is the speaker's wish to escape from earth a death wish? Explain your answer.

10. Explain clearly what you think Frost means in the last eight lines of the poem.

THIRD READING

11. Frost uses the image of girls drying their hair in the sun. Why? How effective is this image?

12. 'One could do worse than be a swinger of birches.' Does the poet present a convincing argument in support of this claim?

13. How does Frost achieve a conversational tone in the poem? Why does he adopt this voice?

FOURTH READING

14. In what way do the boy's actions resemble those of a poet?

15. How does the music in the poem – sounds, metre, etc. – contribute to the atmosphere?

16. Comment on the poet's contrasting use of light and darkness.

17. 'Though much of Frost's poetry is concerned with suffering, he is also capable of capturing moments of unearthly beauty and joy in his work.' Comment on the poem in light of this statement.

Robert Frost

'Out, Out—'

This poem is also prescribed for Ordinary Level exams in 2015 and 2018

The buzz saw snarled and rattled in the yard
And made dust and dropped stove-length sticks of wood,
Sweet-scented stuff when the breeze drew across it.
And from there those that lifted eyes could count
Five mountain ranges one behind the other   5
Under the sunset far into Vermont.
And the saw snarled and rattled, snarled and rattled,
As it ran light, or had to bear a load.
And nothing happened: day was all but done.
Call it a day, I wish they might have said   10
To please the boy by giving him the half hour
That a boy counts so much when saved from work.
His sister stood beside them in her apron
To tell them 'Supper'. At the word, the saw,
As if to prove saws knew what supper meant,   15
Leaped out at the boy's hand, or seemed to leap –
He must have given the hand. However it was,
Neither refused the meeting. But the hand!
The boy's first outcry was a rueful laugh,
As he swung toward them holding up the hand   20
Half in appeal, but half as if to keep
The life from spilling. Then the boy saw all –
Since he was old enough to know, big boy
Doing a man's work, though a child at heart –
He saw all spoiled. 'Don't let him cut my hand off –   25
The doctor, when he comes. Don't let him, sister!'
So. But the hand was gone already.
The doctor put him in the dark of ether.
He lay and puffed his lips out with his breath.
And then – the watcher at his pulse took fright.   30
No one believed. They listened at his heart.
Little – less – nothing! – and that ended it.
No more to build on there. And they, since they
Were not the one dead, turned to their affairs.

Notes

	'Out, Out—':	the title is taken from William Shakespeare's famous tragedy, *Macbeth*: 'Out, Out brief candle; life's but a walking shadow, a poor player that struts and frets his hour upon the stage, and then is heard no more: it is a tale told by an idiot, full of sound and fury, signifying nothing.'
28	**ether:**	an anaesthetic

Explorations

FIRST READING

1. Read the poem aloud. What words and phrases made the greatest impact on your ear? What animals are suggested in the opening line? How are these animals evoked?

2. Why does Frost describe the scenery?

3. Frost refers repeatedly to 'they' and 'them'. Who do you think these people are? What is your impression of them?

4. The poem turns on the word 'supper'. What happens? Is it an appropriate word in the context?

5. 'He saw all spoiled'. In what sense is all spoiled?

6. What is the boy's immediate fear? Refer to the poem to support your answer.

SECOND READING

7. Trace the narrative line in this poem. Were you surprised by the ending? Do you think it is an effective conclusion?

8. Comment on the title. Is it a suitable one? Could you suggest another?

9. 'Little – less – nothing!' Read this line aloud and comment on the rhythm. What is the effect of the exclamation mark?

THIRD READING

10. How effectively does the poet evoke the terror felt by the boy? Examine the techniques used by Frost in your answer.

11. Would you describe the poet as a detached or a sympathetic observer? Is he angered by the incident? How do we know? Comment on the tone.

12. How does the poet engage the reader's sympathies for the boy? Examine the details given, the use of emotive language and the comments made throughout the poem.

FOURTH READING

13. What themes and issues are explored in the poem?

14. Sound plays an important role in the poem. Examine the use of assonance, alliteration and onomatopoeia in 'Out, Out—'.

15. 'In his poetry, Frost confronts the reader with the harsh realities of life.' Discuss this statement in light of your reading of this poem.

16. Identify and discuss some of the distinctive qualities of Frost's style that are evident in this poem.

Robert Frost

The Road Not Taken

Two roads diverged in a yellow wood,
And sorry I could not travel both
And be one traveler, long I stood
And looked down one as far as I could
To where it bent in the undergrowth;   5

Then took the other, as just as fair,
And having perhaps the better claim,
Because it was grassy and wanted wear;
Though as for that, the passing there
Had worn them really about the same,   10

And both that morning equally lay
In leaves no step had trodden black.
Oh, I kept the first for another day!
Yet knowing how way leads on to way,
I doubted if I should ever come back.   15

I shall be telling this with a sigh
Somewhere ages and ages hence:
Two roads diverged in a wood, and I –
I took the one less traveled by,
And that has made all the difference.   20

Explorations

FIRST READING

1. On a first reading, what do you notice about the setting of the poem? What details made the deepest impression on you? Explain.

2. What is the main focus of the speaker's attention throughout the poem?

3. Why does he choose the second road? Are his reasons convincing?

4. Why will the speaker talk about this moment 'ages and ages hence'?

5. What is the difference referred to by Frost in the last line?

SECOND READING

6. Comment on the title of the poem. What does it lead you to expect? Does the poem fulfil your expectations?

7. On a surface level, the speaker is faced with a choice between two paths. On a deeper level, what do the roads symbolise?

8. What is the dominant mood of the poem? What words, phrases and images suggest this mood?

9. What images create an autumnal atmosphere in the poem? Why did Frost choose this time of year?

10. What themes or issues can you identify in 'The Road Not Taken'?

11. Do you find the imagery in this poem effective in conveying the theme? Refer to specific images in your answer.

12. The poem opens and closes on a note of regret. Trace the development of thought and mood throughout the poem.

FOURTH READING

13. Doubt is replaced by certainty in this poem. Examine the movement from one state to the other.

14. What appeals to you about this poem? Consider the theme, images, sounds and particular words or phrases in your answer.

Spring Pools

These pools that, though in forests, still reflect
The total sky almost without defect,
And like the flowers beside them, chill and shiver,
Will like the flowers beside them soon be gone,
And yet not out by any brook or river,   5
But up by roots to bring dark foliage on.

The trees that have it in their pent-up buds
To darken nature and be summer woods –
Let them think twice before they use their powers
To blot out and drink up and sweep away   10
These flowery waters and these watery flowers
From snow that melted only yesterday.

Notes		
6	**foliage:**	the leaves of a tree or plant

Explorations

FIRST READING

1. What do the pools and the flowers have in common?

2. What do you notice about the trees? What characteristic of the trees does the poet focus on, especially in the second stanza? Why?

3. Why should the trees think twice before they drain the pools and overshadow the flowers?

Robert Frost

4. Outline the argument of the poem. Would you agree that it is condensed with considerable skill? What is the effect of this on the reader?

5. What image made the greatest impression on you? Explain your choice.

6. How important are the sounds of words in creating the atmosphere in this poem?

7. What mood is evoked by this scene? How is this mood created?

8. 'The beauty of this poem lies in the aptness of the descriptions and the clarity of the language.' Do you agree? Explain your answer.

9. Fragility and strength are contrasted in the poem. Where is this contrast most evident? What is the effect? How is this effect achieved?

10. Discuss the techniques Frost uses in this poem to depict the changing nature of the world. Support your answer by quotation or reference.

11. 'Frost is a master of the lyric form, his images are sensuous, his language clear and his tone controlled.' Examine 'Spring Pools' in light of this statement.

12. Give your personal reaction to the poem.

Acquainted with the Night

I have been one acquainted with the night.
I have walked out in rain – and back in rain.
I have outwalked the furthest city light.

I have looked down the saddest city lane.
I have passed by the watchman on his beat   5
And dropped my eyes, unwilling to explain.

I have stood still and stopped the sound of feet
When far away an interrupted cry
Came over houses from another street,

But not to call me back or say good-by;   10
And further still at an unearthly height,
One luminary clock against the sky

Proclaimed the time was neither wrong nor right.
I have been one acquainted with the night.

| 12 | **luminary:** | something that gives light, especially a heavenly body |

Explorations

FIRST READING

1. Describe the scene in your own words.

2. Examine the images used. What do they have in common? Do they provide an insight as to the central idea of the poem?

3. How would you describe the poet's mood?

SECOND READING

4. What do you think is the main theme of the poem? Explain your answer.

5. Do you think the imagery used is effective in illustrating the theme? Which images are most appropriate, in your opinion?

6. What feelings does the poem arouse in you? How does it do this?

THIRD READING

7. What do you notice about the verbs in the poem? What tense is it written in? What purpose might this serve?

8. This poem can be read at more than one level. Suggest another reading of 'Acquainted with the Night'.

FOURTH READING

9. Note the repetitions in the poem. What effect do they have?

10. How does Frost evoke the atmosphere of the urban landscape?

11. There is a deep sense of isolation in this poem. Do you agree? Where is it most evident, in your opinion?

12. ' "Acquainted With the Night" is a tribute to the triumph of the human spirit in the face of adversity, rather than a record of the defeat of the soul at its darkest hour.'
Discuss the poem in light of this statement.

Design

I found a dimpled spider, fat and white,
On a white heal-all, holding up a moth
Like a white piece of rigid satin cloth –
Assorted characters of death and blight
Mixed ready to begin the morning right,   5
Like the ingredients of a witches' broth –
A snow-drop spider, a flower like a froth,
And dead wings carried like a paper kite.

Robert Frost

What had that flower to do with being white,
The wayside blue and innocent heal-all?   10
What brought the kindred spider to that height,
Then steered the white moth thither in the night?
What but design of darkness to appall? –
If design govern in a thing so small.

Notes		
2	**heal-all:**	a common flower used for medicinal purposes, usually blue or violet in colour

Explorations

FIRST READING

1. What do you normally associate with the word 'dimpled'?

2. What images in the octave captured your attention? What do they suggest about the subject matter of the poem?

3. The poet raises several issues in the sestet. What are these issues and what conclusion, if any, does he reach?

4. Jot down the words or phrases that best describe your response to this poem on a first reading.

SECOND READING

5. How does the octet–sestet division mark the development of thought in the poem?

6. Describe the poet's mood in the sestet.

7. What is the effect of the scene on the speaker? Does he find it repulsive,

horrifying, interesting, puzzling? Refer to the text to support your answer.

8. Briefly outline the main argument in this poem.

9. Discuss the poet's use of colour.

10. Would you describe this as a nature poem? Explain your answer.

11. What view of life and death is expressed in the poem? Where is this most evident?

12. Comment on the way the imagery in the poem forges the link between evil and beauty, innocence and death.

13. What is your own reaction to 'Design'?

14. Briefly compare the portrayal of nature in this poem with its portrayal in another poem by Frost on your course.

Provide, Provide

The witch that came (the withered hag)
To wash the steps with pail and rag
Was once the beauty Abishag,

The picture pride of Hollywood.
Too many fall from great and good   5
For you to doubt the likelihood.

Die early and avoid the fate.
Or if predestined to die late,
Make up your mind to die in state.

Make the whole stock exchange your own!   10
If need be occupy a throne,
Where nobody can call *you* crone.

Some have relied on what they knew,
Others on being simply true.
What worked for them might work for you.   15

No memory of having starred
Atones for later disregard
Or keeps the end from being hard.

Better to go down dignified
With boughten friendship at your side   20
Than none at all. Provide, provide!

Robert Frost

Notes

1	**hag:**	an ugly old woman, a witch
3	**Abishag:**	(I Kings 1: 2–4) 'Having searched for a beautiful girl throughout the territory of Israel, they found Abishag of Shunem and brought her to the king. The girl was of great beauty. She looked after the king and waited on him ...'
12	**crone:**	a withered old woman

Explorations

BEFORE READING

1. Read the title only. Jot down what you imagine the poem is about before reading the poem itself.

FIRST READING

2. The idea that youth rapidly fades is introduced in the opening stanza. What images convey this?

3. What advice does Frost offer as to how to avoid the worst aspects of old age?

4. How can one avoid being called a 'crone'?

5. Imagine you are the old woman in the poem. Write your response to 'Provide, Provide'.

SECOND READING

6. Can memories offer comfort to the old?

7. Has 'boughten friendship' any advantages according to the poet? What is his tone here?

8. What do you think is meant by the title of the poem?

THIRD READING

9. Is the poem intended to teach us a lesson? Comment on the moral.

10. Do you think Frost is being serious or humorous here? Examine the tone throughout the poem.

FOURTH READING

11. Do you think there is an important theme in the poem? Explain your answer.

12. Examine the contrasts in the poem. State what they are and whether or not you think they are effective.

13. Did you enjoy this poem? Why?

14. 'Realism rather than pessimism is a hallmark of Frost's poetry.'
Discuss this statement in light of your reading of this poem.

T.S. Eliot

(1888–1965)

Prescribed for Higher Level exams in 2016 and 2017

Thomas Stearns Eliot was born on 26 September 1888 in St Louis, Missouri, in the US. He was the youngest of seven children. His father, Henry, was a brick manufacturer and his mother, Charlotte, was a teacher who also wrote poetry and supported social reform.

His father's ancestors had emigrated from East Coker, near Yeovil in Somerset, England, to Boston, Massachusetts in the late 17th century. T.S. Eliot's grandfather, William, moved to St Louis after he graduated from Harvard University in the 1830s. William became a prominent figure in St Louis, speaking out against slavery and promoting women's rights. He also established the first Unitarian Church there. T.S. Eliot's mother encouraged her son's reverence for his grandfather and it is perhaps this influence which adds the almost missionary zeal to some of his poetry, seeking to bring a message to Western civilisation, which he saw as a moral and cultural wasteland. The family's contact with Boston and the New England coast was maintained through summer visits. These were happy times for the young T.S. Eliot and it is not surprising that sea imagery and themes are prominent throughout his poetry.

Eliot entered Harvard University on 26 September 1906, his 18th birthday. He published frequently in the *Harvard Advocate*, an undergraduate literary magazine, of which he also became editor. In Harvard, Professor Irving Babbit influenced Eliot through his classicism and emphasis on tradition while George Santayana, the Spanish-born philosopher, awakened a love of philosophy in Eliot which led to Eliot's own study of the British philosopher Bradley, who exercised considerable influence on Eliot's thoughts. He also studied the Italian poet Dante, who remained a lifelong source of inspiration. Eliot spent the academic year 1910–11 in Paris, where he studied in the Sorbonne. During this time Eliot became fascinated with the sordid squalor of much of urban life. This was to become part of his poetic trademark. He also came under the influence of the French symbolist poets, in particular Baudelaire (1821–67). Intending to study in Germany in 1914, the outbreak of World War I forced him to go to England instead, where he met the American poet Ezra Pound, who would exert a considerable influence over his work and his literary career. At the insistence of Pound, the editor of the magazine *Poetry* agreed to publish 'The Love Song of J. Alfred

T.S. Eliot

Prufrock', from which one can date the beginning of modern poetry in English. This poem became the central piece of *Prufrock and Other Observations*, published in 1917.

In 1915, Eliot married Vivienne Haigh-Wood. The marriage was to be difficult, leading to the nervous breakdown of both and the permanent illness of Vivienne. (In 1933, Eliot legally separated from her.) Eliot worked as a teacher for a year (1915–16), leaving teaching to work in Lloyd's Bank until 1925, when he joined the publishing firm now known as Faber & Faber. 'The Wasteland' was published in 1922 and was immediately denounced as impenetrable and incoherent by conservative critics, but its depiction of a sordid society, empty of spiritual values, appealed to the poetry-reading public. The spiritual questing that informed this poem and others, such as 'Journey of the Magi', led in 1927 to Eliot's baptism into the Anglican Church, whose Anglo Catholicism satisfied his spiritual and emotional needs. Religious themes became increasingly important to him, leading to the publication of, among others, the poetic drama 'Murder in the Cathedral' (1935), which deals with the assassination of St Thomas à Becket, and to the 'Four Quartets', a philosophic sequence dealing with issues of spiritual renewal and of time. These sufficiently consolidated his reputation to the extent that he was awarded the Nobel Prize for Literature in 1948. Following his wife's death, Eliot married his secretary at Faber & Faber, which brought him great personal happiness. He died on 4 January 1965, after several years of declining health, from emphysema. His ashes are buried in East Coker in Somerset, England.

Eliot's importance to 20th-century poetry can hardly be overstated. Through his critical essays and especially through his own poetic practice, he played a considerable role in establishing the modern conception of poetry – impersonal but packed with powerful reserves of private emotions, learned, allusive and organised by associative connections. On a lighter note, his lifelong love of cats lead to his publication of *Old Possum's Book of Practical Cats* (1939), which was the basis for *Cats*, a spectacular musical comedy of the 1980s.

The Love Song of J. Alfred Prufrock

Let us go then, you and I,
When the evening is spread out against the sky
Like a patient etherised upon a table;
Let us go, through certain half-deserted streets,
The muttering retreats   5
Of restless nights in one-night cheap hotels
And sawdust restaurants with oyster-shells:
Streets that follow like a tedious argument
Of insidious intent
To lead you to an overwhelming question ...   10
Oh, do not ask, 'What is it?'
Let us go and make our visit.

In the room the women come and go
Talking of Michelangelo.

The yellow fog that rubs its back upon the window-panes,   15
The yellow smoke that rubs its muzzle on the window-panes,
Licked its tongue into the corners of the evening,
Lingered upon the pools that stand in drains,
Let fall upon its back the soot that falls from chimneys,
Slipped by the terrace, made a sudden leap,   20
And seeing that it was a soft October night,
Curled once about the house, and fell asleep.

And indeed there will be time
For the yellow smoke that slides along the street
Rubbing its back upon the window-panes;   25
There will be time, there will be time
To prepare a face to meet the faces that you meet;
There will be time to murder and create,
And time for all the works and days of hands
That lift and drop a question on your plate;   30
Time for you and time for me,

T.S. Eliot

And time yet for a hundred indecisions,
And for a hundred visions and revisions,
Before the taking of a toast and tea.

    In the room the women come and go   35
Talking of Michelangelo.

    And indeed there will be time
To wonder, 'Do I dare?' and, 'Do I dare?'
Time to turn back and descend the stair,
With a bald spot in the middle of my hair –   40
(They will say: 'How his hair is growing thin!')
My morning coat, my collar mounting firmly to the chin,
My necktie rich and modest, but asserted by a simple pin –
(They will say: 'But how his arms and legs are thin!')
Do I dare   45
Disturb the universe?
In a minute there is time
For decisions and revisions which a minute will reverse.

    For I have known them all already, known them all –
Have known the evenings, mornings, afternoons,   50
I have measured out my life with coffee spoons;
I know the voices dying with a dying fall
Beneath the music from a farther room.
    So how should I presume?

    And I have known the eyes already, known them all –   55
The eyes that fix you in a formulated phrase,
And when I am formulated, sprawling on a pin,
When I am pinned and wriggling on the wall,
Then how should I begin
To spit out all the butt-ends of my days and ways?   60
    And how should I presume?

    And I have known the arms already, known them all –
Arms that are braceleted and white and bare
(But in the lamplight, downed with light brown hair!)
Is it perfume from a dress   65
That makes me so digress?
Arms that lie along a table, or wrap about a shawl.
    And should I then presume?
    And how should I begin?

Shall I say, I have gone at dusk through narrow streets   70
And watched the smoke that rises from the pipes
Of lonely men in shirt-sleeves, leaning out of windows?...

   I should have been a pair of ragged claws
Scuttling across the floors of silent seas.

   And the afternoon, the evening, sleeps so peacefully!   75
Smoothed by long fingers,
Asleep ... tired ... or it malingers,
Stretched on the floor, here beside you and me.
Should I, after tea and cakes and ices,
Have the strength to force the moment to its crisis?   80
But though I have wept and fasted, wept and prayed,
Though I have seen my head (grown slightly bald) brought in upon a platter,
I am no prophet – and here's no great matter;
I have seen the moment of my greatness flicker,
And I have seen the eternal Footman hold my coat, and snicker,   85
And in short, I was afraid.

   And would it have been worth it, after all,
After the cups, the marmalade, the tea,
Among the porcelain, among some talk of you and me,
Would it have been worth while,   90
To have bitten off the matter with a smile,
To have squeezed the universe into a ball
To roll it towards some overwhelming question,
To say: 'I am Lazarus, come from the dead,
Come back to tell you all, I shall tell you all' –   95
If one, settling a pillow by her head,
   Should say: 'That is not what I meant at all.
   That is not it, at all.'

   And would it have been worth it, after all,
Would it have been worth while,   100
After the sunsets and the dooryards and the sprinkled streets,
After the novels, after the teacups, after the skirts that trail along the floor –
And this, and so much more? –
It is impossible to say just what I mean!
But as if a magic lantern threw the nerves in patterns on a screen: 105
Would it have been worth while
If one, settling a pillow or throwing off a shawl,
And turning toward the window, should say:

T.S. Eliot

'That is not it at all,
    That is not what I meant, at all.'   110

    No! I am not Prince Hamlet, nor was meant to be;
Am an attendant lord, one that will do
To swell a progress, start a scene or two,
Advise the prince; no doubt, an easy tool,
Deferential, glad to be of use,   115
Politic, cautious, and meticulous;
Full of high sentence, but a bit obtuse;
At times, indeed, almost ridiculous –
Almost, at times, the Fool.

    I grow old ... I grow old ...   120
I shall wear the bottoms of my trousers rolled.

    Shall I part my hair behind? Do I dare to eat a peach?
I shall wear white flannel trousers, and walk upon the beach.
I have heard the mermaids singing, each to each.

I do not think that they will sing to me.   125

I have seen them riding seaward on the waves
Combing the white hair of the waves blown back
When the wind blows the water white and black.

We have lingered in the chambers of the sea
By sea-girls wreathed with seaweed red and brown   130
Till human voices wake us, and we drown.

Notes

	S'i, credesse ...:	from Dante (*Inferno* XXVII, 61–6), spoken by the warrior Count Guido do Montefeltro, in Hell for the false advice he gave to the Pope. It reads in English: 'If I believed that my reply would be to one who would return to the world, this flame would tremble no more; but as no one ever returns alive from this depth, if what I hear is true, without fear of disgrace I answer you.'
14	**Michelangelo:**	the Italian painter and sculptor; a heroic contrast to Prufrock
23	**And indeed there will be time:**	echoes the Old Testament, Ecclesiastes 3: 1–8
29	**works and days:**	the title of a didactic poem by the Greek writer Hesiod, 8th century BC

52	a dying fall:	the description of a piece of music by Duke Orsino in Shakespeare's *Twelfth Night*
82	my head ... platter:	Matthew's Gospel 14: 3–11. The head of John the Baptist was brought thus to Salome as a reward for her dancing in front of Herod.
85	eternal Footman:	A personification of death; see John Bunyan's *The Pilgrim's Progress* (1678)
92	squeezed ... ball:	a reference to Andrew Marvell's (1621–78) poem of seduction, 'To His Coy Mistress'
94	Lazarus:	the dead man whom Jesus raised from the dead; see St John's Gospel 11: 1–44
111	Prince Hamlet:	in Shakespeare's play of the same name, Hamlet agonises about being indecisive
113	To swell a progress:	in Elizabethan times, a state or royal journey
117	Full of high sentence:	a description of the talk of the Clerk in Chaucer's (1343–1400) *The Canterbury Tales*
119	the Fool:	the court jester in Shakespeare's *King Lear*, a sort of idiot savant
124	mermaids singing:	a reference to John Donne's (1576–1631) poem 'Song'; also in contrast to the sirens of Greek legend who led sailors to their deaths

Explorations

FIRST READING

1. The 'J. Alfred Prufrock' of the title is the speaker in the poem. Knowing this, how do you visualise him? What words or phrases make images for you? Is he the sort of person you would expect to sing a love song?

2. What is the mood of the speaker in the poem: anger, despair, regret or fear?

T.S. Eliot

3. Would you agree that Prufrock is trying to come to some decision? What do you think this is? What, if anything, does Prufrock have to look forward to?

SECOND READING

4. The Italian epigraph comes from Dante's *The Divine Comedy*. It is spoken by one of the damned souls in the Inferno. What sort of expectations does this arouse for you?

5. Who do you think is the 'you' of the first line? Is it the reader or is it another side of Prufrock's personality?

6. Would you agree that the dramatic scene outlined from lines 1–12 suggests some inner sickness or sordid lifestyle? How does the language used here add to this understanding?

7.

a In lines 13–14, what does the naming of Michelangelo mean to you?

b What do the rhythm and rhyme of these lines suggest to you? Why are they repeated later?

8.

a Would you agree that the image of the fog in lines 15–22 also suggests a cat? What have cats traditionally been associated with?

b What does the rhyming of 'leap' and 'sleep' suggest to you?

9.

a The motif of time is particularly strong in lines 23–4. Where else does it occur in the poem?

b What does 'To prepare a face to meet the faces that you meet' mean to you?

10. Prufrock seems particularly self-conscious and indecisive in lines 37–48. Is there an incongruity between this and his apparent wish to 'disturb the universe'?

11. Would you agree that Prufrock is more disillusioned than angry at the meaninglessness of his life, as described in lines 49–54?

12.

a What fears are expressed by Prufrock in lines 55–69?

b Does Prufrock show a simultaneous attraction for and revulsion of women? How is this shown?

13.

a Do you agree that the question raised in lines 70–4 adds to our understanding of Prufrock's predicament?

b What does the image of 'ragged claws | Scuttling' tell us about his state of mind?

c What is the tone here: embarrassment, distress, self-irony? How does the language used add to the tone?

14.

a Some of the major themes of the poem come together in lines 75–86. What images suggest these themes?

b Would you agree that this section marks a turning point, where Prufrock accepts his inadequacy?

15.

a   What does the reference to Lazarus in lines 94–110 mean to you?

b   Is it fear of rejection alone that makes Prufrock indecisive?

16. What does the line 'But as if a magic lantern threw the nerves in patterns on a screen' suggest to you?

17.

a   How does Prufrock see himself in lines 111–19?

b   Explain the references to 'Prince Hamlet' and 'the Fool'. Is there a tone of resignation here?

18. In lines 120–31, Prufrock seems to be making some decisions at last. What is the quality of these decisions?

19. Would you agree that the reference to the sea and mermaids is an escape into a dream world? What brings him back to reality?

THIRD READING

20. What do you think is the 'overwhelming question' of the poem?

21. Show how the distrustful attitude of Prufrock towards others is seen in the ironical transitions in the poem.

22. Discuss the view that Prufrock's confusion and self-doubt are reflected in the apparent incoherence of the poem.

FOURTH READING

23. 'Eliot's main concern in his poetry is the human condition in the modern world.'
Discuss this view with references to both 'The Love Song of J. Alfred Prufrock' and 'A Game of Chess'.

24. The poet Ezra Pound called Prufrock a portrait of failure and futility. Would you agree?

25. Discuss the possibilities of dramatising this poem, either on stage or on film. What difficulties would it present? How could these be overcome?

Preludes

This poem is also prescribed for Ordinary Level exams in 2016 and 2017

I

The winter evening settles down
With smell of steaks in passageways.
Six o'clock.
The burnt-out ends of smoky days.
And now a gusty shower wraps   5
The grimy scraps
Of withered leaves about your feet
And newspapers from vacant lots;

T.S. Eliot

The showers beat
On broken blinds and chimney-pots,   10
And at the corner of the street
A lonely cab-horse steams and stamps.

And then the lighting of the lamps.

                    II
The morning comes to consciousness
Of faint stale smells of beer   15
From the sawdust-trampled street
With all its muddy feet that press
To early coffee-stands.

With the other masquerades
That time resumes,   20
One thinks of all the hands
That are raising dingy shades
In a thousand furnished rooms.

                    III
You tossed a blanket from the bed,
You lay upon your back, and waited;   25
You dozed, and watched the night revealing
The thousand sordid images
Of which your soul was constituted;
They flickered against the ceiling.
And when all the world came back   30
And the light crept up between the shutters,
And you heard the sparrows in the gutters,
You had such a vision of the street
As the street hardly understands;
Sitting along the bed's edge, where   35
You curled the papers from your hair,
Or clasped the yellow soles of feet
In the palms of both soiled hands.

                    IV
His soul stretched tight across the skies
That fade behind a city block,   40
Or trampled by insistent feet
At four and five and six o'clock;
And short square fingers stuffing pipes,
And evening newspapers, and eyes

Assured of certain certainties,   45
The conscience of a blackened street
Impatient to assume the world.

I am moved by fancies that are curled
Around these images, and cling:
The notion of some infinitely gentle   50
Infinitely suffering thing.

Wipe your hand across your mouth, and laugh;
The worlds revolve like ancient women
Gathering fuel in vacant lots.

'The Street': painting by George Grosz (1893-1959) representing the dysfunctional urban landscape described by Eliot.

T.S. Eliot

Notes

19	**masquerades:**	false pretenses, disguises
22	**shades:**	window blinds
36	**curled the papers from your hair:**	paper was used to curl hair before the arrival of manufactured curlers
54	**vacant lots:**	empty building sites

Explorations

FIRST READING

1. The four sections here are snapshots of modern urban life, where the observer is like a camera moving through the streets. Imagine yourself as that observer. What do you see, hear and smell as you read the poem?

2. Did anything unexpected strike you?

SECOND READING

First prelude

3. In the first prelude, would you agree that the image of 'The burnt-out ends of smoky days' (line 4) evokes a feeling of disgust at a useless end to a useless day? What other words and phrases emphasise the speaker's sense of staleness?

4. How is the sense of cramped conditions indoors evoked?

5. Lines 11–12 picture a 'lonely cab-horse', who is obviously also impatient and uncomfortable. Can this be seen as symbolic of urban life?

6. 'And then the lighting of the lamps' perhaps suggests an introduction to some dramatic events, but these possibilities are not fulfilled. Would you agree that the irony here contributes to the speaker's sense of aimless endurance?

Second prelude

7. Would you agree that the atmosphere of the second prelude is oppressive and empty of charm? How is the morning rush hour conveyed?

8. The same sense of cramped indoor conditions seen in the first prelude is continued here. What images suggest these?

9. For the speaker, the rush of urban life is a 'masquerade'. It is a performance put on to give life an apparent meaning and purpose. Does anything lie behind this performance or is the speaker suggesting that the performance is all there is to life?

Third prelude

10.

a   The third prelude begins with the image of a woman whose sluggish, half-conscious mind projects her interior being. What impression of the woman do we get here and later in this prelude as she prepares for life's 'masquerade'?

b   What vision of the street does she have?

c   Can morning be seen almost as an intruder?

d Would you agree that the proper reaction to what is portrayed is disgust?

Fourth prelude

11.

a In the fourth prelude, the street is personified. Its soul and the souls of the passers-by are fused. How is the suffering of both conveyed?

b Is the speaker being ironic when he says 'and eyes | Assured of certain certainties'?

12. The speaker is momentarily moved to pity in the face of human suffering when he says, 'I am moved ... thing'. Are you shocked by his immediate turn to cynicism when he says, 'Wipe your hand across your mouth, and laugh'? Does he mean us to laugh at the plight of the 'ancient women | Gathering fuel'? Or is he suggesting that in the face of the meaninglessness and suffering of life, pity is too easy an emotion?

THIRD READING

13. Discuss how Eliot depersonalises the observer/speaker.

14. What vital impulses, if any, animate the lives of the characters in the poems?

15. Compare the imagery Eliot uses here with that used in 'The Love Song of J. Alfred Prufrock'.

16. In the art of music, a prelude is a short introductory piece. Examine the musical effects of the poems, particularly the use of rhythm and rhyme.

Aunt Helen

This poem is also prescribed for Ordinary Level exams in 2016 and 2017

Miss Helen Slingsby was my maiden aunt,
And lived in a small house near a fashionable square
Cared for by servants to the number of four.
Now when she died there was silence in heaven
And silence at her end of the street. 5
The shutters were drawn and the undertaker wiped his feet –
He was aware that this sort of thing had occurred before.
The dogs were handsomely provided for,
But shortly afterwards the parrot died too.
The Dresden clock continued ticking on the mantelpiece, 10
And the footman sat upon the dining-table
Holding the second housemaid on his knees –
Who had always been so careful while her mistress lived.

T.S. Eliot

Explorations

FIRST READING

1. What do you notice about the setting of the poem? List the things that made an immediate impression on you.

SECOND READING

2. What is the reaction to Aunt Helen's death? Does anyone mourn her? Does the poet mourn her?

3. Would the footman and housemaid have behaved as described in lines 11–12 when she was alive? Why are they behaving like this now?

4. Would you agree that Aunt Helen had a rather false sense of values? If so, how is this shown? Would you like her lifestyle?

THIRD READING

5. This poem is seen as a mockery of conventional middle-class life in the early 20th century. Do you think Eliot is mocking the person of his aunt or is he satirising the external realities that surround her? Would you agree that her world is one of lifeless artifice, symbolised by a Dresden clock?

6. Eliot's poetic technique included presenting us with a gallery of comic types where (a) places and people are suggested in a few strokes but (b) gain their final tone and significance from the poem as a whole. Comment

   on his descriptions of the characters in the poem under these headings.

7. Do you find any trace of the personality or the feelings of the poet in this poem?

8. Do you think that there is anything in the structure of the poem that mimics the speech or tone of Aunt Helen?

from The Waste Land: II. A Game of Chess

The Chair she sat in, like a burnished throne,
Glowed on the marble, where the glass
Held up by standards wrought with fruited vines
From which a golden Cupidon peeped out
(Another hid his eyes behind his wing)   5
Doubled the flames of sevenbranched candelabra
Reflecting light upon the table as
The glitter of her jewels rose to meet it,
From satin cases poured in rich profusion.
In vials of ivory and coloured glass   10
Unstoppered, lurked her strange synthetic perfumes,
Unguent, powdered, or liquid – troubled, confused
And drowned the sense in odours; stirred by the air
That freshened from the window, these ascended
In fattening the prolonged candle-flames,   15
Flung their smoke into the laquearia,
Stirring the pattern on the coffered ceiling.
Huge sea-wood fed with copper
Burned green and orange, framed by the coloured stone,
In which sad light a carvèd dolphin swam.   20
Above the antique mantel was displayed
As though a window gave upon the sylvan scene
The change of Philomel, by the barbarous king
So rudely forced; yet there the nightingale
Filled all the desert with inviolable voice   25
And still she cried, and still the world pursues,
'Jug Jug' to dirty ears.
And other withered stumps of time
Were told upon the walls; staring forms
Leaned out, leaning, hushing the room enclosed.   30
Footsteps shuffled on the stair.
Under the firelight, under the brush, her hair
Spread out in fiery points
Glowed into words, then would be savagely still.

'My nerves are bad tonight. Yes, bad. Stay with me.   35
Speak to me. Why do you never speak? Speak.
   What are you thinking of? What thinking? What?
I never know what you are thinking. Think.'

   I think we are in rats' alley

T.S. Eliot

Where the dead men lost their bones.   **40**

  'What is that noise?'
               The wind under the door.
'What is that noise now? What is the wind doing?'
               Nothing again nothing.

                                'Do   **45**
You know nothing? Do you see nothing? Do you remember
'Nothing?'

  I remember
Those are pearls that were his eyes.
'Are you alive, or not? Is there nothing in your head?'   **50**
                      But
O O O O that Shakespeherian Rag –
It's so elegant
So intelligent
'What shall I do now? What shall I do?   **55**
I shall rush out as I am, and walk the street
With my hair down, so. What shall we do tomorrow?
What shall we ever do?'
                The hot water at ten.
And if it rains, a closed car at four.   **60**
And we shall play a game of chess,
Pressing lidless eyes and waiting for a knock upon the door.

  When Lil's husband got demobbed, I said –
I didn't mince my words, I said to her myself,
HURRY UP PLEASE ITS TIME   **65**
Now Albert's coming back, make yourself a bit smart.
He'll want to know what you done with that money he gave you
To get yourself some teeth. He did, I was there.
You have them all out, Lil, and get a nice set,
He said, I swear, I can't bear to look at you.   **70**
And no more can't I, I said, and think of poor Albert,
He's been in the army four years, he wants a good time,
And if you don't give it him, there's others will, I said.
Oh is there, she said. Something o' that, I said.
Then I'll know who to thank, she said, and give me a straight look.   **75**
HURRY UP PLEASE ITS TIME
If you don't like it you can get on with it, I said.
Others can pick and choose if you can't.
But if Albert makes off, it won't be for lack of telling.

You ought to be ashamed, I said, to look so antique.   80
(And her only thirty-one.)
I can't help it, she said, pulling a long face,
It's them pills I took, to bring it off, she said.
(She's had five already, and nearly died of young George.)
The chemist said it would be all right, but I've never been the same. 85
You *are* a proper fool, I said.
Well, if Albert won't leave you alone, there it is, I said,
What you get married for if you don't want children?
HURRY UP PLEASE ITS TIME
Well, that Sunday Albert was home, they had a hot gammon,   90
And they asked me in to dinner, to get the beauty of it hot –
HURRY UP PLEASE ITS TIME
HURRY UP PLEASE ITS TIME
Goonight Bill. Goonight Lou. Goonight May. Goonight.
Ta ta. Goonight. Goonight.   95
Good night, ladies, good night, sweet ladies, good night, good night.

Notes

	A Game of Chess:	the title alludes to two plays by Thomas Middleton (1570–1627), *A Game of Chess* and *Women Beware Women*. Both of these involve sexual intrigue. In the latter play, a young woman is raped while her mother, quite unaware, plays a game of chess downstairs. The allusion refers to the theme of lust without love. The title could refer to Shakespeare's play *The Tempest*, in which two lovers play a game of chess which is associated with fertility and genuine love. *The Tempest* is referred to again later in the poem.
1	**The Chair she sat in, like a burnished throne:**	This refers to Shakespeare's *Antony and Cleopatra*, Act II, scene ii, recalling Enarbarbus's long description of Cleopatra's first meeting with Antony.
4	**Cupidon:**	a 'beau' or 'Adonis', a handsome young man; also has echoes of Cupid
12	**Unguent:**	in ointment form
16	**laquearia:**	meaning a panelled ceiling; taken from the Roman poet Virgil's 'Aeneid', where he describes the banquet given by Dido, queen of Carthage, for Aeneas, with whom she fell in love
22	**sylvan scene:**	this is taken from Milton's *Paradise Lost*, IV, 140. The phrase occurs in the description of the Garden of Eden as Satan looks at it for the first time.

T.S. Eliot

23	Philomel:	a Greek legend recalled in the Roman writer Ovid's *Metamorphoses VI*. Philomel was raped by her sister Procne's husband, Tereus, King of Thrace, who also cut off Philomel's tongue to prevent her telling. Philomel wove her story into a garment to inform Procne, who in revenge killed Tereus's son and served him as a dish to Tereus at a banquet. The sisters fled, pursued by Tereus, but the gods changed all three into birds; Tereus became a hawk, Procne a swallow and Philomel a nightingale. Poets often refer to a nightingale as 'Philomel'. The reference to the legend here may be to underscore secret or hidden lustful practices.
42	**The wind under the door:**	a reference to John Webster's (1578–1632) play *The Devil's Law Case*, a tragi-comedy
49	**Those are pearls that were his eyes:**	from Shakespeare's *The Tempest*; Ariel's song that speaks of drowning
62	**Pressing lidless eyes … the door:**	a reference to the game of chess in Middleton's play *Women Beware Women*
96	**Good night, ladies … good night:**	The last words spoken by Ophelia, heroine of Shakespeare's play *Hamlet*, who drowned, driven mad by love and by a time that is out of joint

Background note

This poem is Section II of *The Waste Land*, published in 1922. *The Waste Land* summed up the disillusionment and disgust of the post-World War I generation, who saw the standardised civilisation that was developing as barren and who saw 20th-century man as condemned to a living death. Such attitudes can also be seen in 'Preludes' and in 'The Love Song of J Alfred Prufrock'. At the centre of this living death lay an inability to love and a confusion between love and lust. 'A Game of Chess' depicts the stunting effects of lust mistaken for love. In the poem, we see people as pawns moving about in two games that end not in checkmate, but in stalemate.

Explorations

FIRST READING

1.   The first scene of the poem is set in a wealthy lady's boudoir (lines 1–62). What strikes you immediately about this scene?

2.   The second scene (lines 63–96) is set in a public house. Try reading this scene aloud in a 'cockney' or 'scouser' accent. What impression of the women do you get?

SECOND READING

3.   The opening section of the poem has been called a scene of splendid clutter. List some of these cluttering items. Would you find these attractive?

4. The immediate opening section, picturing the lady seated at her dressing table, is a reference to Cleopatra. Why do you think the poet makes this reference?

5. What does the description of the cupidons suggest to you? Is there any hint of the lady's behaviour here?

6. Examine the description of the lady's perfumes. Is the poet suggesting her ability to seduce or is he describing by implication a deeply disturbed person? Look in particular at the choice of verbs.

7. Would you agree that the description of the ceiling adds a claustrophobic atmosphere to this decadent and sensuous scene?

8. Lines 21–4 refer to the Greek legend of Philomel, who was changed into a nightingale following her rape. How does this fit into the overall theme of the poem?

9. What does the description of the lady brushing her hair mean to you?

10.

a Lines 35–62 constitute a 'dialogue' between the lady and an apparently silent male protagonist. Would you agree that she is seen as quite neurotic here? What in the language used suggests this?

b Would you agree that his situation is as desperate as hers?

c Is the reference to Shakespeare elegant?

11. This setting closes with a deep feeling of purposelessness. What images particularly contribute to this theme of sterility?

12. The second scene (lines 63–96), narrated by an unidentified lower-class lady in a pub at closing time, is overheard by the protagonist. Tell the story narrated by the lady in your own words. Would you regard this story as gossip?

13. In what ways are the themes of sterility, emptiness and lust continued here?

14. The barman's words have an immediate meaning but they also have longer-term implications. What do you think these are?

15. The last line is taken from Shakespeare's *Hamlet* and is spoken by Ophelia, whom many see as having died for love. Why do you think it is included here?

THIRD READING

16. Examine the poem as a piece of social satire. What does it have to teach us?

17. Discuss the interweaving of past and present in the poem. How do the references to classical literature, legend, etc. add to our understanding of the poem?

18. Examine the use of rhythm and repetition in the poem. Would you describe the poem as musical?

19. Would you agree that both settings in the poem have all the elements of good drama?

FOURTH READING

20. Explore the relationship between sensuality and culture in this poem.

21. 'Eliot is the poet of psychological turmoil, cultural decay and moral degeneracy.' Discuss this view in reference to this poem. Where else in Eliot's poetry can this be seen?

22. 'The lives of Eliot's characters are ultimately sterile.' Discuss this statement with reference to this poem and to others.

T.S. Eliot

Journey of the Magi

'A cold coming we had of it,
Just the worst time of the year
For a journey, and such a long journey:
The ways deep and the weather sharp,
The very dead of winter.'   5
And the camels galled, sore-footed, refractory,
Lying down in the melting snow.
There were times we regretted
The summer palaces on slopes, the terraces,
And the silken girls bringing sherbet.   10
Then the camel men cursing and grumbling
And running away, and wanting their liquor and women,
And the night-fires going out, and the lack of shelters,
And the cities hostile and the towns unfriendly
And the villages dirty and charging high prices: 15
A hard time we had of it.
At the end we preferred to travel all night,
 Sleeping in snatches,
With the voices singing in our ears, saying
That this was all folly.   20

   Then at dawn we came down to a temperate valley,
Wet, below the snow line, smelling of vegetation,
With a running stream and a water-mill beating the darkness,
And three trees on the low sky.
And an old white horse galloped away in the meadow.   25
Then we came to a tavern with vine-leaves over the lintel,
Six hands at an open door dicing for pieces of silver,
And feet kicking the empty wine-skins.
But there was no information, and so we continued
And arrived at evening, not a moment too soon   30
Finding the place; it was (you may say) satisfactory.

   All this was a long time ago, I remember,
And I would do it again, but set down
This set down
This: were we led all that way for   35
Birth or Death? There was a Birth, certainly,
We had evidence and no doubt. I had seen birth and death,
But had thought they were different; this Birth was
Hard and bitter agony for us, like Death, our death.

We returned to our places, these Kingdoms,   40
But no longer at ease here, in the old dispensation,
With an alien people clutching their gods.
I should be glad of another death.

Notes

	Magi:	the Magi were the Three Wise Men who brought gifts to the infant Jesus
1-5	'A cold ... of winter':	taken from the 1622 Christmas Day sermon of Bishop Launcelot Andrewes
41	the old dispensation:	life pre-Christ

Explorations

BEFORE READING

1. The Magi are the Three Wise Men or kings who visited the infant Jesus at his birth in Bethlehem. Knowing this, what does the title of the poem lead you to expect?

FIRST READING

2. Were any of your expectations met on reading the poem?

SECOND READING

3.

a The poem is the monologue of an old man reviewing the past. What did he and the others have to struggle with in making this journey? What forsaken luxuries did they still yearn for?

b Where does it suggest that they had deep doubts about their desire to witness a birth?

4.

a At the end of the second section of the poem, the Magi arrive at

T.S. Eliot

Christ's birthplace after some fruitless searching. Could the imagery at the beginning of this section symbolise a birth or a new beginning?

b These are followed by symbols surrounding Christ's death. Can you identify these?

5. In the last book of the Bible, Revelations 19: 11, Christ is seen riding a white horse in glory. Is there anything glorious about the image of the white horse here?

6. Would you agree that the last line of the second section is something of an anticlimax? Why is there no sense of awe or celebration?

7. In the final section, the Magus philosophically reflects on the significance of what he had seen. Birth (capitalised) is the birth of Christ, which also brought a death. What is this death – Christ's Death or the death of an old way of life, or both? Is this why the Magi were no longer at ease in their own kingdoms? Why should the Magus be glad of another death?

THIRD READING

8. Eliot's theme is that death is the way to rebirth. Is this a paradox? Examine how the cycle of birth and death are suggested throughout the poem.

9. The poem can also be seen as representing Eliot's own spiritual journey from agnosticism to faith. He wrote it at the time of his baptism into the Anglican Church in 1927. Does the poem suggest a readiness to believe, an assertion of belief or indeed a sense of being conditioned by fate as much as faith?

10. How would you describe the tone of this poem?

from Landscapes: III. Usk

Do not suddenly break the branch, or
Hope to find
The white hart behind the white well.
Glance aside, not for lance, do not spell
Old enchantments. Let them sleep.   5
'Gently dip, but not too deep',
Lift your eyes
Where the roads dip and where the roads rise
Seek only there
Where the grey light meets the green air   10
The hermit's chapel, the pilgrim's prayer.

Notes

	Usk:	an area in Wales, about 15 km north of Newport
3	hart:	a male deer or stag
6	'Gently dip, but not too deep':	from a song by George Peele (1558–96), appropriate because of the song's suggestion of folk rituals
11	hermit:	one who chooses to live a life of isolation and prayer
11	pilgrim:	one who goes on a spiritual journey

Explorations

FIRST READING

1. From the set of poems called 'Landscapes', Eliot wrote this following a holiday in Wales in 1935. In it, the poet evokes some images of the past. What are these images? What period do they refer to?

2. There is also a sense of movement in the poem. What images give the poem that sense?

SECOND READING

3.

a The first line exhorts the viewer not to break the peace of the scene, yet the next few lines forbid him to dwell on resurrecting the past. Is this a contradiction?

b Would you agree that the quoted line (line 6) shows the poet's true intention towards the past?

4. The last five lines suggest a more active journey. What will it lead to? What kind of journey is this for the poet?

5. 'Where the grey light meets the green air'.

Examine this line. Could this symbolise a moment of clarification for the poet? What do the colours mean to you?

THIRD READING

6. Is there a sense of transition in this poem?

7. Comment on the use of colour in the poem. Does it help to enliven the atmosphere or indeed the sense of the poet as painter?

8. Examine the lyrical qualities of the poem. How do they contribute to the energy that surrounds this poem?

9. Compare and contrast this poem with 'Rannoch, by Glencoe'.

T.S. Eliot

from Landscapes: IV. Rannoch by Glencoe

Here the crow starves, here the patient stag
Breeds for the rifle. Between the soft moor
And the soft sky, scarcely room
To leap or soar. Substance crumbles, in the thin air
Moon cold or moon hot. The road winds in   5
Listlessness of ancient war,
Languor of broken steel,
Clamour of confused wrong, apt
In silence. Memory is strong
Beyond the bone. Pride snapped,   10
Shadow of pride is long, in the long pass
No concurrence of bone.

Notes

	Rannoch, by Glencoe:	an area of the Scottish Highlands south of Fort William. This poem, like 'Usk', is from a set of poems called 'Landscapes'.

Explorations

BEFORE READING

1. What are your visions of the Scottish Highlands? What do they symbolise for you?

FIRST READING

2. Were your views confirmed by this poem?

3. List the images of violence and death you see here. Are these images from the past or the present?

4. What sounds does the poet evoke?

SECOND READING

5. In the first few lines of the poem, how does Eliot suggest a sense of barrenness and oppressiveness?

6.

a   The road appears to wander with no purpose. What words in particular evoke this lack of energy? Is the poet suggesting that a depressing sense of history is causing it?

b   Compare the road here to that in 'Usk'.

7. The memory of past rivalries and wrongs is strong in this landscape. What is the poet's attitude to these? Is he suggesting that pride is that which keeps old rivalries from being resolved? Is this what he also means by 'No concurrence of bone'?

THIRD READING

8. Examine how Eliot creates a feeling of place in this poem. Would you agree that he creates a landscape that, paradoxically, is both austere and rich? How does he do this? What other paradoxes do you see in the poem?

9. We get little, if any, sense of the poet's presence in the poem. Why do you think he has this sense of detachment?

10. Discuss the feelings of constriction evident here. Examine where else in Eliot's poetry such feelings exist.

11. Would you consider this to be a lyrical poem?

12. Discuss this poem and 'Usk' under the heading 'Life and Death'.

from Four Quartets: East Coker IV.

The wounded surgeon plies the steel
That questions the distempered part;
Beneath the bleeding hands we feel
The sharp compassion of the healer's art
Resolving the enigma of the fever chart.   5

Our only health is the disease
If we obey the dying nurse
Whose constant care is not to please
But to remind of our, and Adam's curse,
And that, to be restored, our sickness must grow worse.   10

T.S. Eliot

The whole earth is our hospital
Endowed by the ruined millionaire,
Wherein, if we do well, we shall
Die of the absolute paternal care
That will not leave us, but prevents us everywhere.   15

The chill ascends from feet to knees,
The fever sings in mental wires.
If to be warmed, then I must freeze
And quake in frigid purgatorial fires
Of which the flame is roses, and the smoke is briars.   20

The dripping blood our only drink,
The bloody flesh our only food:
In spite of which we like to think
That we are sound, substantial flesh and blood –
Again, in spite of that, we call this Friday good.   25

Background note

'East Coker', from which this poem is taken, is in turn one of 'The Four Quartets' written between 1935 and 1942. The main theme of 'East Coker' is that true wisdom is humility and that at a certain stage in its spiritual progress, the soul must put itself in the hands of God and die in order to be reborn. This is best exemplified by Jesus' death on the Cross. This theme of death and rebirth is also seen in 'The Journey of the Magi' and 'Usk'. In order to achieve one's rebirth, or full spiritual potential, one must first endure the 'Dark Night of the Soul', a time of emptiness and suffering but also of heightened awareness, so called by St John of the Cross, to whom Eliot is indebted.

Notes

	East Coker:	a village near Yeovil in Somerset, England, from which Eliot's direct ancestor, Andrew Eliot, left for the New World around 1699. T.S. Eliot's ashes were buried there after his death in 1965.
1	steel:	the surgeon's scalpel, similar to the 'dart of love' described by St John of the Cross in the 'living Flame of love'
15	prevents:	used here in the 17th-century sense of 'to go before with spiritual guidance' or 'to predispose to repentance'
19	purgatorial fires:	purgatory is a temporary state or place where the soul is purified by punishment

Explorations

1. Have you ever wondered why we call Good Friday 'good', when on that day Jesus was tortured horribly and killed? Is this a paradox? Think about this for awhile.

2. The poem is full of paradoxes. List these. Do they help us to understand the notion of 'necessary evil', a perhaps temporary evil that will be for our ultimate good?

SECOND READING

3. The 'wounded surgeon' in the first stanza is Jesus. To what extent is He being compared to a physical surgeon? Why is His compassion 'sharp'? Why is the fever chart described as an 'enigma'?

4. The image of a hospital is continued in the second stanza, where the nurse is the church. In what sense is she dying? What is her role? What was the curse put on Adam as he left the Garden of Eden?

5.

a The 'ruined millionaire' of the third stanza is Adam. Why is he called this? What was his legacy to the world?

b What is the desired outcome of doing well in this 'hospital'?

c If God is the provider of 'paternal care', what is His role?

6. The fourth stanza suggests a process of purgation. Is this the 'Dark Night of the Soul', i.e. a period of black despair before life is rediscovered? How complete is this process? Is there any sense in which this purgation leads to healing?

7. The fifth stanza refers to both the Crucifixion and the Eucharist. In what ways is the imagery linked to the idea that suffering is the basis of our cure, seen throughout the poem? Is this why we call Good Friday good?

THIRD READING

8. Look again at Question 2 and your list of paradoxes. Would you agree that physical suffering can lead to a spiritual good?

9. Examine the lyrical qualities of the poem. To what extent do these aid the devotional tone of the poem?

10. Would you consider this to be an emotional or intellectual poem?

11. The style of this poem reflects the style of 17th-century metaphysical poetry, such as that of Donne, Herbert or Marvell. Research the features of this style of poetry and indicate to what extent Eliot is using such a style here.

T.S. Eliot

Elizabeth Bishop
(1911–79)

Prescribed for Higher Level exams in 2016 and 2017

Elizabeth Bishop was born on 8 February 1911 in Worcester, Massachusetts. Her father died when she was eight months old. Her mother never recovered from the shock and for the next five years was in and out of mental hospitals. In 1916 she was institutionalised and separated from her daughter, whom she was never to see again – she died in 1934.

Elizabeth was reared for the most part by her grandparents in Great Village, Nova Scotia. The elegy 'First Death in Nova Scotia' draws on some childhood memories. 'Sestina' also evokes the sadness of this period. Yet her recollections of her Nova Scotia childhood were essentially positive and she had great affection for her maternal grandparents, aunts and uncles in this small agricultural village.

She went to boarding school and then attended Vassar College, a private university in New York, from 1930 to 1934. She graduated in English literature (but also took Greek and music), always retaining a particular appreciation for Renaissance lyric poetry and for the works of Gerard Manley Hopkins. It was at Vassar that she first began to publish stories and poems in national magazines and where she met the poet Marianne Moore, who became an important influence on her career as a poet and with whom she maintained a lifelong friendship and correspondence. It was also at Vassar that she formed her first lesbian relationship, and here too, on her own admission, her lifelong problem with alcohol addiction began.

In 1939 she moved to Key West, Florida, a place she had fallen in love with over the previous years. 'The Fish' reflects her enjoyment of the sport of fishing at that time. Key West became a sort of refuge and base for Bishop over the next 15 years. In 1945 she won the Houghton Mifflin Poetry Award. In 1946 her first book of poetry, *North and South*, was published and was well received by the critics. 'The Fish' is among its 30 poems.

The years 1945 to 1951, when her life was centred on New York, were very unsettled. She felt under extreme pressure in a very competitive literary circle and drank heavily. 'The Bight' and 'The Prodigal' reflect this dissolute period of her life.

In 1951 she left for South America on the first stage of a writer's trip round the world. She was fascinated by Brazil and by Lota Soares, on old acquaintance with whom she began a relationship that was to last until the latter's death in 1967. 'Questions of Travel' and 'The Armadillo' reflect this period of her life. In 1970 she was appointed poet in residence at Harvard, where she taught advanced verse writing and studies in modern poetry for her first year and, later, poets and their letters. She began to do a good many public readings of her poetry to earn a living. She continued to do public readings, punctuated by spells in hospital with asthma, alcoholism and depression. She died suddenly of a brain aneurysm on 6 October 1979.

The Fish

This poem is also prescribed for Ordinary Level exams in 2016 and 2017

I caught a tremendous fish
and held him beside the boat
half out of water, with my hook
fast in a corner of his mouth.
He didn't fight.   5
He hadn't fought at all.
He hung a grunting weight,
battered and venerable
and homely. Here and there
his brown skin hung in strips   10
like ancient wallpaper,
and its pattern of darker brown
was like wallpaper:
shapes like full-blown roses
stained and lost through age.   15
He was speckled with barnacles,
fine rosettes of lime,
and infested
with tiny white sea-lice,
and underneath two or three   20
rags of green weed hung down.
While his gills were breathing in
the terrible oxygen
– the frightening gills,
fresh and crisp with blood,   25
that can cut so badly –
I thought of the coarse white flesh
packed in like feathers,
the big bones and the little bones,
the dramatic reds and blacks   30

Elizabeth Bishop

of his shiny entrails,
and the pink swim-bladder
like a big peony.
I looked into his eyes
which were far larger than mine 35
but shallower, and yellowed,
the irises backed and packed
with tarnished tinfoil
seen through the lenses
of old scratched isinglass. 40
They shifted a little, but not
to return my stare.
– It was more like the tipping
of an object toward the light.
I admired his sullen face, 45
the mechanism of his jaw,
and then I saw
that from his lower lip
– if you could call it a lip –
grim, wet, and weaponlike, 50
hung five old pieces of fish-line,
or four and a wire leader
with the swivel still attached,
with all their five big hooks
grown firmly in his mouth. 55
A green line, frayed at the end
where he broke it, two heavier lines,
and a fine black thread
still crimped from the strain and snap
when it broke and he got away. 60
Like medals with their ribbons
frayed and wavering,
a five-haired beard of wisdom
trailing from his aching jaw.
I stared and stared 65
and victory filled up
the little rented boat,
from the pool of bilge
where oil had spread a rainbow
around the rusted engine 70
to the bailer rusted orange,
the sun-cracked thwarts,
the oarlocks on their strings,
the gunnels – until everything

was rainbow, rainbow, rainbow!
And I let the fish go.

Notes

40	isinglass:	a semi-transparent form of gelatine extracted from certain fish and used in making jellies, glue, etc.

Explorations

FIRST READING

1. How do you visualise the fish? Think of it as a painting or a picture. What details strike you on a first reading?

2. What is your initial impression of the speaker in this poem?

SECOND READING

3. Consider in detail the description of the fish. Which elements of the description could be considered objective or factual? Which elements could be seen as purely subjective on the part of the poet? Which are imagined or aesthetic elements in the description?

4. Do you think the poet's re-creation of the fish is a good one? Explain your views.

THIRD READING

5. Explore the attitude of the speaker towards the fish over the entire length of the poem. What changes do you notice, and where?

6. Why do you think she released the fish? Explore the text for possible reasons.

7. Do you think this is an important moment for the poet? What does she

Elizabeth Bishop

learn or discover? Where in the text is this suggested?

8. Is the poet excited by this experience? Where in the text is this suggested? Comment on the tone of the poem.

FOURTH READING

9. What issues does this poem raise? Consider what the poem has to say about:

- Our relationship with the natural world

- The nature of creativity

- Moments of insight and decision

- Other themes hinted at

10. Do you think the imagery is effective in getting across a real understanding of the fish and an awareness of the poet's mood? Explore any two relevant images and explain how they function.

11. This is quite a dramatic poem. Explain how the dramatic effect is created. Consider such elements as the way the narrative builds to a climax, the ending, the effect of the short enjambed lines and the speaker's interior debate.

12. What did you like about this poem?

The Bight

On my birthday

At low tide like this how sheer the water is.
White, crumbling ribs of marl protrude and glare
and the boats are dry, the pilings dry as matches.
Absorbing, rather than being absorbed,
the water in the bight doesn't wet anything,   5
the color of the gas flame turned as low as possible.
One can smell it turning to gas; if one were Baudelaire
one could probably hear it turning to marimba music.
The little ocher dredge at work off the end of the dock
already plays the dry perfectly off-beat claves.   10
The birds are outsize. Pelicans crash
into this peculiar gas unnecessarily hard,
it seem to me, like pickaxes,
rarely coming up with anything to show for it,
and going off with humorous elbowings.   15
Black-and-white man-of-war birds soar
on impalpable drafts
and open their tails like scissors on the curves
or tense them like wishbones, till they tremble.
The frowsy sponge boats keep coming in   20
with the obliging air of retrievers,
bristling with jackstraw gaffs and hooks
and decorated with bobbles of sponges.
There is a fence of chicken wire along the dock
where, glinting like little plowshares,   25
the blue-gray shark tails are hung up to dry
for the Chinese-restaurant trade.
Some of the little white boats are still piled up
against each other, or lie on their sides, stove in,
and not yet salvaged, if they ever will be, from the last bad storm,   30
like torn-open, unanswered letters.
The bight is littered with old correspondences.
Click. Click. Goes the dredge,
and brings up a dripping jawful of marl.
All the untidy activity continues,   35
awful but cheerful.

Notes

	Bight:	recess of coast, bay
2	**marl:**	soil composed of clay and lime, sometimes used as fertiliser
3	**pilings:**	heavy beams driven into the sea bed as support for a jetty or dock
7	**Baudelaire:**	Charles-Pierre Baudelaire (1821–67), French lyric poet, author of *Les Fleurs du Mal*
8	**marimba:**	type of xylophone used in African or South American music
9	**ocher [ochre]:**	orange-brown colour
10	**claves [clefs]:**	symbols of musical notation; there are three clefs, C, G and F, which, when placed on a particular line of a stave of music, show the pitch of the notes
17	**impalpable:**	not easily grasped; imperceptible to touch
20	**frowsy:**	slovenly, unkempt

Explorations

FIRST READING

1. Think of the poem as a painting. Describe it as you see it laid out: background, foreground, centre, left side, right side.

2. What mood is suggested by the scene? Explain.

SECOND READING

3. In what ways do you think it differs from a chocolate-box painting?

4. Is the reader-viewer encouraged to view the scene in a new and fresh way? Where and how does this happen? Examine the details of the descriptions. What is unusual about them?

THIRD READING

5. What do you think is the impact of the subtitle, 'On my birthday'? Might it be significant that she marks her birthday in this way, viewing this scene? How might she identify with the scene? From the evidence of the text, what do you think her mood is?

FOURTH READING

6. Consider the style of the versification. Concentrate on such aspects as metre, rhyme or the lack of it, the organisation of sentence or sense units, etc. What does the form of the poem contribute to its effectiveness?

7. Would you consider it accurate to suggest that the poem moves along in bursts of poetic intensity, punctuated by more prosaic reflections? Discuss.

At the Fishhouses

Although it is a cold evening,
down by one of the fishhouses
an old man sits netting,
his net, in the gloaming almost invisible,
a dark purple-brown,   5
and his shuttle worn and polished.
The air smells so strong of codfish
it makes one's nose run and one's eyes water.
The five fishhouses have steeply peaked roofs
and narrow, cleated gangplanks slant up   10
to storerooms in the gables
for the wheelbarrows to be pushed up and down on.
All is silver: the heavy surface of the sea,
swelling slowly as if considering spilling over,
is opaque, but the silver of the benches,   15
the lobster pots, and masts, scattered
among the wild jagged rocks,
is of an apparent translucence
like the small old buildings with an emerald moss
growing on their shoreward walls.   20
The big fish tubs are completely lined
with layers of beautiful herring scales
and the wheelbarrows are similarly plastered
with creamy iridescent coats of mail,
with small iridescent flies crawling on them.   25
Up on the little slope behind the houses,
set in the sparse bright sprinkle of grass,
is an ancient wooden capstan,
cracked, with two long bleached handles
and some melancholy stains, like dried blood,   30
where the ironwork has rusted.
The old man accepts a Lucky Strike.
He was a friend of my grandfather.
We talk of the decline in the population
and of codfish and herring   35
while he waits for a herring boat to come in.
There are sequins on his vest and on his thumb.
He has scraped the scales, the principal beauty,
from unnumbered fish with that black old knife,
the blade of which is almost worn away.   40

Elizabeth Bishop

Down at the water's edge, at the place
where they haul up the boats, up the long ramp
descending into the water, thin silver
tree trunks are laid horizontally
across the gray stones, down and down   45
at intervals of four or five feet.

Cold dark deep and absolutely clear,
element bearable to no mortal,
to fish and to seals ... One seal particularly
I have seen here evening after evening.   50
He was curious about me. He was interested in music;
like me a believer in total immersion,
so I used to sing him Baptist hymns.
I also sang 'A Mighty Fortress Is Our God.'
He stood up in the water and regarded me   55
steadily, moving his head a little.

Then he would disappear, then suddenly emerge
almost in the same spot, with a sort of shrug
as if it were against his better judgment.
Cold dark deep and absolutely clear,   60
the clear gray icy water ... Back, behind us,
the dignified tall firs begin.
Bluish, associating with their shadows,
a million Christmas trees stand
waiting for Christmas. The water seems suspended   65
above the rounded gray and blue-gray stones.
I have seen it over and over, the same sea, the same,
slightly, indifferently swinging above the stones,
icily free above the stones,
above the stones and then the world.   70
If you should dip your hand in,
your wrist would ache immediately,
your bones would begin to ache and your hand would burn
as if the water were a transmutation of fire
that feeds on stones and burns with a dark gray flame.   75
If you tasted it, it would first taste bitter,
then briny, then surely burn your tongue.
It is like what we imagine knowledge to be:
dark, salt, clear, moving, utterly free,
drawn from the cold hard mouth   80
of the world, derived from the rocky breasts
forever, flowing and drawn, and since
our knowledge is historical, flowing, and flown.

'Nova Scotia Landscape', a watercolour by Elizabeth Bishop.

Explorations

FIRST READING

1. On a first reading, what do you notice about the setting of the poem? List the things that make an immediate impression on you.

2. Examine in detail what is being described in the first section. What is your impression of the atmosphere of the place?

3. What do you suppose is the writer's attitude to that scene in the first section? Does she find it repulsive, or awe-inspiring, or is she completely unaffected by it? Comment, with reference to the text.

4. What aspect of the scene draws the poet's main focus of attention during the entire poem?

SECOND READING

5. List all the characteristics or facets of the sea alluded to or reflected on by the poet throughout the poem.

6. Do you think she manages to effectively evoke the mysterious power of the sea? Comment.

THIRD READING

7. Bishop's poetic technique involved (a) detailed description and (b) making the familiar strange or unusual so that we see it afresh. Comment under these headings on her description of the sea.

8. How would you assess the mood of this poem? Take into consideration both the landscape and the poet.

9. The poem is written in free verse. What does this contribute to the effect of the poem? What else do you notice about the technique of this poem?

FOURTH READING

10. The poem builds to a moment of insight for the poet. Where is this and what is the insight? Describe, in as much depth as you can, what she comes to learn from the sea.

11. Outline the main issues raised by this poem.

12. Do you find any trace of the personality or feelings of the poet in this poem? Comment.

The Prodigal

This poem is also prescribed for Ordinary Level exams in 2016 and 2017

The brown enormous odor he lived by
was too close, with its breathing and thick hair,
for him to judge. The floor was rotten; the sty
was plastered halfway up with glass-smooth dung.
Light-lashed, self-righteous, above moving snouts,   5
the pigs' eyes followed him, a cheerful stare –
even to the sow that always ate her young –
till, sickening, he leaned to scratch her head.
But sometimes mornings after drinking bouts
(he hid the pints behind a two-by-four),   10
the sunrise glazed the barnyard mud with red;
the burning puddles seemed to reassure.
And then he thought he almost might endure
his exile yet another year or more.

But evenings the first star came to warn.   15
The farmer whom he worked for came at dark
to shut the cows and horses in the barn
beneath their overhanging clouds of hay,
with pitchforks, faint forked lightnings, catching light,
safe and companionable as in the Ark.   20
The pigs stuck out their little feet and snored.
The lantern – like the sun, going away –
laid on the mud a pacing aureole.
Carrying a bucket along a slimy board,
he felt the bats' uncertain staggering flight,   25
his shuddering insights, beyond his control,
touching him. But it took him a long time
finally to make his mind up to go home.

Notes

23	**aureole:**	a halo of light around the sun or moon

Explorations

1. What does the title of the poem lead you to expect?

FIRST READING

2. Were any of your expectations met on reading the poem?

3. How do you see the character in this poem?

- What is he doing? How does he live?

- Why is he there?

- Does he find any satisfaction in his work?

- What helps him endure his exile?

4. What details of the scene affected you most?

SECOND READING

5. Examine the final five lines. What do you think the 'shuddering insights, beyond his control' might be? Re-create his thoughts as you imagine them here.

6. Bishop appeals to a range of senses – smell, sight, sound, touch – to re-create the atmosphere of the place. Examine a sample of each type of image and discuss the effect.

7. How would you describe the atmosphere of the place? Is it one of unrelieved misery or is there some contentment in it? Refer to the text.

8. Examine the poet's attitude to the prodigal. Do you think she is condemnatory, sympathetic or neutral? Discuss, with reference to the text.

9. What is your own attitude to the prodigal?

THIRD READING

10. What are the main human issues raised by this poem?

11. Briefly express the theme of the poem.

12. Bishop's poetic technique involved really looking at the detail of her subject matter. Where do you think this works best in 'The Prodigal'?

Elizabeth Bishop

There are too many waterfalls here; the crowded streams
hurry too rapidly down to the sea,
and the pressure of so many clouds on the mountaintops
makes them spill over the sides in soft slow-motion,
turning to waterfalls under our very eyes. 5
– For if those streaks, those mile-long, shiny, tearstains,
aren't waterfalls yet,
in a quick age or so, as ages go here,
they probably will be.
But if the streams and clouds keep travelling, travelling, 10
the mountains look like the hulls of capsized ships,
slime-hung and barnacled.

Think of the long trip home.
Should we have stayed at home and thought of here?
Where should we be today? 15
Is it right to be watching strangers in a play
in this strangest of theatres?
What childishness is it that while there's a breath of life
in our bodies, we are determined to rush
to see the sun the other way around? 20
The tiniest green hummingbird in the world?
To stare at some inexplicable old stonework,
inexplicable and impenetrable,
at any view,
instantly seen and always, always delightful? 25
Oh, must we dream our dreams
and have them, too?
And have we room
for one more folded sunset, still quite warm?

But surely it would have been a pity 30
not to have seen the trees along this road,
really exaggerated in their beauty,
not to have seen them gesturing
like noble pantomimists, robed in pink.
– Not to have had to stop for gas and heard 35
the sad, two-noted, wooden tune
of disparate wooden clogs
carelessly clacking over
a grease-stained filling-station floor.

(In another country the clogs would all be tested.   40
Each pair there would have identical pitch.)
– A pity not to have heard
the other, less primitive music of the fat brown bird
who sings above the broken gasoline pump
in a bamboo church of Jesuit baroque: 45
three towers, five silver crosses.
– Yes, a pity not to have pondered,
blurr'dly and inconclusively,
on what connection can exist for centuries
between the crudest wooden footwear   50
and, careful and finicky,
the whittled fantasies of wooden cages.
– Never to have studied history in
the weak calligraphy of songbirds' cages.
– And never to have had to listen to rain   55
so much like politicians' speeches:
two hours of unrelenting oratory
and then a sudden golden silence
in which the traveller takes a notebook, writes:

'Is it lack of imagination that makes us come   60
to imagined places, not just stay at home?
Or could Pascal have been not entirely right
about just sitting quietly in one's room?

Continent, city, country, society:
the choice is never wide and never free.   65
And here, or there … No. Should we have stayed at home,
wherever that may be?'

Notes

45	baroque:	the style of art that developed in the 17th century after the Renaissance, characterised by massive, complex and ornate design
62	Pascal:	Blaise Pascal (1623–62), French mathematician, physicist and philosopher, author of *Pensées*, who commented, 'I have discovered that all human evil comes from this, man's being unable to sit still in a room.'

Elizabeth Bishop

'Brazilian Landscape', a watercolour by Elizabeth Bishop.

Explorations

1. This is a travel poem with a difference. What are the elements found here that one would normally expect of a travel poem and what elements do you find different or unusual?

2. Follow the traveller's eye. What does she notice in particular about the geography and culture of Brazil?

3. What impression of Brazilian culture do you get? Examine the references in detail.

SECOND READING

4. Do you think the poet feels comfortable in this place? What is her attitude to what she sees? Do you think she is just the usual tired, grumpy traveller or something else?

5. One critic has said that Bishop is essentially a poet of the domestic because she feels estranged in the greater world. Comment on that statement in light of your reading of this poem.

6. What bothers her about travel? Jot down your ideas on this.

THIRD READING

7. List the main issues raised in this poem.

8. What do you notice about the style in which the poem is written? Comment critically on it.

The Armadillo

for Robert Lowell

This is the time of year
when almost every night
the frail, illegal fire balloons appear.
Climbing the mountain height,

rising toward a saint   5
still honored in these parts,
the paper chambers flush and fill with light
that comes and goes, like hearts.

Once up against the sky it's hard
to tell them from the stars –   10
planets, that is – the tinted ones:
Venus going down, or Mars,

or the pale green one. With a wind,
they flare and falter, wobble and toss;
but if it's still they steer between   15
the kite sticks of the Southern Cross,

receding, dwindling, solemnly
and steadily forsaking us,
or, in the downdraft from a peak,
suddenly turning dangerous.   20

Last night another big one fell.
It splattered like an egg of fire
against the cliff behind the house.
The flame ran down. We saw the pair

of owls who nest there flying up   25
and up, their whirling black-and-white
stained bright pink underneath, until
they shrieked up out of sight.

The ancient owls' nest must have burned.
Hastily, all alone,   30
a glistening armadillo left the scene,
rose-flecked, head down, tail down,

and then a baby rabbit jumped out,
short-eared, to our surprise.
So soft! – a handful of intangible ash   35
with fixed, ignited eyes.

Too pretty, dreamlike mimicry!
O falling fire and piercing cry
and panic, and a weak mailed fist
clenched ignorant against the sky!   40

Notes		
3	**fire balloons:**	St John's Day (24 June) was celebrated by releasing these fire balloons in a type of local religious worship. Air currents took them up the mountainside, where they sometimes became a hazard to houses. Bishop's partner, Lota Soares, had a sprinkler system installed on the roof to counter the danger.
16	**Southern Cross:**	a constellation of stars in the Southern Hemisphere

Explorations

FIRST READING

1. Trace the sequence of events in the poem.

2. What images strike you most forcibly?

3. What is your first impression of the location in this poem? How do you imagine it?

SECOND READING

4. Do you think it would be correct to say that the poet is ambivalent in her attitude to the fire balloons? Discuss.

5. Trace the development of the fire imagery throughout the poem. How does the poet link it with the natural world?

6. Where do you think the poet's sympathies lie in this poem? Explain.

THIRD READING

7. Examine the poet's outlook on life here. What image of the local people is presented? What view of humanity in general informs this poem? Can you discern a philosophy of life behind it? Note your impressions, however tentative, then formulate your thoughts in a more organised way.

8. Would you say the poet is uncharacteristically emotional here? Explain your views.

9. What else do you notice about the style of this poem?

FOURTH READING

10. Why do you think this might be considered an important poem?

Sestina

September rain falls on the house.
In the failing light, the old grandmother
sits in the kitchen with the child
beside the Little Marvel Stove,
reading the jokes from the almanac,   5
laughing and talking to hide her tears.

She thinks that her equinoctial tears
and the rain that beats on the roof of the house
were both foretold by the almanac,
but only known to a grandmother.   10
The iron kettle sings on the stove.
She cuts some bread and says to the child,

It's time for tea now; but the child
is watching the teakettle's small hard tears
dance like mad on the hot black stove,   15
the way the rain must dance on the house.
Tidying up, the old grandmother
hangs up the clever almanac

on its string. Birdlike, the almanac
hovers half open above the child,   20
hovers above the old grandmother
and her teacup full of dark brown tears.
She shivers and says she thinks the house
feels chilly, and puts more wood in the stove.

It was to be, says the Marvel Stove.   25
I know what I know, says the almanac.
With crayons the child draws a rigid house
and a winding pathway. Then the child
puts in a man with buttons like tears
and shows it proudly to the grandmother   30

But secretly, while the grandmother
busies herself about the stove,
the little moons fall down like tears
from between the pages of the almanac
into the flower bed the child   35
has carefully placed in the front of the house.

Elizabeth Bishop

Time to plant tears, says the almanac.
The grandmother sings to the marvellous stove
and the child draws another inscrutable house.

Explorations

FIRST READING

1. What is the prevailing atmosphere in this poem? What elements chiefly contribute to this?

2. What are the recurring elements in this poem?

SECOND READING

3. How do you see the grandmother?

4. How do you see the child here?

5. Is the child completely unhappy? Are there any alleviating soft elements in her life?

6. What do you think is absent from the child's picture of life?

THIRD READING

7. Do you understand how the poem is constructed? Explain briefly.

8. Trace the progression of the tear imagery throughout the poem, from the reference to 'September rain' in the first stanza. How do you interpret this in the context of the statement the poet is making about her childhood?

9. Examine the references to her drawings of the house. What do they suggest to you about the child and her environment?

FOURTH READING

10. What thoughts does this poem spark off about childhood and about domestic relationships?

11. Do you think Bishop has made a successful re-creation of a child's world? Examine the actions and the diction in particular.

12. Would you consider this to be a sentimental poem? The term 'sentimental' can be read neutrally as 'emotional thought expressed in literature' or more negatively as 'showing emotional weakness, mawkish tenderness'. Which, if either, description applies? Discuss.

First Death in Nova Scotia

In the cold, cold parlor
my mother laid out Arthur
beneath the chromographs:
Edward, Prince of Wales,
with Princess Alexandra,   5
and King George with Queen Mary.
Below them on the table
stood a stuffed loon
shot and stuffed by Uncle
Arthur, Arthur's father.   10

Since Uncle Arthur fired
a bullet into him,
he hadn't said a word.
He kept his own counsel
on his white, frozen lake,   15
the marble-topped table.
His breast was deep and white,
cold and caressable;
his eyes were red glass,
much to be desired.   20

'Come,' said my mother,
'Come and say good-bye
to your little cousin Arthur.'
I was lifted up and given
one lily of the valley   25
to put in Arthur's hand.
Arthur's coffin was
a little frosted cake,
and the red-eyed loon eyed it
from his white, frozen lake.   30

Elizabeth Bishop

Arthur was very small.
He was all white, like a doll
that hadn't been painted yet.
Jack Frost had started to paint him
the way he always painted   35
the Maple Leaf (Forever).
He had just begun on his hair,
a few red strokes, and then
Jack Frost had dropped the brush
and left him white, forever.   40

The gracious royal couples
were warm in red and ermine;
their feet were well wrapped up
in the ladies' ermine trains.
They invited Arthur to be   45
the smallest page at court.
But how could Arthur go,
clutching his tiny lily,
with his eyes shut up so tight
and the roads deep in snow?   50

Notes

3	chromograph:	printed reproduction of a colour photograph
8	loon:	a diver, a kind of bird, noted for its clumsy gait on land
36	Maple Leaf:	national emblem of Canada
42	ermine:	white fur with black spots, from a type of stoat, used in monarchs' robes

Explorations

FIRST READING

1. First decide who is speaking. Where and when was the event depicted and what age is the speaker?

2. What do you find unusual or confusing on a first reading?

3. If we consider the speaker to be a young child, does this help you come to grips with the poem? Reread it.

SECOND READING

4. What is most noticeable about the scene here?

5. What is the atmosphere in the parlour?

6. How do you think the child speaker feels? Discuss.

THIRD READING

7. Examine the title. Why 'first death'? Discuss the many possible connotations of this.

8. Comment on the use of colour in the poem.

9. Comment on the versification.

FOURTH READING

10. Do you think the poet has managed to successfully re-create the young child's experience?

11. Contrast this poem with Seamus Heaney's poem 'Mid-Term Break'.

12. What did you learn about Elizabeth Bishop from reading this poem?

Filling Station

This poem is also prescribed for Ordinary Level exams in 2016 and 2017

Oh, but it is dirty! *Everthing covered in oil*
– this little filling station,
oil-soaked, oil-permeated
to a disturbing, over-all
black translucency. 5
Be careful with that match! *– humeor*

Father wears a dirty, *focus on people / family*
oil-soaked monkey suit
that cuts him under the arms,
and several quick and saucy 10
and greasy sons assist him
(it's a family filling station),
all quite thoroughly dirty.

Do they live in the station? *Question what she sees*
It has a cement porch 15
behind the pumps, and on it
a set of crushed and grease-
impregnated wickerwork; *→ Garden furniture*
on the wicker sofa *reflect*
a dirty dog, quite comfy. *– homely* 20

Some comic books provide *Takes note of colours*
the only note of color –
of certain color. They lie
upon a big dim doily
draping a taboret 25
(part of the set), beside
a big hirsute begonia. *Attention to detail*

Elizabeth Bishop
217

Why the extraneous plant?
Why the taboret?
Why, oh why, the doily? 30
(Embroidered in daisy stitch
with marguerites, I think,
and heavy with gray crochet.)

Somebody embroidered the doily.
Somebody waters the plant, 35
or oils it, maybe. Somebody
arranges the rows of cans
so that they softly say:
ESSO–SO–SO–SO
to high-strung automobiles. 40
Somebody loves us all.

Someone cares about the shop, tried to improve it

- -

Explorations

BEFORE READING

1. Think about the title. What do you see?

FIRST READING

2. Describe the atmosphere this poem creates for you. What details do you think are significant in creating this? Discuss them.

SECOND READING

3. Plan the shots you would use if you were making a film of this scene. Describe what you see in each shot and explain your choice in detail.

4. Is there any progression, development of complexity, etc. in this film? How do you understand it?

5. What do the doily, the taboret and the begonia add to the atmosphere?

THIRD READING

6. What is it about this scene that fascinates the poet: the forecourt, the domestic details or something else? Discuss.

7. How do you understand the 'somebody' in stanza 6?

FOURTH READING

8. Do you think the poet is discovering a truth and making a statement about life? If so, what? Discuss.

9. Write up your own notes on the theme of the poem, the poet's philosophy of life, her poetic method and the style and tone of the poem.

10. 'The details of Bishop's poems are always compelling but never the whole point.'
Discuss, with reference to the text.

11. 'This is a poem that manages to create poignancy and wit simultaneously.'
Discuss.

In the Waiting Room

In Worcester, Massachusetts,
I went with Aunt Consuelo
to keep her dentist's appointment
and sat and waited for her
in the dentist's waiting room.   5
It was winter. It got dark
early. The waiting room
was full of grown-up people,
arctics and overcoats,
lamps and magazines.   10
My aunt was inside
what seemed like a long time
and while I waited I read
the *National Geographic*
(I could read) and carefully   15
studied the photographs:
the inside of a volcano,
black, and full of ashes;
then it was spilling over
in rivulets of fire.   20
Osa and Martin Johnson
dressed in riding breeches,
laced boots, and pith helmets.
A dead man slung on a pole
– 'Long Pig,' the caption said.   25
Babies with pointed heads
wound round and round with string;
black, naked women with necks
wound round and round with wire
like the necks of light bulbs.   30
Their breasts were horrifying.
I read it right straight through.
I was too shy to stop.
And then I looked at the cover:
the yellow margins, the date.   35

Suddenly, from inside,
came an *oh!* of pain
– Aunt Consuelo's voice –
not very loud or long.
I wasn't at all surprised;   40
even then I knew she was

Elizabeth Bishop

a foolish, timid woman.
I might have been embarrassed,
but wasn't. What took me
completely by surprise   45
was that it was *me*:
my voice, in my mouth.
Without thinking at all
I was my foolish aunt,
I – we – were falling, falling,   50
our eyes glued to the cover
of the *National Geographic*,
February, 1918.

I said to myself: three days
and you'll be seven years old.   55
I was saying it to stop
the sensation of falling off
the round, turning world
into cold, blue-black space.
But I felt: you are an *I*,   60
you are an *Elizabeth*,
you are one of *them*.
Why should you be one, too?
I scarcely dared to look
to see what it was I was.   65
I gave a sidelong glance
– I couldn't look any higher –
at shadowy gray knees,
trousers and skirts and boots
and different pairs of hands   70
lying under the lamps.
I knew that nothing stranger
had ever happened, that nothing
stranger could ever happen.
Why should I be my aunt,   75
or me, or anyone?
What similarities –
boots, hands, the family voice
I felt in my throat, or even
the *National Geographic*   80
and those awful hanging breasts –
held us all together
or made us all just one?
How – I didn't know any

word for it – how 'unlikely' ...   85
How had I come to be here,
like them, and overhear
a cry of pain that could have
got loud and worse but hadn't?

The waiting room was bright   90
and too hot. It was sliding
beneath a big black wave,
another, and another.

Then I was back in it.
The War was on. Outside,   95
in Worcester, Massachusetts,
were night and slush and cold,
and it was still the fifth
of February, 1918.

Background note

This poem was probably written around 1970 and was published in the *New Yorker* on 17 July 1971. It is the opening poem of Bishop's collection *Geography III*, published in 1976.

Notes

21	**Osa and Martin Johnson:**	American photographers and explorers; Bishop first saw the Johnsons' jungle film *Baboons* in the winter of 1935

Explorations

11. What themes or issues are raised by this poem? Explain how the poet deals with some of the following:

- A child's realisation of selfhood

- The poet's uncomfortable connection with the rest of humanity

- The variety and strangeness of the world of which one is a part

- That we are always at risk of being ambushed by the unfamiliar, even in the security of the domestic

- That the chief lessons of childhood are learning to deal with pain and mortality and accepting unity in spite of difference

- Any others

12. What is your own reaction to this poem? Structure your thoughts in the form of questions.

13. Comment on the structure of the poem (five sections) and the type of verse used.

BEFORE READING

1. What might you expect from this title?

2. Do you remember what it was like as a child to sit in a dentist's waiting room? Re-create such an experience. Make brief notes for yourself.

FIRST READING

3. In the poem, what elements of the waiting room experience are all too familiar to you?

4. Who is the speaker in this poem? Assemble as much information, factual and impressionistic, as you can.

SECOND READING

5. After the familiar, what is encountered by the child?

6. Which event most unnerves her? Can you suggest why she is unnerved?

7. What is the child's reaction to this experience?

THIRD READING

8. What is your understanding of the experience described in this poem? Comment briefly.

9. What view of women does Bishop project in this poem?

10. Comment on the experience of childhood reflected here.

Philip Larkin

(1922–85)

Prescribed for Higher Level exams in 2016 and 2018

Philip Arthur Larkin was born in Coventry in 1922, the son of Eva Larkin and Sydney Larkin, the city treasurer. He attended King Henry VIII High School, where he was an avid reader and had some poems and humorous prose printed in the school magazine. In 1940 he went to study English at St John's College, Oxford. He is remembered as a shy, introverted person with a speech impediment. He was a prominent member of the Jazz Club and the English Society. As it was wartime, Larkin expected to be called up, but he failed his medical and so managed to spend a full three years at Oxford. Among his contemporaries were John Wain and Kingsley Amis.

In 1943 Larkin was awarded a first-class degree in English language and literature and the same year had three poems included in *Oxford Poetry, 1942-43*. From 1943 to 1946 he was a librarian at Wellington, Shropshire, where he reorganised the library and managed to write a good deal. It was here that he first became involved in a relationship with Ruth Bowman.

Some of his poems were included in the anthology *Poetry from Oxford in Wartime*, published in 1945 by Fortune Press, which also brought out Larkin's first collection, *The North Ship*, the same year. In 1946 his first novel, *Jill*, was published. In September that year he took up a position as assistant librarian at the University College of Leicester. There he met Monica Jones, a lecturer in the English department, with whom he began a relationship that was to last, on and off, for the rest of his life.

His second novel, *A Girl in Winter*, was published in 1947. In 1948 his father died and Larkin went back to live with his mother. He became engaged to Ruth Bowman, but the engagement was broken off in 1950. In that year Larkin went to Belfast to become the sub-librarian at Queen's University. He enjoyed living in Belfast and he wrote a good deal.

In April 1951 Larkin had 20 of his early poems privately printed as *XX Poems*. These included 'Wedding-Wind' and 'At Grass' (both included in his later volume, *The Less Deceived*). His emotional life became a bit of a tangle. He developed particular relationships with Patsy Strang and Winifred Arnott, who worked in the library, and Monica Jones came to visit.

In 1955 his collection *The Less Deceived* was published. This included the poem 'Toads', a protest against the daily grind of work. Going for interview for the job of librarian at the University of Hull later that year, Larkin feared the board would have seen his poem as representative of his attitude to his job, but he was appointed and, with brief absences, he spent the rest of his life in this position. Here he met Maeve Brennan.

In 1964 *The Whitsun Weddings* was published and in 1965 Larkin was awarded the Queen's Gold Medal for Poetry. *All That Jazz*, a selection of his jazz reviews, was published in 1970. He was a visiting fellow at All Souls College, Oxford, for the academic year 1970–71 and he edited *The Oxford Book of Twentieth-Century Verse* (1973).

In 1974 *High Windows* was published and Larkin bought his first house, opposite the university, where he lived for the rest of his life. His mother died in 1977. In 1982 Monica Jones became ill and Larkin brought her to live at his home.

Required Writing: Miscellaneous Pieces, 1955–82 was published in 1982. In 1984 Larkin refused the offer of appointment as Poet Laureate. He died on 2 December 1985.

Wedding-Wind

The wind blew all my wedding-day,
And my wedding-night was the night of the high wind;
And a stable door was banging, again and again,
That he must go and shut it, leaving me
Stupid in candlelight, hearing rain,   5
Seeing my face in the twisted candlestick,
Yet seeing nothing. When he came back
He said the horses were restless, and I was sad
That any man or beast that night should lack
The happiness I had.   10
                              Now in the day
All's ravelled under the sun by the wind's blowing.
He has gone to look at the floods, and I
Carry a chipped pail to the chicken-run,
Set it down, and stare. All is the wind   15
Hunting through clouds and forests, thrashing
My apron and the hanging cloths on the line.
Can it be borne, this bodying-forth by wind
Of joy my actions turn on, like a thread
Carrying beads? Shall I be let to sleep   20
Now this perpetual morning shares my bed?
Can even death dry up
These new delighted lakes, conclude
Our kneeling as cattle by all-generous waters?

Explorations

FIRST READING

1. List what you notice on a first reading of this poem.

2. Who is the speaker?

3. What scene is the speaker describing (a) in the first stanza and (b) in the second stanza?

SECOND READING

4. How is the woman feeling in the first stanza? What words and phrases indicate her feelings? Explore in detail the nuances and changes of the speaker's mood in the first stanza.

5. What is revealed about her lifestyle in the second stanza? What unanswered questions do you have about her and about her circumstances?

6. What is her mood and what are her feelings in the second stanza? How do we know? Does she interpret her feelings through other means? Explain.

7. Do you think her mood is one of unqualified optimism? Explain.

THIRD READING

8. Briefly outline Larkin's view of marriage and love as you understand it from this poem.

9. Do you think he is successful at interpreting the woman's viewpoint in this poem? Explain.

10. Do you find the setting appropriate to this theme? Comment.

11. Examine the effectiveness of the imagery. Consider in particular the symbolism of storm and of floods. Explore also what the other images contribute to this poem.

Philip Larkin

At Grass

The eye can hardly pick them out
From the cold shade they shelter in,
Till wind distresses tail and mane;
Then one crops grass, and moves about
– The other seeming to look on –   5
And stands anonymous again.

Yet fifteen years ago, perhaps
Two dozen distances sufficed
To fable them: faint afternoons
Of Cups and Stakes and Handicaps,   10
Whereby their names were artificed
To inlay faded, classic Junes –

Silks at the start: against the sky
Numbers and parasols: outside,
Squadrons of empty cars, and heat,   15
And littered grass: then the long cry
Hanging unhushed till it subside
To stop-press columns on the street.

Do memories plague their ears like flies?
They shake their heads. Dusk brims the shadows.   20
Summer by summer all stole away,
The starting-gates, the crowds and cries –
All but the unmolesting meadows.
Almanacked, their names live; they

Have slipped their names, and stand at ease,   25
Or gallop for what must be joy,
And not a fieldglass sees them home,
Or curious stop-watch prophesies:

Only the groom, and the groom's boy,
With bridles in the evening come.   30

Explorations

FIRST READING

1. On a first reading, what do you notice about (a) the setting or scene (b) the horses (c) the time of day and (d) the general mood of the poem?

SECOND READING

2. In the first stanza, did you notice the quiet, undramatic opening? How is this achieved? What words or phrases contribute to it? Explain.

3. Do you find that this poem offers a realistic description of grazing racehorses? Explain, with reference to particular words and phrases.

4. Are there any details that slightly spoil the romantic scene of gently grazing retired horses? Explore this possibility.

5. What elements of a typical race meeting do you think are well caught in stanzas 2–3?

THIRD READING

6. It is as if this scene is viewed from a distance by the poet. Explore how the sense of distance is created in the first three stanzas. What effect does this have on the tone of the poem?

7. Explore the poetic use of language in the fourth stanza.

a What atmosphere do you think is evoked by line 20?

b Technically, how is the sense of easeful and untraumatic departure communicated in line 21? Examine the sounds of the words.

c What is suggested to you by 'the unmolesting meadows'? Do you find this phrase in any way startling or slightly disturbing?

d What part does rhyme play in the creation of atmosphere?

e Consider the phrase 'their names live; they ...'. What do you think is the effect of the punctuation of that phrase and of its particular place in the stanza?

8. How would you describe the atmosphere in stanza 5? Consider the phrases 'Have slipped their names' and 'not a fieldglass sees them home' in this context. What is the effect of the poet's presumption that they gallop 'for what must be joy'?

9. Examine the natural, homely, undistressing evocation of death in the last two lines. It comes not as the Grim Reaper, but as the unthreatening and completely familiar 'groom' and 'groom's boy'. The long vowels of these words are soothing, and semantically they suggest care, comfort, feeding. Yet the finality of it is not disguised. The inverted word order of the final line emphasises that all activity ends in that final verb. Do you think this portrayal of death is effective and suitable in the context of the poem?

Philip Larkin

10. Would you agree that the tone of this poem is unemotional and detached? How is this achieved? Consider the speaking voice (first person, third person, etc.), the sense of distance or perspective and the effect of the style of description (a succession of brief pictures, often unconnected, like a series of untitled photographs).

11. Comment on the sources and effectiveness of the imagery.

12. What do you particularly like about this poem? Or what do you find less than satisfactory?

Church Going

Once I am sure there's nothing going on
I step inside, letting the door thud shut.
Another church: matting, seats, and stone,
And little books; sprawlings of flowers, cut
For Sunday, brownish now; some brass and stuff   5
Up at the holy end; the small neat organ;
And a tense, musty, unignorable silence,
Brewed God knows how long. Hatless, I take off
My cycle-clips in awkward reverence,

Move forward, run my hand around the font.   10
From where I stand, the roof looks almost new –
Cleaned, or restored? Someone would know: I don't.
Mounting the lectern, I peruse a few
Hectoring large-scale verses, and pronounce
'Here endeth' much more loudly than I'd meant.   15
The echoes snigger briefly. Back at the door
I sign the book, donate an Irish sixpence,
Reflect the place was not worth stopping for.

Yet stop I did: in fact I often do,
And always end much at a loss like this,   20
Wondering what to look for; wondering, too,
When churches fall completely out of use
What we shall turn them into, if we shall keep
A few cathedrals chronically on show,
Their parchment, plate and pyx in locked cases,   25
And let the rest rent-free to rain and sheep.
Shall we avoid them as unlucky places?

Or, after dark, will dubious women come
To make their children touch a particular stone;
Pick simples for a cancer; or on some   30
Advised night see walking a dead one?
Power of some sort or other will go on
In games, in riddles, seemingly at random;
But superstition, like belief, must die,
And what remains when disbelief has gone?   35
Grass, weedy pavement, brambles, buttress, sky,

A shape less recognisable each week,
A purpose more obscure. I wonder who
Will be the last, the very last, to seek
This place for what it was; one of the crew   40
That tap and jot and know what rood-lofts were?
Some ruin-bibber, randy for antique,
Or Christmas-addict, counting on a whiff
Of gowns-and-bands and organ-pipes and myrrh?
Or will he be my representative,   45

Bored, uninformed, knowing the ghostly silt
Dispersed, yet tending to this cross of ground
Through suburb scrub because it held unspilt
So long and equably what since is found
Only in separation – marriage, and birth,   50
And death, and thoughts of these – for which was built
This special shell? For, though I've no idea
What this accoutred frowsty barn is worth,
It pleases me to stand in silence here;

A serious house on serious earth it is,   55
In whose blent air all our compulsions meet,
Are recognised, and robed as destinies.
And that much never can be obsolete,
Since someone will forever be surprising
A hunger in himself to be more serious,   60
And gravitating with it to this ground,
Which, he once heard, was proper to grow wise in,
If only that so many dead lie round.

Philip Larkin

Notes

10	**font:**	ornate container, usually of marble or stone and raised on a pedestal, that holds the baptismal water
13	**lectern:**	raised podium or desk from which the reading is done in a church
15	**'Here endeth':**	from the archaic phrase 'Here endeth the Lesson', used at the end of scripture readings
25	**parchment:**	literally animal skin prepared for writing on, here used to signify all church paper, books and records
25	**plate:**	silver and gold vessels
25	**pyx:**	a container for the consecrated Communion wafers
30	**simples:**	an archaic word for herbs
41	**tap:**	perhaps to strike gently or to bore a hole containing an internal screw thread
41	**jot:**	to write brief notes; can also mean to bump or jolt. He may be using both 'tap' and 'jot' in their meaning 'to strike gently', referring to the tapping done by experts who examine timbers in old buildings.
41	**rood-lofts:**	screened galleries separating the nave of a church from the choir
44	**myrrh:**	a perfumed gum-resin used in incense
53	**accoutred:**	richly attired
56	**blent:**	archaic form of 'blended'

Explorations

FIRST READING

Stanzas 1–2

1. This is a first-person narrative poem, so follow the incident with the speaker. See it through his eyes. Step inside the church with him. What is to be seen in the first two stanzas? List everything you notice. What picture of the church do you get? Is it in use, is it well cared for, etc.?

2. What do you notice about the speaker – dress, actions, attitude to the place? What sort of character is he? How does he see himself? What words and phrases do you think are most revealing about the character of the speaker? Explain.

SECOND READING

Stanzas 3–5

3. Is there a change of tone and attitude on the part of the speaker in stanza 3? Explain.

4. Is there a change of style or mode of telling in stanza 3? Explain what you notice.

5. In your own words, trace the speaker's thoughts through stanzas 3–5.

6. What value does the speaker see in the institution of the church? Why does he still find himself 'tending to this cross of ground'? Examine the speaker's thought in stanza 6.

7. 'A serious house on serious earth it is' (stanza 7).
   What do you think the speaker means by 'serious' in the context of this stanza and of the poem as a whole?

THIRD READING

8. Trace the speaker's shifting attitudes to religion and to the church throughout this poem.

9. Can you state briefly what the poem is about?

10. What appeals to you about it?

11. Comment on Larkin's philosophy as it is revealed in this poem.

FOURTH READING

12. Andrew Motion talks about the 'self-mocking, detail-collecting, conversational manner' of this poem. Examine these three aspects of Larkin's style in the poem.

An Arundel Tomb

Side by side, their faces blurred,
The earl and countess lie in stone,
Their proper habits vaguely shown
As jointed armour, stiffened pleat,
And that faint hint of the absurd –   5
The little dogs under their feet.

Such plainness of the pre-baroque
Hardly involves the eye, until
It meets his left-hand gauntlet, still
Clasped empty in the other; and   10
One sees, with a sharp tender shock,
His hand withdrawn, holding her hand.

They would not think to lie so long.
Such faithfulness in effigy
Was just a detail friends would see: 15
A sculptor's sweet commissioned grace
Thrown off in helping to prolong
The Latin names around the base.

Philip Larkin

They would not guess how early in
Their supine stationary voyage   20
The air would change to soundless damage,
Turn the old tenantry away;
How soon succeeding eyes begin
To look, not read. Rigidly they

Persisted, linked, through lengths and breadths   25
Of time. Snow fell, undated. Light
Each summer thronged the glass. A bright
Litter of birdcalls strewed the same
Bone-riddled ground. And up the paths
The endless altered people came,   30

Washing at their identity.
Now, helpless in the hollow of
An unarmorial age, a trough
Of smoke in slow suspended skeins
Above their scrap of history,   35
Only an attitude remains:

Time has transfigured them into
Untruth. The stone fidelity
They hardly meant has come to be
Their final blazon, and to prove   40
Our almost-instinct almost true:
What will survive of us is love.

Notes

	Arundel Tomb:	the monument to the Earl and Countess of Arundel in Chichester Cathedral
7	**pre-baroque:**	the baroque was a style in art predominant from 1600 to 1720, characterised by massive, complex and ornate design. 'Pre-baroque' suggests a more simple design.
40	**blazon:**	coat of arms

Explorations

BEFORE READING

1. When did you last visit a graveyard, an old church or a commemorative monument of any kind? Perhaps it was a famous monument like Kilmainham Jail or just an old church. Visualise it and write brief notes on what you remember.

2. Discuss your experiences in Question 1 or compose a diary extract on your visit.

FIRST READING

3. If possible, listen to the poem read aloud. Close your eyes. What do you see in the poem? In discussion, share what you particularly noticed.

Stanzas 1–2

4. What is the poet looking at? What absorbs his attention?

5. What specific details attract his attention in stanza 2? How does he feel on seeing this? What words or phrases suggest this?

6. How do you react to this detail? Do you share his attitude?

SECOND READING

Stanza 3–4

7. Examine stanza 3. If they could see it, how do you think the earl and countess would view this pose and the detail of the effigy?

8. What does the poet think was the original reason for the detail of the hands? Examine the last two lines of stanza 3.

9. How is the passage of time evoked in stanza 4? Is it violent or gently insidious? Does the passage of time have any social and cultural implications here? Explain.

10. Explore the connotations of 'supine stationary voyage'. What does it suggest to you?

11. If the earl and countess were aware of what has happened up to now and could somehow communicate, what would they say to a visitor to Chichester Cathedral? Choose the view of either figure.

12. Reread stanzas 1–4. What do you think is the underlying issue that preoccupies the poet here?

Philip Larkin

233

Stanzas 5–7

13. What pictures or images do you notice in particular in stanza 5? What is the effect of these images?

14. Examine from 'Rigidly they' (line 24) to 'Washing at their identity' (line 31). If you had a camera to film this section as a sequence of shots, how would you do it? Do you think shots of contrasting images would create an atmosphere true to the verse? Outline the sequence.

15. What words in stanza 6 best describe the predicament of the earl and countess? Explain.

16. What attitude to life and human enterprise underpins stanza 6, in your opinion?

17. Read the 'Background' section in the Critical Commentary. Does this throw any light on your understanding of stanza 7? Attempt to restate the message of stanza 7 in your own words.

FOURTH READING

18. Compose extracts from an imaginary diary that Larkin might have written about this event and that show how he was affected by this experience.

19. Briefly, what are the main themes or issues raised by the poem?

20. Larkin concludes with a seemingly positive statement: 'What will survive of us is love.' Is this sentiment justified by the poem as a whole? Review the evidence throughout the poem.

21. How does this poem make you feel and how does it do that?

22. Briefly compare Larkin's treatment of the possible survival of love against the ravages of time with other poems of a similar theme.

The Whitsun Weddings

That Whitsun, I was late getting away:
  Not till about
One-twenty on the sunlit Saturday
Did my three-quarters-empty train pull out,
All windows down, all cushions hot, all sense   5
Of being in a hurry gone. We ran
Behind the backs of houses, crossed a street
Of blinding windscreens, smelt the fish-dock; thence
The river's level drifting breadth began,
Where sky and Lincolnshire and water meet.   10

All afternoon, through the tall heat that slept
  For miles inland,
A slow and stopping curve southwards we kept.
Wide farms went by, short-shadowed cattle, and

Canals with floatings of industrial froth;   15
A hothouse flashed uniquely: hedges dipped
And rose: and now and then a smell of grass
Displaced the reek of buttoned carriage-cloth
Until the next town, new and nondescript,
Approached with acres of dismantled cars.   20

At first, I didn't notice what a noise
    The weddings made
Each station that we stopped at: sun destroys
The interest of what's happening in the shade,
And down the long cool platforms whoops and skirls   25
I took for porters larking with the mails,
And went on reading. Once we started, though,
We passed them, grinning and pomaded, girls
In parodies of fashion, heels and veils,
All posed irresolutely, watching us go,   30

As if out on the end of an event
    Waving goodbye
To something that survived it. Struck, I leant
More promptly out next time, more curiously,
And saw it all again in different terms: 35
The fathers with broad belts under their suits
And seamy foreheads; mothers loud and fat,
An uncle shouting smut; and then the perms,
The nylon gloves and jewellery-substitutes,
The lemons, mauves, and olive-ochres that   40

Marked off the girls unreally from the rest.
    Yes, from cafés
And banquet-halls up yards, and bunting-dressed
Coach-party annexes, the wedding-days
Were coming to an end. All down the line   45
Fresh couples climbed aboard: the rest stood round;
The last confetti and advice were thrown,
And, as we moved, each face seemed to define
Just what it saw departing: children frowned
At something dull; fathers had never known   50

Success so huge and wholly farcical;
    The women shared
The secret like a happy funeral;
While girls, gripping their handbags tighter, stared

Philip Larkin

235

At a religious wounding. Free at last,   55
And loaded with the sum of all they saw,
We hurried towards London, shuffling gouts of steam.
Now fields were building-plots, and poplars cast
Long shadows over major roads, and for
Some fifty minutes, that in time would seem   60

Just long enough to settle hats and say
  I nearly died,
A dozen marriages got under way.
They watched the landscape, sitting side by side
– An Odeon went past, a cooling tower,   65
And someone running up to bowl – and none
Thought of the others they would never meet
Or how their lives would all contain this hour.
I thought of London spread out in the sun,
Its postal districts packed like squares of wheat: 70

There we were aimed. And as we raced across
  Bright knots of rail
Past standing Pullmans, walls of blackened moss
Came close, and it was nearly done, this frail
Travelling coincidence; and what it held   75
Stood ready to be loosed with all the power
That being changed can give. We slowed again,
And as the tightened brakes took hold, there swelled
A sense of falling, like an arrow-shower
Sent out of sight, somewhere becoming rain.   80

Explorations

FIRST READING

1. Where is the speaker in this poem?

2. What is happening?

3. What images or pictures particularly catch your eye?

SECOND READING

4. Get on the train with the poet and observe what he sees on the journey. List the kinds of things he notices (categories rather than individual sights) and the order in which he sees them.

5. Note the sections you do not understand.

6. What mood is the speaker in at the start of the journey (stanzas 1–2)? What words or phrases lead you to this view?

THIRD READING

7. Is the poet immediately fascinated by the happenings on the station platforms? What is Larkin's initial attitude to the wedding guests? What details strike him in stanzas 3–6?

8. When does he make an effort to understand them, to get inside their thinking? Does his attitude change then? Explain.

9. What is his attitude to the couples? What words or phrases lead you to this conclusion?

10. What do you think is the significance of the weddings for the poet?

FOURTH READING

11. From your reading of this poem, what do you conclude about Larkin's views on weddings and marriage?

12. What picture of England emerges from the poem? Examine stanzas 1, 2, 6 and 7 in particular.

13. What has a reading of this poem added to your understanding of Philip Larkin, man and poet?

14. What questions do you have about this poem?

Philip Larkin

MCMXIV

Those long uneven lines
Standing as patiently
As if they were stretched outside
The Oval or Villa Park,
The crowns of hats, the sun   5
On moustached archaic faces
Grinning as if it were all
An August Bank Holiday lark;

And the shut shops, the bleached
Established names on the sunblinds,   10
The farthings and sovereigns,
And dark-clothed children at play
Called after kings and queens,
The tin advertisements
For cocoa and twist, and the pubs   15
Wide open all day;

And the countryside not caring:
The place-names all hazed over
With flowering grasses, and fields
Shadowing Domesday lines   20
Under wheat's restless silence;
The differently-dressed servants
With tiny rooms in huge houses,
The dust behind limousines;

Never such innocence,   25
Never before or since,
As changed itself to past
Without a word – the men
Leaving the gardens tidy,
The thousands of marriages   30
Lasting a little while longer:
Never such innocence again.

Notes		
MCMXIV:	1914	

15	twist:	probably a twist of tobacco, i.e. tobacco sold in a rope-shaped piece
20	**Domesday (pronounced 'doomsday'):**	the Domesday Book was the record of the great survey of the lands of England ordered by William the Conqueror in 1086, so this reference communicates an awareness of the country's history and a sense of continuity with the past

Explorations

FIRST READING

1. It might be helpful if you were to think of this poem as a picture:

- Centre and foreground: stanza 1

- Right side: stanza 2

- Left side: stanza 3

- Background: stanza 4

   Describe what you see in each part of the picture.

2. Describe the atmosphere in each part of this picture. What words or phrases suggest it?

SECOND READING

3. Concentrate on stanzas 1 and 4, the central line of the picture. What image of humanity comes across from these sections?

4. Jot down words or phrases that you think best describe the atmosphere in the entire picture (all four stanzas).

5. What questions could you ask about any of the events or scenes in the poem? Do you think the style of the poem encourages you to question and speculate? Explain.

THIRD READING

6. Examine the attitude or tone of voice of the poet during this poem. Would you describe him as a detached observer, a sympathetic viewer, cynical, nostalgic or something else? Do you think his attitude changes during the course of the poem? Explain your opinion, with reference to the text.

7. What point or points do you think the poet is making in the poem?

8. Compose a new title for the poem and justify it with reference to the text.

9. Do you know any other poems dealing with a similar theme? Which poem do you prefer and why?

10. Do you find this poem different in any way from the other Larkin poems you have read? Explain, with reference to particular lines or details of poems.

11. 'The grim reality of human suffering and the transience of all things is hidden behind a veneer of nostalgia in "MCMXIV".'
Discuss this view of the poem, with suitable reference to the text.

12. 'Despite a naïve, idealistic view of humankind, Larkin shows some awareness of social problems in "MCMXIV".'
Explore this opinion of the poem.

13. When asked to select two of his poems for an anthology in 1973,

Larkin opted for 'MCMXIV' and 'Send No Money', saying:

'They might be taken as representative examples of the two kinds of poem I sometimes think I write: the beautiful and the true ... I think a poem usually starts off either from the feeling "How beautiful that is" or from the feeling "How true that is". One of the jobs of the poem is to make the beautiful seem true and the true beautiful, but in fact the disguise can usually be penetrated.'
(James Gibson (editor), *Let the Poet Choose*)

a   In what ways do you think 'MCMXIV' might be considered to exemplify the beautiful?

b   Do you think it makes the beautiful seem true and the true beautiful? Discuss this with reference to the text.

Ambulances

This poem is also prescribed for Ordinary Level exams in 2016 and 2018

Closed like confessionals, they thread
Loud noons of cities, giving back
None of the glances they absorb.
Light glossy grey, arms on a plaque,
They come to rest at any kerb: 5
All streets in time are visited.

Then children strewn on steps or road,
Or women coming from the shops
Past smells of different dinners, see
A wild white face that overtops   10
Red stretcher-blankets momently
As it is carried in and stowed,

And sense the solving emptiness
That lies just under all we do,
And for a second get it whole,   15
So permanent and blank and true.
The fastened doors recede. *Poor soul*,
They whisper at their own distress;

For borne away in deadened air
May go the sudden shut of loss   20
Round something nearly at an end,
And what cohered in it across
The years, the unique random blend
Of families and fashions, there

At last begin to loosen. Far   25
From the exchange of love to lie
Unreachable inside a room
The traffic parts to let go by
Brings closer what is left to come,
And dulls to distance all we are.   30

Explorations

FIRST READING

1. What is happening in this poem?

2. Follow the ambulance through the streets. Describe what you see.

3. What is the reaction of the onlookers?

SECOND READING

4. Read the first stanza carefully. What is suggested about the ambulances? Consider in particular the connotations of each of the following phrases: 'Closed like confessionals', 'they thread', 'giving back | None of the glances', 'come to rest', 'All streets in time are visited'.

Philip Larkin

5. Read the second stanza carefully. What do we learn about the victims? Consider the connotations of 'children strewn', 'a wild white face', 'stowed'.

6. In the third stanza the victims are frightened because they sense the answer to the question of the meaning 'That lies just under all we do'. What is the answer sensed here?

7. In the first three lines of stanza 4, what words or phrases indicate the seriousness of the situation?

8. What does the use of 'something' and 'it' suggest to you when used to describe the victim?

9. In what sense does the phrase 'begin to loosen' describe death in the poem?

10. The syntax of the last stanza is deliberately scrambled. Why do you think this might be? If you read 'a room | The traffic parts to let go by' as a metaphorical rendering of 'an ambulance', does the sense become clearer?

THIRD READING

11. What view of death comes from this poem? Support your opinion with reference to the text.

12. How would you describe the poet's attitude to death?

13. What view of life is intimated in this poem?

14. Explain your own response to the poem's philosophy and its view of death.

FOURTH READING

15. 'The awful ordinariness of death is one of Larkin's chief preoccupations in this poem.' Discuss this statement with reference to the text.

16. 'The poem becomes a celebration of the values of consciousness' (Andrew Motion). Examine the poem from this perspective.

The Trees

The trees are coming into leaf
Like something almost being said;
The recent buds relax and spread,
Their greenness is a kind of grief.

Is it that they are born again   5
And we grow old? No, they die too.
Their yearly trick of looking new
Is written down in rings of grain.

Yet still the unresting castles thresh
In fullgrown thickness every May.   10
Last year is dead, they seem to say,
Begin afresh, afresh, afresh.

Explorations

FIRST READING

1. What do you notice about the trees on a first reading of this poem?

2. What phrases do you find perplexing?

3. Is it your first impression that this is a predominantly sad or a predominantly happy poem?

SECOND READING

4. What aspect or quality of the trees does the poet focus on throughout these verses? Explain, with reference to specific words or phrases, etc.

5. 'The trees are coming into leaf | Like something almost being said'. What does this simile suggest about the process of foliation? From your own experience, do you think this is an accurate observation? Explain.

6. 'Their greenness is a kind of grief.' How could this be? Do you think the 'grief' applies to the trees or to the poet? How do you interpret the line?

7. What do the trees have in common with humanity? Is this a source of comfort or of despair to the poet? Explain.

8. What is your reaction to the description of the trees as 'unresting castles'?

9. Trace the poet's mood in each of the stanzas. What words or phrases carry this mood?

THIRD READING

10. Explore the relationship between the poet and nature in this poem.

11. What do you think is the essential wisdom or truth of this poem?

12. Would you agree that Larkin's attitude here is one of 'grudging optimism'? Explain your views with reference to the poem.

13. Read 'The Trees' in conjunction with 'Ambulances'. Do you find the outlook on life in both poems similar or different? Explain. Which poem, in your opinion, exhibits more of a longing for life? Explain.

Philip Larkin

The Explosion

This poem is also prescribed for Ordinary Level exams in 2016 and 2018

On the day of the explosion
Shadows pointed towards the pithead:
In the sun the slagheap slept.

Down the lane came men in pitboots
Coughing oath-edged talk and pipe-smoke,   5
Shouldering off the freshened silence.

One chased after rabbits; lost them;
Came back with a nest of lark's eggs;
Showed them; lodged them in the grasses.

So they passed in beards and moleskins,   10
Fathers, brothers, nicknames, laughter,
Through the tall gates standing open.

At noon, there came a tremor; cows
Stopped chewing for a second; sun,
Scarfed as in a heat-haze, dimmed.   15

The dead go on before us, they
Are sitting in God's house in comfort,
We shall see them face to face –

Plain as lettering in the chapels
It was said, and for a second   20
Wives saw men of the explosion

Larger than in life they managed –
Gold as on a coin, or walking
Somehow from the sun towards them,

One showing the eggs unbroken.   25

Explorations

FIRST READING

1. On a first reading, what details made the most impression on you?

2. What happens in the poem?

SECOND READING

3. What do you notice about the village? Examine all details carefully.

4. What information are we given about the miners? Explore details of dress, habit, manner, mood, philosophy, etc.

5. Are there any hints, either in the imagery or the method of narration, that a tragedy was about to happen? Examine stanzas 1–4 for any signs of the ominous.

6. Do you think the poet's description of the explosion is effective? Explain your thinking on this.

7.

a The fifth stanza marks a division between two quite different halves in this poem. How do the last 10 lines differ from the first four stanzas?

b How would you describe the atmosphere in the last 10 lines? What words or phrases contribute to this?

8. What is suggested in stanza 8? What is the effect of the imagery in this stanza?

9. What do you think is the effect of the last line?

THIRD READING

10. What does the poet want us to feel in this poem and how does he achieve this?

11. What statement about life, society and people do you think the poet is making here? Refer to details in the poem.

12. Is this a poem you might remember five years from now? Why?

Philip Larkin

Cut Grass

Cut grass lies frail:
Brief is the breath
Mown stalks exhale.
Long, long the death

It dies in the white hours   5
Of young-leafed June
With chestnut flowers,
With hedges snowlike strewn,

White lilac bowed,
Lost lanes of Queen Anne's lace,   10
And that high-builded cloud
Moving at summer's pace.

Notes

10	**Queen Anne's lace:**	wild carrot, a plant sometimes used in herbal medicine and reputed to have contraceptive properties

Explorations

BEFORE READING

1. From your own experiences, list what you have noticed about a June day in the countryside.

FIRST READING

2. What elements of nature's activity does the poet focus on?

3. Do you find the poet's attitude to the cut grass particularly sensitive? Explain.

4. What is suggested by the image of the 'white hours' of 'young-leafed June'?

5. 'Lost lanes of Queen Anne's lace'. What do you see when you read this line? What atmosphere does it conjure up?

SECOND READING

6. What exactly is Larkin's main idea about the season, as communicated in this poem? State it briefly in your own words.

7. What part do the sounds of words play in the creation of atmosphere in the poem?

8. 'While the main focus may be on the exuberance of nature in June, we are also aware of the transience of life, the swift passage of time and the changing seasons in this poem.' Comment.

THIRD READING

9. Do you think this poem is effective? Explain your own reaction to it.

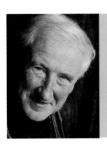

John Montague

(1929–)

Prescribed for Higher Level exams in 2015 and 2018

John Montague was born on 28 February 1929 into a family struggling to survive in a turbulent world.

His father James, a Catholic Nationalist, was unable to find work in the new state of Northern Ireland, so he decided to follow his brother and other members of the Montague family to New York in an effort to provide for his family. His wife, Molly, and his two sons remained in County Tyrone until 1928, when they were finally able to join him in New York. The following year, John Montague was born in St Catherine's Hospital, Brooklyn: a new child for a new beginning for the Montague family.

Sadly, this new beginning was destined to fail. The times proved to be just as turbulent in America as they had been in Ireland. Some eight months after John's birth, in October 1929, the New York stock market collapsed and the Great Depression hit America. John's father lost his job and his mother became ill. The family relied on the support of John's uncle, who ran two 'speakeasies' – illegal drinking dens. When John's uncle died, any hope of a new beginning disappeared and the Montague family separated once again.

At the age of four, John left his mother and father in Brooklyn and travelled with his two older brothers to a new life in County Tyrone. While his brothers went to live with his maternal grandmother, John was sent to the Garvaghey home of his father's two unmarried sisters. He would never again live with his mother, father and brothers as a family unit under one roof. His mother returned to Northern Ireland when John was seven, but did not reclaim him. Instead, she lived some eight miles away and the pair met only infrequently. His father did not come home until some years later.

John proved to be a very able student and read History and English at UCD, where he achieved a double First. He continued his studies in America and lived in France before returning to Ireland.

Resolving not to rely on poetry for his income, John Montague has worked in a variety of areas: as a journalist, a critic and a teacher at Berkeley, UCD and UCC amongst others, while publishing a substantial body of writing. His contribution to the world of letters has been widely recognised and he has won a number of awards.

He retired from teaching in 1988 and now divides his time between France and Ireland. He continues to work with words.

The noise.

He was pulled out, squealing,
an iron cleek sunk in the roof
of his mouth.

(Don't say they are not intelligent: 5
they know the hour has come
and they want none of it;
they dig in their little trotters,

will not go dumb or singing
to the slaughter.)   10

That high pitched final effort,
no single sound could match it –
a big plane roaring off,
a *diva* soaring towards her last note,
the brain-chilling persistence of an electric saw, 15
scrap being crushed.

Piercing & absolute,
only high heaven ignores it.

Then a full stop.
Mickey Boyle plants   20
a solid thump of the mallet
flat between the ears.

Swiftly the knife seeks the throat;
swiftly the other cleavers work
till the carcass is hung up   25
shining and eviscerated as
a surgeon's coat.

A child is given
the bladder to play with.
But the walls of the farmyard   30
still hold that scream,
are built around it.

Notes

3	**cleek:**	hook
14	**diva:**	a famous woman singer
24	**cleavers:**	heavy chopping tools often used by butchers
26	**eviscerated:**	intestines and bowels removed

Explorations

FIRST READING

1. What is your reaction to this poem? Do you feel that the killing of a pig is a suitable subject for a poem? Why?

2. Montague begins the poem with two words: 'The noise'. In your own words, describe the noise. How does his use of metaphors help you to imagine the noise? How does Montague convey the noise the pig makes as he is dragged to the slaughter?

3. 'Then a full stop.' Why does the 'squealing' noise stop? What sounds take its place? Which sound do you find the most disturbing? Why?

4.

a How does Montague describe the killing of the pig? What is your reaction to the image of 'a surgeon's coat'?

b Do you find it easy or difficult to read lines 19–27? Give reasons for your answer.

SECOND READING

5.

a What are your feelings for the pig when you read the line 'they dig in their little trotters'?

b Does the gift of the pig's bladder to the child as a plaything tell you anything about the people's attitude to the pig's death?

John Montague

c How do you feel about the way that the people in the poem react to the pig's death?

6. 'But the walls of the farmyard | still hold that scream, | are built around it.' Can you explain what Montague means by these lines? Would you agree that suffering and death are indeed part of farming?

7.

a Is this poem simply about a particular incident, the killing of a pig, or does it have a reference to life in general?

b What do you think the theme of this poem is?

8. Sounds play a big part in this poem. Examine the contribution that alliteration and assonance make to the effectiveness of this poem.

9. Discuss Montague's use of line length to reinforce line meaning in the poem. Use quotations from the poem to support your discussion.

10. John Montague wrote of his descriptions of the County Tyrone countryside of his youth: 'one must avoid seeing all this through a haze of nostalgia'. What is nostalgia? Would you have preferred a bit more of the 'haze of nostalgia' in this poem or does the stark realism give it a greater impact?

The Trout

For Barrie Cooke

Flat on the bank I parted
Rushes to ease my hands
In the water without a ripple
And tilt them slowly downstream
To where he lay, tendril light,   5
In his fluid sensual dream.

Bodiless lord of creation
I hung briefly above him
Savouring my own absence,
Senses expanding in the slow   10
Motion, the photographic calm
That grows before action.

As the curve of my hands
Swung under his body
He surged, with visible pleasure.   15
I was so preternaturally close
I could count every stipple
But still cast no shadow, until

The two palms crossed in a cage
Under the lightly pulsing gills.   20
Then (entering my own enlarged
Shape, which rode on the water)
I gripped. To this day I can
Taste his terror on my hands.

Notes

	Barrie Cooke:	an artist living in Ireland who uses nature as the subject matter for many of his paintings
5	**tendril:**	a slender, leafless shoot, a line or curl of hair
16	**preternatural:**	supernatural, outside the normal range of nature

Explorations

BEFORE READING

1. Have you ever sat looking into water, watching fish swimming, or tried to catch a fish? Take a moment to think about your experience, then try writing a short passage recreating it.

FIRST READING

2. Compare Montague's description with your own piece. Are there any similarities or differences?

3. In your own words, give a description of the fish. How does Montague want us to feel about the fish? What words or phrases does he use to make us feel this way?

4. 'Bodiless lord of creation | I hung briefly above him | Savouring my own absence'.
   What do these lines tell you about the boy's feelings? Can you suggest why he feels like this?

5.

a 'I gripped. To this day I can | Taste his terror on my hands.'
   How do the boy's feelings change when he catches the fish? Are you surprised by this change?

b Do you find Montague's description of the boy catching the fish realistic? Give reasons for your answer.

6. Describe the mood that is conveyed in each of the four stanzas. In each case, choose one line or phrase that you feel communicates the mood.

SECOND READING

7.

a What senses does Montague appeal to in his descriptions in order to make the scene in this poem come alive?

b 'Taste his terror on my hands'.
   Can you explain what Montague is trying to suggest in this line?

c Discuss how Montague's use of sensory images helps the reader to become involved in this poem. Use references to support your view.

John Montague

251

8.

a   The first two stanzas are really two long sentences with very little punctuation. Read these two stanzas aloud and discuss the effect that this structure has on the rhythm and tone of the reading. The third and fourth stanzas are written in shorter sentences. Can you suggest why there is this change?

b   How does Montague's use of punctuation help to convey what happens in the poem?

9.   How do the sounds of the words contribute to the effectiveness of the poem? You might like to include the poet's use of assonance and alliteration, vowels and consonants in your consideration.

THIRD READING

10.

a   In an interview with Dennis O'Driscoll, John Montague commented on the way he wrote poetry: '... from time to time a poem will start to arrive and I try to get it all out. The metaphor I've used for years has been fishing, trying to get the fish out on to the bank.' Do you think that fishing is a good metaphor for writing a poem? Why?

b   Trace how 'The Trout' could be a metaphor for the creative process.

11.   Robert Welch admires John Montague's poetry because of 'the brilliant suddenness of its responses to the touch, feel, look and shock of the actual'. Discuss this statement with regard to 'Killing the Pig' and 'The Trout'.

The Locket   Track 2

This poem is also prescribed for Ordinary Level exams in 2015 and 2018

Sing a last song
for the lady who has gone,
fertile source of guilt and pain.
The worst birth in the annals of Brooklyn,
that was my cue to come on,   5
my first claim to fame.

Naturally, she longed for a girl,
and all my infant curls of brown
couldn't excuse my double blunder
coming out, both the wrong sex,   10
and the wrong way around.
Not readily forgiven,

So you never nursed me
and when all my father's songs
couldn't sweeten the lack of money,   15
'when poverty comes through the door
love flies up the chimney',
your favourite saying,

Then you gave me away,
might never have known me,   20
if I had not cycled down
to court you like a young man,
teasingly untying your apron,
drinking by the fire, yarning

Of your wild, young days   25
which didn't last long, for you,
lovely Molly, the belle of your small town,
landed up mournful and chill
as the constant rain that lashes it
wound into your cocoon of pain.   30

Standing in that same hallway,
'Don't come again,' you say, roughly,
'I start to get fond of you, John,
and then you are up and gone';
the harsh logic of a forlorn woman   35
resigned to being alone.

And still, mysterious blessing,
I never knew, until you were gone,
that, always around your neck,
you wore an oval locket   40
with an old picture in it,
of a child in Brooklyn.

John Montague

Explorations

1. John Montague said that the song 'The Tri-coloured Ribbon' was in his mind when he wrote this poem. Listen to this song or read the lyrics if possible.

2. How did you feel when you had finished reading this poem? Choose two images that you found emotionally affecting and explain how and why they touched you.

3. Examine the first three stanzas. What reasons does Montague give for his mother's rejection of him when he was born? Do you feel that they were valid reasons for her behaviour or is he simply trying to find excuses?

4. 'Fertile source of guilt and pain.' Why would Montague's mother be the source of 'guilt and pain' for him? Would you feel 'guilt and pain' if you were Montague?

5.

a In the fourth stanza, Montague describes the efforts he made to form some sort of relationship with his mother. Does he use words that you would normally associate with a mother–child relationship? Is there a connection between this stanza and his use of the word 'lady' in the second line of the poem?

b How does Montague describe his relationship with his mother when he was older and went to visit her?

6.

a The fifth and sixth stanzas tell us more about the poet's mother. Do you feel more sympathetic towards her having read these stanzas? Do they help you to understand her actions better or do you feel that Montague is once again trying to excuse her?

b Imagine that you are Montague's mother. Write the story in this poem in the way she might see it.

7.

a Did the final stanza surprise you? Why? Consider how the phrase 'mysterious blessing' might be interpreted.

b Do you find the seventh stanza a successful conclusion to the poem? Give reasons for your opinion.

8. Montague uses a conversational style to recount his relationship with his mother. What effect does it have on the impact of the poem? Is this style as simple as it appears?

9.

a John Montague has said that he tends not to read this poem aloud to an audience because he feels that it is too private. Do you understand his feelings? Would you find it easier

to write something emotional rather
than to say it?

b   Write and present a short speech
     either for or against the following
     motion: 'Emotions are better
     expressed through the spoken word
     than through the written word.'

10. 'For a man, the death of a mother can
     be quite central ... the death of the
     woman who gave you birth is a very
     deep experience.'

In light of these comments by John
Montague, consider how effectively
this poem expresses his 'very deep
experience' of his mother's death.

11. The song 'The Tri-Coloured Ribbon'
     tells of a girl losing her lover in the
     fight for Ireland's freedom. Consider
     the ways in which the political
     situation in Ireland affected the
     relationship between Montague and
     his mother.

The Cage

 Track 3

This poem is also prescribed for Ordinary Level exams in 2015 and 2018

My father, the least happy
man I have known. His face
retained the pallor
of those who work underground:
the lost years in Brooklyn   5
listening to a subway
shudder the earth.

But a traditional Irishman
who (released from his grille
in the Clark Street IRT)   10
drank neat whiskey until
he reached the only element
he felt at home in
any longer: brute oblivion.

And yet picked himself   15
up, most mornings,
to march down the street
extending his smile
to all sides of the good
(all-white) neighbourhood   20
belled by St. Teresa's church.

John Montague

When he came back
we walked together
across fields of Garvaghey
to see hawthorn on the summer   25
hedges, as though
he had never left;
a bend of the road

which still sheltered
primroses. But we   30
did not smile in
the shared complicity
of a dream, for when
weary Odysseus returns
Telemachus should leave.   35

Often as I descend
into subway or underground
I see his bald head behind
the bars of the small booth;
the mark of an old car   40
accident beating on his
ghostly forehead.

Notes

3	**pallor:**	paleness
10	**IRT:**	Interborough Rapid Transit Subway Company, the first subway company in New York
34	**Odysseus:**	The hero of the 'Odyssey', who married Penelope, the cousin of Helen of Troy, and fought bravely in the Trojan War. After many adventures, lasting some 20 years, he finally returned home to Penelope.
35	**Telemachus:**	son of Odysseus and Penelope. He was a baby when Odysseus left to fight in the Trojan War. When Odysseus returned after 20 years he sent Telemachus into exile because he had been warned that he should not trust his son. Unfortunately, the warning referred to another of Odysseus' sons, who later accidentally killed Odysseus. Telemachus then returned and became king.

Explorations

1. Imagine that you are phoning someone to arrange to have John Montague's father collected at the airport. Using the details given in the poem, write a short passage outlining the description you would give to ensure that the right person is met.

2. How did Montague's father earn his living in Brooklyn? From the descriptions in the poem, do you think he worked in a pleasant place?

3.

a   What was 'the only element | he felt at home in'? Look up the words 'brute' and 'oblivion' in the dictionary. Do the meanings of these words suggest that he really 'felt at home' or found comfort there? This was a man who had been actively involved in Republican activities when he was young; how do you think he would have felt about the way his life had developed?

b   Imagine that you meet Montague's father and you ask him to talk about his life. Write a passage to express what you think he would say. You will find your work on Questions 2 and 3(a) helpful.

4. 'the good | (all-white) neighbourhood | belled by St. Teresa's church.' What sort of a neighbourhood did Montague's father live in? Can you suggest why Montague put the words 'all-white' in brackets? You might find it helpful to think about the position of black people in America in the first half of the 20th century.

5. From his description, do you think that Montague enjoyed the walk with his father? Use quotations from the poem to support your view.

6.

a   Images of being below and above ground fill this poem. Examine the way that Montague describes each place. What effects did each place have on his father?

b   How do you feel about Montague's father when you read about his life in Brooklyn?

7.

a   The cage mentioned in the title appears twice in the poem itself. What impression do you get of this cage from these descriptions? Consider what cages are used for. For instance, do they protect or do they trap? Might there be a connection between the cage and being underground?

b   Do you think 'The Cage' is a suitable title for this poem? Why?

8.

a   Montague once referred to his father as 'my poor old battered father' and he ends the poem with the memory of the scar on his father's head. Is this the only type of injury that this man suffered?

b   Write and present a short speech on the following topic: 'In his poetry, John Montague shows us that psychological wounds can often be more damaging than physical ones.' Support your

John Montague

argument with quotations from relevant poems.

9. It is clear that Montague confronts some very personal issues in 'The Cage' and in 'The Locket'.

a How does he describe his relationship with (i) his mother and (ii) his father?

b Consider the implications of his use of imagery based on (i) courtly love when writing about his mother and (ii) classical literature in connection with his father.

c Do you think Montague develops an understanding of the reasons for his parents' behaviour? Why?

10. 'Montague uses his own family situation as a metaphor for the suffering brought about by the political turmoil in Northern Ireland.' Discuss, with reference to 'The Cage' and 'The Locket'.

Windharp

for Patrick Collins

The sounds of Ireland,
that restless whispering
you never get away
from, seeping out of
low bushes and grass,   5
heatherbells and fern,
wrinkling bog pools,
scraping tree branches,
light hunting cloud,
sound hounding sight,   10
a hand ceaselessly
combing and stroking
the landscape, till
the valley gleams
like the pile upon   15
a mountain pony's coat.

Notes

	Windharp:	an open box with strings stretched across it, played by the wind
	Patrick Collins:	(1910–94) a painter whose work seeks to evoke misty Celtic landscapes
6	heatherbells:	heather with bell-shaped flowers
11	ceaselessly:	without end
15	pile	a velvet-like surface

Explorations

BEFORE READING

1. Make an audio tape of the wind and listen to it before reading this poem. Write a list of the words that occur to you as you listen to the tape. What does the list reveal about your thoughts on the wind? Do you see it as a positive or negative force, a constructive or destructive energy?

FIRST READING

2.

a What do you notice about the punctuation of this poem? Read the poem aloud, then change all the commas to full stops and read the poem aloud again. What effect did the change in punctuation have on the way that the poem was read? Can you suggest why Montague chose to punctuate his poem in this way?

b How does Montague use punctuation to help convey his impression of the wind?

3.

a Given that the wind cannot be seen, how does Montague set about creating a visual 'pen picture' of it?

What aspect of the wind does he concentrate on? Pick out two lines that you find particularly effective.

b Do you find Montague's description of the wind successful? Refer to the poem in your answer.

4. Apart from showing us the visual effects of the wind, Montague also helps us to 'hear' the wind. Examine the way that he suggests the changing speed of the wind by his use of (i) the sibilant (hissing) 's', alliteration, assonance and internal rhyme; and (ii) the rhythm of the lines.

5. What type of words does Montague use in lines 7–12 to suggest the sensation of feeling the wind blowing? Would you say it is a pleasant or unpleasant feeling? Why?

SECOND READING

6. 'light hunting cloud, | sound hounding sight'.
Write a passage describing what you imagine when you read these lines. How is Montague's style of writing different to yours? Can you think of three words to describe his style?

John Montague

7.

a   How does John Montague seek to make the ordinary more noticeable in 'Windharp'?

b   Based on your points in part (a) and using references from 'Windharp' and one other poem by John Montague, write an article for a literary magazine entitled 'John Montague's Poetry Makes Me See My World in a New Light'.

8.

a   What did you think when you saw the title of this poem? How does the wind interact with a windharp? How does the wind interact with the Irish landscape? Can you suggest a connection between the two?

b   Working in pairs, imagine that John Montague has just read this poem to you and tells you that he is thinking of calling it 'Windharp'. With one of you writing as Montague and one of you as yourself, write out the conversation that the two of you have, beginning with:

JM: So I was thinking that I'd call this poem 'Windharp'. What do you think?

You: Well, John, I think that ...

THIRD READING

9.   As always with John Montague, this poem has many layers. In your own words, explain the themes of 'Windharp'. You may find it helpful to refer back to Questions 7 and 8.

10. Montague regarded himself as a 'bewildered boy [who] had lost and refound himself in nature'. With reference to 'Killing the Pig', 'The Trout' and 'Windharp', discuss how nature helps Montague to make important discoveries that help him to understand his world.

11. Look at the list of words that you made as you listened to the tape of the wind. Having worked on the poem, do you want to change the list in any way, either by adding or deleting words, in order to more fully express your thoughts on the wind? Can you explain the reasons for your changes?

All Legendary Obstacles

All legendary obstacles lay between
Us, the long imaginary plain,
The monstrous ruck of mountains
And, swinging across the night,
Flooding the Sacramento, San Joaquin,   5
The hissing drift of winter rain.

All day I waited, shifting
Nervously from station to bar
As I saw another train sail
By, the San Francisco Chief or   10
Golden Gate, water dripping
From great flanged wheels.

At midnight you came, pale
Above the negro porter's lamp.
I was too blind with rain   15
And doubt to speak, but
Reached from the platform
Until our chilled hands met.

You had been travelling for days
With an old lady who marked   20
A neat circle on the glass
With her glove to watch us
Move into the wet darkness
Kissing, still unable to speak.

Notes

1	**legendary:**	having a connection with legends/myths
1	**obstacles:**	something or someone that blocks progress
3	**ruck:**	a crease or a wrinkle
5	**the Sacramento:**	the longest river in California
5	**San Joaquin:**	the second longest river in California
12	**flanged:**	having a projecting rim

Explorations

BEFORE READING

1. Think back to a time when you were looking forward to meeting someone. Try to remember how you felt as you were waiting. Were you excited, anxious, impatient? Perhaps you felt a mixture of emotions.

FIRST READING

2.

a   Does the first stanza of this poem make a successful opening? Why? Choose the words or phrases that you feel play a key part in the first stanza.

b   Write a short piece beginning with the following words: 'When I read the first stanza of "All Legendary Obstacles", I felt ...'. You might like to share some of your thoughts with the class.

3. How does Montague feel in the second stanza as he waits for his lover to arrive? What are the clues that convey his feelings?

4. Describe what Montague does when his lover finally arrives. Use quotations to support your description. Are you surprised by his behaviour? Why?

5.

a   Who is introduced into the scene in the final stanza? Are there any clues given as to the type of person she is? Do you

think she would have made a good
travelling companion 'for days'? Would
you be comfortable being watched by
her? Why?

b Imagine that you are the old lady.
Describe the journey and the meeting
of the two lovers from your point of
view.

SECOND READING

6. 'All legendary obstacles lay between |
Us'.
Describe in your own words all the
obstacles that the lovers face.

7. 'The monstrous ruck of mountains';
'The hissing drift of winter rain'.
How does Montague's use of sound in
these lines help you to visualise what is
being described?

8. 'Move into the wet darkness | Kissing,
still unable to speak.'
Do you think these lines indicate a
happy ending for the couple? Does the
poem support a happy ending or is it
less certain?

THIRD READING

9. Montague has commented that the
story of Orpheus and Eurydice lies
behind this poem. Orpheus doomed
Eurydice to death and the Underworld
when he looked back at her despite
being warned not to by Hades, the god
of the Underworld. What implications
does this story have for Montague's
feelings about his relationship?

10. 'This poem begins with a specific
incident in a particular relationship, but
ends by revealing something of the
nature of love itself.'
Discuss.

11. Montague said of 'All Legendary
Obstacles', 'It's a complicated poem.'
Write a letter to John Montague
explaining why you agree or disagree
with his assessment.

The Same Gesture

There is a secret room
of golden light where
everything – love, violence,
hatred is possible;
and, again, love.   5

Such intimacy of hand
and mind is achieved
under its healing light
that the shifting of
hands is a rite   10

like court music.
We barely know our

selves there though
it is what we always were –
most nakedly are –   15

and must remember
when we leave, re-
suming our habits
with our clothes:
work, phone, drive   20

through late traffic
changing gears with
the same gesture as
eased your snowbound
heart and flesh.   25

Notes

10	rite:	a religious or solemn action

Explorations

FIRST READING

1. Begin a sentence with 'I found this poem…' and add in your response to this poem, then follow it with 'because…' and explain what it was in the poem that made you respond in this way. You might like to share your response with the class.

2. 'There is a secret room | of golden light', 'under its healing light'.

a What do the words 'secret', 'golden', 'healing' and 'light' suggest about this room? Do these words tell you anything about the nature of the relationship that takes place in this room?

b Describe in your own words how you imagine the 'secret room'.

SECOND READING

3. In the first stanza, Montague lists the emotions that the couple experience in this room. Are you surprised by the emotions that are grouped together? Why? Can you see any connection between the three ('love, violence, | hatred')? Are they the emotions you would expect to occur in the room that you imagined?

4. How does Montague convey the close intimacy of their relationship in the second stanza? Is it simply a physical relationship or does it have a deeper quality? What do you think Montague is trying to convey about their relationship by using the word 'rite'?

5. 'We barely know our | selves there though | it is what we always were | – most nakedly are –'.

John Montague

a   When Montague uses the word 'nakedly', does he just mean a physical nakedness?

b   How does Montague portray the love that is shared by the lovers in the first three stanzas of the poem? Use quotations to support your view. You will find it helpful to refer back to your work on Questions 3 and 4.

6. How do the couple prepare to leave the room? Can you suggest a connection between the 'clothes' image and the image of 'nakedness' that you considered in Question 5? What happens to the intimacy that the couple shared when they leave the room?

7. Using your work on Question 6, can you explain the theme of this poem in your own words?

8. With reference to lines 6–15 and lines 16–25, examine how Montague uses the pace and rhythm of his writing to suggest the different ways that the lovers feel in (i) the 'secret room' and (ii) the outside world.

THIRD READING

9. Compare Montague's description of two lovers in an intimate setting with that of John Donne in his poem 'The Sun Rising' (also in this anthology). Which one do you prefer? Why?

10. 'In his poems "All Legendary Obstacles" and "The Same Gesture", Montague reveals Truths about Love that challenge us to reassess our expectations of what "being in love" truly means.'
    Discuss, using quotations from both poems to support your answer.

Like Dolmens Round My Childhood

This poem is also prescribed for Ordinary Level exams in 2015 and 2018

Like dolmens round my childhood, the old people.

Jamie MacCrystal sang to himself,
A broken song without tune, without words;
He tipped me a penny every pension day,
Fed kindly crusts to winter birds.   5
When he died his cottage was robbed,
Mattress and money box torn and searched.
Only the corpse they didn't disturb.

Maggie Owens was surrounded by animals,
A mongrel bitch and shivering pups,   10
Even in her bedroom a she-goat cried.
She was a well of gossip defiled,
Fanged chronicler of a whole countryside;
Reputed a witch, all I could find
Was her lonely need to deride.   15

The Nialls lived along a mountain lane
Where heather bells bloomed, clumps of foxglove.
 All were blind, with Blind Pension and Wireless.
Dead eyes serpent-flickered as one entered
To shelter from a downpour of mountain rain.   20
Crickets chirped under the rocking hearthstone
Until the muddy sun shone out again.

Mary Moore lived in a crumbling gatehouse,
Famous as Pisa for its leaning gable.
Bag-apron and boots, she tramped the fields   25
Driving lean cattle from a miry stable.
A byword for fierceness, she fell asleep
Over love stories, *Red Star* and *Red Circle*,
Dreamed of gypsy love-rites, by firelight sealed.

Wild Billy Eagleson married a Catholic servant girl   30
When all his Loyal family passed on:
We danced around him shouting 'To hell with King Billy,'
And dodged from the arc of his flailing blackthorn.
Forsaken by both creeds, he showed little concern
Until the Orange drums banged past in the summer   35
And bowler and sash aggressively shone.

Curate and doctor trudged to attend them,
Through knee-deep snow, through summer heat,

John Montague

From main road to lane to broken path,
Gulping the mountain air with painful breath. 40
Sometimes they were found by neighbours,
Silent keepers of a smokeless hearth,
Suddenly cast in the mould of death.

Ancient Ireland, indeed! I was reared by her bedside,
The rune and the chant, evil eye and averted head, 45
Fomorian fierceness of family and local feud.
Gaunt figures of fear and of friendliness,
For years they trespassed on my dreams
Until once, in a standing circle of stones,
I felt their shadows pass 50

Into that dark permanence of ancient forms.

Notes

1	**dolmens:**	megalithic tombs consisting of upright stones capped by a large flat stone
12	**defiled:**	corrupted, dirtied, polluted
13	**Fanged:**	with sharp, large wolf- or dog-like teeth
13	**chronicler:**	a person who keeps track of or records events
14	**Reputed:**	generally considered
15	**deride:**	ridicule, make fun of
18	**Wireless:**	a radio
21	**hearthstone:**	the area in front of the fireplace
26	**miry:**	muddy, dirty
31	**Loyal:**	Loyalists, owing allegiance to the sovereign
33	**flailing:**	swinging wildly
33	**blackthorn:**	a stick made from the wood of the blackthorn shrub
45	**rune:**	early Germanic alphabet often believed to have magical significance
45	**chant:**	piece spoken in sing-song voice
45	**evil eye:**	a gaze believed to be able to cause harm
45	**averted:**	turned away
46	**Fomorian:**	in Irish mythology, a gruesome and disfigured race who inhabited Ireland. They lived in the sea and had Tory Island as their base.
47	**Gaunt:**	lean and exhausted looking

Explorations

BEFORE READING

1. Have you ever seen a dolmen? Describe what it looked like. Or have you visited any of Ireland's ancient heritage sites, such as Newgrange or Carrowmore? How did you feel when you were there? Did you feel closer to the past?

FIRST READING

2. Imagine that you are writing for a local newspaper. Choose one of the people described in stanzas 1–5 and write an obituary (death notice) for him/her. Give an honest account of what he/she was like and how he/she lived.

3. Which of the five people do you least like? Explain the reasons behind your choice, using quotations to support your views.

4. Does Montague tell us everything about 'the old people'? Why do you think that he chose to use only a few details in his descriptions?

5.

a Which of the following words would you use to sum up the old people's lifestyles: lonely, contented, isolated, harsh, peaceful? How do you feel about the way they lived?

b How do Montague's descriptions make us believe that 'the old people' were real people with real lives? You will find your work on part (a) and Question 4 helpful.

SECOND READING

6. What images does Montague use in the final stanza to convey ancient Ireland? Based on these images, how do you imagine ancient Ireland? What sort of people would have survived in such a world?

7.

a 'Ancient Ireland, indeed! I was reared by her bedside'.
What do you think Montague is saying here about the connection between his life in the present and Ireland's past?

b How does Montague's attitude to 'the old people' change in the final four lines of the poem? Is this change

John Montague

in his view of 'the old people' related to how he sees the connection between the past and the present?

8. Using your work for Questions 5 and 6, write a short piece for presentation to the class beginning with the sentence: 'Montague thinks that "the old people" are like dolmens because …'. After the class has listened to the pieces, you might like to arrive at an agreed explanation of the connection.

THIRD READING

9. Do you think Montague wrote this poem when he was a child or did he write it as an adult remembering back to his childhood? Refer to the poem to support your decision.

10. 'In Montague's poetry, we can always hear the voice of his four-year-old abandoned self asking the question, "Where do I belong?" '
Discuss with reference to at least three poems by Montague that you have studied.

11. 'With Montague, personal experience is inextricably interwoven with national politics and the truths of our human existence.'
Consider this statement, using quotations from the poems you have studied to support your view.

The Wild Dog Rose

1

I go to say goodbye to the *Cailleach,*
that terrible figure who haunted my childhood
but no longer harsh, a human being
merely, hurt by event.
         The cottage,   5
circled by trees, weathered to admonitory
shapes of desolation by the mountain winds,
straggles into view. The rank thistles
and leathery bracken of untilled fields
stretch behind with – a final outcrop –   10
the hooped figure by the roadside,
its retinue of dogs
            which give tongue
as I approach, with savage, whinging cries
so that she slowly turns, a moving nest   15
of shawls and rags, to view, to stare
the stranger down.
         And I feel again
that ancient awe, the terror of a child
before the great hooked nose, the cheeks
dewlapped with dirt, the staring blue   20

of the sunken eyes, the mottled claws
clutching a stick
                    but now hold
and return her gaze, to greet her,   25
as she greets me, in friendliness.
Memories have wrought reconciliation
between us, we talk in ease at last,
like old friends, lovers almost,
sharing secrets   30
                    of neighbours
she quarrelled with, who now lie
in Garvaghey graveyard, beyond all hatred;
of my family and hers, how she never married,
though a man came asking in her youth.   35
'You would be loath to leave your own'
she sighs, 'and go among strangers' –
his parish ten miles off.
                    For sixty years
since, she has lived alone, in one place.   40
Obscurely honoured by such confidences,
I idle by the summer roadside, listening,
while the monologue falters, continues,
rehearsing the small events of her life.
The only true madness is loneliness,   45
the monotonous voice in the skull
that never stops
                    because never heard.

        2
And there
where the dog rose shines in the hedge   50
she tells me a story so terrible
that I try to push it away,
my bones melting.
                    Late at night
a drunk came beating at her door   55
to break it in, the bolt snapping
from the soft wood, the thin mongrels
rushing to cut, but yelping as
he whirls with his farm boots
to crush their skulls.   60
                    In the darkness
they wrestle, two creatures crazed
with loneliness, the smell of the

John Montague

decaying cottage in his nostrils
like a drug, his body heavy on hers,   65
the tasteless trunk of a seventy-year-
old virgin, which he rummages while
she battles for life
                    bony fingers
reaching desperately to push   70
against his bull neck. 'I prayed
to the Blessed Virgin herself
for help and after a time
I broke his grip.'
                    He rolls   75
to the floor, snores asleep,
while she cowers until dawn
and the dogs' whimpering starts
him awake, to lurch back across
the wet bog.   80

              3
                    And still
the dog rose shines in the hedge.
Petals beaten wide by rain, it
sways slightly, at the tip of a
slender, tangled, arching branch   85
which, with her stick, she gathers
into us.
        'The wild rose
is the only rose without thorns,'
she says, holding a wet blossom   90
for a second, in a hand knotted
as the knob of her stick.
'Whenever I see it, I remember
the Holy Mother of God and
all she suffered.'   95
                    Briefly
the air is strong with the smell
of that weak flower, offering
its crumbling yellow cup
and pale bleeding lips   100
 fading to white
                    at the rim
of each bruised and heart-
shaped petal.

- -

Notes

1	*Cailleach:*	from the Celtic, originally meant 'the veiled one'. It has a number of interpretations, including an old woman, a hag (a Celtic teacher of wisdom) and a witch (someone who practises magic).
6	admonitory:	reproving, rebuking
12	retinue:	a group of attendants waiting on an important person
21	dewlapped:	a dewlap is a loose fold of skin hanging from an animal's throat
22	mottled:	marked with spots or patches
27	wrought:	beaten out, hammered into shape
36	loath:	reluctant
41	Obscurely:	not easily understood, vaguely
43	monologue:	a person speaking alone
77	cowers:	shrinks back or crouches in fear

Explorations

FIRST READING

1. Having read 'The Wild Dog Rose', read 'Like Dolmens Round My Childhood'. Are there any similarities that immediately strike you between the descriptions of the old people in 'Like Dolmens Round My Childhood' and the description of the old woman in section 1 of 'The Wild Dog Rose'?

2. Describe in your own words where the old woman lives. Can you suggest reasons why she continued living in such an environment, on her own, for over 60 years? Does

John Montague

her rejection of the marriage offer because she was 'loath to leave [her] own' tell you anything about her attitude to the wider world?

3.

a   'a final outcrop – | the hooped figure by the roadside'.
     What does Montague's use of the phrase 'a final outcrop' suggest to you about the old woman's appearance? Are there any other words or phrases in section 1 that help you to imagine how she looked?

b   Imagine that you pass by the old woman as she waits for Montague. Write a description of what you think of her.

4.   Do you, like the poet, find section 2 of the poem 'a story so terrible'? Why?

SECOND READING

5.

a   Montague wrote that 'Ireland has often been seen as feminine ... and her colonisation has aspects of rape – becoming even more complicated when colonial England became Protestant and Ireland remained Roman Catholic, attached to the medieval ethos of the Virgin Mary'. How does this statement affect your approach to the poem?

b   Examine the old woman's attitude to the Virgin Mary in section 2 and discuss what she feels when she thinks about Her.

6.

a   The wild dog rose is described in section 3. How does it compare to the surrounding vegetation that Montague described in lines 5–9 of section 1?

b   What do you think the word 'shines' conveys about the wild rose? Is it really a 'weak' flower or does it have an unexpected strength?

7.

a   Consider the image of the old woman gaining the strength to resist her attacker from her belief in the Virgin Mary and the image of the wild dog rose. What do you think these two images suggest about Montague's attitude to England's colonisation of Ireland?

b   Do you feel that the poem ends on a positive or a negative tone?

THIRD READING

8.   'The only true madness is loneliness'. Discuss Montague's depiction of loneliness and the effects it has on those who endure it in 'Like Dolmens Round My Childhood' and 'The Wild Dog Rose'.

9.   Write an article for a literary magazine entitled 'Women in John Montague's Poetry'. Use references from relevant poems by John Montague on your course.

10. 'a human being | merely, hurt by event.'
     Consider these lines with reference to three of Montague's poems.

A Welcoming Party

Wie war das möglich?

That final newsreel of the war:
A welcoming party of almost shades
Met us at the cinema door
Clicking what remained of their heels.   5

From nests of bodies like hatching eggs
Flickered insectlike hands and legs
And rose an ululation, terrible, shy;
Children conjugating the verb 'to die'.

One clamoured mutely of love   10
From a mouth like a burnt glove;
Others upheld hands bleak as begging bowls
Claiming the small change of our souls.

Some smiled at us as protectors.
Can those bones live?   15
Our parochial brand of innocence
Was all we had to give.

To be always at the periphery of incident
Gave my childhood its Irish dimension; drama of unevent:
Yet doves of mercy, as doves of air,   20
Can falter here as anywhere.

That long dead Sunday in Armagh
I learnt one meaning of total war
And went home to my Christian school
To belt a football through the air.   25

Notes

	Wie war das möglich?:	How was it possible?
1	**newsreel:**	a short film of news items
2	**shades:**	ghosts
7	**ululation:**	wailing

8	**conjugating:**	giving different forms of a verb
9	**clamoured:**	shouted loudly
9	**mutely:**	silently
15	**parochial:**	local, narrow
17	**periphery:**	outer region

Explorations

BEFORE READING

1. How do you feel when you see images of war on television news programmes? Do you think that some images should be censored or should all images be shown? Can viewers become accustomed to images of war, so that what they once considered shocking becomes ordinary? Does showing these pictures actually have any effect?

FIRST READING

2. Can you suggest why Montague begins this poem with a question in German? Do you think it makes a good opening for the poem? Why?

3. How old do you think the poet and his friends were when this incident occurred? From your reading of the first stanza, describe how you imagine the boys acted as they watched these images in the cinema.

4. How does Montague convey the horror of the scenes in the newsreel in stanzas 2–3? Choose two images that you find especially effective and explain why you chose them.

5. 'Claiming the small change of our souls.'
Does this line suggest a response in terms of money or emotions? What do you think the 'almost shades' were 'begging' for?

6.

a What does the boys' question, 'Can those bones live?', indicate about their reaction to what they were seeing? When Montague returned to his school, he played football. Why do you think he did this?

b Using your work on Questions 2–5, write the conversation that you imagine Montague and his friends had after they left the cinema and were on their way back to school.

SECOND READING

7.

a 'To be always at the periphery of incident | Gave my childhood its Irish dimension; drama of unevent'. What reason does Montague give in these lines for the boys' limited reaction to the newsreel? In your opinion, has Ireland become more involved with world affairs since Montague was young, during the 1940s? Do you think that young people nowadays would have a different response to a similar newsreel?

b Write a speech for presentation to the class for or against the motion: 'The Ireland that John Montague describes is dead and gone.'

8. 'Yet doves of mercy, as doves of air, |
   Can falter here as anywhere.'
   Try to explain these lines in your own
   words. What might the 'doves of
   mercy' be? How are they connected
   to the boys? Does the fact that the
   'doves of mercy' 'falter' have anything
   to do with the boys playing football in
   the final line of the poem?

THIRD READING

9. 'For Montague, the experiences of
   childhood have resonances in the
   world of the adult.'
   Discuss with reference to at least
   three poems by Montague that you
   have studied.

10. 'I learnt one meaning'.
    Montague sees poetry as the learning
    and acceptance of meaning, no
    matter how difficult that meaning
    may be. Consider how this concept
    informs Montague's work, supporting
    your argument by quotations from
    the Montague poems on your course.

11. 'John Montague's poetry acts like a
    prism, revealing the layers of universal
    truths contained in the individual's
    experience of ordinary life.'
    Discuss, with reference to the poems
    that you have studied.

Sylvia Plath

(1932–63)

Prescribed for Higher Level exams in 2015, 2016 and 2017

Sylvia Plath was born in Boston, Massachusetts, on 27 October 1932 to Aurelia Schober Plath and Otto Plath, professor of biology and German at Boston University. In 1940 Otto died after a long illness, a tragedy that haunted Sylvia throughout her life. From a young age, Sylvia wanted above all else to be a writer. Already writing at the age of five, she had her first poem published in the children's section of the *Boston Herald* at the age of eight. She was a brilliant high school student, consistently earning A grades, and also led a busy social life. She had a number of stories and poems published – and also got many rejection slips; this pattern recurred throughout her writing life. In 1950 she entered the prestigious women's university, Smith College, Massachusetts.

In 1952 Plath was selected to work as one of 20 'guest editors' with *Mademoiselle* magazine in New York City. On her return to Wellesley she suffered a serious bout of depression, for which she was given electric shock treatment. However, this seems to have deepened her depression and she attempted suicide in August, leading to a four-month spell in a psychiatric hospital. She resumed her studies in Smith College in January 1953, graduating with honours in 1955, and winning a Fulbright scholarship to study in Cambridge, England. There she met Ted Hughes, a young English poet, whom she married in June 1956.

Sylvia and Ted worked and wrote in the US for two years and returned to London in December 1959. 'Black Rook in Rainy Weather' and 'The Times Are Tidy' date from this period. Her first book, *The Colossus and Other Poems*, was published in February 1960 but received disappointing reviews. April 1960 saw the birth of their daughter, Frieda. The following year they moved to Devon, where their son, Nicholas, was born in January 1962. Throughout this time, Sylvia was writing poetry (including 'Morning Song', 'Finisterre', 'Mirror', 'Pheasant' and 'Elm'), some of which was published in magazines in Britain and the US. Her semi-autobiographical novel, *The Bell Jar*, was published in 1963.

Shortly after Nicholas's birth, Ted and Sylvia separated. She remained in Devon, caring for her children and writing despite poor health and recurring depression. She completed most of the poems that made up her second book, *Ariel* (published posthumously), among them 'Poppies in July' and 'The Arrival of the Bee Box'. In mid-December 1962, she moved to London with her children. The poems she wrote at this time include 'Child', written on 28 January 1963. However, unable to cope with the many difficulties facing her, she took her own life on 11 February 1963. Since her death her writing has received wide acclaim, including the prestigious Pulitzer Prize, an award rarely bestowed posthumously.

Black Rook in Rainy Weather

On the stiff twig up there
Hunches a wet black rook
Arranging and rearranging its feathers in the rain.
I do not expect a miracle
Or an accident   5

To set the sight on fire
In my eye, nor seek
Any more in the desultory weather some design,
But let spotted leaves fall as they fall,
Without ceremony, or portent.   10

Although, I admit, I desire,
Occasionally, some backtalk
From the mute sky, I can't honestly complain:
A certain minor light may still
Lean incandescent   15

Out of kitchen table or chair
As if a celestial burning took
Possession of the most obtuse objects now and then –
Thus hallowing an interval
Otherwise inconsequent   20

By bestowing largesse, honor,
One might say love. At any rate, I now walk
Wary (for it could happen
Even in this dull, ruinous landscape); skeptical,
Yet politic; ignorant   25

Sylvia Plath

Of whatever angel may choose to flare
Suddenly at my elbow. I only know that a rook
Ordering its black feathers can so shine
As to seize my senses, haul
My eyelids up, and grant   30

A brief respite from fear
Of total neutrality. With luck,
Trekking stubborn through this season
Of fatigue, I shall
Patch together a content   35

Of sorts. Miracles occur,
If you care to call those spasmodic
Tricks of radiance miracles. The wait's begun again,
The long wait for the angel,
For that rare, random descent.   40

Notes

2	**rook:**	crow
8	**desultory:**	without method, disjointed
10	**portent:**	omen of some possibly calamitous event
15	**incandescent:**	glowing, brilliant
19	**hallowing:**	making sacred
21	**largesse:**	a generously given present
25	**politic:**	prudent
31	**respite:**	brief period of relief

Explorations

1. What picture does the title create for you? Does it suggest a particular mood?

FIRST READING

2. The poem is set against a very definite landscape: read the poem and describe the scene as accurately as you can. Build your picture from the poet's words and phrases.

3. What does the narrator seem to be doing in this poem? What thoughts does this lead to?

4. Describe the atmosphere the poem creates for you. What details are most important in setting this atmosphere?

SECOND READING

5. There is an abrupt change between lines 3 and 4. What is it?

6. The narrator claims that 'I do not expect ... nor seek' (lines 4–7). What does she neither expect nor seek?

7. What does she 'admit' to desiring? How does she convey the idea that it may not be possible to get what she desires?

8. Can you find other places in the poem where she makes a statement and then qualifies it – 'neutralises' it? What do such statements tell us about the narrator's frame of mind?

9. The 'minor light' of line 14 'may' have an extraordinary effect: read lines 14–22 carefully and explain this effect in your own words.

10. Can you explain how the 'rook | Ordering its black feathers can .... grant | A brief respite' to the speaker? A brief respite from what?

11. In the final lines, the poet is waiting for the 'rare, random descent' of the angel. What might the angel bring? What examples of this has she already given?

12. The angel's 'rare, random descent' is a metaphor: what do you think it represents? Look at references to other heavenly phenomena before answering.

THIRD READING

13. Comment on the effect of the repetition of the sound 'rain' in line 3.

14. Look through the poem again and pick out words connected with darkness and light. Compare the images or words used. Can you find any pattern?

15. The narrator does not 'seek ... design' in things around her. How does the language reflect that lack of design, the accidental nature of what happens? A good starting point might be to identify the words associated with time or chance.

16. There is a mixture of the everyday/ earthly and the extraordinary/ miraculous here. How is this effect achieved? You might find it helpful to contrast concrete descriptions with references to the sacred.

FOURTH READING

17. Examine the rhyme scheme. What pattern do you find? What is the effect of this careful sound pattern?

Sylvia Plath

18. Write a note on the style of the poem, looking at tone, language, imagery and structure.

19. Throughout her life, Plath was preoccupied with the conflict between her ambitions to be a poet and the expectations of a society that defined women as homemakers. Reread this poem with this in mind. Would you agree that this could be one theme of the poem? Are there other possibilities? Write about what you consider to be the main themes of this poem.

The Times Are Tidy

Unlucky the hero born
In this province of the stuck record
Where the most watchful cooks go jobless
And the mayor's rôtisserie turns
Round of its own accord.   5

There's no career in the venture
Of riding against the lizard,
Himself withered these latter-days
To leaf-size from lack of action:
History's beaten the hazard.   10

The last crone got burnt up
More than eight decades back
With the love-hot herb, the talking cat,
But the children are better for it,
The cow milks cream an inch thick.   15

Notes

4	rôtisserie:	a rotating spit, traditionally used to roast whole animals. Often a communal service used by peasants who would not own an oven or a spit.
11	crone:	witch

Explorations

1. Think back to folk tales or legends you have read or heard involving knights in armour, witches and monsters. What can you remember about their world or the adventures described?

2. Jot down whatever comes into your mind when you hear the word 'tidy'.

3. The poem puts two eras side by side. What can you learn from the poem about each of them?

4. Which era sounds more appealing to you? Why? Which does the author seem to favour? Refer to the poem to support your impression.

5. Try to mentally recapture the effect of listening to a stuck record. What do you think the poet is telling you about 'this province' when she uses this image? Do you think this links in any way with 'tidy'?

6. The poem was written about a particular phase in American political life. In light of this, suggest what the 'mayor's rôtisserie' might represent. Who might the 'cooks' be?

7. We are told that the jobless cooks are the 'most watchful': why then are they jobless? By choice? Because they have been sacked?

8. What mythical creature does the lizard resemble? Think of medieval knights and the creatures they did battle with. What is there in this stanza to show that the poet intends this connection to be made?

9. In what way has 'History' 'beaten the hazard'?

10. What association exists between the crone and the 'love-hot herb', the 'talking cat' and the 'cream an inch thick'?

11. What do the crone, the hero and the lizard have in common? How does their absence affect the 'times'?

12. Most of the poem focuses on what this age has lost: the last two lines suggest a gain. What is this? Do you think the poet is being serious here or is she being ironic? Explain your answer.

13. Two eras are contrasted in the poem. How do they differ? Be precise – refer to the text for each point you make.

14. Choose the image(s) you consider to be most effective. Explain your choice.

15. Keeping in mind the title, the images used and the comparisons made, write a note on the tone of the poem.

16. 'This poem is an ironic commentary on an era of smug, self-satisfied complacency in American life.' Discuss this statement, referring to imagery, language and tone.

Sylvia Plath

Love set you going like a fat gold watch.
The midwife slapped your footsoles, and your bald cry
Took its place among the elements.

Our voices echo, magnifying your arrival. New statue.
In a drafty museum, your nakedness   5
Shadows our safety. We stand round blankly as walls.

I'm no more your mother
Than the cloud that distills a mirror to reflect its own slow
Effacement at the wind's hand.

All night your moth-breath   10
Flickers among the flat pink roses. I wake to listen:
A far sea moves in my ear.

One cry, and I stumble from bed, cow-heavy and floral ✳ *Feminist*
In my Victorian nightgown.
Your mouth opens clean as a cat's. The window square   15

Whitens and swallows its dull stars. And now you try
Your handful of notes;
The clear vowels rise like balloons.

Explorations

BEFORE READING

1. Look at the title of this poem: jot down the ideas you associate with both words. What mood do they evoke?

FIRST READING

2. Stanzas 1–3 centre on the infant taking her place in the world. How do others respond to her? Which emotions come across most clearly?

3. How do you understand the image of the baby as a 'New statue' taking its place in a 'drafty museum'? How does nakedness 'shadow' the safety of the onlookers? (There are a number of possibilities.)

4. Explain in your own words what happens in stanzas 4–6. Do you find the description realistic?

SECOND READING

5. What emotions does the opening line suggest to you? Look at the first word, the image, the rhythm. Do you think it is an effective opening line? Why?

6. Identify the noises named in the poem. Name the source of each

sound. Who is listening to them? What impression do they create? How do they contribute to the texture of the poem?

THIRD READING

7. This poem is rich in vivid imagery and word-pictures. Identify these.

8. Say what each image or word-picture suggests about the baby, about the mother and about the world they inhabit. How is this suggested? Refer to the language, the juxtaposition of images and the associations implied.

9. Explain the cloud/mirror/wind image used in stanza 3. What does the comparison suggest about the narrator's feelings about motherhood?

FOURTH READING

10. 'Morning Song' is a tender evocation of a simple, daily event. Examine how the writer conveys the mood of tenderness while avoiding sentimentality.

11. Compare this poem with 'Child' in terms of theme, tone, language and imagery. Which of the two poems do you prefer? Why?

Finisterre

This was the land's end: the last fingers, knuckled and rheumatic,
Cramped on nothing. Black
Admonitory cliffs, and the sea exploding
With no bottom, or anything on the other side of it,
Whitened by the faces of the drowned.   5
Now it is only gloomy, a dump of rocks –
Leftover soldiers from old, messy wars.
The sea cannons into their ear, but they don't budge.
Other rocks hide their grudges under the water.

The cliffs are edged with trefoils, stars and bells   10
Such as fingers might embroider, close to death,
Almost too small for the mists to bother with.
The mists are part of the ancient paraphernalia –
Souls, rolled in the doom-noise of the sea.
They bruise the rocks out of existence, then resurrect them.   15
They go up without hope, like sighs.
I walk among them, and they stuff my mouth with cotton.
When they free me, I am beaded with tears.

Our Lady of the Shipwrecked is striding toward the horizon,
Her marble skirts blown back in two pink wings.   20
A marble sailor kneels at her foot distractedly, and at his foot

Sylvia Plath

283

A peasant woman in black
Is praying to the monument of the sailor praying.
Our Lady of the Shipwrecked is three times life size,
Her lips sweet with divinity.   25
She does not hear what the sailor or the peasant is saying –
She is in love with the beautiful formlessness of the sea.

Gull-colored laces flap in the sea drafts
Beside the postcard stalls.
The peasants anchor them with conches. One is told: 30
'These are the pretty trinkets the sea hides,
Little shells made up into necklaces and toy ladies.
They do not come from the Bay of the Dead down there,
But from another place, tropical and blue,
We have never been to.   35
These are our crêpes. Eat them before they blow cold.'

Notes

	Finisterre:	the westernmost tip of Brittany – literally 'land's end'
3	**Admonitory:**	giving a warning
10	**trefoils:**	three-leaved plants
13	**paraphernalia:**	belongings, bits and pieces, ornaments
14	**doom:**	judgement, punishment
30	**conches:**	spiral shells
36	**crêpes:**	light, lacy, crisp pancakes – a speciality of Brittany

Explorations

1. What kind of landscape/seascape do the place names 'Finisterre' and 'land's end' suggest? How do you visualise it – the colours, shapes, sounds, weather, etc.?

FIRST READING

Stanza 1

2. Read stanza 1. What overall picture do you form of the scene? What words or images do you find most striking? Is the personification effective?

3. How is language used to create the impression of an attack, a battle? Does this description of a headland create a familiar picture for you?

Stanza 2

4. What does stanza 2 describe? How does it connect with stanza 1? Notice how language and imagery are used to create links.

5. What qualities do you usually associate with mist? Which of these qualities does this mist share? What other qualities does the narrator attribute to it? Do these add anything new?

6. What is your impression of the atmosphere in this place? How is it created?

SECOND READING

Stanza 3

7. Describe in your own words the scene depicted in stanza 3. What

connection is there with the first two stanzas?

8. The perspective in this stanza has changed: the poet is showing us things from a different angle. How is this indicated?

9. This stanza tells a little story within the poem. Tell it in your own words.

Stanza 4

10. The stalls in stanza 4 are suggested through a few precise details. Look at the description – can you picture them?

11. This stanza differs remarkably from the preceding stanzas. In what way?

12. Identify the ideas/words/images that link stanza 4 with the earlier stanzas. Explain the connection.

13. We now learn that the bay is named the Bay of the Dead: does the name fit, in your opinion? Why do you think the poet did not name it until the end of the poem?

THIRD READING

14. Comment on the effect of the image in lines 1–2. How is this image developed in the rest of this stanza and in stanza 2?

15. Stanza 3 opens with a description of the monument. Contrast the 'I' of stanza 2 with Our Lady of the Shipwrecked. What is the impact of the contrast? What is the narrator's attitude to Our Lady?

16. Comment on the language used to describe the scene – the details given and the intentions or qualities attributed to each figure. Where does the narrator fit into this scene?

Sylvia Plath

What does she seem to be saying about prayer?

17. The author broadens the scope of the poem through the stall-keeper's comments, which reflect quite a different response to the bay. How? What is the effect of the wider canvas?

18. How does the final line strike you? Would you agree that there is a slightly ironic note here? What effect does this have on your reading of the poem?

FOURTH READING

[handwritten: mirror Symbolic of Plath's relationship with herself]

19. Write a note on the tone of the poem. Be aware of the gradual change in tone, reflected in the language and imagery. *[handwritten: and how she dealt with her failings]*

Note the differences between the narrator's attitude and that of the other figures in the poem.

20. Trace the progress of thought from the opening line to the end of the poem. Focus on how the author moves from the inner thoughts of the narrator to a more objective view. Note where the changes occur.

21. Plath once commented that 'a poem, by its own system of illusions, can set up a rich and apparently living world within its particular limits'. Write about 'Finisterre' in light of this comment, looking at her choice of words, images, sound effects and point of view.

Mirror

[handwritten: Speaker = mirror]   *[handwritten: Theme Identity + Image]*

I am silver and exact. I have no preconceptions.   *[handwritten: reflects the truth nothing else]*
Whatever I see I swallow immediately   *[handwritten: +unusual]*
Just as it is, unmisted by love or dislike. — *[handwritten: if it likes you or not – swallow image]*
I am not cruel, only truthful –
The eye of a little god, four-cornered.   *[handwritten: worship there image]*   *[handwritten: 5]*
Most of the time I meditate on the opposite wall.   *[handwritten: Mirror in love with opposite wall. emotion impact on what we see]*
It is pink, with speckles. I have looked at it so long   *[handwritten: Intense observe]*
I think it is a part of my heart. But it flickers.
Faces and darkness separate us over and over.   *[handwritten: In love]*

Now I am a lake. A woman bends over me,   *[handwritten: Searching for her Identity]*   *[handwritten: 10]*
Searching my reaches for what she really is.
Then she turns to those liars, the candles or the moon.   *[handwritten: Soft gentle light]*
I see her back, and reflect it faithfully.
She rewards me with tears and an agitation of hands.   *[handwritten: her form happy/sad]*
I am important to her. She comes and goes. —
Each morning it is her face that replaces the darkness.   *[handwritten: 15]*   *[handwritten: obsession wanting her youth trying to find herself]*
In me she has drowned a young girl, and in me an old woman
Rises toward her day after day, like a terrible fish.   *[handwritten: old age waiting for her]*

[handwritten: Simile]

Notes

11	reaches:	stretch of water, depths

Explorations

BEFORE READING

1. Think for a minute about a mirror. Write down quickly all the words, ideas and associations that come to mind.

FIRST READING

2. Listen to this poem a number of times. What is it saying?

3. Write a note on the form of the poem: number of stanzas, number of lines, etc.

4. Pick out all the 'I' statements. How many are there? What effect do they have?

5. Identify the qualities the mirror claims to possess. What overall impression is created by these attributes?

6. Notice the position of the words 'a little god': they are at the exact centre of stanza 1. Can you suggest why the poet placed them just there?

7. What impression is created by the description of 'the opposite wall'?

8. In stanza 2, the mirror states that it is now 'a lake'. What similarities are there between a lake and a mirror? What differences are there? How does this new image expand the mirror image?

9. Why do you think the narrator describes the candles and the moon as 'liars'?

10. What might cause the woman's tears and agitation? How does this point broaden the scope of the poem?

11. The mirror/lake contains three phases of the woman's life: what are these?

SECOND READING

12. The focus – the point of view – changes between stanzas 1 and 2. How has the centre of consciousness changed? What is the effect of this?

13. Write a note about what you think the 'terrible fish' might be.

14. 'I am important to her': this is a very strong statement. How could a mirror be important to the woman? What do you think the mirror may represent to the narrator? (Try to move beyond the most obvious points.)

THIRD READING

15. Compare the opening lines (1–3) with the final lines. Trace the progress of thought through the poem, showing how the narrator moves from the opening statement to the conclusion. Note the changes in tone that occur.

16. The poem concludes on a note of desperation. How is this prepared for in the poem as a whole?

17. Do you agree that the narrator has 'no preconceptions', as stated in line 1? What evidence can you find to support your opinion? Look especially at phrases like 'I think', 'those liars', etc.

18. While the poem is unrhymed, Plath uses a variety of sound effects. Identify some of these and say what effect they create.

FOURTH READING

19. Many writers and artists use the mirror as a symbol – for example, of

Sylvia Plath

the self, the alter ego, the 'dark side of the soul'. Reread the poem with this idea in mind. How does it colour your reading of the poem? Does it fit the poem?

20. It has been argued that in this poem, Plath is addressing the conflict between what a woman was expected to be (smooth, unruffled, reflecting the image the world wanted to see) and her true nature (struggling to be heard, seen for what it is: the 'terrible fish'). Reread the poem in light of this and write your response.

Pheasant

You said you would kill it this morning.
Do not kill it. It startles me still,
The jut of that odd, dark head, pacing

Through the uncut grass on the elm's hill.
It is something to own a pheasant,   5
Or just to be visited at all.

I am not mystical: it isn't
As if I thought it had a spirit.
It is simply in its element.

That gives it a kingliness, a right.   10
The print of its big foot last winter,
The tail-track, on the snow in our court –

The wonder of it, in that pallor,
Through crosshatch of sparrow and starling.
Is it its rareness, then? It is rare.   15

But a dozen would be worth having,
A hundred, on that hill – green and red,
Crossing and recrossing: a fine thing!

It is such a good shape, so vivid.
It's a little cornucopia.   20
It unclaps, brown as a leaf, and loud,

Settles in the elm, and is easy.
It was sunning in the narcissi.
I trespass stupidly. Let be, let be.

Notes

14	crosshatch:	criss-cross pattern
20	cornucopia:	a mythical horn, always full of flowers and fruit. A symbol of plenty.

Explorations

FIRST READING

1. The poem opens very abruptly: it plunges the reader right into the narrator's preoccupation. What is this? Why do you think she repeats the word 'kill'?

2. Lines 3–4 present a graphic picture. What scene is evoked?

3. The speaker's attitude towards the pheasant is clearly signaled in lines 5–6. What is it? Can you find any further echo of this feeling in the poem?

4. In stanzas 4–5 the poet pictures the pheasant. How does she underline its difference from the other birds that visit her yard?

5. Stanza 7 moves back to the present: the pheasant's 'clap' draws her attention. What was it doing before it flew up into the elm?

6. She loves the colour, the shape, the sound of the pheasant. Identify where each of these is praised.

SECOND READING

7. In stanza 3 the narrator explains why she feels so honoured by the visit of the pheasant. Identify what 'it is' and what 'it isn't' that touches her. Why do you think she tells us that she is 'not mystical'?

Sylvia Plath

8. In what sense is she trespassing? What does this word suggest about her attitude to the pheasant?

9. How do the final words link back to the opening statement and request? Do you feel the narrator has got her way at the end? Explain.

10. What is the tone/mood of the poem? Use the text to support your points, paying attention to the narrator's relationship with 'you'.

THIRD READING

11. Plath describes the pheasant as 'vivid'. The same word could apply to this poem: it is strong, vigorous and sinewy. Write about this quality of the poem. Look at language – verbs, nouns, adjectives – as well as imagery, structure, rhythm and rhyme.

After the breakdown of her marriage

Elm

For Ruth Fainlight

Tree talking   *women in great desporhon*   *she hit rock bottom*

I know the bottom, she says. I know it with my great tap root: *Comparison of tree with plath*
It is what you fear.
I do not fear it: I have been there.

Elm tree doesn't fear rock bottom
                sorrow
Is it the sea you hear in me,   *Tree is tormenting plath with noises it makes*
Its dissatisfactions?
Or the voice of nothing, that was your madness? — *make will of her*   5

Elm mocking   *emptiness - numb*
her Love is a shadow/ *worthless illusion*
How you lie and cry after it — *lying crying after her heartbreac*
Listen: these are its hooves: it has gone off, like a horse.   *Tone mocking to cruel*
Cruly tells that her love is gone like a horse
All night I shall gallop thus, impetuously, — *All night it makes the* 10
                noises
Till your head is a stone, your pillow a little turf, → *Listen to the noises until her*   ""
Echoing, echoing.

Elm talking about itself
Or shall I bring you the sound of poisons? *Elm tortured by toxic rain*
This is rain now, this big hush.   *its fruit has gone poisonous*
And this is the fruit of it: tin-white, like arsenic.   15

I have suffered the atrocity of sunsets.
Scorched to the root   *describn buring of the hot sunsets*
My red filaments burn and stand, a hand of wires.
Branches being burnt by the sun
Now I break up in pieces that fly about like clubs. *very strong winds*
A wind of such violence   *Breack him into pieces*   20
Will tolerate no bystanding: I must shriek.
Cry out in agony

New Explorations

The moon, also, is merciless: she would drag me
Cruelly, being barren.

[handwritten: moon burns the elm / brightness]
[handwritten: — moon jealous barren place]

Her radiance scathes me. Or perhaps I have caught her.

[handwritten: moon is jealous of lovely elm tree]

I let her go. I let her go

[handwritten: moon was caught by the elm tree 25 and left diminished]

Diminished and flat, as after radical surgery.

※ How your bad dreams possess and endow me.

[handwritten: Speaking to plath — her bad dreams possess the tree]

I am inhabited by a cry.

[handwritten: — Creature in the elm tree]

Nightly it flaps out
Looking, with its hooks, for something to love.   30

I am terrified by this dark thing

[handwritten: elm is terrified of the creature on its tree]

That sleeps in me;

[handwritten: — evil sleeps in it all day]
[handwritten: — Searching for something to love — plath]

All day I feel its soft, feathery turnings, its malignity.

Clouds pass and disperse.

[handwritten: Bird]
[handwritten: Cloud breaks up like when]

Are those the faces of love, those pale irretrievables?

[handwritten: relationship 35 does never be the same again]

Is it for such I agitate my heart?

[handwritten: × love is a shadow]
[handwritten: mocking the women for caring about love]

I am incapable of more knowledge.
What is this, this face
So murderous in its strangle of branches? –

Its snaky acids hiss.

[handwritten: Acid comes from its mouth]   40

It petrifies the will. These are the isolate, slow faults

[handwritten: negative feelings cannot deal with it]

That kill, that kill, that kill.

[handwritten: Women kills herself / she commit sui...]

Notes

15	arsenic:	lethal poison
18	filaments:	thread-like conductors of electrical current
24	scathe:	to hurt or injure, especially by scorching
35	irretrievables:	cannot be recovered or won back

Explorations

FIRST READING

1. Listen to the poem a number of times. What sounds are most striking? Which words stay in your mind? Jot down your impressions.

2. What attitude does 'I' seem to adopt towards 'you' in stanza 3?

3. Stanzas 5–8 introduce rain, sunset, wind and moon. How is each one presented? How do they affect 'I'?

Sylvia Plath

4. What change seems to occur in 'I' in stanzas 9–14? Can you identify at what point the change began?

5. Would you agree that the latter half of the poem powerfully conveys a nightmare world? Which images and phrases are most effective in building this impression?

SECOND READING

6. 'Elm' opens on a confident, objective note, as if the narrator is quite detached from 'you'. How is this achieved?

7. Trace the references to love in the poem. How does the narrator view love? Is it important to her?

8. There are several references to violence, both physical and mental. Select those you consider most powerful. What is the source of the violence?

9. Compare the force of love with the force of evil. Which comes across as the more powerful? Explain how this is achieved.

THIRD READING

10. Plath uses many rich and powerful images. The central image is the elm, the 'I' persona. Trace the elm's feelings and mood through the poem. What do you think the elm may symbolise to the poet? In answering this, reflect on the tone, the utter weariness, the feelings of anguish, the growing terror and the role 'you' plays in generating these feelings.

11. The moon is another important image in the poem. Reread the stanzas describing it (8, 9, 13). What qualities are attributed to it? What do you think

it symbolises? Can you explain the seeming contradictions?

FOURTH READING

12. The poet uses rich sound effects throughout the poem. Note where she uses rhyme, assonance, repetition, cacophony and soft sounds. How do these affect the reader/listener?

13. The poem opens with a calm, confident voice and a sense of control: 'I know ... | I do not fear'. It closes on a note of hysterical despair and total loss of control: 'It petrifies the will. These are the isolate, slow faults | That kill, that kill, that kill.' Trace the change through the poem. Describe how this transformation is achieved.

FIFTH READING

14. 'Plath infuses this poem with a strong sense of vulnerability pitted against destructive energy.'
What is your response to this statement? Use detailed reference to the poem in support of each point you make.

15. ' "Elm" is a powerful, urgent statement spoken by a narrator who has been abandoned by the person she loves.' Discuss this view of the poem.

16. 'This poem has the surreal quality of a nightmare in which the smallest objects seem fraught with hidden significance.' Discuss how this effect is achieved, basing each point you make on specific reference to the poem.

This poem is also prescribed for Ordinary Level exams in 2015, 2016 and 2017

Little poppies, little hell flames, — *sinister – hell*
Do you do no harm? — *rhetorical question*

You flicker. I cannot touch you. → *self harm* *Frightning image* *trying to feel something*
I put my hands among the flames. Nothing burns.

And it exhausts me to watch you *worn out be the pain – hurt* 5
Flickering like that, wrinkly and clear red, like the skin of a mouth.

A mouth just bloodied. *violent image Deep red lip stick*
Little bloody skirts! *She wants to punch her in the mouth* *Angry + rage*

(margin: Speaking to husband/affair words) *(to poppies)*

There are fumes that I cannot touch.
Where are your opiates, your nauseous capsules? — *rather be dead* 10

If I could bleed, or sleep! – *longs to escape numbness*
If my mouth could marry a hurt like that! *consume enough opium*

poppy
Or your liquors seep to me, in this glass capsule, — *trapped – "child's" ceiling* *wants to escape*
Dulling and stilling.

But colorless. Colorless. – *Death* *she longs for the end* 15

Sylvia Plath

293

Notes

10	opiates:	narcotics, drugs that induce sleep, dull feelings
10	nauseous:	causing vomiting or illness

Explorations

BEFORE READING

1. Imagine a poppy. What qualities do you associate with it? Think of colour, texture and shape.

FIRST READING

2. The poem opens with a question. What does it suggest to you?

3. Describe what the narrator is doing in this poem. What thoughts are triggered by her actions?

4. Identify the words associated with fire in lines 1–6. What is the narrator's feeling about this fire/these poppies? What does fire symbolise? Do you see any of these qualities reflected here?

5. Which qualities of the poppies might make the narrator think of a mouth?

6. What could 'bloody' a mouth? Do any of the other words suggest violence?

7. Lines 9–15 focus on another aspect of poppies. What is this?

8. Looking at the various descriptions of the poppies, try to explain the author's attitude to them.

SECOND READING

9. What feelings does the narrator convey in this poem? Say how each feeling is suggested, referring to specific words and images.

10. There is a strong contrast between lines 1–8 and lines 9–15. How is this effected? Look at how words, images and tone contribute to the contrast.

11. The narrator seems to imply an answer to the question posed in stanza 1. How does she answer it?

THIRD READING

12. While there is no end rhyme in this poem, the poet uses quite intricate sound effects, including repetition. Trace these, noting the effect they have.

13. Write a paragraph about the poet's use of colour in the poem, noting how she moves from the vividness of the early stanzas to the final repeated 'colorless'. What might the loss of colour say about the narrator's feelings?

14. The poem moves from the outside world to the inner world of the narrator. Chart this movement through the poem. How does she connect one to the other?

FOURTH READING

15. Do you think the intensity of the feeling conveyed is consistent with a simple description of poppies? What underlying emotion do you think might cause such intense anguish? Discuss this point, referring to the text in support of your arguments.

16. In both 'Poppies in July' and 'Elm', Plath takes a simple natural object and invests it with intense feelings, creating a metaphor for personal suffering – the inner struggle to come to terms with an overwhelming problem. Write a comparison of the two poems.

The Arrival of the Bee Box

This poem is also prescribed for Ordinary Level exams in 2015, 2016 and 2017

I ordered this, this clean wood box
Square as a chair and almost too heavy to lift.
I would say it was the coffin of a midget
Or a square baby
Were there not such a din in it.   5

Dangerous – link with coffin

The box is locked, it is dangerous.
I have to live with it overnight
And I can't keep away from it.
There are no windows, so I can't see what is in there.
There is only a little grid, no exit.   10

cannot shy away from the box

I put my eye to the grid.
It is dark, dark,
With the swarmy feeling of African hands
Minute and shrunk for export,
Black on black, angrily clambering.   15

African slaves being transported
Bee's – rage, angy, stuck in the box

How can I let them out?
It is the noise that appalls me most of all,
The unintelligible syllables.
It is like a Roman mob,
Small, taken one by one, but my god, together!   20

threatened by the swarm of bees

I lay my ear to furious Latin.
I am not a Caesar.
I have simply ordered a box of maniacs.
They can be sent back.
They can die, I need feed them nothing, I am the owner.   25

Description of sound
King - power

I wonder how hungry they are.
I wonder if they would forget me
If I just undid the locks and stood back and turned into a tree.
There is the laburnum, its blond colonnades,

Sylvia Plath

295

And the petticoats of the cherry.   30

They might ignore me immediately
In my moon suit and funeral veil.
I am no source of honey
So why should they turn on me?
Tomorrow I will be sweet God, I will set them free.   35

The box is only temporary.

Notes

22	**Caesar:**	Roman emperor
28	**turned into a tree:**	a reference to the Greek myth of Daphne, who was chased by Apollo. She pleaded with the gods to help her escape and they changed her into a tree.
32	**moon suit and funeral veil:**	protective clothing worn by beekeepers

Explorations

1. Stanza 1 gives the background to the arrival of the bee box and the narrator's reaction. Which feeling is most obvious? Have you ever felt this way about bees, wasps, etc.?

2. How does she seem to relate to the bees in stanzas 3–5?

3. Stanza 5 concludes with the statement 'They can die'. Do you actually believe she means this? How does she undermine her statement? Be precise.

4. How does she propose to escape the bees' wrath if she releases them?

5. She describes her clothing as a 'moon suit'. What ideas does this image suggest?

6. Comment on the contradiction between 'I am no source of honey' and 'I will be sweet God'. Note the play on words – what is the tone of these lines? How can she be 'sweet God' to the bees?

7. What happens in this poem? What part does the 'I' of the poem play in the event?

SECOND READING

8. The language used to describe the bee box is strong, suggesting something sinister and dangerous. Select the words or images that help to create this impression.

9. There is a contradiction between the image of a coffin and the intense life within the box. Which idea – death or life – is implied with more strength in the rest of the poem? Be precise.

10. In stanza 3 the writer creates a graphic metaphor for the bees and their sound. Identify these and note the common link between them. What do they tell us about the narrator?

11. In stanzas 4–5 the bees have become a metaphor for the narrator's words. Explain the image, trying to convey some of the feeling she captures. What relationship is suggested between the narrator and her words in these two stanzas?

12. The image of turning into a tree is associated with the Greek myth of the god Apollo and Daphne: she turned into a tree to escape his attentions. What does this association say about the narrator's attitude to the bees?

13. Write a detailed description of the changes in the narrator's attitude between stanza 1 and stanza 7.

14. The final line stands alone, separated from the rest of the poem, which is arranged in five-line stanzas. What does the line suggest? How does it colour the reader's response to the poem as a whole?

THIRD READING

15. Plath makes extensive use of internal rhyme, assonance and word play. One example is 'Square as a chair'. Here, 'chair' suggests the homely and ordinary, while 'square' implies honest, straightforward, exact. The rhyme almost echoes the box's shape – its regularity and squareness. Identify other examples of sound effects and word-play in the poem. Comment on their use.

Sylvia Plath

16. This poem moves between the real and familiar world and the symbolic. Can you identify what is real and ordinary, what happens on the surface?

17. On the symbolic level, what is suggested by the poem? Look at the metaphors used for the bee box, the bees and the 'I' persona. Be aware of the feelings conveyed throughout.

Deals with enadiges she had about motherhood

18. There is a touch of dark humour and self-mockery running through the poem. Where is this most obvious? What effect does it have on the reader?

19. What do you consider to be the central theme of the poem? In answering, refer to the writer's tone and the images used. Look also at your answers to Questions 16 and 17.

Child

2 weeks before she killed herself

This poem is also prescribed for Ordinary Level exams in 2015, 2016 and 2017

innocent *only ture thing there is*
Your clear eye is the one absolutely beautiful thing.
I want to fill it with color and ducks, — *Childrens toys*
The zoo of the new
new and amazing

grows in hard condition) Whose names you meditate – – *names you consider*
★April snowdrop, Indian pipe, – *tough*   5
Little

Innocenen of the child
Stalk without wrinkle,
Pool in which images → *retrene to eyes wants child to expriea*
Should be grand and classical *classcal images*

hoplemes *Shes depressed*
Not this troublous — *feels hes giving her child darbage*
Wringing of hands, this dark   10
Ceiling without a star.
No hope

★wants her child to be close to nature

Link with morning Star

Explorations

FIRST READING

1. Read this poem aloud and listen to its lyrical tone. What is your first impression of the speaker's feeling for her child? Try to imagine the speaker and child – what image do you see?

2. What pictures does she create for the child's 'eye'?

3. Which words here remind you of childlike things? What mood is usually associated with these?

4. How do you interpret the final stanza? Does it affect your reading of the rest of the poem?

5. What feelings does the narrator display toward the child in the opening stanzas?

6. Does the narrator's focus remain consistent throughout the poem? Where do you think the change occurs? Look at the verb tenses used when answering this.

7. How is the adult/narrator/mother contrasted with the child?

THIRD READING

8. What is the effect of line 1 on the reader? Examine how this is achieved.

9. Write a paragraph showing how this contrasts with the final lines. Look at language, imagery and tone.

10. The language of the poem is fresh, clear and simple. What is the effect of this?

11. Write a note about the impressions created by this poem for you.

Sylvia Plath

Eiléan Ní Chuilleanáin

(1942–)

Prescribed for Higher Level exams in 2015, 2016 and 2018

Eiléan Ní Chuilleanáin was born in Cork in 1942, the eldest of three children. Her father was Cormac Ó Cuilleanáin, a noted academic and professor of Irish at University College Cork. Her mother was Eilis Dillon, who wrote over 50 books, including detective stories, historical novels and children's stories. On leaving school, Eiléan Ní Chuilleanáin attended University College Cork and was awarded a BA in English and History in 1962, a Master's degree in 1964 and a Bachelor of Letters in 1968, following a period of study in Oxford.

She won her first prize for poetry in 1966, the Irish Times Award for Poetry. This was followed in 1973 by the Patrick Kavanagh Poetry Award for her first collection of poetry. In 1975, her commitment to the Irish literary scene led her to co-found the literary magazine *Cyphers* with Macdara Woods, Leland Bardwell and Pearse Hutchinson, which is still being published today. She has continued to win prizes for her poetry and in 2010 she won the International Griffin Poetry Prize.

Eiléan Ní Chuilleanáin has worked as an academic in Trinity College Dublin since 1966, when she was appointed to a Junior Lectureship in English, specialising in Renaissance literature, and she is now a Fellow Emeritus. In 1978 she married fellow poet Macdara Woods and they have a son Niall, who is a musician.

The Bend in the Road

This poem is also prescribed for Ordinary Level exams in 2015, 2016 and 2018

This is the place where the child
Felt sick in the car and they pulled over
And waited in the shadow of a house.
A tall tree like a cat's tail waited too.
They opened the windows and breathed   5
Easily, while nothing moved. Then he was better.

Over twelve years it has become the place
Where you were sick one day on the way to the lake.
You are taller now than us.
The tree is taller, the house is quite covered in   10
With green creeper, and the bend
In the road is as silent as ever it was on that day.

Piled high, wrapped lightly, like the one cumulus cloud
In a perfect sky, softly packed like the air,
Is all that went on in those years, the absences,   15
The faces never long absent from thought,
The bodies alive then and the airy space they took up
When we saw them wrapped and sealed by sickness
Guessing the piled weight of sleep
We knew they could not carry for long;   20
This is the place of their presence: in the tree, in the air.

Eiléan Ní Chuilleanáin

13	cumulus:	a type of cloud formation that appears as a mass of rounded clouds, like cotton wool, piled on top of a flat base. This formation is often associated with fine weather.

Explorations

1.

a Family memories play an important part in this poem. Does your family have a particular memory that they always recall when they meet up? If so, perhaps you might like to share it with the class.

b How do you feel about family memories – do you like hearing about them? Why or why not?

2. Choose one phrase or image from this poem that you particularly like and explain why you chose it.

3.

a Why do the people stop at the bend in the road?

b From your reading of lines 3–6, describe in your own words how you imagine the bend in the road.

4. 'Over twelve years it has become the place | Where you were sick one day on the way to the lake.'

a What made this place become somewhere to be remembered for the people? Refer to the lines quoted above in your answer.

b Based on your reading of lines 9–12, describe the changes that have taken place in this 12-year period.

5.

a 'The faces never long absent from thought'.
This line is taken from the final section of the poem (lines 13–21). In your own words, explain what changes are described in this section.

b What does this line tell you about the people's reaction to these changes?

6. 'Piled high, wrapped lightly, like the one cumulus cloud | In a perfect sky, softly packed like the air, | Is all that went on in those years'.

a Discuss how the poet appeals to the senses of sight and touch in these lines in order to create a vivid image of a cloud.

b Explain how these lines could be a comparative image describing the way in which memories of 'all that went on in those years' are stored by the people.

7.

a 'This is the place where the child | Felt sick in the car and they pulled over'.
Describe the tone (the emotion in the voice) of these lines.

b 'Where you were sick one day on the way to the lake. | You are taller now than us.'
How is the tone in these lines different to the one that you described in part (a)?

c   Can you suggest why this change in tone takes place? You might find it helpful to refer back to your work for Question 4.

THIRD READING

8. This poem begins with the real and concrete image of people travelling in a car and then goes on to explore the abstract idea of life. Can you explain how a family living their life together could be compared to them taking a car journey? Support your answer by reference to the poem.

9. 'This is the place of their presence: in the tree, in the air.'

a   What is it about the bend in the road that encourages the people to think about their memories of their loved ones who are dead?

b   What do you think Eiléan Ní Chuilleanáin wants to suggest to us about the importance to family life of having a shared family history made up of memories?

10. Imagine that you have been asked to suggest a poem for a new collection entitled *The Importance of Memories*. Write a piece explaining why you would choose this poem as part of the collection.

To Niall Woods and Xenya Ostrovskaia, married in Dublin on 9 September 2009 Track 6

This poem is also prescribed for Ordinary Level exams in 2015, 2016 and 2018

When you look out across the fields
And you both see the same star
Pitching its tent on the point of the steeple –
That is the time to set out on your journey,
With half a loaf and your mother's blessing.   5

Leave behind the places that you knew:
All that you leave behind you will find once more,
You will find it in the stories;
The sleeping beauty in her high tower
With her talking cat asleep   10
Solid beside her feet – you will see her again.

When the cat wakes up he will speak in Irish and Russian
And every night he will tell you a different tale
About the firebird that stole the golden apples,
Gone every morning out of the emperor's garden,   15
And about the King of Ireland's Son and the Enchanter's Daughter.

Eiléan Ní Chuilleanáin

The story the cat does not know is the Book of Ruth
And I have no time to tell you how she fared
When she went out at night and she was afraid,
In the beginning of the barley harvest,   20
Or how she trusted to strangers and stood by her word:

You will have to trust me, she lived happily ever after.

Notes

	Niall Woods:	this poem is addressed to Eiléan Ní Chuilleanáin's son, Niall Woods, on the occasion of his marriage
3	**Pitching:**	setting up
3	**steeple:**	a tall tower with a tapering roof, usually found on churches
9	**sleeping beauty:**	a beautiful princess is cursed and sleeps for many years. She is awakened by a kiss from a prince who has been on a long and difficult quest to reach her and they marry.
14	**the firebird:**	a bird with glowing feathers that steals golden apples from the tsar's garden in a Russian folktale. Prince Ivan, his son, sets out on a long and difficult quest to find the bird. He is successful and he also meets and marries a beautiful princess.
16	**the King of Ireland's Son:**	a prince of Ireland marries the Enchanter's Daughter, Fedelma, but she is stolen from him. The prince goes on a long and difficult quest and eventually finds her.
17	**the Book of Ruth:**	a story from the Old Testament about Ruth, who because of her loyalty to her dead husband's mother leaves her home country and goes to Bethlehem with her. There, Ruth helps to harvest the barley in the fields belonging to a man called Boaz who is impressed by her loyalty and courage. In time, Ruth and Boaz marry. Considered by some to be a type of folktale.

Explorations

BEFORE READING

1.

a   Folktales and fairytales have been told since ancient times not only in Ireland, but all over the world. Working in pairs, choose a folktale or a fairytale that you remember and write a short summary (four to seven sentences) outlining the beginning of the narrative or story (the main characters, the incident that triggers the rest of the narrative or story), the middle of the narrative (what happens next to the characters) and the end of the narrative or story (which of the characters are happy, sad, dead, etc.; what future they will have).

b   Share your summaries, discussing and noting down the features that the folktales and fairytales have in common.

2. What two words or phrases would you use to describe this poem? Support your two words by reference to the poem.

3. Pick out the phrases and images in lines 1–5 that remind you of a folktale or fairytale. Discuss the reasons for your selection.

4.

a The poet compares her son's marriage to a 'journey' in line 4. In your own words, explain how getting married could be seen as setting out on a journey or a quest.

b Can you suggest how the idea of a journey or a quest could be connected to folktales? You should find your work on Question 1 helpful.

SECOND READING

5.

a 'Leave behind the places that you knew'.
In this line, the poet says that the young couple's lives will change after their marriage. What sort of changes do you think she might be referring to in this line?

b How do you think the young couple might be feeling about having to make these changes?

6.

a 'All that you leave behind you will find once more, | You will find it in the stories'.
In your own words, explain how the poet is trying to reassure her son and daughter-in-law in the lines above about the changes they will have to make.

b Are you surprised by this advice that she gives to them? Why?

7. In lines 9–21, Ní Chuilleanáin refers to some folktales and fairytales. Using the brief summaries of the narratives of these folktales (see the Notes) and your work for Question 1, as a class discuss what messages you think the young couple might find in these folktales and fairytales about how to live their lives successfully as a married couple.

8.

a 'You will have to trust me, she lived happily ever after.'
Explain in your own words what the connection is between the idea of living 'happily ever after' and the messages that you found in the folktales and fairytales during your discussion for Question 7.

b Suggest how the idea of living 'happily ever after' can be connected to the poet as a mother attending the marriage of her son.

THIRD READING

9.

a Examine how the influence of the past on the present, through folktales and fairytales, is explored in this poem.

b Examine how the influence of the past on the present, in the form of memories that create a shared family history, is explored in 'The Bend in the Road'.

10. 'Folktales and Fairytales in Today's World' is the title of an article you have been asked to write for your school magazine. In your article, discuss your views on whether there is or is not a place for folktales and fairytales in today's world.

Eiléan Ní Chuilleanáin

The Second Voyage

Odysseus rested on his oar and saw
The ruffled foreheads of the waves
Crocodiling and mincing past: he rammed
The oar between their jaws and looked down
In the simmering sea where scribbles of weed defined   5
Uncertain depth, and the slim fishes progressed
In fatal formation, and thought
                     If there was a single
Streak of decency in these waves now, they'd be ridged
Pocked and dented with the battering they've had,   10
And we could name them as Adam named the beasts,
Saluting a new one with dismay, or a notorious one
With admiration; they'd notice us passing
And rejoice at our shipwreck, but these
Have less character than sheep and need more patience.   15

I know what I'll do he said;
I'll park my ship in the crook of a long pier
(And I'll take you with me he said to the oar)
I'll face the rising ground and walk away
From tidal waters, up riverbeds   20
Where herons parcel out the miles of stream,
Over gaps in the hills, through warm
Silent valleys, and when I meet a farmer
Bold enough to look me in the eye
With 'where are you off to with that long   25
Winnowing fan over your shoulder?'
There I will stand still
And I'll plant you for a gatepost or a hitching-post
And leave you as a tidemark. I can go back
And organise my house then.   30
                But the profound
Unfenced valleys of the ocean still held him;
He had only the oar to make them keep their distance;
The sea was still frying under the ship's side.

He considered the water-lilies, and thought about fountains   35
Spraying as wide as willows in empty squares,
The sugarstick of water clattering into the kettle,
The flat lakes bisecting the rushes. He remembered spiders
   and frogs

Housekeeping at the roadside in brown trickles floored
   with mud,
Horsetroughs, the black canal, pale swans at dark: **40**
His face grew damp with tears that tasted
Like his own sweat or the insults of the sea.

Notes

1	**Odysseus:**	the King of Ithaca and hero of Homer's 'The Odyssey'. Because he offends Poseidon, the god of the sea, Odysseus encounters many difficulties on his sea journey back home after the Trojan War. On one occasion, he goes down into the underworld and speaks to the spirit of the blind seer, Tiresias. Tiresias tells Odysseus that when he is once again King of Ithaca he must take an oar and walk away from Ithaca until he meets a man who knows nothing about the sea. This man will think that the oar is a winnowing fan used to separate grain from the husks. Odysseus should stick the oar into the ground at this place and make offerings to the god Poseidon. If he does this, Odysseus will live a long life as King of Ithaca. This quest has been referred to as Odysseus' 'Second Voyage'.
3	**Crocodiling:**	possibly as when used to describe the surface of paint cracking so that it looks like the scales of crocodile skin; possibly as when used to describe a line of paired children walking one after the other; possibly linking to 'foreheads' (line 2) to suggest the movement of a hunting crocodile through water with only the bumps of his eyes and upper head above water
3	**mincing:**	walking in an exaggerated and affected way in small short steps
10	**Pocked:**	pockmarked with spots from chickenpox or smallpox
12	**notorious:**	known for being bad
17	**crook:**	a curve, as at the top of a shepherd's crook
24	**Bold:**	brave, courageous
26	**Winnowing fan:**	a fan used to blow air to separate wheat grains from the outer dry husks
28	**hitching-post:**	a post to which animals are tied to stop them from wandering off
29	**tidemark:**	a mark left by the tide at its highest point
31	**profound:**	stretching to a great depth
37	**sugarstick:**	a striped candy stick
38	**bisecting:**	cutting into two equal parts

Eiléan Ní Chuilleanáin

Explorations

1. This is a poem that is filled with vivid images that appeal to the reader's senses. Choose two images from the poem that you find particularly striking and explain the reasons for your choices.

2. What do Odysseus' actions in lines 1–6 suggest to you about his attitude to the sea? Refer to the poem in your answer.

3. Explain in your own word show lines 8–15 convey that Odysseus wants to gain power over the waves and the sea and also that Odysseus feels contempt for the waves. Support your answers by reference to the poem.

SECOND READING

4. Both Odysseus and the sea are established as the two key characters in this poem. What qualities of Odysseus' personality are conveyed in lines 1–15? What qualities of the sea are conveyed in lines 1–15? Support your answers by reference to the poem.

5.

a Based on your work for Questions 2–4, can you suggest why Odysseus decides that his second voyage will be on land?

b How is his attitude to the land, described in lines 16–29, different to his attitude to the sea? Refer to the poem in your answers.

6. 'But the profound | Unfenced valleys of the ocean still held him; He had only the oar to make them keep their distance'.

a What do these lines tell you about the true state of the balance of power between Odysseus and the sea?

b What phrases or images in these lines convey Odysseus' lack of power to you?

7. How do the images that Odysseus recalls in lines 35–40 suggest that he believes that water is more easily controlled on land?

THIRD READING

8. 'His face grew damp with tears that tasted | Like his own sweat or the insults of the sea.' Examine the different ways in which the final two lines of this poem can be interpreted. Do you find these lines a satisfactory conclusion to the poem? Why?

9. Discuss how Eiléan Ní Chuilleanáin uses changes in the focus of this poem to increase the effect that it has on the reader. Support your answers by reference to the poem.

10. 'Eiléan Ní Chuilleanáin's poetry reminds us that the past, in the forms of folktales, fairytales and myths, can still have an influence on our lives in the present.'
Write your response to this statement, supporting your answer with suitable reference to the poems 'To Niall Woods and Xenya Ostrovskaia, married in Dublin on 9 September 2009' and 'The Second Voyage'.

This poem is also prescribed for Ordinary Level exams in 2015, 2016 and 2018

He fell in love with the butcher's daughter
When he saw her passing by in her white trousers
Dangling a knife on a ring at her belt.
He stared at the dark shining drops on the paving-stones.

One day he followed her   5
Down the slanting lane at the back of the shambles.
A door stood half-open
And the stairs were brushed and clean,
Her shoes paired on the bottom step,
Each tread marked with the red crescent   10
Her bare heels left, fading to faintest at the top.

Notes

6	**shambles:**	a 16th-century English word for a slaughterhouse where animals are killed for food
10	**tread:**	the flat, horizontal part of a step
10	**crescent:**	a curved shape like that of a new moon

Explorations

BEFORE READING

1. Many of our television series come from the US, where often a series will be cancelled if it is not successful before it reaches the end of its narratives, or stories.

a Have you ever watched a series that was cancelled and, as a result, the stories were left unfinished? How did you feel about this situation?

b Which sort of narrative do you prefer when you are watching television or a film or reading a book – a narrative that has an ending where there are no mysteries or puzzles left or an ending that leaves some mysteries or puzzles unsolved?

c Do you think that unsolved mysteries and puzzles are part of our experience of living life in the real world? Why?

FIRST READING

2. How do you feel about the way in which this poem finishes in line 11? Explain why you feel this way.

3.

a Describe how you imagine 'the butcher's daughter' based on your reading of lines 1–3.

Eiléan Ní Chuilleanáin

b   What would your reaction be if you saw a woman like this passing you by in the street? Why would you react like this?

4.   'He fell in love with the butcher's daughter', 'One day he followed her'. What impression do these lines give you of the man in this poem? Are you surprised by the way he behaves? Why?

SECOND READING

5.

a   In your own words, describe what the man sees when he looks inside the half-open door in lines 7–11.

b   How would you feel if you saw this? Why?

6.

a   Explain the connection you think the poet is suggesting that we could make between the girl, who is a 'butcher's daughter', her 'knife' in line 3, the 'dark shining drops' in line 4 and the 'red crescent' in line 10.

b   Can you think of any other ways in which this connection might be explained?

7.   In this poem, there are objects, ways of behaving and incidents that are familiar and understandable, but also objects, ways of behaving and incidents that are mysteriously puzzling.

a   Working in pairs, make a list of the objects, ways of behaving and incidents that you think are familiar and understandable and a second list of the objects, ways of behaving and incidents that you think are mysterious and puzzling.

b   As a class, share your lists and discuss what you think the poet is trying to suggest about life by featuring this mixture in this poem.

THIRD READING

8.   From the phrases below, choose one which, in your opinion, best describes this poem:

•   It is a frightening poem.

•   It is an annoying poem.

•   It is a thought-provoking poem.

     Explain the reasons for your choice with reference to the poem.

9.   In her poetry, Eiléan Ní Chuilleanáin often uses real, concrete images to represent abstract human emotions or qualities. Explain how the concrete images of passing through a doorway, or over a threshold, and climbing up a flight of stairs are used in this poem to suggest the abstract process of change, or transition, from one state to another in a person.

10. 'The traditional roles for men and women are no longer relevant in the Irish society of today.'
     Write out the speech that you would make for or against this proposition. As a class you might like to present your speeches and discuss the various views expressed regarding this topic.

One hare, absorbed, sitting still,
Right in the grassy middle of the track,
I met when I fled up into the hills, that time
My father was dying in a hospital –
I see her suddenly again, borne back   5
By the morning paper's prize photograph:
Two greyhounds tumbling over, absurdly gross,
While the hare shoots off to the left, her bright eye
Full not only of speed and fear
But surely in the moment a glad power,   10

Like my father's, running from a lorry-load of soldiers
In nineteen twenty-one, nineteen years old, never
Such gladness, he said, cornering in the narrow road
Between high hedges, in summer dusk.
                        The hare   15
Like him should never have been coursed,
But, clever, she gets off; another day
She'll fool the stupid dogs, double back
On her own scent, downhill, and choose her time
To spring away out of the frame, all while   20
The pack is labouring up.
                     The lorry was growling
And he was clever, he saw a house
And risked an open kitchen door. The soldiers
Found six people in a country kitchen, one   25
Drying his face, dazed-looking, the towel
Half covering his face. The lorry left,
The people let him sleep there, he came out
Into a blissful dawn. Should he have chanced that door?
If the sheltering house had been burned down, what good   30
Could all his bright running have done
For those that harboured him?
                    And I should not
Have run away, but I went back to the city
Next morning, washed in brown bog water, and   35
I thought about the hare, in her hour of ease.

Eiléan Ní Chuilleanáin

Notes

	Killer Instinct:	an instinctive tendency to kill or be ruthless
7	absurdly:	ridiculously
7	gross:	disgusting
16	coursed:	hunted
32	harboured:	sheltered

Explorations

BEFORE READING

1.

a   As a class, agree on your own definition of the term 'killer instinct' and note it down.

b   With your agreed definition in mind, discuss the answer to the following question: Who do you think has the most power: those having the killer instinct or those 'lacking the killer instinct'? If possible, see if you can agree as a class on who has the most power. If not, note down the numbers for the two options.

FIRST READING

2.

a   The poem opens with a description, in lines 1–4, of a memory from Ní Chuilleanáin's past concerning the time when her father was dying in 1970. In your own words, explain what she recalls in this narrative fragment. Your answer should make close reference to the text.

b   How is the hare's state different to the poet's state in these lines?

3.

a   According to lines 5–10, the poet, in the present, saw a photograph of another hare in the newspaper and this triggered her 1970 memory. How is the hare in the photograph different to the one in 1970?

b   Explain how the idea of death and the idea of running away on a quest for escape link the newspaper photograph in the present to the poet's memory set in 1970. Refer to the text in your answer.

4.

a   In lines 11–14, we are presented with another memory from the past, set in 1921, as the poet remembers her father telling her about an incident from his youth. Summarise in one sentence the incident described in this narrative fragment.

b   Can you suggest what two ideas connect this memory to the present in lines 5–10 and to the memory set in 1970, in lines 1–4? Support your answer by reference to the text.

SECOND READING

5.

a   'The hare | Like him should never have been coursed'.
What impression do you get from these lines of the poet's attitude to

those who were hunted (her father and the hare) and those who were hunting (the greyhounds and the soldiers)?

b   What ability do the hare and her father share, in lines 15–29, that enables them to escape from their hunters? Explain in your own words how this ability actually helped the hare and her father to escape.

c   How does this ability change the balance of power between the hunted and the hunters?

6.

a   'But, clever, she gets off; another day | She'll fool the stupid dogs'.
How does the poet feel about the photographed hare's escape in these lines?

b   As well as the fact that she was clever, can you suggest what basic instinct may have also helped the hare to escape?

7.

a   Along with his cleverness, what basic instinct do you think may have helped the poet's father to escape?

b   What decision did he make that enabled him to escape?

c   How does the poet feel about this decision? Your answer should make close reference to the text.

THIRD READING

8.

a   How is the poet's attitude towards what the hare did to escape different to her attitude towards what her father did to escape? Support the points you make by reference to the poem.

b   Do you think there are different codes of right behaviour for animals and humans? Why?

c   Which particular code of right behaviour for human beings do you think the poet feels her father broke by going into the house?

9.   In lines 33–5, the poet refers again to her memory, set in 1970, of running away from her dying father's bedside to 'the hills'.

a   Based on your reading of lines 1–4 and lines 33–5, explain how the world of nature helped her to return to his bedside in 1970.

b   She now recognises that she should have returned to her father because of certain codes of right behaviour. Can you suggest which codes in particular would have made her go back?

10.

a   Based on your work on this poem: do you feel the need to reconsider the view that you held in the discussion for Question 1? Why?

b   There are two groups in this poem: those having the killer instinct (the greyhounds and the soldiers) and those lacking the killer instinct (the hare and the poet's father). Which group would you join? Explain the reasons for your answer by reference to the poem.

Eiléan Ní Chuilleanáin

Deaths and Engines

 Track 9

We came down above the houses
In a stiff curve, and
At the edge of Paris airport
Saw an empty tunnel
– The back half of a plane, black   5
On the snow, nobody near it,
Tubular, burnt-out and frozen.

When we faced again
The snow-white runways in the dark
No sound came over   10
The loudspeakers, except the sighs
Of the lonely pilot.

The cold of metal wings is contagious:
Soon you will need wings of your own,
Cornered in the angle where   15
Time and life like a knife and fork
Cross, and the lifeline in your palm
Breaks, and the curve of an aeroplane's track
Meets the straight skyline.

The images of relief: 20
Hospital pyjamas, screens round a bed
A man with a bloody face
Sitting up in bed, conversing cheerfully
Through cut lips:
These will fail you some time.   25

You will find yourself alone
Accelerating down a blind
Alley, too late to stop
And know how light your death is;
You will be scattered like wreckage,   30
The pieces every one a different shape
Will spin and lodge in the hearts
Of all who love you.

Notes

7	**Tubular:**	shaped like a tube
13	**contagious:**	able to spread to others
23	**conversing:**	in conversation

Explorations

BEFORE READING

1.

a   The title of this poem is 'Deaths and Engines'. Working in pairs and without reading the poem, discuss the possible connections between deaths and engines that could be explored in this poem. Share your ideas with the class and write up bullet-point summaries of them on the board.

b   Based on this title and your ideas, do you think this will be a happy poem or a sad poem? Why?

FIRST READING

2.   Select an image or a phrase from the poem that you think is particularly effective in suggesting a feeling or a sensation and explain the reasons for your choice.

3.   From you reading of lines 1–12, what impression do you get of the effect that seeing the plane wreckage had on those who were landing in 'Paris airport'? Support your answer by referring to the poem.

4.

a   'Soon you will need wings of your own'.
Explain in your own words what the poet is referring to in this line.

b   Choose one of the images that the poet uses in lines 15–19. Write the image down and discuss how it refers to death.

5.

a   'The images of relief'.
How can the images in lines 21–4 be interpreted as 'images of relief'?

b   What do you think the poet is suggesting about these 'images of relief' in the line 'These will fail you some time'? Support your answers by reference to the poem.

SECOND READING

6.

a   What emotions do you think the poet wants her readers to feel when they read lines 26–8? Refer to the particular word or image that you think creates each of the emotions that you have suggested.

b   What emotions do you think she wants her readers to feel in lines 29–33? Again, refer to the particular word or image that you think creates each of the emotions that you have suggested.

7.   Do you think reading this poem would result in the reader developing a positive or a negative attitude towards death? Refer to the poem to support your viewpoint.

Eiléan Ní Chuilleanáin

8.

a Based on your work for Questions 1 and 7, do you think that 'Deaths and Engines' is a suitable title for the poem or can you suggest another title that you feel would be more suitable? You may like to select a phrase from the poem or to compose a new title.

b Whether you decide to keep Eiléan Ní Chuilleanáin's title or to suggest an alternative title, explain why you think your choice of title is appropriate to the poem.

9. In this poem, Ní Chuilleanáin clearly feels that memories of loved ones who are dead can have an important influence on those still living in the present. Discuss how recalling memories of loved ones who are dead affects those living in the present in 'The Bend in the Road' and 'On Lacking the Killer Instinct'.

10. Write a personal response to this poem. Your answer should make close reference to the text.

Fireman's Lift

I was standing beside you looking up
Through the big tree of the cupola
Where the church splits wide open to admit
Celestial choirs, the fall-out of brightness.

The Virgin was spiralling to heaven,   5
Hauled up in stages. Past mist and shining,
Teams of angelic arms were heaving,
Supporting, crowding her, and we stepped

Back, as the painter longed to
While his arm swept in the large strokes.   10
We saw the work entire, and how the light

Melted and faded bodies so that
Loose feet and elbows and staring eyes
Floated in the wide stone petticoat
Clear and free as weeds.   15

This is what love sees, that angle:
The crick in the branch loaded with fruit,
A jaw defining itself, a shoulder yoked,

The back making itself a roof
The legs a bridge, the hands   20
A crane and a cradle.

Their heads bowed over to reflect on her
Fair face and hair so like their own
As she passed through their hands. We saw them
Lifting her, the pillars of their arms   25

(Her face a capital leaning into an arch)
As the muscles clung and shifted
For a final purchase together
Under her weight as she came to the edge of the cloud.

Parma 1963–Dublin 1994

Eiléan Ní Chuilleanáin

Notes

	Fireman's Lift:	a particular way of lifting an incapable person
2	cupola:	a rounded dome that forms a roof
4	Celestial:	heavenly
5	The Virgin:	Correggio's fresco, in the cathedral of Parma, depicts the Christian belief that the Virgin, i.e. Mary, Christ's mother, was taken up into heaven when her life on earth was over. This is called the Annunciation.
14	petticoat:	an underskirt
17	crick:	a painful cramp in a muscle
26	capital:	the top part of a pillar
28	purchase:	a firm hold

Explorations

BEFORE READING

1.

a   Look at the photograph that accompanies this poem of Correggio's *Assumption of the Virgin* in Parma Cathedral. What three words would you use to describe this fresco? Take it in turns to write one of your words on the board.

b   Based on these words, do you find it surprising that this fresco is located in a cathedral? Why? Share and discuss your thoughts as a class.

FIRST READING

2.

a   In your work on Question 1, did you notice any of the images that Ní Chuilleanáin describes in lines 2–15 of this poem? If so, which ones?

b   Choose one image from the poem that you feel is an effective and vivid description of a part of the fresco that you can see in the photograph.

Explain the reasons for your choice.

3.   In lines 2–15, pick out the words or images that are drawn from a religious context and the words or images that are humorous. Are you surprised by this combination? Why?

SECOND READING

4.   What impression do you get of the process of lifting 'the Virgin' up into heaven from lines 2–15? Your answer should make close reference to the words and images in these lines that you feel convey this impression.

5.

a   In lines 22–25, what words and images does the poet use to convey the effort that the nurses had to put in when they were lifting her dying mother?

b   Using your work for Question 4 and part (a) of this question, discuss the similarities that the poet sees between the situation of 'the Virgin' and her mother's situation. Refer to the poem to support your answer.

6.

a   'This is what love sees, that angle'. What part does love play in the two lifting processes involving a person that are described in the poem?

b   Explain how each of the images in lines 17–21 effectively convey this process of lifting by appealing to the senses of sight and touch.

THIRD READING

7.

a   'as she came to the edge of the cloud'.
From your reading of this poem, what do you think 'the cloud' image represents for the poet's dying mother? Give reasons for your answer.

b   In your own words, explain how this 'cloud' can be seen as another example of Ní Chuilleanáin's use of the image of a threshold to suggest the process of changing from one state to another in a person.

8.   Ní Chuilleanáin has described this poem as a 'cheering-up poem'. Based on your work on this poem, do you agree or disagree with her description? Why? Your answer should make close reference to the text of the poem.

9.   Discuss how memories drawn from her shared family history help Ní Chuilleanáin to cope with her mother's death in 'Fireman's Lift' and her father's death in 'On Lacking the Killer Instinct' and 'Deaths and Engines'.

10.   Do you find 'Fireman's Lift' an easy or a difficult poem to understand? Why? Support your answer with suitable reference to the poem.

Translation   ⦿ Track 10

for the reburial of the Magdalenes

The soil frayed and sifted evens the score –
There are women here from every county,
Just as there were in the laundry.

White light blinded and bleached out
The high relief of a glance, where steam danced   5
Around stone drains and giggled and slipped across water.

Assist them now, ridges under the veil, shifting,
Searching for their parents, their names,
The edges of words grinding against nature,

As if, when water sank between the rotten teeth   10
Of soap, and every grasp seemed melted, one voice
Had begun, rising above the shuffle and hum

Eiléan Ní Chuilleanáin

319

Until every pocket in her skull blared with the note –
Allow us now to hear it, sharp as an infant's cry
While the grass takes root, while the steam rises: 15

      Washed clean of idiom · the baked crust
      Of words that made my temporary name ·
      A parasite that grew in me · that spell
      Lifted · I lie in earth sifted to dust ·
      Let the bunched keys I bore slacken and fall ·   20
      I rise and forget · a cloud over my time.

Notes

	Translation:	possibly as when used to describe changing words in one language into another language; possibly as when used to describe being moved from one place to another
	Magdalenes:	in 1993, the remains of the bodies of 155 women who had lived and worked in appalling conditions over the previous 100 years were found in unmarked graves during building work on the site of a Magdalene laundry in a convent in Dublin. As most of their names were unknown and with death certificates for only some of them, 154 of the bodies were cremated and reburied in a mass grave in Glasnevin Cemetery in Dublin. Eiléan Ní Chuilleanáin read this poem at the reburial ceremony.
1	**frayed:**	tattered; torn with ragged edges
5	**relief:**	possibly as when used to describe the ending of something unpleasant or stressful, such as pain or distress; possibly as in 'high relief', when used to describe a design that stands out from the surface and closely represents the object it depicts
16	**idiom:**	possibly as when used to describe a specialised vocabulary peculiar to a specific group of people, either in a particular occupation or institution, e.g. the Catholic Church; possibly as when used to describe a phrase with a meaning that is not literal because it does not come from the individual words but from understood usage of the phrase, e.g. 'fallen women' was often used to describe the Magdalene women, indicating that they had been judged to be in some way connected to 'sin'
18	**parasite:**	an organism that lives on or inside another and thrives at the expense of its host
20	**slacken:**	loosen

Explorations

BEFORE READING

1.

a   Before you read 'Translations', read the note given for the word 'Magdalenes' in the Notes. What is your reaction to this event?

b   How many in the class already knew about this event or about the Magdalene laundries or the women who worked in them? As a class, share and discuss what you know about the women who worked in the Magdalene laundries.

FIRST READING

2.

a   What impression of the women's working conditions do you get from reading this poem?

b   Choose one image that you feel is particularly effective in conveying these conditions. Explain your choice.

3.

a   Look at the photograph that accompanies this poem of a Magdalene Laundry. What similarities and differences are there between the photograph and the poem?

b   Which of the two has more of an impact on you? Why?

4.

a   'Searching for their parents, their names'.
Explain in your own words what this line suggests about the two changes that were made to the women's lives when they were committed to one of these institutions.

b   What effect do you think taking a girl away from her parents, and the rest of her family, would have on the place that she had in her community or society?

c   What effect would changing her name have on her sense of identity?

5.   'White light blinded and bleached out | The high relief of a glance'. A glance can be very expressive, communicating our thoughts and emotions to others. What impression do you get from the lines quoted above of the attitude to self-expression in the Magdalene laundries?

Eiléan Ní Chuilleanáin

6.

a   Sound and silence play an important part in this poem. What are the sounds heard in the laundry?

b   Given that this is a group of women working together, what sounds would you expect to hear in the laundry?

c   What does the absence of such sounds tell you about how the women were treated?

7.

a   In lines 11–14, the poet imagines one of the women working in the laundry screaming. Explain how the images in these lines suggest the psychological and emotional distress that this scream expresses.

b   Bearing in mind your work for Question 5, do you think any of the women would have actually screamed like this? Why?

c   Which do you find most disturbing, the scream or the silence? Why?

8.

a   'Assist them now', 'Allow us now to hear it'.
    What do these phrases suggest to you about how the poet expects those of us who live in Irish society in the present to react to the way in which the Magdalene women were treated in Irish society in the past?

b   Why do you think the poet feels that it is important for us to react in this way?

THIRD READING

9.   In lines 16–21, the poet creates a persona, one of the Magdalene women reburied in Glasnevin Cemetery, to express the thoughts and emotions of these women after this event.

a   Given the fact that these women were prevented from speaking for much of their lives, how does the poet convey that these words are spoken by someone who is not used to speaking? You might find it helpful to read these lines aloud.

b   Based on your work for Questions 5 and 6, can you suggest why Ní Chuilleanáin decided to end the poem in this way?

9.   'Washed clean of idiom · the baked crust | Of words that made my temporary name · | A parasite that grew in me.'

a   Explain in your own words how these lines could be interpreted as a reference to the Magdalene woman finally being freed from the name that she was given when she entered the laundry.

b   What does her use of the word 'parasite' suggest to you about how she felt about the name that she was given?

10.   '· that spell
    Lifted · I lie in earth sifted to dust ·
    Let the bunched keys I bore slacken
        and fall ·
    I rise and forget · a cloud over my
        time.'

a   Discuss how a sense of release could be suggested by three of the images in these lines.

b   Explain what you think these lines mean.

Kilcash

from the Irish, c. 1800

What will we do now for timber
With the last of the woods laid low –
No word of Kilcash nor its household,
Their bell is silenced now,
Where the lady lived with such honour,   5
No woman so heaped with praise,
Earls came across oceans to see her
And heard the sweet words of Mass.

It's the cause of my long affliction
To see your neat gates knocked down,   10
The long walks affording no shade now
And the avenue overgrown,
The fine house that kept out the weather,
Its people depressed and tamed;
And their names with the faithful departed,   15
The Bishop and Lady Iveagh!

The geese and the ducks' commotion,
The eagle's shout, are no more,
The roar of the bees gone silent,
Their wax and their honey store   20
Deserted. Now at evening
The musical birds are stilled
And the cuckoo is dumb in the treetops
That sang lullaby to the world.

Even the deer and the hunters   25
That follow the mountain way
Look down upon us with pity,
The house that was famed in its day;
The smooth wide lawn is all broken,
No shelter from wind and rain;   30
The paddock has turned to a dairy
Where the fine creatures grazed.

Mist hangs low on the branches
No sunlight can sweep aside,
Darkness falls among daylight   35
And the streams all run dry;
No hazel, no holly or berry,

Eiléan Ní Chuilleanáin

Bare naked rocks and cold;
The forest park is leafless
And all the game gone wild.   40

And now the worst of our troubles:
She has followed the prince of the Gaels –
He has borne off the gentle maiden,
Summoned to France and to Spain.
Her company laments her   45
That she fed with silver and gold:
One who never preyed on the people
But was the poor souls' friend.

My prayer to Mary and Jesus
She may come safe home to us here   50
To dancing and rejoicing
To fiddling and bonfire
That our ancestors' house will rise up,
Kilcash built up anew
And from now to the end of the story   55
May it never again be laid low.

Notes

2	**woods laid low:**	in the 18th and 19th centuries, many Irish people blamed the new 'English' landowners who took over from the accepted and integrated Anglo-Norman landowners for the loss of the Irish forests. Thus, the loss of the forests became a metaphor for the loss of the old Anglo-Norman way of life.
3	**Kilcash:**	now a ruined castle in South Tipperary, but until the end of the 18th century it was the main residence of a branch of the Butler family, one of the powerful Anglo-Norman dynasties
16	**Lady Iveagh:**	the original poem, written in Irish, lamented the death of Margaret Butler, Viscountess Iveagh, who died in 1744

Explorations

1. Look at the two photographs that accompany this poem. As a class, brainstorm ideas about the ways in which these two photographs could be connected. Write the points on the board as you go along and then note them down.

FIRST READING

2. In stanzas 1–2 (lines 1–16), the bard refers to two people who represent the two key social structures that used to provide his Anglo-Norman society with a sense of order.

   a Explain who these two people were and what social structures they represented in this society.

   b How do lines 1–2 signal that this poem is about a change in Irish society?

3. Although this poem seems to lament the death of Lady Iveagh, the widespread changes that are described by the bard in stanzas 2–5 (lines 9–40) indicate that he is lamenting the breakdown in order caused by the loss of the old Anglo-Norman world and society in Ireland. Explain how this disorder is conveyed in two images connected to (i) the Kilcash house and gardens in stanza 2 (lines 9–16) (ii) the world of nature in stanzas 3–4 (lines 17–32) and (iii) the weather in stanza 5 (lines 33–40).

4. How does the bard convey his longing for the return of the old Anglo-Norman way of life to Irish society in stanza 7 (lines 49–56)?

Your answer should make close reference to the images and phrases in stanza 7.

SECOND READING

5. 'What will we do now for timber'

   'It's the cause of my long affliction'

   'And now the worst of our troubles'

   'My prayer to Mary and Jesus'

   a What impression do you get of the bard's emotional and mental state from these lines?

   b Do you think that great changes in society can affect people in these ways? Why?

6.

   a What is an allegory? In your own words, explain how 'Kilcash' is an allegory for the great changes that took place in Irish society during the Celtic Tiger years.

   b What effect do you think Eiléan Ní Chuilleanáin wanted this poem to have on Irish people who were living at the time of the Celtic Tiger?

7.

   a Following your work on 'Kilcash', would you make any deletions or additions to the notes that the class made for Question 1? Why?

   b Explain how the two photographs that accompany this poem can be seen as representing the Irish society of the late 1700s to early 1800s and as the Irish society of the Celtic Tiger years.

Eiléan Ní Chuilleanáin

8. It is not surprising that Eiléan Ní Chuilleanáin uses allegory in this poem, as she has already used concrete images to express human emotions in many of her other poems. Choose three examples, from three different poems, of her use of concrete images to express human emotions and qualities that you find particularly effective. Explain the reasons for your choice.

9. Ní Chuilleanáin believes that the world of nature and the lives of human beings are closely connected. Discuss how this connection is portrayed in 'Kilcash' and in three of her other poems that you have studied. Support your answer with suitable reference to the poems.

10.

a   Look at the notes that you made about the two photographs accompanying this poem for Question 1. Were any of the brainstorm ideas similar to the ideas expressed in 'Kilcash'?

b   Write a short paragraph explaining how these two photographs relate to Eiléan Ní Chuilleanáin's poem 'Kilcash'.

Following

 Track 11

So she follows the trail of her father's coat through the fair
Shouldering past beasts packed solid as books,
And the dealing men nearly as slow to give way –
A block of a belly, a back like a mountain,
A shifting elbow like a plumber's bend –   5
When she catches a glimpse of a shirt-cuff, a handkerchief,
Then the hard brim of his hat, skimming along,

Until she is tracing light footsteps
Across the shivering bog by starlight,
The dead corpse risen from the wakehouse   10
Gliding before her in a white habit.
The ground is forested with gesturing trunks,
Hands of women dragging needles,
Half-choked heads in the water of cuttings,
Mouths that roar like the noise of the fair day.   15

She comes to where he is seated
With whiskey poured out in two glasses
In a library where the light is clean,
His clothes all finely laundered,
Ironed facings and linings.   20
The smooth foxed leaf has been hidden

In a forest of fine shufflings,
The square of white linen
That held three drops
Of her heart's blood is shelved   25
Between the gatherings
That go to make a book –
The crushed flowers among the pages crack
The spine open, push the bindings apart.

Notes

10	wakehouse:	the house where the dead body was being kept for the wake
12	gesturing:	making expressive movements
14	cuttings:	where parts of the bog have been cut away for use
21	foxed:	discoloured with brownish stains
29	spine:	the part of a book where the pages have been bound together

Explorations

BEFORE READING

1. Have you ever become separated
from your family or your friends
and found yourself on your own in
a crowd of strangers? How did it
happen? What did you feel? How did
your family or friends react when you
were reunited with them? As a class,
share your stories.

FIRST READING

2. Based on the experiences that you
shared before reading this poem, do
you think the poet's description of
the daughter being separated from
her father in lines 1–7 is effective
and realistic? Support your view by
reference to lines 1–7.

3.

a What emotions do you think the poet
wants to convey in the nightmarish
images in lines 8–15?

Eiléan Ní Chuilleanáin

b   Can you suggest how these emotions are connected to the daughter's experience of being left behind by her father in lines 1–7?

4.

a   How do the 'dealing men' in line 3 treat the daughter?

b   How does the father behave towards his daughter at the fair, in lines 1–7, and react when his daughter catches up with him again, as described in lines 16–18?

c   How might these incidents be interpreted as representing the types of roles assigned by society in the past to men and women?

SECOND READING

5.   There is very little information given in the poem about the father, but we do learn about his clothes. What impression do you get of the father from the description of his clothes? Support your points with suitable reference to the poem.

6.   In the final section of the poem, lines 16–29, we see the father in his library of books.

a   What do you think the father most enjoys doing: reading the books or organising them in an orderly way? Refer to the poem in your answer.

b   Using your work for Question 5, can you suggest how the father's attitude to his books can be connected to his attitude to his clothes?

7.   'The smooth foxed leaf has been hidden | In a forest of fine shufflings'. Explain how this images can be interpreted in two ways that both

suggest that the father represses his emotions. Refer to the lines quoted above in your answer.

8.   'The square of white linen
      That held three drops
      Of her heart's blood is shelved'

a   How does this image suggest that the daughter wanted to connect emotionally with her father?

b   How does this image suggest that the father was unable to connect emotionally with his daughter? Support your answers by reference to the lines quoted above.

THIRD READING

9.   'The crushed flowers among the pages crack | The spine open, push the bindings apart.'
      These lines act as an enigmatic ending to the poem because they can be interpreted in a number of ways.

a   Examine the different interpretations that could be applied to these lines.

b   Do you think this enigmatic ending reflects the reality of life? Why?

10.   Write a personal response to this poem, highlighting the impact it makes on you. Your answer should make close reference to the text.

Once beyond the gate of the strange stableyard, we dismount.
The donkey walks on, straight in at a wide door
And sticks his head in a manger.

The great staircase of the hall slouches back,
Sprawling between warm wings. It is for you.   5
As the steps wind and warp
Among the vaults, their thick ribs part; the doors
Of guardroom, chapel, storeroom
Swing wide and the breath of ovens
Flows out, the rage of brushwood,   10
The roots torn out and butchered.

It is for you, the dry fragrance of tea-chests
The tins shining in ranks, the ten-pound jars
Rich with shrivelled fruit. Where better to lie down
And sleep, along the labelled shelves,   15
With the key still in your pocket?

Notes

6	**warp:**	twist
7	**vaults:**	arched roofs
7	**ribs:**	long, curved, narrow strips of stonework that help to support the vaults

Explorations

FIRST READING

1. Choose one image from the poem that appealed to you. Explain your choice.

2.

a   Lines 1–3 form the narrative fragment of this poem. In your own words, describe what happens in these lines.

b   Can you clearly imagine this scene based on lines 1–3? Why or why not?

3.

a   What does the donkey do in lines 1–3 that suggests he is familiar with this place? Refer to the poem in your answer.

b   What does the word 'strange' in line 1 indicate to you about the people who have just arrived?

4. The poem moves inside a building in lines 4–11.

a   What type of a building do you think it is? Refer to the text to support your answer.

Eiléan Ní Chuilleanáin

329

b   What impression do you get of this building from lines 4–8?

5.

a   It is clear from line 1 that at the beginning of the poem, the people are arriving at a place they do not know. What does the phrase 'Where better to lie down | And sleep' suggest to you about how they feel about the place at the end of the poem?

b   What aspects of this place have helped the people to feel at home? Make reference to the poem in your answer.

6.

a   The phrase 'It is for you' is used in lines 5 and 12. What do you think this phrase suggests about why the people who have just arrived are there?

b   How would you feel if someone said this to you about a building?

7.

a   Why do you think it is important that the person has 'the key still in your pocket' when he/she goes asleep?

b   Do you think the people feel completely safe in this place? Why?

8.

a   'Flows out, the rage of brushwood, | The roots torn out and butchered.' Which words in these lines might indicate that violence is a part of this place?

b   Are there any other indications in this poem that power is linked to physical force in this world? Refer to the poem in your answer.

9.   What mood or atmosphere is created in this poem? Your answer should make close reference to the text.

10.   Do you find this poem fascinating or irritating? Support your answer with suitable reference to the poem.

Lucina Schynning in Silence of the Nicht

◉ Track 13

Moon shining in silence of the night
The heaven being all full of stars
I was reading my book in a ruin
By a sour candle, without roast meat or music
Strong drink or a shield from the air   5
Blowing in the crazed window, and I felt
Moonlight on my head, clear after three days' rain.

I washed in cold water; it was orange, channelled down bogs
Dipped between cresses.
The bats flew through my room where I slept safely.   10
Sheep stared at me when I woke.

Behind me the waves of darkness lay, the plague
Of mice, plague of beetles
Crawling out of the spines of books,
Plague shadowing pale faces with clay   15
The disease of the moon gone astray.

In the desert I relaxed, amazed
As the mosaic beasts on the chapel floor
When Cromwell had departed, and they saw
The sky growing through the hole in the roof.   20

Sheepdogs embraced me; the grasshopper
Returned with lark and bee.
I looked down between hedges of high thorn and saw
The hare, absorbed, sitting still
In the middle of the track; I heard   25
Again the chirp of the stream running.

Notes

	Lucina Schynning in Silence of the Nicht:	this is a line taken from a poem by a Scottish poet, William Dunbar, who died before 1530. Lines 1–2 of Ní Chuilleanáin's poem are a modern English translation of this line and another line from Dunbar's poem. Lucina is another name for Diana, the goddess of the moon.
6	crazed:	possibly marked with fine surface cracks; possibly made insane
9	cresses:	a plant with edible leaves
12	plague:	around 1650, many people in Ireland died from the plague
14	Crawling out:	a reference to spontaneous generation, i.e. the belief that life could suddenly appear from sources that were not parents, eggs or seeds, such as mud or books. This was accepted as fact until the late Renaissance.
19	Cromwell:	Oliver Cromwell, who landed in Ireland in 1649 with a large army. The war that followed his arrival led to great destruction, many deaths and famine in Ireland.

Eiléan Ní Chuilleanáin

Explorations

BEFORE READING

1. In this poem, nature is shown as having a positive effect on human emotions. Do you agree or disagree with this idea? Why?

FIRST READING

2. What is your first reaction to this poem? Do you like or dislike it? Why? Refer to the text to support your opinion.

3.

a How do the images in lines 3–6 convey the speaker's negative and depressed emotions?

b Line 7 suggests that her emotions begin to change. In what way have they changed? What has caused this change?

4.

a 'I washed in cold water; it was orange, channelled down bogs | Dipped between cresses.'
   What senses are appealed to in this image?

b What does this image suggest to you about the state of the speaker's emotions at this point?

c How do the images that follow in lines 10–11 also convey this state?

5. Although she has now put her negative and depressed emotions behind her, in lines 12–16 the speaker uses a series of images to show just how nightmarish they were. Choose one image from these lines that you feel is particularly effective in doing this. Explain the reasons for your choice.

SECOND READING

6. In lines 17–20, the speaker compares her 'amazed' feelings to the 'mosaic beasts on the chapel floor'. In your own words, explain how this comparison works.

7.

a How would you describe the effect that the world of nature has on the speaker's feelings in lines 21–26?

b Do you think this is an effective ending for this poem? Why?

THIRD READING

8. 'I was reading my book in a ruin | By a sour candle, without roast meat or music', 'the plague | Of mice, plague of beetles | Crawling out of the spines of books'.

a What impression do you get of the speaker's attitude to books and their contents from these lines?

b Do you think this is a fair representation of books? Why?

9. Discuss how the world of nature is shown to have a positive effect on human emotions in 'Lucina Schynning in Silence of the Nicht' and two of Eiléan Ní Chuilleanáin's other poems.

10. Having explored this poem, do you still have the same reaction to this poem as you did for Question 2? Why?

Eavan Boland

(1944–)

Prescribed for Higher Level exams in 2017 and 2018

Eavan Boland was born in Dublin in 1944, daughter of the painter Frances Kelly and the diplomat Frederick Boland. She was educated at Holy Child Convent, Killiney, and Trinity College, Dublin. For some years she lectured at Trinity College in the English department before becoming a literary journalist, chiefly with *The Irish Times* but also with RTÉ, where she produced award-winning poetry programmes for radio. She married the novelist Kevin Casey, exchanging the Dublin literary scene for family life in the suburbs, where she wrote prolifically.

New Territory (1967) was her first volume of poetry. Her second volume, *The War Horse* (1975), deals with the Northern Ireland 'Troubles' and with the way violence encroaches on our domestic lives. The poem 'Child of Our Time' is taken from this volume. Her third volume, *In Her Own Image* (1980), explores the darker side of female identity, 'woman's secret history'; it deals with real but taboo issues such as anorexia, infanticide, mastectomy, menstruation and domestic violence. The fourth collection, *Night Feed* (1982),

celebrates the ordinary, everyday, domestic aspect of woman's identity. The fifth volume, *The Journey* (1986), and the sixth, *Outside History* (1990), consider the image of women in Irish history as illustrated in painting and in literature – a tale of exploitation and repression, of being marginalised and kept from the centre of influence. The seventh collection, *In a Time of Violence* (1994), deals specifically with Irish national and historical issues such as the Famine, agrarian violence and the Easter Rising. It also focuses on the theme of women as mothers and the relationship between mothers and daughters. The poem 'This Moment' is taken from this volume.

The place of the woman writer in Irish literature, mythology and history is a prominent theme in Boland's poetry and other writings. Her pamphlet *A Kind of Scar* (1989) examines this issue. Her collection of autobiographical prose, published in 1995, is entitled *Object Lessons: The Life of the Woman and the Poet in Our Time*. In 1980 she was joint founder of Arlen House, a feminist publishing company.

The War Horse

This dry night, nothing unusual
About the clip, clop, casual

[handwritten annotations: onomatopeia, relaxed image, Alliteration, contrast – stamps Death]

Iron of his shoes as he stamps death
Like a mint on the innocent coinage of earth.

I lift the window, watch the ambling feather   5
Of hock and fetlock, loosed from its daily tether

[handwritten annotation: setting / modern]

In the tinker camp on the Enniskerry Road,
Pass, his breath hissing, his snuffling head

Down. He is gone. No great harm is done.
Only a leaf of our laurel hedge is torn –   10

Of distant interest like a maimed limb,
Only a rose which now will never climb

The stone of our house, expendable, a mere
Line of defence against him, a volunteer

You might say, only a crocus, its bulbous head   15
Blown from growth, one of the screamless dead.

But we, we are safe, our unformed fear
Of fierce commitment gone; why should we care

If a rose, a hedge, a crocus are uprooted
Like corpses, remote, crushed, mutilated?   20

He stumbles on like a rumour of war, huge
Threatening. Neighbours use the subterfuge

Of curtains. He stumbles down our short street
Thankfully passing us. I pause, wait,

Then to breathe relief lean on the sill   25
And for a second only my blood is still

With atavism. That rose he smashed frays
Ribboned across our hedge, recalling days

Of burned countryside, illicit braid:
A cause ruined before, a world betrayed.   30

Background note

This poem stems from an incident when the front garden of Boland's new house in the suburbs was invaded a number of times by a stray horse, presumed to belong to local Travellers. Perhaps the horse had lived there when the site was open fields.

Notes

4	mint:	place where money is coined
6	hock:	joint on a horse's leg corresponding to the human ankle
6	fetlock:	tuft of hair above and behind the horse's hoof
27	atavism:	resemblance to remote ancestors; in this instance the horse's violation of the domestic garden stirs race memories of English colonial violence and the destruction of Irish homesteads
29	braid:	anything plaited or interwoven, such as hair or ribbon, or the gold and silver thread decoration on uniforms; it might refer to rebel uniforms

Explorations

FIRST READING

1. On a first reading, what do you see? Visualise the night, the garden, the atmosphere, the animal. What sounds are there in this scene?

2.

a At one level, this horse is made real to the reader. How is this realised? What words best convey the shape, size, movement, etc. of the animal to us? Explore sounds of words as well as visual images.

b What is your first impression of the horse?

3. Do you think this horse carries a sense of menace or threat? Examine the first four couplets in particular. Explore the imagery, the sounds of

words and the rhythm of the piece in coming to a conclusion.

4. How is the fragility of the domestic garden conveyed to us? What words or images suggest this?

SECOND READING

5. What do you notice about the speaker's reactions to this intrusion? Do they change as the poem progresses? Make specific references to the text.

6.

a Could this piece be read as a political poem, with the horse as a symbol of violence? What evidence do you find in the poem for this reading?

b At a symbolic level, what is being suggested here about the nature of violence?

Eavan Boland

7. How do you read the poem? What themes do you find it deals with and what levels of meaning do you notice?

The Famine Road

'Idle as trout in light Colonel Jones,
these Irish, give them no coins at all; their bones
need toil, their characters no less.' Trevelyan's
seal blooded the deal table. The Relief
Committee deliberated: 'Might it be safe,   5
Colonel, to give them roads, roads to force
from nowhere, going nowhere of course?'

    'one out of every ten and then
    another third of those again
    women – in a case like yours.'   10

Sick, directionless they worked; fork, stick
were iron years away; after all could
they not blood their knuckles on rock, suck
April hailstones for water and for food?
Why for that, cunning as housewives, each eyed –   15
as if at a corner butcher – the other's buttock.

    'anything may have caused it, spores,
    a childhood accident; one sees
    day after day these mysteries.'

Dusk: they will work tomorrow without him.   20
They know it and walk clear. He has become
a typhoid pariah, his blood tainted, although
he shares it with some there. No more than snow
attends its own flakes where they settle
and melt, will they pray by his death rattle.   25

    'You never will, never you know
    but take it well woman, grow
    your garden, keep house, good-bye.'

'It has gone better than we expected, Lord
Trevelyan, sedition, idleness, cured   30
in one; from parish to parish, field to field,
the wretches work till they are quite worn,
then fester by their work; we march the corn
to the ships in peace; this Tuesday I saw bones
out of my carriage window, your servant Jones.'   35

*'Barren, never to know the load
of his child in you, what is your body
now if not a famine road?'*

Notes

	Famine Road:	in the Great Famine of 1845–48, the potato crop failed and the people were left destitute and starving. Among the relief works organised to allow the hungry to earn money was road construction, but these roads were rarely meant to be used and often ended uselessly in a bog or field. Thus, the famine road might be read as a symbol of unfulfilled lives that go nowhere.

Eavan Boland

1	**Colonel Jones:**	Lieutenant-Colonel Jones was one of the officers in charge of relief works around Newry. There exists a letter from him to Trevelyan reporting on work carried out during the winter of 1846; this may be the source of the exchange here.
3	**Trevelyan:**	Charles Trevelyan was a senior British civil servant, Assistant Secretary to the Treasury, in charge of relief works in Ireland at the outbreak of the Great Famine in 1845. At first his approach was dominated by the laissez-faire (non-intervention) policy popular at the time and he was concerned that the Irish might be demoralised by receiving too much government help. Later he came to realise that they would not survive without it, but he never really warmed to the Irish, speaking of 'the selfish, perverse and turbulent character of the people'.
4-5	**Relief Committee:**	committees that organised local schemes to try to alleviate the starvation
22	**pariah:**	outcast
30	**sedition:**	conduct or language directed towards the overthrow of the state
33-4	**corn to the ships:**	despite the starvation, normal commerce was carried on and corn was exported as usual, though grain carts now needed protection against the local population

Explorations

FIRST READING

1. Read aloud Trevelyan's letter in the first three lines of the poem. How do you think it should sound? Consider the tone. What is Trevelyan's attitude? What words or phrases convey his attitude particularly well? What do Trevelyan's gestures add to the tone of this? Read it as you think he would say it.

2. Read aloud the Relief Committee's speech to Colonel Jones as you imagine it said. Pay attention to the tone of 'Might it be safe' and 'going nowhere of course'.

3. Read stanzas 3 and 5 (beginning 'Sick' and 'Dusk', respectively). What do you notice about the relief work and the condition of the people?

4. Consider Colonel Jones's letter to Trevelyan ('It has gone better'). What does it reveal about the writer – his priorities, his attitude to the Irish, his awareness of the famine, etc.? Is there evidence of sympathy or of superiority and indifference? Consider phrases such as 'the wretches', 'fester by their work', 'march ... in peace'. What is the effect of the hollow rhyme 'bones'/'Jones'? Read the letter aloud as you think he might say it.

SECOND READING

5. In the third stanza, how is the desperate bleakness of the people's situation conveyed? What image in particular conveys the depth of their degradation? Explain your thinking.

6. Illness isolates and degrades human beings. How is this portrayed in the

fifth stanza? Consider the effect of the imagery and the sounds of words.

THIRD READING

7. Now explore the woman's story (stanzas 2, 4, 6 and 8).

a Who is speaking in the first three stanzas? Which words suggest that?

b Consider the tone and read these three stanzas aloud.

c Who speaks the last stanza? How does the speaker feel? Which words best convey the feelings?

8. Write an extract from that woman's diary as she might compose it following that meeting. Fill it with the thoughts you imagine going through her head as she listened to the consultant.

FOURTH READING

9. What statement do you think this poem makes on the status of women?

10. Explain the comparisons implied in the poem between the experience of women and the treatment of the Famine people. Do you find it enlightening? Explain.

11. In her writings, Boland has often expressed concern that history is sometimes simplified into myth.

'Irish poets of the nineteenth century, and indeed their heirs in this century, coped with their sense of historical injury by writing of Ireland as an abandoned queen or an old mother. My objections to this are ethical. If you consistently simplify women by making them national icons in poetry or drama you silence a great deal of the actual women in that past, whose sufferings and complexities are part of that past, who intimately depend on us, as writers, not to simplify them in this present.' (From the interview in *Sleeping with Monsters*)

Do you think 'The Famine Road' shows an awareness of the real complexity of actual lives from history? Explain, with reference to the text.

12. What sense of national identity or Irishness comes across from 'The Famine Road'?

Child of Our Time   ● Track 14

(for Aengus)   [handwritten: Dual narrative   angry, sad, regretful]

This poem is also prescribed for Ordinary Level exams in 2017 and 2018

Yesterday I knew no lullaby — [handwritten: She is not a mother]
But you have taught me overnight to order   [handwritten: She is guna right a song (poem)]
This song, which takes from your final cry   [handwritten: Not guna be a happy poem]
Its tune, from your unreasoned end its reason,
Its rhythm from the discord of your murder
Its motive from the fact you cannot listen.   [handwritten: angry tone, baby dead (cannot listen)]

[handwritten: Wants us to think about violence]

Eavan Boland

339

A We who should have known how to instruct
B With rhymes for your waking, rhythms for your sleep,
C Names for the animals you took to bed,
a Tales to distract, legends to protect,
D Later an idiom for you to keep   10
L And living, learn, must learn from you, dead,
    Alliteration

A To make our broken images, rebuild   — need to come together
B Themselves around your limbs, your broken   — violent, disturbing   Shes, Brave
C Image, find for your sake whose life our idle   women 1970
D Talk has cost, a new language. Child   — gossip   15   women
  Of our time, our times have robbed your cradle.
positive Sleep in a world your final sleep has woken.   Our problems robbed
pleading   your life
tone

handwritten margin notes:
We try to create safe place for children but you cant always

Background note

This poem was inspired by a press photograph showing a firefighter carrying a
dead child out of the wreckage of the Dublin bombings in May 1974.

Explorations

FIRST READING

1. If you hadn't read the title or the last three lines, what might suggest to you that the poem was written to a child? Examine stanzas 1–2.

2. The speaker acknowledges that it was the child's death that prompted her to compose this poem ('you have taught me overnight to order | This song'). How does she feel about the child's death in the first stanza? Examine the words and phrases describing the death: 'your final cry', 'your unreasoned end', 'the discord of your murder'. What do these phrases tell us about the way the poet views the death?

3. In the second stanza, notice that the main clause consists of the first word

and the final five words in the stanza: 'We ... must learn from you dead'. The rest of the stanza relates to 'we', presumably adult society.

a In what way has adult society failed, according to the poet?

b What particular aspect of childbearing and education does the poet focus on?

c 'Later an idiom for you to keep | And living, learn'.
In your own words, what do you think is meant by this? ('Idiom' here means style of expression.)

4. In the third stanza the child's body is described poetically as 'your broken | Image'. What does this picture suggest to you?

5. What do you think she has in mind when she says that we need to (a)

rebuild 'our broken images ... around your limbs' and (b) 'find ... a new language'?

6. Does the speaker find any ray of hope for the society in which this calamity occurred? Refer to the text of the third stanza.

7. Consider this poem as an elegy, a meditation on death. What ideas on that subject are explored or suggested?

8. Can this be read as a public or political poem? Explain, with reference to the text.

9. Concerning the poet's feelings, do you find here a sense of personal sorrow or community guilt and sorrow? Explain your thinking.

10. The poem might be seen as a mixture of dirge and lullaby. What elements of dirge or of lullaby do you find? Consider the theme, the choice of language, the imagery, the repetitions, etc.

The Black Lace Fan My Mother Gave Me

It was the first gift he ever gave her,
buying it for five francs in the Galeries
in pre-war Paris. It was stifling.
A starless drought made the nights stormy.

They stayed in the city for the summer.   5
They met in cafés. She was always early.
He was late. That evening he was later.
They wrapped the fan. He looked at his watch.

She looked down the Boulevard des Capucines.
She ordered more coffee. She stood up.   10
The streets were emptying. The heat was killing.
She thought the distance smelled of rain and lightning.

These are wild roses, appliqued on silk by hand,
darkly picked, stitched boldly, quickly.
The rest is tortoiseshell and has the reticent,   15
clear patience of its element. It is

a worn-out, underwater bullion and it keeps,
even now, an inference of its violation.
The lace is overcast as if the weather
it opened for and offset had entered it.   20

Eavan Boland

The past is an empty café terrace.
An airless dusk before thunder. A man running.
And no way now to know what happened then –
none at all – unless, of course, you improvise:

The blackbird on this first sultry morning,   25
in summer, finding buds, worms, fruit,
feels the heat. Suddenly she puts out her wing –
the whole, full, flirtatious span of it.

Explorations

FIRST READING

1. The black lace fan was a present from the poet's father to her mother and was passed on later to the speaker. How do you visualise the fan? What assistance does the poem give us? Examine the details in stanza 4.

2. How do you visualise the scene, the background, the atmosphere of the evening as the woman waits? Look at the details.

3. What do you notice about the man in the poem? What else would you like to know about him? Why is he always late? Is the gift a peace offering or a genuine love token? What does he really feel for her? Can any of these questions be answered from the poem?

4. What do you notice about the woman? Examine the details. What do they suggest about how she is feeling, etc.? While remaining faithful to the text, jot down what you imagine the thoughts inside her head are as she waits.

5. Do you think this was a perfectly matched and idyllic relationship? What is suggested by the poem? Explain.

6. How does the poet think of the fan? Does she see it as more than just the usual love token, a symbol in the sensual ritual? Explore in detail her imaginative apprehension of the fan in stanza 5. For example, what is meant by 'it keeps ... an inference of its violation' and 'The lace is overcast as if the weather ... had entered it'?

7. How do you think the final stanza relates to the rest of the poem? Does the mating display of the blackbird add anything to the connotations of the keepsake?

8. How do you think you would regard the first present from a lover? Were you at all surprised by the fact that the mother in this poem gave away the fan? Explain your thinking.

9. Do you think the poet views the keepsake solely in a romantic or in an erotic way? How do you think she sees it?

10. Examine what the poet herself says (in *Object Lessons*) about the symbol. What does this add to your own thinking on the subject?

'I make these remarks as a preliminary to a poem I wrote about a black lace fan my mother had given me, which my father had given her in a heat wave in Paris in the thirties. It would be wrong to say I was clear, when I wrote this poem, about disassembling an erotic politic. I was not. But I was aware of my own sense of the traditional erotic object – in this case the black fan – as a sign not for triumph and acquisition but for suffering itself.

And without having words for it, I was conscious of trying to divide it from its usual source of generation: the sexualised perspective of the poet. To that extent I was writing a sign which might bring me close to those emblems of the body I had seen in those visionary years, when ordinary objects seemed to warn me that the body might share the world but could not own it. And if I was not conscious of taking apart something I had been taught to leave well alone, nevertheless, I had a clear sense of – at last – writing the poem away from the traditional erotic object towards something which spoke of the violations of love, while still shadowing the old context of its power. In other words, a back-to-front love poem.'

THIRD READING

11. What does the poem say to you about love and time?

12. In your own words, outline the themes you find in this poem.

13. What images appeal to you particularly? Explain why you find them effective.

14. Comment on the use of symbolism in this poem.

FOURTH READING

15. 'The past is an empty café terrace. | An airless dusk before thunder. A man running. | And no way now to know what happened then – | none at all – unless, of course, you improvise'.
In a brief written description, improvise the sequel to the 'empty café terrace' and 'A man running' as you imagine it. Keep faith with the spirit of the poem.

Eavan Boland

The Shadow Doll

They stitched blooms from the ivory tulle
to hem the oyster gleam of the veil.
They made hoops for the crinoline.

Now, in summary and neatly sewn –
a porcelain bride in an airless glamour –   5
the shadow doll survives its occasion.

Under glass, under wraps, it stays
even now, after all, discreet about
visits, fevers, quickenings and lusts

and just how, when she looked at   10
the shell-tone spray of seed pearls,
the bisque features, she could see herself

inside it all, holding less than real
stephanotis, rose petals, never feeling
satin rise and fall with the vows   15

I kept repeating on the night before –
astray among the cards and wedding gifts –
the coffee pots and the clocks and

the battered tan case full of cotton
lace and tissue-paper, pressing down, then   20
pressing down again. And then, locks.

Notes

	Shadow Doll:	this refers to the porcelain doll modelling the proposed wedding dress, under a dome of glass, sent to the 19th-century bride by her dressmaker
1	tulle:	soft, fine silk netting used for dresses and veils
2	oyster:	off-white colour
12	bisque:	unglazed white porcelain used for these models
14	stephanotis:	tropical climbing plant with fragrant white flowers

Explorations

FIRST READING

1. The function of the doll is explained above in the Notes, but what does the title 'Shadow Doll' suggest to you?

2. What do you notice about the model dress?

3. 'A porcelain bride in an airless glamour' – what does this suggest to you about the poet's view of the doll?

4. Do you think the poet understands the doll's significance in more general terms, as an image of something or a symbol? If so, an image or symbol of what?

SECOND READING

5. What image of woman is portrayed by the doll? Explore stanza 3 in particular.

6. How does this image contrast with the poet's experience of her own wedding? Explore stanzas 5–7.

7. The speaker's reality is more appealing, despite the clutter, but has she anything in common with the 'shadow doll'?

THIRD READING

8. What does the poem say to you about the image of woman? Refer to the text to substantiate your ideas.

9. Explore the significance of colour in this poem.

10. 'In the main, symbol and image carry the main themes of this poem.' Comment, with reference to the text.

White Hawthorn in the West of Ireland

I drove West
in the season between seasons.
I left behind suburban gardens.
Lawnmowers. Small talk.

Under low skies, past splashes of coltsfoot,   5
I assumed
the hard shyness of Atlantic light
and the superstitious aura of hawthorn.

All I wanted then was to fill my arms with sharp flowers,
to seem, from a distance, to be part of   10
that ivory, downhill rush. But I knew,

Eavan Boland

I had always known
the custom was
not to touch hawthorn.   15
Not to bring it indoors for the sake of

the luck
such constraint would forfeit –
a child might die, perhaps, or an unexplained
fever speckle heifers. So I left it   20

stirring on those hills
with a fluency
only water has. And, like water, able
to re-define land. And free to seem to be –

for anglers,   25
and for travellers astray in
the unmarked lights of a May dusk –
the only language spoken in those parts.

Notes		
5	**coltsfoot:**	wild plant with yellow flowers

Explorations

FIRST READING

1.

a   In this migration, what is the speaker leaving behind her?

b   From what little is said in the first stanza, what do you understand of her attitude to life in suburbia?

2.

a   How does her state of mind alter as she drives west?

b   Explore stanzas 2–3. How does this experience contrast with life in suburbia?

3.   According to the poem, what is the significance of hawthorn in folklore?

4.   Water, too, is a deceptive source of hidden energies. What is the poet's thinking on this? Explore stanzas 6–7.

SECOND READING

5.   'The speaker's attitude to the hawthorn is a combination of passionate, sensuous attraction balanced by a degree of nervous respect.'
Would you agree? Substantiate your views with reference to the text.

6.   What do you think this poem reveals about the speaker?

7.   What statement is the poet making about our modern way of life?

THIRD READING

8.   List the themes or issues raised by this poem.

9.   What is your personal reaction to this poem?

Outside History **Track 15**

There are outsiders, always. These stars –
these iron inklings of an Irish January,
whose light happened

thousands of years before
our pain did: they are, they have always been   5
outside history.

They keep their distance. Under them remains
a place where you found
you were human, and

a landscape in which you know you are mortal.   10
And a time to choose between them.
I have chosen:

Eavan Boland

out of myth into history I move to be
part of that ordeal
whose darkness is   15

only now reaching me from those fields,
those rivers, those roads clotted as
firmaments with the dead.

How slowly they die
as we kneel beside them, whisper in their ear.   20
And we are too late. We are always too late.

Explorations

1. Boland's argument is that Irish
   history has been turned into myth
   and therefore rendered false and
   remote from real lives. Do you think
   the image of the stars is an effective
   metaphor for historical myths?
   Examine the attributes of the stars as
   suggested in the first two stanzas.

2. In contrast, what aspects of real, lived
   history are emphasised in this poem?

SECOND READING

3. The poet chooses to turn her back
   on myth and this choice brings her,
   and the reader, face to face with the
   unburied dead of history. Does she
   find this an easy choice? Explore her
   feelings on this. What words, phrases,
   gestures, etc. indicate her feelings?

4. What do you think she means by
   the last line of the poem? Explore
   possible interpretations.

THIRD READING

5. On the evidence of this poem as a
   whole, what is the poet's attitude to
   the historical past?

6. Comment on the effectiveness of the
   imagery.

This poem is also prescribed for Ordinary Level exams in 2017 and 2018

A neighbourhood.
At dusk.

Things are getting ready
to happen
out of sight.   5

Stars and moths.
And rinds slanting around fruit.

But not yet.

One tree is black.
One window is yellow as butter.   10

A woman leans down to catch a child
who runs into her arms
this moment.

Stars rise.
Moths flutter.   15
Apples sweeten in the dark.

Explorations

FIRST READING

1. What do you see in this scene? List the items.

2. What senses, other than sight, are involved or hinted at?

3. Do you think this scene is unusual or very ordinary? Explain. What do you think the poet is celebrating here?

4. There is a hint of the mysterious about the scene. Where and what do you think are suggested?

SECOND READING

5. What do you think is the most significant image in the poem? How does the poet draw attention to its importance?

6. Do you notice any sense of dramatic build-up in the poem? Examine the sequence of ideas and images.

7. Explore the imagery. What do the images contribute to the atmosphere? What is suggested, for example, by 'One window is yellow as butter' and by 'Apples sweeten in the dark'?

Eavan Boland

349

8. What is the key moment in this poem all about?

9. What do you think the poem is saying about nature?

10. Do you think it is making a statement about the experience of women? Explain your ideas.

Love

 Track 17

This poem is also prescribed for Ordinary Level exams in 2017 and 2018

once upon a time
Dark falls on this mid-western town *her husband was — personification — metaphor*
where we once lived when myths collided. *her hero*
Dusk has hidden the bridge in the river *Styx-river*
which slides and deepens
to become the water   5
the hero crossed on his way to hell.

Not far from here is our old apartment. *simple solid life they had*
We had a kitchen and an Amish table. *2 gether*
We had a view. And we discovered there
love had the feather and muscle of wings *— metaphor to love they had*
and had come to live with us, *— personifies love*
a brother of fire and air.

We had two infant children one of whom *child survived near death*
was touched by death in this town *experience*
and spared: and when the hero   15
was hailed by his comrades in hell *failure of experience*
their mouths opened and their voices failed and
there is no knowing what they would have asked
about a life they had shared and lost. *more ordinary*

I am your wife. *Trying to convince herself*
It was years ago. *her relationship is OK*   20
Our child is healed. We love each other still.
Across our day-to-day and ordinary distances
we speak plainly. We hear each other clearly.

And yet I want to return to you *She wants to see him*
on the bridge of the Iowa river as you were, *as a hero — sure from*   25 *male*
with snow on the shoulders of your coat
and a car passing with its headlights on:

I see you as a hero in a text –
the image blazing and the edges gilded –   30
and I long to cry out the epic question
my dear companion:

Will we ever live so intensely again?   *love personified*
Will love come to us again and be   *Higher*
so formidable at rest it offered us ascension   *being*   35
even to look at him?

But the words are shadows and you cannot hear me.
You walk away and I cannot follow.

Explorations

FIRST READING

1. The poem is occasioned by a return
    visit to 'this mid-western town' in
    America where they had once lived.
    Which lines refer to present time and
    which refer to that earlier stay?

2. 'When myths collided' – what do you
    think this might refer to?

3. Explore the mood of the opening
    stanza. How is it created and does
    it fit in with the mythical allusions?
    Explain.

4. On a first reading, what issues do you
    notice that preoccupy the poet?

SECOND READING

5. The second stanza contains some
    memories of the speaker's previous
    visit. What was important to her?

6.

(a) What insights about love are
    communicated in the second stanza?

Eavan Boland

b   What is your opinion of the effectiveness of the imagery used?

7.

a   The poet uses allusions from myth to create an awareness of death in the third stanza. What insights on death are communicated to you by this very visual presentation?

b   Do you think this is an effective way of recording the speaker's feelings? Explain your view.

8.   Explore the speaker's feelings for her husband at the present time and contrast them with past emotions. Is she content? What does she yearn for?

THIRD READING

9.   Overall, what does this poem have to say about love? What does she think is important?

10. What other themes do you find are dealt with?

11. What does the poem say about women's experience?

12. What do the mythical allusions contribute to the poem?

13. Comment on the effectiveness of the imagery.

FOURTH READING

14. What did you discover from reading this poem?

The Pomegranate   Track 18

The only legend I have ever loved is
the story of a daughter lost in hell.
And found and rescued there.
Love and blackmail are the gist of it.
Ceres and Persephone the names.   5
And the best thing about the legend is
I can enter it anywhere. And have.
As a child in exile in
a city of fogs and strange consonants,
I read it first and at first I was   10
an exiled child in the crackling dusk of
the underworld, the stars blighted. Later
I walked out in a summer twilight
searching for my daughter at bed-time.
When she came running I was ready   15
to make any bargain to keep her.
I carried her back past whitebeams
and wasps and honey-scented buddleias.
But I was Ceres then and I knew
winter was in store for every leaf   20
on every tree on that road.

Was inescapable for each one we passed.
And for me.
        It is winter
and the stars are hidden.   25
I climb the stairs and stand where I can see
my child asleep beside her teen magazines,
her can of Coke, her plate of uncut fruit.
The pomegranate! How did I forget it?
She could have come home and been safe   30
and ended the story and all
our heart-broken searching but she reached
out a hand and plucked a pomegranate.
She put out her hand and pulled down
the French sound for apple and   35
the noise of stone and the proof
that even in the place of death,
at the heart of legend, in the midst
of rocks full of unshed tears
ready to be diamonds by the time   40
the story was told, a child can be
hungry. I could warn her. There is still a chance.
The rain is cold. The road is flint-coloured.
The suburb has cars and cable television.
The veiled stars are above ground.   45
It is another world. But what else
can a mother give her daughter but such
beautiful rifts in time?
If I defer the grief I will diminish the gift.
The legend will be hers as well as mine.   50
She will enter it. As I have.
She will wake up. She will hold
the papery flushed skin in her hand.
And to her lips. I will say nothing.

Eavan Boland

Notes

	Pomegranate:	the fruit of a North African tree, the size and colour of an orange. In classical mythology it was associated with the underworld.
5	**Ceres and Persephone:**	Ceres in Roman mythology (identified with Demeter in Greek mythology) was the goddess of corn and growing vegetation, an earth goddess. Her daughter by Zeus, Persephone, was carried off to the underworld by Hades. Ceres wandered over the earth in mourning, vainly searching. In grief she made the earth barren for a year. She resisted all entreaties by the gods to allow the earth back to fertility. Eventually Zeus sent his messenger to persuade Hades to release Persephone, which he did, but not before he had given her a pomegranate seed to eat. This fruit was sacred to the underworld, and so Persephone was condemned to spend one-third of each year there with Hades, only appearing back on earth each spring, with the first fertility.

Explorations

FIRST READING

1. The poet says, 'the best thing about the legend is | I can enter it anywhere'. When did she first encounter it and why did she find it relevant to her life?

2. At what other times and in what ways did the legend run parallel to her own situation?

3. How closely do you think the poet identifies with the myth? What evidence is there for this?

SECOND READING

4. What does the poem tell us about the poet's relationship with her daughter?

5. What does the legend contribute to that relationship?

6. What do you think the poet has in common with Ceres?

THIRD READING

7. Where and how do the time zones of past and present fuse and mingle? What does this suggest about the importance of myth in our lives?

8. What statement do you think this poem is making about the significance of legend to ordinary lives? Refer to the text.

9. What truths about human relationships are discovered in this poem?

FOURTH READING

10. Examine the different motifs in the imagery – fruit, darkness, stars, stone, etc. What do these strands of imagery contribute to the atmosphere and the themes?

11. What effect did reading this poem have on you?

Paul Durcan

(1944–)

Prescribed for Higher Level exams in 2016, 2017 and 2018

Paul Durcan was born in Dublin to parents from County Mayo: John Durcan, barrister and judge, and Sheila MacBride Durcan, solicitor. He was raised between Dublin and Turlough, County Mayo, where his aunt ran a pub.

He began to study law and economics in UCD but left in 1964. For a number of years he lived between London, Barcelona and Dublin. When he worked for the North Thames Gas Board in London he used to visit the Tate Gallery at lunchtime to view the paintings of Francis Bacon in particular.

He married Nessa O'Neill. They settled in Cork in 1970 and have two daughters. She worked as a teacher in a prison and he completed a degree in archaeology and medieval history at UCC. The marriage ended in 1984.

Durcan has travelled widely, as the titles of his volumes demonstrate. He has been writer in residence in universities, including the University of Ulster and Trinity College Dublin. He has collaborated with artists and musicians. He was commissioned to write poetry in response to paintings by the National Gallery of Ireland ('Crazy about Women', 1991) and by the National Gallery, London ('Give Me Your Hand', 1994). He held the Irish Chair of Poetry from 2004 to 2007. As a performing poet, he is known for the mesmeric quality of his readings.

Among his many volumes of poetry are the following: *O Westport in the Light of Asia Minor* (1975), *The Berlin Wall Café* (1985), *Going Home to Russia* (1987), *Daddy, Daddy* (1990), *Greetings to Our Friends in Brazil* (1999), *The Laughter of Mothers* (2007) and *Praise in Which I Live and Move and Have My Being* (2012). A selection of his work, *Life Is a Dream: 40 Years Reading Poems 1967–2007*, was published in 2009.

Paul Durcan has won many awards for his poetry, including the Patrick Kavanagh Award, the Irish American Cultural Institute Poetry Award, the Heinemann Award and the Whitbread Poetry Award for 'Daddy, Daddy'.

I met her on the first of August
In the Shangri-La Hotel,
She took me by the index finger
And dropped me in her well.
And that was a whirlpool, that was a whirlpool,   5
And I very nearly drowned.

Take off your pants, she said to me,
And I very nearly didn't;
Would you care to swim, she said to me,
And I hopped into the Irish Sea.   10
And that was a whirlpool, that was a whirlpool,
And I very nearly drowned.

On the way back I fell in the field
And she fell down beside me,
I'd have lain in the grass with her all my life   15
With Nessa:
She was a whirlpool, she was a whirlpool,
And I very nearly drowned.

O Nessa my dear, Nessa my dear,
Will you stay with me on the rocks?   20
Will you come for me into the Irish Sea
And for me let your red hair down?
And then we will ride into Dublin City
In a taxi-cab wrapped up in dust.
Oh you are a whirlpool, you are a whirlpool,   25
And I am very nearly drowned.

Notes

	Background Note:	This is an autobiographical poem about Durcan's first meeting with Nessa O'Neill, whom he later married. He met her on 1 August 1967, sitting at the bar in the Shangri-La Hotel, in the aftermath of a wedding to which he was not invited.
2	**Shangri-La Hotel:**	a well-known hotel, since demolished, that was situated by the seashore in Dalkey, County Dublin

Explorations

BEFORE READING

1. Why do you think we use the expression *'falling* in love'? What does it suggest?

FIRST READING

2. Has the speaker here fallen in love? Discuss.

3. Think of the poem as a succession of still images, as from a film (ignore the refrain for the moment). What do you see? What story do the images tell as you follow the sequence?

4.

a What suggestions does the whirlpool image bring to the relationship?

b How does the whirlpool image change as the story develops?

5. Do you find this account of a first date unusual? Discuss in groups.

SECOND READING

6. What do we learn about the personality of the girl as she is portrayed in this poem?

7. The poem begins with a succession of images that could be read as humorous, zany or even mocking the usual conventions of love poetry, but do you think this gives way to serious honest emotion at a particular point? Think about this and share ideas in a group discussion.

8.

a Read the final stanza carefully. What has changed about the tone of the speaker?

b Has anything altered in the relationship between himself and Nessa?

c What does the last line communicate about the speaker's emotional state?

9. 'And then we will ride into Dublin City | In a taxi-cab wrapped up in dust.'
This is the equivalent of riding off into the sunset, happily ever after. Where do you think he gets the image from? Do you think it works well here?

THIRD READING

10. Who do you think has the most power and influence in this relationship? Why do you think this?

11. What might we understand about Durcan's view of women from this poem?

12. 'This is a most unusual love poem.' Discuss.

Paul Durcan

357

13. 'Yet it is a very honest and effective love poem.' Discuss.

14. Do you think this poem could be made into a short film quite easily? Explain your thinking.

The Girl with the Keys to Pearse's Cottage

to John and Judith Meagher

When I was sixteen I met a dark girl;
Her dark hair was darker because her smile was so bright;
She was the girl with the keys to Pearse's Cottage;
And her name was Cáit Killann.

The cottage was built into the side of a hill;   5
I recall two windows and cosmic peace
Of bare brown rooms and on whitewashed walls
Photographs of the passionate and pale Pearse.

I recall wet thatch and peeling jambs
And how all was best seen from below in the field;   10
I used to sit in the rushes with ledger-book and pencil
Compiling poems of passion for Cáit Killann.

Often she used linger on the sill of a window;
Hands by her side and brown legs akimbo;
In sun-red skirt and moon-black blazer;   15
Looking toward our strange world wide-eyed.

Our world was strange because it had no future;
She was America-bound at summer's end.
She had no choice but to leave her home –
The girl with the keys to Pearse's Cottage.   20

O Cáit Killann, O Cáit Killann,
You have gone with your keys from your own native place.
Yet here in this dark – El Greco eyes blaze black
From your Connemara postman's daughter's proudly mortal face.

Notes

	Pearse:	Padraig Pearse (1879–1916), schoolteacher, writer and iconic leader of the 1916 Rising, for which he was executed
	Pearse's Cottage:	a traditional Irish cottage in Connemara now restored and a tourist venue. It was used by Padraig Pearse as a summer residence and summer school venue for his pupils from St Enda's, the school he ran in Dublin.
	Girl with the Keys:	the girl who unlocked the cottage for visitors
8	**passionate and pale Pearse:**	'passionate' presumably refers to his ardent commitment to Irish independence and in particular his view that the activists needed to sacrifice their lives so that the population at large would be aroused to support the cause of independence
23	**El Greco:**	Domenikos Theotokopoulos (1541–1614) was a major painter of the Spanish Renaissance, who was born in Crete, hence the name El Greco ('the Greek'). He is known for his elongated, tortured-looking figures. Among the many distinctive elements of his figures are large, dark, expressive eyes that seem to communicate the thoughts and feelings of the figures.

Explorations

FIRST READING

1.

a   At one level, this is a poem about a teenager's passionate infatuation with a girl. Who is the girl, Cáit Killann?

b   If you were going to draw a sketch of her or make a painting, what details would you include in order to create a true likeness? Search the poem for all details: what does she look like; does she have a very busy day; is she happy, content or something else; what is she thinking as she is 'Looking towards our strange world wide-eyed', etc.

c   Discuss in groups the aspects that should feature in a true likeness and make a list.

2.   Do you think she is aware of the young poet's feelings towards her? Are there any indications of this in the poem?

3.   This poem is about the relationship from the writer's perspective. What are his feelings on this? Chart the range of emotions he expresses as the poem develops.

4.   Do you think this is a sad love poem? Explain your thinking.

SECOND READING

5.   At another level, this is a poem about political ideals and society. Pearse was an iconic figure who gave his life for Irish independence. The cottage was regarded as a sort of shrine to his memory, a political holy place. Read stanzas 2–3 carefully. What is the writer's experience of the place? Explore the complexity of his thoughts here, in a group discussion.

Paul Durcan

6. Though the terms 'passionate' and 'passion' are used in connection both with Pearse and the young Durcan, it serves to emphasise the differences between their preoccupations and attitudes to life. Would you agree? Discuss their differences.

7. The Proclamation of the Provisional Government of the Irish Republic to the People of Ireland, signed by Pearse and the other leaders in 1916, contains the following political promises:

'The Republic guarantees religious and civil liberty, equal rights and equal opportunities for all its citizens, and declares its resolve to pursue the happiness and prosperity of the whole nation, cherishing all the children of the nation equally...'

On the evidence of this poem, do you think these ambitions for the citizens have been achieved?

8. What political point is Durcan making in this poem? Do you think he is making it in anger or in sadness? Explain your thinking.

9. Is it not highly ironic that Cáit Killann has the keys to Pearse's cottage?

10. Who is Cáit Killann? Do you think she may represent more than just the girl Durcan met when he was 16? Discuss.

THIRD READING

11. What do you like about this poem?

12. Does this poem reflect the thinking, attitudes, values and fears of young people in Ireland in present times? Discuss this and then write a review of the poem under this heading.

The Difficulty That Is Marriage Track 20

We disagree to disagree, we divide, we differ;
Yet each night as I lie in bed beside you
And you are faraway curled up in sleep
I array the moonlit ceiling with a mosaic of question marks;
How was it I was so lucky to have ever met you?   5
I am no brave pagan proud of my mortality
Yet gladly on this changeling earth I should live for ever
If it were with you, my sleeping friend.
I have my troubles and I shall always have them
But I should rather live with you for ever   10
Than exchange my troubles for a changeless kingdom.   .
But I do not put you on a pedestal or throne;
You must have your faults but I do not see them.
If it were with you, I should live for ever.

Notes

4	array:	here it can mean to cover with or adorn; or to set in order, in lines or ranks
7	changeling earth:	a changeling is a person or thing put in place of another. For example, there are references to changeling children in Irish fairytales. The phrase 'changeling earth' embodies a religious philosophy of life, i.e. that our life on earth is a temporary substitute for authentic eternal life.
9	my troubles:	may refer to depression, which the poet has experienced and has written about elsewhere
12	pedestal:	the base for a statue or sculpture

Explorations

BEFORE READING

1. Read only the title. What thoughts, feelings and images would you expect to find in a poem of this title?

FIRST READING

2.

a Focus on lines 1–4. These first four lines set the scene and outline the problem. What do you notice in these lines? Make a list.

b What questions are raised in your mind by these lines? List them.

c Now share your observations and questions in group discussion.

3. Trace the speaker's line of thinking through the rest of the poem. In your own words, note down the main thoughts.

Paul Durcan

4. In the first line, the speaker outlines the issue in a precise, emotionless, almost mathematical-sounding expression. Now, read through the rest of the poem as a neutral observer. What are the differences between husband and wife that you notice?

5. What are the speaker's feelings towards his wife? Carefully consider each reference to her and examine what it suggests.

SECOND READING

6. You have been inside the speaker's head for some time now. What kind of person is he? What would you like to ask him?

7. Durcan is writing personally and quite openly about his marriage, yet he is also articulating a dilemma about marriage in general. After careful consideration of the poem, what do you think is the difficulty about marriage, according to the speaker? Do you think the opinion on this in the Critical Commentary (on the CD) is justified?

8. Is this a poem about the difficulty of marriage or is it a love poem? Or is it both?

THIRD READING

9. Read 'Nessa' in conjunction with this poem. What are the differences and similarities in terms of themes and issues raised, mood and atmosphere, and styles of writing?

10. Could you see the two poems as marking different stages of a relationship? What do they say about each stage?

11. Durcan has been praised by critics for 'his emotional directness when dealing with family relations'. What was your reaction to his emotional directness in this poem?

12. Do you think the conversational style of this poem works well? Explain your views on this.

Wife Who Smashed Television Gets Jail

This poem is also prescribed for Ordinary Level exams in 2016, 2017 and 2018

'She came home, my Lord, and smashed in the television;   Track 21
Me and the kids were peaceably watching *Kojak*
When she marched into the living room and declared
That if I didn't turn off the television immediately
She'd put her boot through the screen;   5
I didn't turn it off, so instead she turned it off –
I remember the moment exactly because Kojak
After shooting a dame with the same name as my wife
Snarled at the corpse – Goodnight, Queen Maeve –
And then she took off her boots and smashed in the television;   10
I had to bring the kids round to my mother's place;
We got there just before the finish of *Kojak*;
(My mother has a fondness for *Kojak*, my Lord);
When I returned home my wife had deposited
What was left of the television into the dustbin,   15
Saying – I didn't get married to a television
And I don't see why my kids or anybody else's kids
Should have a television for a father or mother,
We'd be much better off all down in the pub talking
Or playing bar-billiards –   20
Whereupon she disappeared off back down again to the pub.'
Justice O'Brádaigh said wives who preferred bar-billiards to family television
Were a threat to the family which was the basic unit of society
As indeed the television itself could be said to be a basic unit of the family
And when as in this case wives expressed their preference in forms of violence   25
Jail was the only place for them. Leave to appeal was refused.

Notes

2	*Kojak*:	an American detective series that ran from 1973 to 1978, starring the famous US film and TV actor Telly Savalas. It became hugely popular around the world and had significant cultural influence. People in Ireland used American phrases from it in daily speech.
9	**Queen Maeve:**	from the old Irish Medb (Anglicised Maeve). She was Queen of Connaught in the Ulster cycle of Irish mythology, when she embarked on the Cattle Raid of Cooley (Táin Bó Cuailinge) to steal the prize bull from Conchobar Mac Neasa, King of Ulster and a former husband. She was also famous for the number of her husbands and lovers.

Paul Durcan

Explorations

BEFORE READING

1. You might like to conduct an anonymous survey of your class members about their TV viewing and internet usage. Here are a few suggestions, but you can construct your own questions.

a   How many hours per evening (on average) do you spend (i) watching TV (ii) using the internet?

b   For the most part, do family members (i) watch the TV as they eat (ii) turn off the TV and talk at meals? Tick one answer.

c   Do you watch mostly (i) American (ii) British (iii) Irish TV programmes?

    Rate 1, 2, 3 according to frequency. Discuss the findings of the survey.

2.

a   Where would you expect to read this title: 'Wife Who Smashed Television Gets Jail'?

b   If this was a headline, what might you expect to find in the rest of the article?

FIRST READING

3. Carefully examine the language of the husband's speech, down to line 15.

a   What clues us in to the fact that he is a witness, giving evidence? Look beyond the obvious.

b   Do you think that he deliberately attempts to show himself in a good light and ingratiate himself with the judge? Where? Explain your view

with reference to the language used.

c   How would you describe the tone of his speech – is he justifiably angry, rational and reasonable, self-righteous, etc.? Justify your opinion with references to the phrases used.

4. On the other hand, how does the husband attempt to portray his wife?

5. Examine the wife's speech, as quoted by the husband (lines 16–20). What point is she making? What is your opinion on it?

6. Would you agree that the judge is made to sound delightfully ridiculous by the great disconnection between the type of language he uses (serious-sounding social and moral clichés) and the actual content of what he says? Explore how this is achieved.

SECOND READING

7. Effective comic writing often uses some of the following techniques: exaggeration, inversion of the usual expectations about people's behaviour and values, take-off of accents, take-off of speech patterns and styles of language, etc. What do you find comic about this poem? Is it a light-hearted comedy or does it have a serious point?

8. Satire can be described as the use of ridicule, irony, etc. to expose folly or vice. What is Durcan actually satirising in this poem? Discuss this and write up your views.

THIRD READING

9. The literary critic Lucy Collins, in discussing Durcan's use of humour

to draw attention to social problems in Ireland, writes that 'many of his poems take an apparently absurd premise and develop it to a telling extreme'. Write a short piece discussing the poem from the perspectives of this statement.

10. Do you think this is poetry? Debate this.

11. What do you like about the poetry by Durcan that you have read so far?

Parents

This poem is also prescribed for Ordinary Level exams in 2016, 2017 and 2018

A child's face is a drowned face:
Her parents stare down at her asleep
Estranged from her by a sea:
She is under the sea
And they are above the sea: 5
If she looked up she would see them
As if locked out of their own home,
Their mouths open,
Their foreheads furrowed –
Pursed-up orifices of fearful fish –   10
Their big ears are fins behind glass
And in her sleep she is calling out to them
    Father, Father
    Mother, Mother
But they cannot hear her: 15
She is inside the sea
And they are outside the sea.
Through the night, stranded, they stare
At the drowned, drowned face of their child.

Explorations

BEFORE READING

1. Did you ever look up through the sea and experience how distorted everything appears from that perspective? What did you notice?

2. Have you ever held a newborn baby? What thoughts were going through your head? What did you feel? Talk about this in your groups.

3. What do you imagine the baby was experiencing at that moment? Share your thoughts in the group.

4. Do you know how a newborn baby actually sees the world? Find out.

FIRST READING

5. 'A child's face is a drowned face'. This opening line is dramatic, even shocking, but is there any sense in which the image is not totally unreal?

Paul Durcan

6. The poem is entitled 'Parents'. Consider the references to the perspectives of parents in the poem. What does each image suggest about how they are feeling as they 'stare down at her asleep', 'Estranged', 'As if locked out of their own home', 'mouths open', 'foreheads furrowed', etc.?

7. Now examine the scene from the baby's perspective, as the poet views it. What do you imagine she may be feeling as she looks up from 'under the sea' and sees 'Pursed-up orifices of fearful fish' as 'she is calling out to them ... they cannot hear her'?

SECOND READING

8. Through the overarching metaphor of the sea, a barrier of silence, carrying its images of distorted fish-like and drowned faces, what insights about the experiences of parents and young children does the poet manage to communicate?

9. Eamon Grennan writes, 'A poetic world of such extremities and such simplicities as those constituted by Durcan's metaphors seems designed to make us see our experiences with new born eyes – new born, that is, in spirit and feeling.' Did Durcan's metaphors enable you to experience the poem in this way? Discuss the quotation and the question and then write about how you experienced the images in the poem.

10. 'While the image of the sea in this poem has some similarities with the sea in "Nessa", there are significant differences.'
Talk about this in your discussion groups.

THIRD READING

11. Do you think this is too bleak and disturbing a meditation on the subject or do the insights gained make it worthwhile?

12. Do you think you could write with such honesty?

Track 22

Bring me back to the dark school – to the dark school of childhood:
To where tiny is tiny, and massive is massive.

Notes		
	En Famille:	in or with one's family; at home, informally. It has a suggestion of 'in private'.

Explorations

1. What thoughts are stirred up in your imagination by the image 'the dark school' of 'childhood'? Discuss this in your groups.

2. Are there contradictions between this image and what you might have expected from the title of the poem?

3. What is this poem saying about the writer's experience of childhood and family? Consider both lines.

4. Do you think the brevity works well here? Explain your thinking on this.

Madman

Every child has a madman on their street:
The only trouble about *our* madman is that he's our father.

Explorations

1. Have you ever felt acutely embarrassed by your parents? Write about an incident.

2. As we know from his writing, Durcan had a troubled relationship with his father. Do you think the humour here takes the sting out of the unhappy memory while still making the point?

Paul Durcan

But, then, at the end of the day I could always say –
Well, now, I am going home.
I felt elected, steeped, sovereign to be able to say –
I am going home.
When I was at home I liked to stay at home;   5
At home I stayed at home for weeks;
At home I used sit in a winged chair by the window
Overlooking the river and the factory chimneys,
The electricity power station and the car assembly works,
The fleets of trawlers and the pilot tugs,   10
Dreaming that life is a dream which is real,
The river a reflection of itself in its own waters,
Goya sketching Goya among the smoky mirrors.
The industrial vista was my Mont Sainte-Victoire.
While my children sat on my knees watching TV   15
Their mother, my wife, reclined on the couch
Knitting a bright-coloured scarf, drinking a cup of black coffee,
Smoking a cigarette – one of her own roll-ups.
I closed my eyes and breathed in and breathed out.
It is ecstasy to breathe if you are at home in the world.   20
What a windfall! A home of our own!
Our neighbours' houses had names like 'Con Amore',
'Sans Souci', 'Pacelli', 'Montini', 'Homesville'.
But we called our home 'Windfall'.
'Windfall', 8 Parnell Hill, Cork.   25
In the gut of my head coursed the leaf of tranquillity
Which I dreamed was known only to Buddhist Monks
In lotus monasteries high up in the Hindu Kush.
Down here in the dark depth of Ireland,
Below sea level in the city of Cork,   30
In a city as intimate and homicidal as a Little Marseille,
In a country where all the children of the nation
Are not cherished equally
And where the best go homeless, while the worst
Erect block-house palaces – self-regardingly ugly –   35
Having a home of your own can give to a family
A chance in a lifetime to transcend death.

At the high window, shipping from all over the world
Being borne up and down the busy, yet contemplative, river;
Skylines drifting in and out of skylines in the cloudy valley;   40

Firelight at dusk, and city lights;
Beyond them the control tower of the airport on the hill –
A lighthouse in the sky flashing green to white to green;
Our black-and-white cat snoozing in the corner of a chair;
Pastels and etchings on the four walls, and over the mantelpiece   45
'Van Gogh's Grave' and 'Lovers in Water';
A room wallpapered in books and family photograph albums
Chronicling the adventures and metamorphoses of family life:
In swaddling clothes in Mammy's arms on baptism day;
Being a baby of nine months and not remembering it;   50
Face-down in a pram, incarcerated in a high chair;
Everybody, including strangers, wearing shop-window smiles;
With Granny in Felixstowe, with Granny in Ballymaloe;
In a group photo in First Infants, on a bike at thirteen;
In the back garden in London, in the back garden in Cork;   55
Performing a headstand after First Holy Communion;
Getting a kiss from the Bishop on Confirmation Day;
Straw hats in the Bois de Boulogne, wearing wings at the seaside;
Mammy and Daddy holding hands on the Normandy Beaches;
Mammy and Daddy at the wedding of Jeremiah and Margot;   60
Mammy and Daddy queuing up for *Last Tango in Paris*;
Boating on the Shannon, climbing mountains in Kerry;
Building sandcastles in Killala, camping in Barley Cove;
Picnicking in Moone, hide-and-go-seek in Clonmacnoise;
Riding horses, cantering, jumping fences;   65
Pushing out toy yachts in the pond in the Tuileries;
The Irish College revisited in the Rue des Irlandais;
Sipping an *orange pressé* through a straw on the roof of the Beaubourg;
Dancing in Père Lachaise, weeping at Auvers.
Year in, year out, I pored over these albums accumulating,   70
My children looking over my shoulder, exhilarated as I was,
Their mother presiding at our ritual from a distance –
The far side of the hearthrug, diffidently, proudly.
Schoolbooks on the floor and pyjamas on the couch –
Whose turn is it tonight to put the children to bed?   75

Our children swam about our home
As if it was their private sea,
Their own unique, symbiotic fluid
Of which their parents also partook.
Such is home – a sea of your own –   80
In which you hang upside down from the ceiling
With equanimity, while postcards from Thailand on the mantelpiece
Are raising their eyebrow markings benignly:

                                                    Paul Durcan

Your hands dangling their prayers to the floorboards of your home,
Sifting the sands underneath the surfaces of conversations,   85
The marine insect life of the family psyche.
A home of your own – or a sea of your own –
In which climbing the walls is as natural
As making love on the stairs;
In which when the telephone rings   90
Husband and wife are metamorphosed into smiling accomplices,
Both declining to answer it;
Initiating, instead, a yet more subversive kiss –
A kiss they have perhaps never attempted before –
And might never have dreamed of attempting   95
Were it not for the telephone belling.
Through the banisters or along the banister rails
The pyjama-clad children solemnly watching
Their parents at play, jumping up and down in support,
Race back to bed, gesticulating wordlessly;   100
The most subversive unit in society is the human family.

We're almost home, pet, almost home ...
Our home is at ...
I'll be home ...
I have to go home now ...   105
I want to go home now ...
Are you feeling homesick?
Are you anxious to get home? ...
I can't wait to get home ...
Let's stay at home tonight and ...   110
What time will you be coming home at? ...
If I'm not home by six at the latest, I'll phone ...
We're nearly home, don't worry, we're nearly home ...

But then with good reason
I was put out of my home: 115
By a keen wind felled.
I find myself now without a home
Having to live homeless in the alien, foreign city of Dublin.
It is an eerie enough feeling to be homesick
Yet knowing you will be going home next week;   120
It is an eerie feeling beyond all ornithological analysis
To be homesick knowing that there is no home to go home to:
Day by day, creeping, crawling,
Moonlighting, escaping,

Bed-and-breakfast to bed-and-breakfast;   125
Hostels, centres, one-night hotels.

Homeless in Dublin,
Blown about the suburban streets at evening,
Peering in the windows of other people's homes,
Wondering what it must feel like   130
To be sitting around a fire –
Apache or Cherokee or Bourgeoisie –
Beholding the firelit faces of your family,
Beholding their starry or their TV gaze:
Windfall to Windfall – can you hear me?   135
Windfall to Windfall ...
We're almost home, pet, don't worry anymore, we're almost home.

Notes

13	Goya sketching Goya:	Francisco José de Goya y Lucientes (1746–1828) was a Spanish Romantic painter and royal painter at the Spanish court in Madrid. Perhaps the reference is to a 'Portrait of Francisco Goya' by Vincente López y Portana (1826) that shows Goya with his palette and brushes looking out from the painting as if he is both painter and sitter.
14	Mont Sainte-Victoire:	the 19th-century French post-Impressionist painter Paul Cezanne had a home in Provence with a view of the Sainte-Victoire mountains and he often painted them
22-3	'Con Amore' ... 'Montini'	'Con Amore' means 'with love' (Italian); 'Sans Souci' means 'without worries' (French); 'Pacelli' and 'Montini' are the surnames of Catholic popes
27	Buddhist Monks:	Buddhism is a spiritual way of life that is 2,500 years old and focuses on personal spiritual development and the attainment of enlightenment into the true nature of life. Buddhists meditate in order to still the mind, be at peace and live each moment.
28	lotus monasteries:	the lotus position is a cross-legged position in meditation
28	Hindu Kush:	a mountain range in Central Asia, running through Afghanistan and Pakistan. Ironically, in the context of the poem, this has been an area of military conflict for over two and a half millennia.
32-3	all the children ... equally:	a reference to aspirations in the 1916 Proclamation. Durcan is pointing out the failure to realise these.
34	best go ... worst:	these lines echo the social criticism of W.B. Yeats's poem 'The Second Coming': 'The best lack all conviction, while the worst | Are full of passionate intensity'.

Paul Durcan

45	Pastels:	drawings or pictures done in a type of crayon etchings; engravings created by using acid on a metal plate; also impressions produced from this etched plate
46	'Van Gogh's Grave':	this is a reference to the grave of Vincent Van Gogh (1853–90), a Dutch post-Impressionist painter who spent much of his life in France and is buried at Auvers-sur-Oise, in a Paris suburb
48	metamorphoses:	changes
49	swaddling clothes:	the bandages that were used to wrap up newborn babies tightly, considered good practice in previous centuries
53	Felixstowe:	a seaside town on the coast of Suffolk in the UK
57	kiss ... Confirmation Day:	a reference to what was formerly a liturgical kiss of peace (like the Continental form of greeting – an 'air kiss' on both cheeks). This had been adapted to a pat on the cheek for Confirmation. Perhaps it's a handshake now?
58	Bois de Boulougne:	a famous city park in Paris, also known as one of the city's red light districts
59	Normandy Beaches:	scene of the Normandy landings on 6 June 1944 (D-Day) where the Allies landed on the coast of France in World War II. There are many cemeteries and war memorials in the area, often visited by relatives and other tourists.
61	*Last Tango in Paris*:	an iconic Bertolucci film (1972) starring Marlon Brando and Maria Schneider about the sexual affair between a young Parisian woman and a middle-aged American
63	Killala ... Barley Cove:	seaside villages/townlands in counties Mayo and Cork, respectively
64	Moone ... Clonmacnoise:	historic religious sites, locations of ancient High Cross and monastic ruins in counties Kildare and Offaly, respectively
66	Tuileries:	surviving garden of a destroyed royal palace near the Louvre in Paris
67	The Irish College ... Rue des Irlandais:	founded in the late 16th century, it was a Catholic college of education. In the 18th century this was extended to a second college, built on the Rue des Irlandais. The college now houses the Centre Culturel Irlandais.
68	*orange pressé*:	fresh orange squash
68	Beaubourg:	the Pompidou Centre complex in Paris, known locally as the Beaubourg, is a significant centre of culture. It has views across the rooftops of Paris.
69	Père Lachaise:	a cemetery in Paris containing the graves of many famous artists and writers
69	Auvers:	probably Auvers-sur-Oise, a suburb of Paris associated with famous artists. Vincent Van Gogh is buried in the cemetery there.

78	**symbiotic:**	symbiosis is a mutually advantageous association between organisms or people. There is an echo here too of amniotic fluid, in which a baby is enveloped in the womb.
121	**ornithological analysis:**	the study of birds
132	**Apache:**	the term used to describe several related groups of Native Americans in the south-western United States
132	**Cherokee:**	a Native American people settled in the south-eastern United States
132	**Bourgeoisie:**	middle class

Explorations

Lines 1–14

1. How does the writer feel about the concept of 'home'? What words, phrases and images communicate this?

2. Describe the view from his window.

3. Is there anything to suggest that he finds this view artistically inspiring? Consult the line notes and then outline your view.

Lines 15–37

4. Would you agree that this section begins with a romanticised view of perfect family life? Explain how you see this.

5.

a A 'windfall' can refer to fruit blown down by the wind or unexpected good fortune (such as money). Why do you suppose they named the house 'Windfall'?

b Personalised house names often reflect the philosophies and ideals of their owners. If so, what do we learn about the writer's neighbours?

c Do you think the writer fits in well with this community? Discuss.

6. The writer is obviously delighted at their good fortune: 'A home of our own!' But he also feels a deeper spiritual contentment. Explore the references and images here and try to express what he is experiencing in your own words.

7. Ironically, this experience of contentment leads him to think about the less than ideal society all around. Consult the line references and explain what exactly the writer is criticising here.

Lines 38–75

You could think of this section as organised along cinematic lines in the following way:

- The opening shot shows the view through the window.

- Then the camera pans to take in the room and shows some details, such as the domestic cat and the pictures.

- It then zooms in to examine the details of the photograph albums 'Chronicling the adventures and metamorphoses of family life'. This is the central section.

Paul Durcan

- At the end, the camera pulls back a little to show the attitudes of his children and wife to their family reminiscences.

8.

a   Examine the detail of the photographic history. What does this reveal about the writer's family background and personal experience?

b   What does this add to the understanding of family that is being built up in this poem?

c   What are the attitudes of his wife and children to this reminiscence?

Lines 76–101

9.   Would you agree that 'home' for them is a very personal, private space in which the adults can be uninhibited? Write about what you discover from the poem about this.

10. How does the metaphor of the home as a sea contribute to Durcan's concept of the ideal home as an uninhibiting place?

11. How do you understand the following lines?

'Sifting the sands underneath the surfaces of conversations, | The marine insect life of the family psyche.'

12. Did the children have a happy childhood? Explain your thoughts on this, with reference to the poem.

13. 'The most subversive unit in society is the human family.'
Do you think this is actually true or is it an ideal of Durcan's? Debate the issue.

Lines 102–13

14. Durcan is famous for the quality of his poetry reading. In your groups, plan for and perform aloud the litany of words, the type of chant in this section. Each person reads a line in succession. Read as you think it might be said (imagine someone saying it – who, where?), then have a group discussion on the possible ways of saying each line. When ready, perform the section aloud. What does this section convey about the writer's concept of home?

Lines 114–37

15. 'But then with good reason | I was put out of my home: | By a keen wind felled.' What is your reaction to these lines?

16. What pictures and images of homelessness affect you most in this section? Talk about them.

17. The writer gives a new and bitter twist to the idea of homesickness. What is the effect of this?

18. What does he miss most? What image haunts him?

19. 'Windfall to Windfall – can you hear me? | Windfall to Windfall…' What are your thoughts when you read these lines?

20. Do you find the echo of former times in the final line a consolation or desperately sad?

SECOND READING

21. This poem is both a 'celebration of domesticity' and a record of the poet's feelings after the break-up of his marriage. Critical opinion varies

on the appropriateness of writing about this. Some praise his openness and courage in writing about intimate private life; others feel that continuing to revisit it is exploitative. What do you think?

22. 'But then with good reason | I was put out of my home'.

a   In an online article, critic Alan Dent is trenchant in his criticism:

'Yet this is not an honest appraisal of his shortcomings, it is a self-serving posture. It is a manipulation. The cry of "How unworthy I am!" demands the response "Of course you aren't!" '

Is this a fair criticism or is the critic demanding a different type of poem altogether?

b   Do you think there is a degree of self-pity in this poem?

c   Read the Critical Commentary on the CD to hear what Durcan himself says about the 'good reason'.

23. Collect together all the elements of the ideal home as envisaged by Durcan in this poem. Critique this vision. In what way could it be considered subversive of Irish society?

24. The sea metaphor plays a significant role in imaging the family here. In an interview in the *Irish Times* (10 February 1990), Durcan said, 'To me everything that is good is water-connected or based, even attitudes to life – flowing into things rather than being rigid.'

a   Explore again what Eamon Grennan called 'the extended life of this metaphor' in the third section of this poem (lines 76–86).

b   Explore each of the additions the metaphor gathers as it grows, from 'private sea' → 'symbiotic fluid' → 'home – a sea of your own' → 'hang upside down' → 'hands dangling their prayers to the floorboards' → 'The marine insect life of the family psyche'.

c   What light does this throw on Durcan's concept of the ideal family?

25. 'Even in a poem about private family life, Durcan is aware of wider social issues.'
Discuss this statement.

Paul Durcan

Six Nuns Die in Convent Inferno

To the
happy memory of six Loreto nuns
who died
between midnight and morning of
2 June 1986

I

We resided in a Loreto convent in the centre of Dublin city
On the east side of a public gardens, St Stephen's Green.
Grafton Street – the *paseo*
Where everybody *paseo*'d, including even ourselves –
Debouched on the north side, and at the top of Grafton Street,   5
Or round the base of the great patriotic pebble of O'Donovan Rossa,
Knelt tableaus of punk girls and punk boys.
When I used pass them – scurrying as I went –
Often as not to catch a mass in Clarendon Street,
The Carmelite Church in Clarendon Street,   10
(Myself, I never used the Clarendon Street entrance,
I always slipped in by way of Johnson's Court,
Opposite the side entrance to Bewley's Oriental Café),
I could not help but smile, as I sucked on a Fox's mint,
That for all the half-shaven heads and the martial garb   15
And the dyed hair-dos and the nappy pins
They looked so conventional, really, and vulnerable,
Clinging to warpaint and to uniforms and to one another.
I knew it was myself who was the ultimate drop-out,
The delinquent, the recidivist, the vagabond,   20
The wild woman, the subversive, the original punk.
Yet, although I confess I was smiling, I was also afraid,
Appalled by my own nerve, my own fervour,
My apocalyptic enthusiasm, my other-worldly hubris:
To opt out of the world and to   25
Choose such exotic loneliness,
Such terrestrial abandonment,
A lifetime of bicycle lamps and bicycle pumps,
A lifetime of galoshes stowed under the stairs,
A lifetime of umbrellas drying out in the kitchens.   30

I was an old nun – an agèd beadswoman –
But I was no daw.

I knew what a weird bird I was, I knew that when we
Went to bed we were as eerie an aviary as you'd find
In all the blown-off rooftops of the city: 35
Scuttling about our dorm, wheezing, shrieking, croaking,
In our yellowy corsets, wonky suspenders, strung-out garters,
A bony crew in the gods of the sleeping city.
Many's the night I lay awake in bed
Dreaming what would befall us if there were a fire: 40
No fire-escapes outside, no fire-extinguishers inside;
To coin a Dublin saying,
We'd not stand a snowball's chance in hell. Fancy that!
It seemed too good to be true:
Happy death vouchsafed only to the few.   45
Sleeping up there was like sleeping at the top of the mast
Of a nineteenth-century schooner, and in the daytime
We old nuns were the ones who crawled out on the yardarms
To stitch and sew the rigging and the canvas.
To be sure we were weird birds, oddballs, Christniks,   50
For we had done the weirdest thing a woman can do –
Surrendered the marvellous passions of girlhood,
The innocent dreams of childhood,
Not for a night or a weekend or even a Lent or a season,
But for a lifetime.   55
Never to know the love of a man or a woman;
Never to have children of our own;
Never to have a home of our own;
All for why and for what?
To follow a young man – would you believe it –   60
Who lived two thousand years ago in Palestine
And who died a common criminal strung up on a tree.

As we stood there in the disintegrating dormitory
Burning to death in the arms of Christ –
O Christ, Christ, come quickly, quickly –   65
Fluttering about in our tight, gold bodices,
Beating our wings in vain,
It reminded me of the snaps one of the sisters took
When we took a seaside holiday in 1956
(The year Cardinal Mindszenty went into hiding   70
In the US legation in Budapest.
He was a great hero of ours, Cardinal Mindszenty,
Any of us would have given our right arm
To have been his nun – darning his socks, cooking his meals,
Making his bed, doing his washing and ironing.)   75

Paul Durcan

Somebody – an affluent buddy of the bishop's repenting his affluence –
Loaned Mother Superior a secluded beach in Co. Waterford –
Ardmore, along the coast from Tramore –
A cove with palm trees, no less, well off the main road.
There we were fluttering up and down the beach,   80
Scampering hither and thither in our starched bathing-costumes.
Tonight, expiring in the fire, was quite much like that,
Only instead of scampering into the waves of the sea,
Now we were scampering into the flames of the fire.

That was one of the gayest days of my life,   85
The day the sisters went swimming.
Often in the silent darkness of the chapel after Benediction,
During the Exposition of the Blessed Sacrament,
I glimpsed the sea again as it was that day.
Praying – daydreaming really –   90
I became aware that Christ is the ocean
Forever rising and falling on the world's shore.
Now tonight in the convent Christ is the fire in whose waves
We are doomed but delighted to drown.
And, darting in and out of the flames of the dormitory,   95
Gabriel, with that extraordinary message of his on his boyish lips,
Frenetically pedalling his skybike.
He whispers into my ear what I must do
And I do it – and die.
Each of us in our own tiny, frail, furtive way   100
Was a Mother of God, mothering forth illegitimate Christs
In the street life of Dublin city.
God have mercy on our whirring souls –
Wild women were we all –
And on the misfortunate, poor fire-brigade men   105
Whose task it will be to shovel up our ashes and shovel
What is left of us into black plastic refuse sacks.
Fire-brigade men are the salt of the earth.

Isn't it a marvellous thing how your hour comes
When you least expect it? When you lose a thing,   110
Not to know about it until it actually happens?
How, in so many ways, losing things is such a refreshing experience,
Giving you a sense of freedom you've not often experienced?
How lucky I was to lose – I say, lose – lose my life.
It was a Sunday night, and after vespers   115
I skipped bathroom so that I could hop straight into bed
And get in a bit of a read before lights out:

Conor Cruise O'Brien's new book *The Siege*,
All about Israel and superlatively insightful
For a man who they say is reputedly an agnostic –   120
I got a loan of it from the brother-in-law's married niece –
But I was tired out and I fell asleep with the book open
Face down across my breast and I woke
To the racket of bellowing flame and snarling glass.
The first thing I thought was that the brother-in-law's married niece   125
Would never again get her Conor Cruise O'Brien back
And I had seen on the price-tag that it cost £23.00:
Small wonder that the custom of snipping off the price
As an exercise in social deportment has simply died out;
Indeed a book today is almost worth buying for its price,   130
Its price frequently being more remarkable than its contents.

The strange Eucharist of my death –
To be eaten alive by fire and smoke.
I clasped the dragon to my breast
And stroked his red-hot ears.   135
Strange! There we were, all sleeping molecules,
Suddenly all giving birth to our deaths,
All frantically in labour.
Doctors and midwives weaved in and out
In gowns of smoke and gloves of fire.   140
Christ, like an Orthodox patriarch in his dressing gown,
Flew up and down the dormitory, splashing water on our souls:
Sister Eucharia; Sister Seraphia; Sister Rosario;
Sister Gonzaga; Sister Margaret; Sister Edith.
If you will remember us – six nuns burnt to death –   145
Remember us for the frisky girls that we were,
Now more than ever kittens in the sun.

II

When Jesus heard these words at the top of Grafton Street
Uttered by a small, agèd, emaciated, female punk
Clad all in mourning black, and grieving like an alley cat,   150
He was annulled with astonishment, and turning round
He declared to the gangs of teenagers and dicemen following him:
'I tell you, not even in New York City
Have I found faith like this.'

That night in St Stephen's Green,   155
After the keepers had locked the gates,

Paul Durcan

And the courting couples had found cinemas themselves to die in,
The six nuns who had died in the convent inferno,
From the bandstand they'd been hiding under, crept out
And knelt together by the Fountain of the Three Fates,   160
Reciting the Agnus Dei: reciting it as if it were the torch song
Of all aid – Live Aid, Self Aid, AIDS, and All Aid –
Lord, I am not worthy
That thou should'st enter under my roof;
Say but the word and my soul shall be healed.   165

Notes

3	**Grafton Street:**	well-known shopping street off St Stephen's Green in Dublin
3	*paseo:*	a public place designed for walking; a slow, idle walk
5	**Debouched:**	emerged from a confined space
6	**pebble of O'Donovan Rossa:**	Jeremiah O'Donovan Rossa (1831–1915) was an important Fenian leader. His monument in St Stephen's Green consists of a bronze plaque fixed into a very large piece of stone that could be seen to resemble an enormous pebble.
7	**punk:**	a fast, hard-edged style of rock music that originated in the 1970s; punk fashion among followers involved highly distinctive clothes, hairstyles, body piercing, etc.

10	The Carmelite Church in Clarendon Street:	staffed by the Carmelite community, St Teresa's Church, off Grafton Street, is well known for its midnight mass at Christmastime
13	Bewley's Oriental Café:	also on Grafton Street
14	Fox's mint:	well-known mint sweets, famous for the polar bear icon on the wrapper
20	delinquent:	young offender, hooligan, tearaway
20	recidivist:	person who relapses into crime
20	vagabond:	wanderer, having no settled home
21	subversive:	person trying to overthrow, for instance, the system or the government
24	apocalyptic enthusiasm:	the apocalypse was a revelation about the end of the world; so enthusiasm for the end of the world
24	hubris:	arrogant pride
26	exotic loneliness:	exotic has many shades of meaning, such as foreign, different, unusual
27	terrestrial abandonment:	abandonment of the world, the earth
29	galoshes:	waterproof overshoes
32	no daw:	usually taken to mean 'no fool'
34	as eerie an aviary:	aviary is a large cage for keeping birds; eerie, as an adjective, could mean creepy, frightening, ghostly. But it could also be a word play on 'eyrie', which is the nest of a bird of prey, built high up in trees or cliffs
37	wonky:	slang for unsteady, unreliable
37	suspenders ... garters:	attachments, formerly used to hold up clothes and stockings
38	in the gods:	'the gods' is the term used for the seats at the very top of a steeply raked theatre, giving a bird's eye view of the stage. Here, the dormitory at the top of the house has a similar view of the city.
45	vouchsafed:	conferred as a favour; granted
47	schooner:	a two-masted ship
50	Christniks:	followers of Christ
54	Lent:	religious period (traditionally a time of fasting and penance) between Ash Wednesday and Easter Saturday
61	Palestine:	refers here to what became known as the Holy Land, the region where Christ lived and preached

Paul Durcan

66	bodices:	the part of women's dresses above the waist
70	**Cardinal Mindszenty:**	a Catholic bishop in Hungary who opposed both fascists and Nazis in World War II. After torture and imprisonment he managed to take refuge in the United States legation in 1956.
87–8	**Benediction ... Exposition:**	Benediction is a religious liturgy of prayer where the Blessed Sacrament (Host) is on view (Exposition). It usually ends with a benediction or blessing with the Sacred Host.
95	**Gabriel:**	a reference to the angel Gabriel in the Bible, who was sent by God to tell Mary that she was to be the mother of the Son of God
117	**Conor Cruise O'Brien *The Siege*: ...**	(1917–2008) Irish academic, historian and politician who was a very forthright speaker and writer. One of his most controversial works was *The Siege* (1989), a sympathetic history of Zionism and the state of Israel.
119	agnostic:	a person who believes that the existence of God is not provable
132	**Eucharist:**	in the Catholic faith, this refers to the celebration of the Mass in which the sacrifice and death of Christ is re-enacted. The poet is making a connection between the nun's death and that of Christ. Her death is another sacrifice.
140	**Orthodox patriarch:**	a leader of the Eastern European or Orthodox branch of Christianity, usually seen dressed in elaborate priestly robes
143–4	**Sister Eucharia etc.:**	in former times when a woman became a nun she adopted the name of a saint or holy person as her new religious name. This signified that she had put her former life behind her and was now a member of a new religious family.
148–54	**When Jesus heard these words ... faith like this:**	in this section an episode from the life of Christ in the Gospels is transposed and applied to modern times, with both humorous and serious effects. The incident is told in St Matthew's Gospel, Chapter 8, among others. Jesus was asked by a centurion (an officer of the conquering Roman army that ruled the Jews) to help his servant who was paralysed. Jesus said that he would come and cure him. But the centurion said, 'Lord, I am not fit that you should come in under my roof. But just say a word and my servant will be healed.'... 'Jesus heard this and was astonished; and he said to the people following, "Amen, I tell you, I have not found such faith from anyone in Israel".'

160	**Fountain of the Three Fates:**	This fountain in St Stephen's Green, erected in 1956, was a gift from the people of the German Federal Republic to show their gratitude for Ireland's help after the war of 1939–45. It shows the three legendary Fates spinning and measuring the thread of man's destiny.
161	**Agnus Dei:**	a Latin phrase, translates as 'Lamb of God' and referring to Jesus. It is the opening phrase of a prayer in the Liturgy of the Mass – 'Lamb of God, who takes away the sins of the world, have mercy on us'.

Explorations

Note: Part I of this poem is narrated in the voice of one of the Loreto nuns who lost her life in the fire and it is structured as a reminiscence that is at times realistic and at times imagined.

FIRST READING

Lines 1–30

1. In the first 13 lines the speaker sets the scene, giving us a feeling for the environment around the convent. What details do you notice about the geography of the place, buildings, etc. that she mentions? Use Google Maps to trace her journey from Loreto Convent to the Clarendon Street Church. What do you see?

2. Follow her journey in your mind's eye as you read the poem. Do you see her strolling at leisure, comfortable in her environment, or something else? Examine the detail.

3. She has a particularly good understanding and empathy for the 'tableaus of punk girls and punk boys' she passes on her journey. What particular insights does she articulate about them?

4. In what way might the punks be considered 'conventional'?

5. This leads her to consider her own position. She uses the terms 'delinquent', 'recidivist', 'vagabond', 'wild woman', 'subversive' and 'original punk' and 'ultimate dropout' about herself. Has she lost the plot? Or do you think there is a sense in which these terms could apply to her? How was she more radical than the punks?

6. Did her radical choice lead to an exciting lifestyle?

Lines 31–62

7. 'But I was no daw. | I knew what a weird bird I was'.

a How are these women described as strange or different?

b What is their attitude to death here?

c The strangeness is emphasised in the dream metaphor of the schooner. Do you think this is effective?

8.

a 'For we had done the weirdest thing a woman can do'.
In your own words, explain what this was.

b Nuns have been described as 'brides of Christ'. Does this concept help you understand the nun's motivation here? Discuss.

Paul Durcan

Lines 63–84

9. The first five lines of this section describe the fire taking hold in the disintegrating dormitory. What do you notice about the image of the nuns described here?

10. In a somewhat bizarre memory link, their panic-stricken fluttering about in the dormitory reminds her of fluttering up and down the beach on the one memorable holiday of her life. Carefully read the final three lines of this section. What does this communicate about the nuns' attitude to death?

Lines 84–131

11. She refers to that holiday as 'one of the gayest days of my life'. That seaside experience led her to think of Christ in a new way. Explain this in your own words.

12. 'I became aware that Christ is the ocean
   Forever rising and falling on the world's shore.
   Now tonight in the convent Christ is the fire in whose waves
   We are doomed but delighted to drown.'

   If you refer back to the concept of nuns as 'brides of Christ', does it help you to understand the attitude to death here? Discuss this.

13. Strange dream-like image connections are made here. The angel Gabriel ('Frenetically pedalling his skybike') whispers in her ear, which reminds her of his message to the mother of God. She thinks:

   'Each of us in our own tiny, frail, furtive way

Was a Mother of God, mothering forth illegitimate Christs
In the street life of Dublin city.'

   Though on first reading it may appear shocking, is there a sense in which this explains the religious mission of the nuns? Discuss.

14. Despite the lengthy emphasis on death in the poem, the lively personalities of the nuns and their compassionate understanding for people come across strongly. Do you think this is true of this section? What do you notice about them here?

15.

   a Lines 109–13 give quite a positive, even upbeat view of death. What insights are offered on the subject?

   b What do we learn about the nuns from this?

16. Read lines 114–30. The everyday small talk of the old nun 'wittering on' and the conversational tone of the piece is in stark contrast to the savage, wild animal reality of the fire ('bellowing flame and snarling glass'). What is the resulting effect of this contrast, do you think?

Lines 132–47

17. From the perspective of a religious faith, death is the end of one form of life but the beginning of another. In that sense it is a sort of birth. What are your thoughts on how this is portrayed in the final section of part I?

18. How does the speaker want us to remember them, finally?

Part II

19. Though the first section of part II is narrated with visual and verbal humour, a serious point is still being made. Discuss this.

20. What are your thoughts on the final section of the poem? Does it make a good conclusion? Do you think the nun narrator of part I would enjoy it?

SECOND READING

21. Collect together all the speaker's references to death in the poem. Analyse them and put together a coherent statement on her philosophy of death.

22. Collect together all the references that show the personality of the speaker. Write an obituary for her that does justice to all aspects of her personality.

23. Do you think Durcan understands these women, not only as nuns, but also as human beings? Is he always sympathetic, never critical?

24. Critic Christina Hunt Mahony has written, 'Although Durcan has disdained the term "surreal" as applied to these departures from realism ... the point at which the real and the highly imagined collide is a successful and idiosyncratic feature of many of his poems.' Write up your views on this.

25. 'This poem is enhanced by the humour.'
Write on this.

This poem is also prescribed for Ordinary Level exams in 2016, 2017 and 2018

There were not many fields
In which you had hopes for me
But sport was one of them.
On my twenty-first birthday
I was selected to play   5
For Grangegorman Mental Hospital.
In an away game
Against Mullingar Mental Hospital.
I was a patient
In B Wing.   10
You drove all the way down,
Fifty miles,
To Mullingar to stand
On the sidelines and observe me.

I was fearful I would let down   15
Not only my team but you.
It was Gaelic football.
I was selected as goalkeeper.
There were big country men
On the Mullingar Mental Hospital team,   20
Men with gapped teeth, red faces,
Oily, frizzy hair, bushy eyebrows.
Their full forward line
Were over six foot tall
Fifteen stone in weight.   25
All three of them, I was informed,
Cases of schizophrenia.

There was a rumour
That their centre-half forward
Was an alcoholic solicitor   30
Who, in a lounge bar misunderstanding,
Had castrated his best friend
But that he had no memory of it.
He had meant well – it was said.
His best friend had had to emigrate   35
To Nigeria.

To my surprise,
I did not flinch in the goals.
I made three or four spectacular saves,
Diving full stretch to turn 40
A certain goal around the corner,
Leaping high to tip another certain goal
Over the bar for a point.
It was my knowing
That you were standing on the sideline 45
That gave me the necessary motivation –
That will to die
That is as essential to sportsmen as to artists.
More than anybody it was you
I wanted to mesmerise, and after the game – 50
Grangegorman Mental Hospital
Having defeated Mullingar Mental Hospital
By 14 goals and 38 points to 3 goals and 10 points –
Sniffing your approval, you shook hands with me.
'Well played, son.' 55

I may not have been mesmeric
But I had not been mediocre.
In your eyes I had achieved something at last.
On my twenty-first birthday I had played on a winning team
The Grangegorman Mental Hospital team. 60
Seldom if ever again in your eyes
Was I to rise to these heights.

Notes

6	**Grangegorman:**	St Brendan's Psychiatric Hospital, Grangegorman, was located in north Dublin
25	**schizophrenia:**	a mental disorder marked by disconnection between thoughts, feelings and actions (dictionary definition)
48	**mesmerise:**	hypnotise

Paul Durcan

Explorations

FIRST READING

1. 'There were not many fields
   In which you had hopes for me
   But sport was one of them.'

   What do these opening lines hint about the relationship between father and son?

2. According to the speaker, why did his father come 'all the way down' to the match?

3.

   a Was the match exciting?

   b Did the young man play well?

   c What was his main motivation to play well?

4.

   a What was the father's reaction?

   b The father doesn't say much, but what thoughts may have been going through his mind at this stage? Write them as a diary entry.

5.

   a Read the last stanza (lines 56–62). What are your thoughts and feelings on reading this?

   b What would you like to say to the speaker?

SECOND READING

6. Over half of the poems in the volume *Daddy, Daddy*, from which this poem is taken, are about the troubled relationship with his father. On the evidence of this poem, how would you describe the relationship between father and son?

7. In this poem we mainly get the son's perspective, but could the father have a different view? Discuss this.

8. How is mental illness portrayed in the poem?

9. Do you think the writer deliberately selects details to shock the reader? What may be the purpose of this?

10. Do you think the context in which the game is played is a significant element in the poem?

11. Durcan forces us to look beneath the surface of everyday events to the human unhappiness beneath. Would you agree? Write about this aspect of Durcan's poetry.

Father's Day, 21 June 1992

Just as I was dashing to catch the Dublin–Cork train,
Dashing up and down the stairs, searching my pockets,
She told me that her sister in Cork wanted a loan of the axe;
It was late June and
The buddleia tree in the backyard   5
Had grown out of control.
The taxi was ticking over outside in the street,
All the neighbours noticing it.
'You mean that you want me to bring her down the axe?'
'Yes, if you wouldn't mind, that is –'   10
'A simple saw would do the job, surely to God
She could borrow a simple saw.'
'She said she'd like the axe.'
'OK. There is a Blue Cabs taxi ticking over outside
And the whole world inspecting it,   15
I'll bring her down the axe.'
The axe – all four-and-a-half feet of it –
Was leaning up against the wall behind the settee –
The fold-up settee that doubles as a bed.
She handed the axe to me just as it was,   20
As neat as a newborn babe,
All in the bare buff.
You'd think she'd have swaddled it up
In something – if not a blanket, an old newspaper,
But no, not even a token hanky   25
Tied in a bow round its head.
I decided not to argue the toss. I kissed her goodbye.

The whole long way down to Cork
I felt uneasy. Guilt feelings.
It's a killer, this guilt.   30
I always feel bad leaving her
But this time it was the worst.
I could see she was glad
To see me go away for a while,
Glad at the prospect of being   35
Two weeks on her own,
Two weeks of having the bed to herself,
Two weeks of not having to be pestered
By my coarse advances,
Two weeks of not having to look up from her plate   40

Paul Durcan
389

And behold me eating spaghetti with a knife and fork.
Our daughters are all grown up and gone away.
Once when she was sitting pregnant on the settee
It snapped shut with herself inside it,
But not a bother on her. I nearly died.   45

As the train slowed down approaching Portarlington
I overheard myself say to the passenger sitting opposite me:
'I am feeling guilty because she does not love me
As much as she used to, can you explain that?'
The passenger's eyes were on the axe on the seat beside me.   50
'Her sister wants a loan of the axe ...'
As the train threaded itself into Portarlington
I nodded to the passenger 'Cúl an tSúdaire!'
The passenger stood up, lifted down a case from the rack,
Walked out of the coach, but did not get off the train.   55
For the remainder of the journey, we sat alone,
The axe and I,
All the green fields running away from us,
All our daughters grown up and gone away.

Notes

	Father's Day:	traditionally held in Ireland on the third Sunday in June, it celebrates fatherhood, male parenting and the influence of fathers in society. It complements Mother's Day.
5	buddleia:	a large flowering bush, easy to grow and difficult to kill
23	swaddled:	wrapped up tightly
27	argue the toss:	refuse to accept a decision; quibble over something of little consequence
46	Portarlington:	a town on the borders of counties Laois and Offaly
53	Cúl an tSúdaire:	the Irish for Portarlington, probably visible on the railway station signpost

Explorations

FIRST READING

1.

a   Working in pairs, prepare to read the first section aloud. Choose which part of the dialogue each will read. Think about the frame of mind and mood of each speaker and how each voice should sound. Discuss it and practise before each pair in turn reads aloud for the class.

b   Have a class discussion on the different interpretations and on which interpretation is closest to the text.

2. What did you discover about the two people from this exchange in the poem?

3. Who do you think is the more dominant personality? Explain your views, with reference to the text.

4.

a One of the ways in which humour is created is through sudden unexpected shifts in thought and sometimes in tone. Consider the first three lines, for example. Read them aloud dramatically and you will notice the unexpected shift in line 3.

b Are there other instances of this?

c In what other ways is the humour created?

5. In the second section there is an unexpected and sudden change in tone from the comic to the contemplative and introspective. What do we learn about the couple from this section?

6. How would you rate the self-esteem of the speaker? Explain your thinking.

7. There is another sudden change in tone at the end of this section, just after the plaintive line 'Our daughters are all grown up and gone away' (line 42). Can you think of any reason for this sudden shift?

8. T.S. Eliot once wrote, 'Human kind | Cannot bear very much reality'. For best understanding, act out the last section in pairs. You could substitute a sweeping brush for the axe.

9.

a Picture yourself on the train as the passenger alone in the carriage with the speaker and his axe. What are your thoughts as he speaks to you?

b Why do you stand up and leave when he says 'Cúl an tSúdaire'?

10. Would you describe the comedy in this section as more akin to tragi-comedy than the slapstick fun of the first section? Explain your thinking.

SECOND READING

11. Do you think it ironic that the poem is entitled 'Father's Day'? Write about this.

12. 'Behind the comedy there is always sadness in a Durcan poem.'
Is there a balance here or does this poem lean towards one or the other?

13. The critic Maurice Elliott, when discussing Durcan's changes of tone in musical terms, wrote about 'abrupt and rapid tonal changes in a series of surprises ... which ultimately leave the reader or hearer on a note of tender and, most often, melancholy compassion'. Do you think this is true of 'Father's Day'? Explain how the shifts in tone work in this poem and describe the ultimate effect on the reader.

14. Do you think Durcan is attempting to question the traditional image of fathers here? If so, what is he saying about fathers?

Paul Durcan

after Jan Van Eyck

We are the Arnolfinis.
Do not think you may invade
Our privacy because you may not.

We are standing to our portrait,
The most erotic portrait ever made,   5
Because we have faith in the artist

To do justice to the plurality,
Fertility, domesticity, barefootedness
Of a man and a woman saying 'we':

To do justice to our bed   10
As being our most necessary furniture;
To do justice to our life as a reflection.

Our brains spill out upon the floor
And the terrier at our feet sniffs
The minutiae of our magnitude.   15

The most relaxing word in our vocabulary is 'we'.
Imagine being able to say 'we'.
Most people are in no position to say 'we'.

Are you? Who eat alone? Sleep alone?
And at dawn cycle to work   20
With an Alsatian shepherd dog tied to your handlebars?

We will pause now for the Angelus.
Here you have it:
The two halves of the coconut.

- -

Notes

Jan Van Eyck:	Jan Van Eyck was a Flemish painter (c. 1395–c. 1441) who worked in Bruges and was considered one of the most significant painters of the 15th century
The Arnolfini Marriage:	an oil painting on oak panel, dated 1434, by Jan Van Eyck. It is signed on the back wall of the picture, over the mirror: 'Johannes de eyck, fuit hic 1434' (Jan Van Eyck was here, 1434). And these are the only undisputed facts about the painting! It is also known by other titles: *The Arnolfini Portrait*, *The Arnolfini Wedding*, *The Arnolfini Double Portrait* and *Portrait of Giovanni Arnolfini and His Wife*.
	The Arnolfinis were a wealthy Italian merchant clan who became merchant bankers in Bruges. There has been debate about which of the Arnolfinis is depicted and which of the wives. It is generally accepted to be a portrait of Giovanni di Nicolao Arnolfini and a wife.
	The picture has been variously considered to be an official portrait of a marriage, a portrait of a betrothal and even a memorial portrait of a deceased wife. The woman has been described as pregnant or merely holding up her heavy gown. The man's gesture may be a gesture of dismissal or a sign of welcome to the two people coming in, who are reflected in the mirror, one of whom is believed to be the painter.
	There are many signs of wealth in the portrait: the expensive clothes, the bed (which was not unusual in the living quarters), the brass chandelier, the mirror (a rare domestic luxury) and even the oranges, which were rare and expensive.
	From an artistic point of view, it is generally agreed that the painting was remarkable for its time in the realistic depiction of the people and the room, in the use of detail and in the use of light to create a sense of space.

Paul Durcan

Explorations

BEFORE READING

1. First study the painting, discuss it and read the Notes and other artistic comment on it. What impression of the Arnolfinis and their lifestyle do you form from viewing this painting? Write about this.

FIRST READING

2. What trait or quality of the Arnolfinis does the poet choose to focus on in the first stanza? What elements in the painting could prompt him to this view?

3. Why do you think this is referred to as 'The most erotic portrait ever made'? Do you think it is?

4. In the poem, the Arnolfinis say they have faith in the artist

   'To do justice to the plurality,
   Fertility, domesticity, barefootedness
   Of a man and a woman saying "we".'

a What aspect of their lives do they wish recorded?

b Do you think the painting does this effectively?

5. What other aspects of their lives do the Arnolfinis in the poem wish recorded in order to do them justice?

6. 'The most relaxing word in our vocabulary is "we".
   Imagine being able to say "we".
   Most people are in no position to say "we".'

   What do you think they may mean by this phenomenon, 'we'?

7. Then the Arnolfinis directly challenge the poet, asking if he has this perfect relationship: 'Are you?', etc. What image of the poet is painted here?

SECOND READING

8.

a In creating this poem, Durcan has selected certain elements of the painting and ignored others. What aspects of the painting has he focused on?

b Do you think the resulting poem makes a unified, coherent statement? Explain your thinking.

c What interesting elements of the painting has he ignored?

9. Would you agree with critic Kathleen McCracken that Durcan 'often translates the "story" depicted on the canvas into a contemporary social or personal context'? Write about the poem from the perspective of this statement.

10. Now compose your own poem on the painting.

Paul Durcan

I

That was that Sunday afternoon in May
When a hot sun pushed through the clouds
And you were born!

I was driving the two hundred miles from west to east,
The sky blue-and-white china in the fields   5
In impromptu picnics of tartan rugs;

When neither words nor I
Could have known that you had been named already
And that your name was Rosie –

Rosie Joyce! May you some day in May   10
Fifty-six years from today be as lucky
As I was when you were born that Sunday:

To drive such side-roads, such main roads, such ramps, such roundabouts,
To cross such bridges, to by-pass such villages, such towns
As I did on your Incarnation Day.   15

By-passing Swinford – Croagh Patrick in my rear-view mirror –
My mobile phone rang and, stopping on the hard edge of P. Flynn's highway,
I heard Mark your father say:

'A baby girl was born at 3.33 p.m.
Weighing 7 and a ½ lbs in Holles Street.   20
Tough work, all well.'

II

That Sunday in May before daybreak
Night had pushed up through the slopes of Achill
Yellow forefingers of Arum Lily – the first of the year;

Down at the Sound the first rhododendrons   25
Purpling the golden camps of whins;
The first hawthorns powdering white the mainland;

The first yellow irises flagging roadside streams;

Quills of bog-cotton skimming the bogs;
Burrishoole cemetery shin-deep in forget-me-nots;   30

The first sea pinks speckling the seashore;
Cliffs of London Pride, groves of bluebell,
First fuchsia, Queen Anne's Lace, primrose.

I drove the Old Turlough Road, past Walter Durcan's Farm,
Umbrella'd in the joined handwriting of its ash trees;   35
I drove Tulsk, Kilmainham, the Grand Canal.

Never before had I felt so fortunate
To be driving back into Dublin City;
Each canal bridge an old pewter brooch.

I rode the waters and the roads of Ireland,   40
Rosie, to be with you, seashell at my ear!
How I laughed when I cradled you in my hand.

Only at Tarmonbarry did I slow down,
As in my father's Ford Anglia half a century ago
He slowed down also, as across the River Shannon   45

We crashed, rattled bounced on a Bailey bridge;
Daddy relishing his role as Moses,
Enunciating the name of the Great Divide

Between the East and the West!
We are the people of the West,   50
Our fate to go East.

No such thing, Rosie, as a Uniform Ireland
And please God there never will be;
There is only the River Shannon and all her sister rivers

And all her brother mountains and their family prospects.   55
There are higher powers than politics
And these we call wildflowers or, geologically, people.

Rosie Joyce – that Sunday in May
Not alone did you make my day, my week, my year
To the prescription of Jonathan Philbin Bowman –   60

Paul Durcan

Daymaker!
Daymaker!
Daymaker!

Popping out of my daughter, your mother –
Changing the expressions on the faces all around you –   65
All of them looking like blue hills in a heat haze –

But you saved my life. For three years
I had been subsisting in the slums of despair,
Unable to distinguish one day from the next.

III

On the return journey from Dublin to Mayo   70
In Charlestown on Main Street
I meet John Normanly, organic farmer from Curry.

He is driving home to his wife Caroline
From a Mountbellew meeting of the western Development Commission
Of Dillon House in Ballaghadereen.   75

He crouches in his car, I waver in the street,
As we exchange lullabies of expectancy;
We wet our foreheads in John Moriarty's autobiography.

The following Sunday is the Feast of the Ascension
Of Our Lord into Heaven: 80
Thank You, O Lord, for the Descent of Rosie onto Earth.

Notes

15	Incarnation Day:	in the Christian religion, the Incarnation refers to when Jesus, as the Son of God, took human form ('became flesh'). The writer sees Rosie's birth as an incarnation.
16	Swinford:	a town in County Mayo
16	Croagh Patrick:	Cruach Phádraig (in Irish) is a mountain in County Mayo on which St Patrick is reputed to have fasted for 40 days. Many pilgrims climb the mountain on the last Sunday of July (Reek Sunday).
17	P. Flynn's highway:	Padraig Flynn, a local politician and former Fianna Fáil Minister for the Environment. Presumably the reference is to a new road built in his constituency.

20	Holles Street:	a well-known maternity hospital in Dublin
23	Achill:	Achill Island, County Mayo
24	Arum Lily:	large, trumpet-shaped flowers.
25	the Sound:	Achill Sound, a Gaeltacht village on the east side of Achill Island
25	rhododendrons:	evergreen shrubs with very large, usually pink flowers in May; grows wild in Mayo
26	whins:	a common, thorny, invasive bush that has bright yellow flowers in spring/summer; also called 'gorse' or 'furze'.
27	hawthorn:	a thorny hedgerow shrub that produces clusters of white flowers in May and berries in winter
29	bog-cotton:	a plant of the sedge family that grows in wetland and produces white cotton balls on a long stem
30	Burrishoole cemetery:	is in Newport, County Mayo
31	sea pinks:	also known as thrift, an evergreen, grass-like plant that produces globes of pink flowers on long stalks all summer
32	London Pride:	an evergreen plant that bears pale-pink flowers on tall stalks all summer
33	fuchsia:	a shrub with bell-like flowers
33	Queen Anne's Lace:	a tall plant with long fern-like leaves and clusters of tiny white flowers that look like lace
34	Old Turlough Road:	is near Castlebar, County Mayo. Turlough was one of the places in which Durcan grew up.
36	Tulsk:	a village in County Roscommon
36	Kilmainham:	in Dublin 8, where the famous Kilmainham Gaol is located
36	the Grand Canal:	the southernmost of Dublin's two main canals
39	pewter:	a metal alloy of dull silver colour
39	brooch:	an ornamented hinged pin or clasp; formerly could refer to a necklace or bracelet
43	Tarmonbarry:	a village in County Roscommon on the banks of the River Shannon
44	Ford Anglia:	a popular British-made car. Four different models were produced between 1939 and 1967.
46	Bailey bridge:	a temporary, prefabricated bridge
47	Moses:	in the Old Testament story, Moses led the Jews out of slavery in Egypt and to the Holy Land that God had promised them. God parted the Red Sea to help them escape.

Paul Durcan

60–1	Jonathan Philbin Bowman | *Daymaker*:	this reference is to *A Living Word* programme recorded for RTÉ by the late Jonathan Philbin Bowman on 29 February 2000, in which he described how he received two fun, complimentary emails from different friends on a day he was feeling down. He replied as follows: 'You've just made my day. In fact I have a whole new word for you people. You're day makers.'
71	Charlestown:	a small town in County Mayo, which was the focus of a series of articles by the late John Healy. These were highly critical of government policies towards rural areas and were published in the *Irish Times* in the 1960s and 70s. These were later published in book form as *Death of an Irish Town* in 1968.
72	Curry:	a townland near Castlebar, County Mayo
74	Mountbellew:	a small town in County Galway and the site of a famous Agricultural College
75	Ballaghadreen:	a town in County Roscommon
78	we wet our foreheads:	a version of 'wetting the baby's head', i.e. having a drink to celebrate the birth
78	John Moriarty's autobiography:	the autobiography of the late Irish philosopher John Moriarty is entitled *Nostros*. Durcan called it 'one of the most remarkable autobiographies I have ever read in my life'.
79	Feast of the Ascension:	is celebrated on the 40th day after Easter Sunday and commemorates the Ascension of Christ into Heaven

Explorations

Section I

1. Why do you think the speaker was driving 'two hundred miles from west to east' on that Sunday?

2. The speaker is highly energised and excited. How is this excitement conveyed?

3. The poet vividly records all the details of the journey. What is your reaction to this detail?

4. There is a spiritual or religious aspect to the poet's thinking on this journey. Discuss this.

5.

a The high point of the drama comes in the final stanza of the section. Listen carefully to the content and the language of the mobile message. Do you think it is an effective piece of communication?

b How does it contrast with the rest of section I?

Section II

6. The poet records, with a botanist's eye, the flora that signposts his journey. It is as if the entire countryside is giving birth.

a Search for pictures of these flowers and plants on the internet. Which flowers and plants do you recognise?

b What is the poet celebrating here?

7. His reasons for this frantic journey become apparent in stanza 7 of this section.

a What image of the speaker do you get from this stanza?

b Do you think that this stanza communicates his love effectively? Write your opinions on this.

8. This journey reminds him of the many such childhood journeys he made in the company of his father.

a What was his father's sense of self-identity as an Irish person?

b What impression of the father's personality do we get from the writer's brief vignette here?

9. What concept of Irishness does the writer want Rosie to inherit?

10. Focus on the final stanzas of this section (lines 58–69). The poet has already expressed his great love and affection for his granddaughter. In these stanzas he reveals yet another level of complexity for his joy. Explain this added significance of Rosie for him.

Section III

11. As with all perfect journeys, this too is a circle. Do you think the writer is calmer on the way back? Explain your thinking.

12. Consider the detail of the second to last stanza. Describe the atmosphere of the meeting with John Moriarty. Do you think this would be a typical conversation between farmers?

13. How has the birth of Rosie Joyce affected the writer?

Paul Durcan

14. 'This is a poem of pure joy and celebration.'
    Write about everything that is celebrated in the poem.

15. 'The sense of place is important in Durcan's philosophy.'
    Discuss this.

16. Do you think this poem is infused with both the spirituality and ecology of Ireland?

17. 'The poem has all the qualities of a very good diary.'
    Write your views on this.

Ireland 2002

Do you ever take a holiday abroad?
No, we always go to America.

- -

Explorations

1. What does this say to you about Irish people?

2. Can an overheard snatch of conversation be a poem?

3. What constitutes a poem?

4. What are you discovering about poetry from reading Paul Durcan?

What young mother is not a vengeful goddess
Spitting dynastic as well as motherly pride?
In 1949 in the black Ford Anglia,
Now that I had become a walking, talking little boy,
Mummy drove me out to visit my grand-aunt Maud Gonne   5
In Roebuck House in the Countryside near Dublin,
To show off to the servant of the Queen
The latest addition to the extended family.
Although the eighty-year-old Cathleen Ni Houlihan had taken to her bed
She was keen as ever to receive admirers,   10
Especially the children of the family.
Only the previous week the actor MacLiammóir
Had been kneeling at her bedside reciting Yeats to her,
His hand on his heart, clutching a red rose.
Cousin Seán and his wife Kid led the way up the stairs,   15
Seán opening the door and announcing my mother.
Mummy lifted me up in her arms as she approached the bed
And Maud leaned forward, sticking out her claws
To embrace me, her lizard eyes darting about
In the rubble of the ruins of her beautiful face.   20
Terrified, I recoiled from her embrace
And, fleeing her bedroom, ran down the stairs
Out onto the wrought-iron balcony
Until Seán caught up with me and quieted me
And took me for a walk in the walled orchard.   25
Mummy was a little but not totally mortified:
She had never liked Maud Gonne because of Maud's
Betrayal of her husband, Mummy's Uncle John,
Major John, most ordinary of men, most
Humorous, courageous of soldiers,   30
The pride of our family,
Whose memory always brought laughter
To my grandmother Eileen's lips. 'John,'
She used to cry, 'John was such a gay man.'
Mummy set great store by loyalty; loyalty   35
In Mummy's eyes was the cardinal virtue.
Maud Gonne was a disloyal wife
And, therefore, not worthy of Mummy's love.
For dynastic reasons we would tolerate Maud,
But we would always see through her.   40

Paul Durcan

Notes

3	Ford Anglia:	a popular British-made car, produced from 1939 to 1967
5	grand-aunt Maud Gonne:	Maud Gonne (1865–1953) married Major John MacBride (brother of Joseph MacBride, Paul Durcan's maternal grandfather) in Paris in 1903. They had one son, Seán MacBride ('Cousin Seán'), but the marriage was short lived and the separation was acrimonious. MacBride returned to Dublin in 1905. Gonne raised their son in Paris and did not return to Ireland until 1917.
		Maud Gonne had been a famous beauty in her youth and was the inspiration for some of W.B. Yeats's poems. He was in love with her and asked her to marry him at one stage. She became heavily involved in Irish national and revolutionary politics. In 1902 she played the leading role in *Cathleen Ní Houlihan*, a play written by Yeats and Lady Gregory in which an older woman (an embodiment of Ireland) summons a young man to fight for Irish freedom.
		Gonne's autobiography, published in 1938, was entitled *A Servant of the Queen*, partly a reference to *Cathleen Ní Houlihan* and partly an ironic title, given her nationalist politics.
		She is buried in the Republican Plot in Glasnevin Cemetery.

12	MacLiammóir:	Micheál MacLiammóir (1899–1978) was an English-born Irish actor, dramatist, writer, poet and painter. With his partner, Hilton Edwards, he was co-founder, in 1928, of the Gate Theatre, Dublin. He is best remembered for his one-man show *The Importance of Being Oscar*, on the life and work of Oscar Wilde. A man of wit and humour, he was given to melodramatic poses and performances.
15	Cousin Seán:	Seán MacBride (1904–88) was the son of Major John MacBride and Maud Gonne. He was involved in republican politics from an early age, joining the Irish Volunteers in 1919. A member of the IRA, he was at one time Chief of Staff and was imprisoned many times.
		In 1925 he married Kid Bulfin. He had studied law in UCD and was called to the bar in 1937. He resigned from the IRA when the 1937 Constitution was enacted.
		He was Minister for External Affairs in the First Inter-Party Government of 1948. He played leading roles in many international organisations, including the Council of Europe, the United Nations and Amnesty International. In 1974 he received the Nobel Peace Prize.
28	Mummy's Uncle John:	Paul Durcan's mother, Sheila MacBride, was a niece of Major John MacBride (1868–1916). From Westport in County Mayo, MacBride became a member of the Irish Republican Brotherhood. He went to South Africa, fought in the second Boer War against the British and was given the rank of major in the Boer Army.
		As already noted, he married Maud Gonne. He was second in command to Thomas Mac Donagh at Jacob's Factory in the 1916 Rebellion and was executed on 5 May in the aftermath.
33	Eileen:	Paul Durcan's maternal grandmother, Eileen, married Joseph MacBride

Explorations

FIRST READING

1. What connotations does the term 'dynasty' have for you?

2. 'What young mother is not a vengeful goddess | Spitting dynastic as well as motherly pride?'
Examine the language carefully. What does it suggest about the tone or atmosphere of the upcoming visit?

3. 'She was keen as ever to receive admirers'.
Comment on the writer's choice of words here. What does it suggest about his attitude to Maud Gonne?

4. 'Only the previous week the actor MacLiammóir
Had been kneeling at her bedside reciting Yeats to her,
His hand on his heart, clutching a red rose.'

Paul Durcan

a What does this add to the picture of Maud Gonne that is being developed here?

b What poem do you think he may have recited?

5. 'Cousin Seán and his wife Kid led the way up the stairs, | Seán opening the door and announcing my mother.' How would you describe the atmosphere here? What does it convey about the household of Maud Gonne?

6. The young boy is obviously frightened by the figure of the old woman in the bed. Do you think this is a less than kind description of her? Discuss this.

7. Why was Mummy only 'a little but not totally mortified'?

8. Examine the character portrait of Major John MacBride that is described here. How is he remembered and whose viewpoint is it?

9. Explain Mummy's attitude to Maud Gonne.

10. 'For dynastic reasons we would tolerate Maud, | But we would always see through her.' What do you think the writer means by this?

SECOND READING

11. Consider the title again. Do you think it is an apt one for the poem? Explain your thinking.

12. Consider again the first two lines. From your reading of the poem, describe what these lines mean to you now.

13. How is Maud Gonne portrayed in this poem? Write about this, with reference to the details.

14.

a Would you agree that the portrayal of Maud Gonne is unashamedly biased? Where does this bias show?

b How would you describe the tone of the portrayal?

15. What impression of 'Mummy' do you get from the poem?

16. What insight into the nature of clans or dynasties do we get from a reading of this poem?

17. 'One of the most effective technical features of this poem is the realistic, almost photographic detail of some images.'
Write about this.

Ordinary Level: Poems

George Herbert

(1593–1633)

George Herbert came from an aristocratic family in the Welsh border country. An outstanding scholar, he was educated at Westminster and at Trinity College, Cambridge, where he was public orator from 1619 to 1627. His initial hopes of a political appointment were not fulfilled. In 1630 he was ordained a priest in the Anglican ministry and became rector of Bemerton, near Salisbury. None of his poetry was published during his lifetime, but when he knew that he was dying he sent a collection of his verse to his friend George Ferrar with the advice to 'publish or burn' depending on his judgement of the poems. The collection was published under the title *The Temple*.

The Collar

Prescribed for exams in 2015 and 2018

I struck the board and cry'd, 'No more;
        I will abroad!
  What? shall I ever sigh and pine?
My lines and life are free; free as the road,
  Loose as the wind, as large as store.   **5**
        Shall I be still in suit?
  Have I no harvest but a thorn
  To let me blood, and not restore
What I have lost with cordiall fruit?
        Sure there was wine   **10**
Before my sighs did dry it; there was corn
        Before my tears did drown it.
  Is the year only lost to me?
        Have I no bays to crown it,
No flowers, no garlands gay? All blasted?   **15**
        All wasted?
  Not so, my heart; but there is fruit,
        And thou hast hands.

Recover all thy sigh-blown age
On double pleasures: leave thy cold dispute   20
Of what is fit, and not. Forsake thy cage,
            Thy rope of sands,
Which petty thoughts have made, and made to thee
        Good cable, to enforce and draw,
                And be thy law,   25
While thou didst wink and wouldst not see.
                Away! take heed;
                I will abroad.
Call in thy death's-head there; tie up thy fears.
                He that forbears   30
        To suit and serve his need,
            Deserves his load.'
But as I raved and grew more fierce and wild
            At every word,
Methoughts I heard one calling, *Child!*   35
        And I replied, *My Lord.*

Notes

	The Collar:	this could refer to a clerical collar, but more likely to a restraining band or strap
2	**abroad:**	be free
6	**in suit:**	in bondage, a servant
8	**To let me blood:**	to bleed me
9	**cordiall:**	healing
14	**bays:**	bay leaves, used in a victory crown in classical times
15	**blasted:**	infected by blight
20	**double pleasures:**	by throwing off the restraints he feels and enjoying new experiences
20	**dispute:**	debate
23	**petty:**	minor, insignificant
29	**death's-head:**	human skull as an emblem of mortality

Explorations

Lines 1–16

1. How would you describe the poet's feelings in these lines? Choose images and lines that you think best catch the poet's feelings and discuss what they suggest about his mood.

2. Are there any hints to suggest possible reasons for his bleak state of mind? Discuss.

SECOND READING

Lines 17–32

3. How does the poet's mood change in this section?

4. What advice does he give himself in his effort to break free and rebel? In your own words, list the sequence of his thoughts.

THIRD READING

5. What happens in the last four lines? Is this unexpected?

6. On a rereading of the poem, list everything the poet feels himself deprived of.

7. The collar can be read as a symbol of religious and moral restraint. What other images in the poem portray freedom and restraint? Are these images linked?

FOURTH READING

8. What do you think the poet is rebelling against?

9. Do you find this a dramatic poem? What makes it so?

10. Metaphysical poets are renowned for being clever and witty in their use of words and images. What evidence of this do you find here?

11. Can you sympathise with the poet here? Discuss your feelings about his feelings.

12. Write about the view that this poem discusses an issue that affects every human life.

John Milton
(1608–74)

John Milton was born in London of well-to-do parents who appear to have given him a good basic education, especially in music and literature. He attended St Paul's School and later graduated with BA and MA degrees from Cambridge. Milton was appointed 'Latin secretary of the council of state' by Oliver Cromwell in 1649 because of his fluency in Latin, the language of diplomacy at that time.

He wrote extensively on religious and political matters as well as writing poetry in Latin and English. His eyesight, which had been failing for some time, failed him completely when he was aged 44. From then on he dictated his work to his secretaries and family members. In his masterpiece, the epic *Paradise Lost*, which was published in 1667, he attempted 'to justify the ways of God to men'. The restoration of the monarchy briefly threatened Milton with execution for regicide and brought an end to his political career in 1660. Having been granted a royal pardon, he retired to concentrate on writing and published the sequel to *Paradise Lost*, called *Paradise Regained*, and, in 1671, a drama called *Samson Agonistes*. A revised volume of his collected poetry appeared the following year. Milton died of gout in 1674.

When I Consider How My Light is Spent

Prescribed for the exam in 2017

When I consider how my light is spent,
   E're half my days, in this dark world and wide,
   And that one Talent which is death to hide,
   Lodg'd with me useless, though my Soul more bent
To serve therewith my Maker, and present   5
   My true account, least he returning chide,
   Doth God exact day-labour, light deny'd,
   I fondly ask; But Patience to prevent
That murmur, soon replies, God doth not need
   Either man's work or his own gifts, who best   10
   Bear his milde yoak, they serve him best, his State
Is Kingly. Thousands at his bidding speed
   And post o'er Land and Ocean without rest:
   They also serve who only stand and waite.

Notes

3	**Talent:**	gift, faculty; also a unit of currency in New Testament times
4	**bent:**	determined
8	**fondly:**	foolishly
11	**yoak:**	yoke, burden

Explorations

FIRST READING

1.

a What is Milton saying about his blindness in the opening three lines?

b How do you imagine 'this dark world'?

2.

a Does Milton take the parable of the Talents seriously?

b What is the implication of 'which is death to hide'?

3. What does Milton's soul incline to do? What does this tell us about him?

4.

a 'Doth God exact day-labour, light deny'd'.
What is your understanding of this line?

b What does the question tell us about Milton's attitude to God?

5.

a What does 'Patience' reply to the question posed in the first eight lines?

b According to Milton, does God need man's work? Does He need man's gifts?

6. According to Milton, how do people best serve God? How can God be served passively?

SECOND READING

7. Read the poem aloud. What do you notice about its sounds and rhythm? How many full stops appear in the text? Does this affect how you read the poem? What tone of voice should you adopt?

8. Comment on the financial terminology: 'spent', 'Talent', 'Lodg'd', 'account'. What is Milton saying with this choice of words?

9. How do you see John Milton on the evidence of the poem? What kind of person do you think he was? Does he display any self-pity or sense of injustice? What comment would you make on how he deals with his disability?

10. How would you summarise the octet?

11. Describe how Milton resolves his difficulties in the sestet. Do you find his conclusion convincing?

12. How does Milton feel towards God in the poem? What words and images convey his emotions?

THIRD READING

13. Examine how images of light and darkness are used in the first eight lines. Do you consider such imagery to be appropriate?

14. How is the majesty of God conveyed in the final six lines?

15. Would you agree that this poem's language has a biblical quality? What words or phrases would you highlight for comment?

16. What do you think of Milton's portrayal of God? Is this interpretation of God one you are comfortable with?

17. How would you describe the mood of the final line? Has the conclusion been anticipated in the poem?

18. Write a paragraph giving your personal response to the poem.

John Milton

Percy Bysshe Shelley

(1792–1822)

The son of an English country gentleman, Shelley was educated at Eton and Oxford, where he spent a rebellious and unhappy youth. Revolutionary in thought, he was anti-religious and anti-monarchy and wrote and spoke publicly on the need for radical social and political reforms. He felt it was the role of the poet to be prophetic and visionary. He lived a fairly unconventional family life, much of it in Italy, where the Shelleys seemed dogged by illness and death. It was here that he wrote some of his best-known poems, such as 'Stanzas Written in Dejection Near Naples', 'Ode to the West Wind', 'Ode to a Skylark' and 'Prometheus Unbound'.

Ozymandias

Prescribed for the exam in 2016

I met a traveller from an antique land
Who said: Two vast and trunkless legs of stone
Stand in the desert ... Near them, on the sand,
Half sunk, a shattered visage lies, whose frown,
And wrinkled lip, and sneer of cold command,   5
Tell that its sculptor well those passions read
Which yet survive, stamped on these lifeless things,
The hand that mocked them, and the heart that fed:
And on the pedestal these words appear:
'My name is Ozymandias, king of kings: 10
Look on my works, ye Mighty, and despair!'
Nothing beside remains. Round the decay
Of that colossal wreck, boundless and bare
The lone and level sands stretch far away.

Notes

	Ozymandias:	another name for Pharaoh Ramses II of Egypt (13th century BC), whose great tomb at Thebes was shaped like a sphinx. It was the historian Diodorus the Sicilian who first referred to it as the tomb of Ozymandias.
1	**antique:**	ancient
4	**visage:**	face
8	**The hand that mocked:**	the hand that imitated, referring to the hand of the sculptor
8	**the heart that fed:**	the king's heart, which gave life to these qualities and passions that were captured in stone by the sculptor

Explorations

FIRST READING

1. The poem is in the form of a narrative or story told by a traveller who had been to 'an antique land'. What suggestions and pictures does this phrase conjure up for you?

2.

a What did the traveller actually see, as reported in lines 2–4?

b What is your first reaction to this scene: interesting, pathetic, grotesque or something else?

c Why do you think he might consider this worth reporting?

3. Where is this scene? What impressions of the land do we get?

4. Does the poet tell us the name of the place? Why do you think this is?

SECOND READING

5. What do we learn of the king from this sculpture: his qualities, character traits, etc.?

6. Do you think Shelley appreciates the sculptor's skill? Explain.

7. Relate lines 4–8 in your own words and as simply as possible.

THIRD READING

The sestet

8. What was your own reflection on reading the words on the pedestal?

9.

a Explore the final two and a half lines. What do you see? Really look.

b What atmosphere is created here?

c What statement do you think is being made?

10. What do you think this poem is saying about human endeavour and about power? Explain with reference to specific phrases, etc.

11. Consider the imagery. Do you think the imagery is appropriate to the theme? Explain. What pictures do you find most effective?

Percy Bysshe Shelley

413

12. How does the poet make use of irony to communicate his theme? Do you find this effective?

13. Would you agree that this poem embodies Shelley's view that the poet should really be a kind of prophet or wise person in society? Discuss this with reference to the text.

14. What features of the sonnet do you notice in the poem? Do you think it is a good sonnet?

15. Do you think this poem was worth reading? Why or why not?

William Carlos Williams
(1883–1963)

The early poetic work of William Carlos Williams shows the influence of two of the major poets of the 20th century, Ezra Pound and T.S. Eliot. However, he eventually felt limited by this and searched for an authentic American expression in poetry. He found this in writing about commonplace objects and the lives of ordinary people. In this way, he managed to bring out the significance of people and things we might otherwise take for granted. He has been an inspiration for some major poets, particularly Allen Ginsberg. His output includes stories and plays as well as his five well-known books of poetry.

This Is Just to Say

Prescribed for the exam in 2018

I have eaten
the plums
that were in
the icebox

and which   5
you were probably
saving
for breakfast

Forgive me
they were delicious   10
so sweet
and so cold

Explorations

BEFORE READING

1. Imagine that you have just eaten a large, and very delicious, bar of chocolate that your best friend had been saving to eat at lunchtime. Write a short note to explain what happened and to apologise for what you have done. You might like to read aloud some of the notes written by the class and discuss the various approaches taken.

FIRST READING

2.

a   While you were reading 'This Is Just to Say', did you notice any differences between the poem and your piece of writing?

b   Which of the two pieces do you think works better as an explanation and an apology? Give reasons for your answer.

3.

a   In your own words, summarise the main point that Williams makes in each of the three stanzas of this poem.

b   Do you think he has the points in the best sequence in order to gain forgiveness or would you rearrange the sequence?

4.   Williams breaks up his message into very short phrases written on separate lines with no punctuation. Experiment with reading this poem aloud to see what effect this has on the pace, or speed, that should be used when reading this poem and the tone of voice.

5.

a   Williams rarely uses capital letters in his poetry, so there are only two capital letters employed in this poem: 'I' and 'Forgive'. Why do you think he decided to use capital letters for these particular words?

b   Do these words help you to explain what the theme of this poem is? Explain your answer.

6.   'Forgive me | they were delicious | so sweet | and so cold'

a   Alliteration is when two or more words close together begin with the same letter. Can you pick out Williams's use of alliteration in this stanza?

b   In what ways does his use of alliteration help you to imagine how the plums tasted?

c   Why do you think he emphasises how 'delicious' the plums were in his message?

THIRD READING

7.   Which one of the following statements do you think best describes Williams's motivation for writing this poem?

•   He wanted to leave a note reminding the person to buy more plums.

•   He felt guilty about eating the plums but was too embarrassed to speak to the person who had put the plums in the icebox.

•   He wanted to show the person who had put the plums in the icebox that he was genuinely sorry by leaving the poem as a gift to make up for the missing plums.

8.

a   If you received this poem, would you forgive Williams? Why or why not?

b   Write a short reply to Williams explaining how you feel.

9.   Williams said of his poetry, 'I try to say it straight, whatever is to be said.' In what ways could this poem be said to be a 'straight' piece of writing? You might like to consider (a) the language he uses (b) the form of the poem and (c) the theme.

10.

a   This poem, including the title, consists of 33 words. Do you think this piece is too short to be a poem?

b   In your view, what turns a piece of writing into a poem? Is it the language, the use of rhyme, the emotions expressed or something else?

Francis Ledwidge

(1887–1917)

Francis Ledwidge was born, the eighth of nine children, in Slane, County Meath. His father died when he was four and Francis had to leave school at the age of 14 to find work to help to support his family. He played an active part in his local community, both culturally, setting up the Slane Drama Group, and politically, joining the local labour union and the Irish Volunteers.

From an early age, Ledwidge enjoyed writing poetry to entertain his friends and he worked hard at developing his poetic skills. Lord Dunsany was so impressed by his work that he introduced Ledwidge to the Dublin literary scene, which included such writers as W.B. Yeats and Thomas MacDonagh. Although Ledwidge was a nationalist, he joined the British army in 1914 shortly after World War I began. There are some suggestions that he did this because he had been disappointed in love, but Francis himself wrote, 'I joined the British army because she stood between Ireland and an enemy common to our civilization.' However, his attitude changed following the execution of the 1916 leaders, when he declared, 'if someone were to tell me that the Germans were coming over our back wall, I wouldn't lift a finger to stop them'. Nevertheless, he courageously fought on with the British army through the horrors of the war until he was killed by an exploding shell near Ypres, in Belgium.

Lament for Thomas MacDonagh

Prescribed for the exam in 2016

He shall not hear the bittern cry
In the wild sky, where he is lain,
Nor voices of the sweeter birds
Above the wailing of the rain.

Nor shall he know when loud March blows   5
Thro' slanting snows her fanfare shrill,
Blowing to flame the golden cup
Of many an upset daffodil.

But when the Dark Cow leaves the moor
And pastures poor with greedy weeds,   10
Perhaps he'll hear her low at morn
Lifting her horn in pleasant meads.

Notes

	Thomas MacDonagh:	one of the leaders of the 1916 Easter Rising, also a teacher, a poet and a playwright. He was imprisoned and executed in Kilmainham Jail. Because the British authorities were anxious that the funerals and graves of the 1916 leaders might increase anti-British feeling, his body, along with those of the other leaders, was buried in Arbour Hill Cemetery, the cemetery for British soldiers from the nearby Royal Barracks. This is now Collins Barracks where the National Museum is located.
1	**bittern:**	a type of large brown heron. The males have a loud, booming mating call. Thomas MacDonagh translated an 18th-century Irish poem, *'An Bonnán Buí'*, into English under the title 'The Yellow Bittern'.
6	**fanfare:**	a sounding of trumpets during a ceremony
9	**Dark Cow:**	a secret name for Ireland used by Irish people in the 18th century when the country was under British rule
10	**pastures:**	grassy lands used for grazing animals
12	**meads:**	meadows, an area of grassland often used for hay

Explorations

FIRST READING

1.

a   Take it in turns to sum up in one sentence how this poem made you feel. Begin with the phrase 'This poem made me feel ...'. List each feeling on the board.

b   What feeling did the majority of the class experience when they read this poem for the first time?

2.

a   Choose one phrase or line in the poem that makes you feel the emotion that you named in Question 1.

b   Explain why the line or phrase makes you feel this way.

3.   From the phrases below, choose two that, in your opinion, best describe the language used in this poem:

- It is difficult to understand.
- It is easy to understand.
- It describes images (word-pictures) that I can imagine easily.
- It describes images that I find it difficult to imagine.

   Explain your choice of phrases by reference to the poem.

SECOND READING

4.

a   In stanzas 1 and 2 (lines 1–8), the poet describes some of the experiences that Thomas MacDonagh will no longer have because he is dead. In your own words, explain what these experiences are.

b   What senses does the poet appeal to in his descriptions of these experiences?

Francis Ledwidge

5.

a   How would you describe the mood (feelings and atmosphere) in lines 1–8? Give reasons for your answer based on your reading of these lines.

b   Do you think the images the poet uses in lines 1–8 convey the mood in a way that is easy to understand? Why?

6.

a   In stanza 3 (lines 9–12), the poet describes the 'Dark Cow', a secret name for Ireland in the 18th century. What do you think Ledwidge is hoping will happen to Ireland when he refers to the 'Dark Cow' moving to 'pleasant meads'?

b   Based on your answer to part (a), can you suggest what Ledwidge hopes that Thomas MacDonagh will know about, even though he is dead, in the final two lines of the poem?

c   Do you think the mood of lines 9–12 is different to the mood of lines 1–8? Why? Refer to the poem in support of your answer.

7.   Look back at the feeling that the majority of the class experienced when they read this poem for the first time. Based on your work for Questions 5 and 6, do you agree that this majority feeling describes the mood of the whole poem? Or do you think that you need to add in another feeling? Explain your answer with reference to the poem.

THIRD READING

8.

a   Working in pairs with one of you as the reporter and the other as Francis Ledwidge, imagine that you are interviewing Francis Ledwidge. From your reading of the poem, write out the answers that you both think he would give to the following questions:

•   How do you feel about Thomas MacDonagh's death?

•   What do you think about where he was buried?

•   What is your attitude to Ireland becoming an independent country?

•   Why do you hope that Thomas MacDonagh might somehow know when Irish freedom is achieved?

b   As a class, listen to some of the interviews and discuss whether you agree or disagree with the answers that are given.

9.   Do you think a reader of this poem needs to know the historical facts that it refers to (for example, what happened to Thomas MacDonagh in 1916 and what the 'Dark Cow' stands for) in order to understand fully what the poet is trying to express? Explain your view and support it by reference to the poem.

10.   This poem was written about 100 years ago. Do you think it should be studied by Irish students in the 21st century? Why or why not?

Patrick Kavanagh

(1904–67)

Patrick Kavanagh was born on 21 October 1904. He was the fourth child and the eldest son of James and Bridget (née Quinn), born in the townland of Mucker, Inniskeen parish, County Monaghan. From the age of 12 Kavanagh started writing verse and collected it in a copybook. His brother Peter later published this juvenilia in his *Collected Poems*. Kavanagh was keen to use the things around him in his poems, no matter how mundane they might seem to others. Regular trips to Dundalk brought him into contact with literature, especially with the literary journals of the time, such as *Poetry* and the *Irish Statesman*. He entered the joint trades of cobbler and small farmer, like his father before him, but also began to see himself as someone different from the regular farmers. He now began to see himself as a poet.

His first volume of poetry, *Ploughman and Other Poems*, was published in 1936. It contained many of the ideas that would remain central to his poetry for the rest of his life. His poetry in this book examined not only his surrounding area, but also poetry itself, the nature of the poet and the creative act. In 1939 Kavanagh made a major change to his life by giving up farming and concentrating on writing as a career, moving to Dublin in the process. He wrote a number of regular columns as well as book and film reviews at the time. In addition to his poetry he also produced a novel, *Tarry Flynn*. He also ventured into publishing, producing a newspaper called *Kavanagh's Weekly* in 1952. Its stated purpose was 'to introduce the critical constructive note into Irish thought'. Kavanagh put every aspect of Irish life under scrutiny. The newspaper was both loved and hated at the time. Kavanagh himself was put under scrutiny later that year when an article in *The Leader* criticised his work. He sued *The Leader* for libel but lost.

Soon after this period, he entered the Rialto hospital with lung cancer. Against great odds, he made a heroic recovery and spent the summer of 1955 regaining his strength on the banks of the Grand Canal in Dublin. He described this period as his 'rebirth'. Kavanagh's health began to decline again in the late 1950s. He returned to journalism. On 19 April 1967 he married Katherine Moloney, whom he had known for a number of years, and on 30 November in that year he died at the age of 63.

Shancoduff

Prescribed for the exam in 2016

My black hills have never seen the sun rising,
Eternally they look north towards Armagh.
Lot's wife would not be salt if she had been
Incurious as my black hills that are happy
When dawn whitens Glassdrummond chapel.   5

My hills hoard the bright shillings of March
While the sun searches in every pocket.
They are my Alps and I have climbed the Matterhorn
With a sheaf of hay for three perishing calves
In the field under the Big Forth of Rocksavage.   10

The sleety winds fondle the rushy beards of Shancoduff
While the cattle-drovers sheltering in the Featherna Bush
Look up and say: 'Who owns them hungry hills
That the water-hen and snipe must have forsaken?
A poet? Then by heavens he must be poor.'   15
I hear and is my heart not badly shaken?

Notes

10-12	Rocksavage/ Shancoduff/ Featherna Bush:	places in County Monaghan near the poet's father's farm

Explorations

FIRST READING

1.

a The title of the poem is taken
from the name of the place where
Kavanagh's family had a farm. It is
derived from two Irish words, 'Sean'
and 'Dubh'. Do you know what these
words mean? If not, find out.

b What sort of a place would you
expect from such a name?

SECOND READING

2. How does Kavanagh describe this
place? Draw a picture or describe
the scene in your own words as you
imagine it.

3. What is the cattle-drovers' attitude to
the hills?

4. What is the poet's reaction to this?

THIRD READING

5. The poet personifies the place. How
does he do this? What effect does it
have?

6. He names a lot of specific places
in the poem, e.g. Glassdrummond,
Rocksavage, Featherna Bush. Why
does he do this?

7. He repeatedly uses the possessive
'my' when talking about the hills.
What does it tell us about the
narrator?

8. Do you think the cattle-drovers place
any value on poetry? Examine their
words carefully.

FOURTH READING

9. In an earlier version of the poem,
Kavanagh used the word 'faith'
instead of the word 'heart' in the last
line of the poem. Why do you think
he made that change? What effect
does it have? Do you think it was a
good change to make?

10. In another poem, Kavanagh says,
'Naming a thing is the love act and
the pledge'. Relate that statement to
'Shancoduff'.

11. ' "Shancoduff" is a love poem.'
Do you agree?

Patrick Kavanagh

W.H. Auden
(1907–73)

Wystan Hugh Auden was born in York on 21 February 1907 and educated at Oxford and Berlin. He is considered one of the most important English poets of the 1930s, writing on political and social themes. A prolific poet, he wrote in a variety of verse forms, composing both humorous and serious poetry. 'Funeral Blues', originally a song in one of his plays, is taken from the volume *Another Time* (1940), which contains many of his best-known poems, such as 'September 1939' and 'Lullaby'. Auden spent much of his life in the United States, becoming an American citizen in 1946.

Funeral Blues

Prescribed for the exam in 2015

Stop all the clocks, cut off the telephone,
Prevent the dog from barking with a juicy bone,
Silence the pianos and with muffled drum
Bring out the coffin, let the mourners come.

Let aeroplanes circle moaning overhead   5
Scribbling on the sky the message He Is Dead,
Put crêpe bows round the white necks of the public doves,
Let the traffic policemen wear black cotton gloves.

He was my North, my South, my East and West,
My working week and my Sunday rest,   10
My noon, my midnight, my talk, my song;
I thought that love would last for ever: I was wrong.

The stars are not wanted now: put out every one;
Pack up the moon and dismantle the sun;
Pour away the ocean and sweep up the wood.   15
For nothing now can ever come to any good.

Explorations

FIRST READING

1. What images grab your attention?

2. What do you think is happening in this poem?

3. Do you find it unusual in any way? Explain.

SECOND READING

4. The first two stanzas create the atmosphere of a funeral. What sights and sounds of a funeral do you notice?

5. It used to be the custom that clocks were stopped in a house where a death had occurred. As well as marking the time of death, this signified that time stood still for the grieving family. Do you think the signs of mourning have been carried to extremes in the first two stanzas? Examine the actions called for.

6. How do you think the first stanza should be read: in a low, defeated tone, semi-hysterical or something else? Read it aloud.

7. Read the second stanza aloud.

8. Do you think there might be a change of tone from the third stanza on? Read stanzas 3–4 aloud.

9. Are you sympathetic to the speaker in this poem?

THIRD READING

10. What does the third stanza suggest about the relationship between the speaker and the person mourned? Examine each line in detail for the kernel of truth behind the clichés.

11. How do you understand the speaker's state of mind, particularly in the last verse?

12.
   a Do you take this poem to be a serious statement about loss and bereavement or do you find it exaggerated and over the top? Explain your opinion.

   b Do you think it could be read as a satire, i.e. a poem ridiculing, in this case, the public outpouring of emotion at the funerals of famous people? Read the poem again.

FOURTH READING

13. What do you think the poem is saying?

14. Look at the imagery again. How does it fit in with what the poem is saying?

15. Find out what you can about blues music and lyrics. What elements of a blues song do you find in the poem?

16. What do you like about this poem?

W.H. Auden

William Stafford

(1914–93)

William Stafford was born in Kansas in 1914. Although the family suffered financially during the American Depression, Stafford's parents consistently encouraged their three children to develop an independently moral view of life through reading and discussion.

This tendency towards independence led the teenage Stafford to embark on a camping trip, during which he developed a close spiritual connection with the natural world: 'The earth was my home; I would never feel lost while it held me.' Later, as a conscientious objector during the Second World War, he refused to fight but did work in areas such as fire-fighting and building roads.

In 1948 he began teaching at Lewis and Clark College, Oregon, a position that he retained until his retirement despite travelling widely to share his work with others. It was not until he was in his forties that his first anthology of poetry, *Traveling through the Dark*, was published, which subsequently won the 1963 National Book Award. Until his death in 1993, Stafford maintained the daily habit of rising at four in the morning to write poetry because he found it 'a confirming, satisfying activity to do'.

Traveling through the Dark

Prescribed for exams in 2016 and 2017

Traveling through the dark I found a deer
dead on the edge of the Wilson River road.
It is usually best to roll them into the canyon:
that road is narrow; to swerve might make more dead.

By glow of the tail-light I stumbled back of the car   5
and stood by the heap, a doe, a recent killing;
she had stiffened already, almost cold.
I dragged her off; she was large in the belly.

My fingers touching her side brought me the reason –
her side was warm; her fawn lay there waiting,   10
alive, still, never to be born.
Beside that mountain road I hesitated.

The car aimed ahead its lowered parking lights;
under the hood purred the steady engine.
I stood in the glare of the warm exhaust turning red;   15
around our group I could hear the wilderness listen.

I thought hard for us all – my only swerving –,
then pushed her over the edge into the river.

Notes

3	**canyon:**	a deep and narrow opening running between hills

Explorations

FIRST READING

1.

a   Based on the clues in the first and
    second stanzas, describe in your own
    words how you picture 'the Wilson
    River road'.

b   Would you like to drive along it in the
    dark? Why or why not? Use references
    from the poem to support your view.

2.

a   What reason does the poet give
    for saying about the dead deer, 'It
    is usually best to roll them into the
    canyon'?

b   Do you agree with his attitude? Why
    or why not?

3.

a   What does the poet discover that
    causes him to hesitate in the third
    stanza?

b   Can you understand why he pauses?
    Explain your answer.

4.

a   Were you shocked when you read the
    final line of the poem? If so, why?

William Stafford

b   Would you have preferred the poem to end in another way? Describe the ending that you would prefer.

SECOND READING

5.

a   The poet's emotions change a number of times during his experience on the Wilson River road. Go through the poem and trace the emotions he feels.

b   Based on what you have learned about his feelings, would you consider the poet to be a kind or unkind person? Give reasons for your answer.

6.   How does the poet use the senses of sight, touch and hearing in order to make this scene more vivid and easy to imagine? Use references from the poem in your answer.

7.

a   Although this scene takes place at night, Stafford still includes some colours in his poem. What colours appear in the poem?

b   Why do you think he refers only to these colours in the poem?

THIRD READING

8.   It has been suggested that in this poem, Stafford portrays his view of the relationship between the world of nature, represented by the deer, and the world of technology, represented by the car. What do you think this poem says to us about this relationship?

9.   Although this poem is written in everyday, conversational language, Stafford uses words and phrases that have layers of meaning.

a   Discuss the different meanings the word 'still' can have in the following lines: 'her fawn lay there waiting, | alive, still, never to be born.'

b   In a similar way, consider how the title of the poem, 'Traveling through the Dark', can be interpreted in a number of ways.

10.   Imagine that you live on the Wilson River road and you are very concerned about the dangers posed both to people and to deer by the driving conditions in this area at night. Write a letter to the local newspaper trying to persuade the readers that something has to be done to improve the situation.

Edwin Morgan
(1920–2010)

Morgan was born in Glasgow, was first published in 1952 and was still being published in 2007. Such a long career is marked by an ability and vision to write poetry inspired by a wide and varied list of subjects, from space travel to mythological goddesses. His prolific output includes libretti, plays, criticism and translations from Anglo-Saxon and Russian. His poems are as varied in form as they are in material, showing, for example, similarities to medieval Latin writing on the one hand and e.e. cummings on the other.

Strawberries

Prescribed for the exam in 2015

There were never strawberries
like the ones we had
that sultry afternoon
sitting on the step
of the open french window   5
facing each other
your knees held in mine
the blue plates in our laps
the strawberries glistening
in the hot sunlight   10
we dipped them in sugar
looking at each other
not hurrying the feast
for one to come
the empty plates   15
laid on the stone together
with the two forks crossed
and I bent towards you
sweet in that air
in my arms   20
abandoned like a child
from your eager mouth
the taste of strawberries

in my memory
lean back again let me love you   25

let the sun beat
on our forgetfulness
one hour of all
the heat intense
and summer lightning   30
on the Kilpatrick hills

let the storm wash the plates

Explorations

FIRST READING

1.

a   The poet suggests that food connected with special moments has a special taste. Do you agree with him?

b   Do you have any special memories where the food seemed to taste particularly good?

2.

a   What impression do you get of the setting for this poem?

b   Do you find it a surprising setting for a poem? Why?

3.   What sort of a relationship do you think these two people have? Choose two phrases from the poem to support your view.

SECOND READING

4.   What is the weather like as the couple eat the strawberries? Does it tell you anything about their feelings?

5.   'the empty plates | laid on the stone together | with the two forks crossed'.

a   Why do you think the poet introduces this image into the poem at this point?

b   Does it have any connection with the couple?

6.

a   How does the poet use the weather to suggest the intensifying of their emotions?

b   Do you think this is a successful device or is it rather over-dramatic?

THIRD READING

7.

a   'not hurrying the feast | for one to come'.
Eating is a sensual experience. Can the 'feast' of strawberries be seen as a preparation for another equally sensual 'feast'?

b   What is your reaction to this connection of ideas?

8.

a   Eating is also an important social activity. Can you think of occasions where sharing food has a special significance, perhaps even suggesting a change in the nature of a relationship?

b   How would you feel if you had to share a table in a restaurant with a stranger or if you were invited to a friend's home for a meal?

9.   Why do you think the poet chose to write this poem without any punctuation? Was he trying to suggest something about the moment or perhaps about the way that he remembers the moment?

10.

a   This is a remembered moment. Do you think this affects the way the poet views the scene?

b   Can memories be trusted? Does it matter if they are unreliable?

Howard Nemerov
(1920–91)

Howard Nemerov was born in New York in 1920. After he graduated from Harvard in 1941, he served as a pilot in the Royal Canadian unit of the US Army Air Force. He flew throughout the Second World War and he became a first lieutenant. He married in 1944.

Following the end of the war, Nemerov taught in a number of American universities while writing poetry, novels, short stories, essays and criticism. He was awarded numerous prizes for his poetry, including the prestigious Pulitzer Prize for Poetry in 1978 for *The Collected Poems of Howard Nemerov.*

Nemerov became the third Poet Laureate of the United States of America in 1988. He died in 1991.

The Vacuum

Prescribed for the exam in 2018

The house is so quiet now
The vacuum cleaner sulks in the corner closet,
Its bag limp as a stopped lung, its mouth
Grinning into the floor, maybe at my
Slovenly life, my dog-dead youth.   5

I've lived this way long enough,
But when my old woman died her soul
Went into that vacuum cleaner, and I can't bear
To see the bag swell like a belly, eating the dust
And the woolen mice, and begin to howl   10

Because there is old filth everywhere
She used to crawl, in the corner and under the stair.
I know now how life is cheap as dirt,
And still the hungry, angry heart
Hangs on and howls, biting at air.   15

Notes

2	**closet:**	cupboard
5	**Slovenly:**	always very untidy
7	**my old woman:**	wife

Explorations

BEFORE READING

1.

a   Imagine that you want to sell an electrical appliance in your house, such as a toaster, a washing machine, a television, etc. Write a short paragraph describing its appearance, what it does and how you feel about its performance.

b   As a class, read out some of the paragraphs and discuss whether they would encourage people to buy the appliance.

FIRST READING

2.

a   Did you notice any difference between the way in which you described your appliance and the way in which the vacuum cleaner is described in this poem? Explain what the difference is.

b   Personification is where a writer gives human feelings and characteristics to something that is not human. Pick out lines and images from the poem where you think personification is used in the description of the vacuum cleaner.

3.

a   What impression do you get of the man's feelings towards the vacuum cleaner from the description of it? Support your answer by reference to the poem.

b   Do you think the death of his wife has anything to do with how he feels about the vacuum cleaner? Why?

c   Does the fact that he thinks about the vacuum cleaner as having human characteristics suggest to you that the man is lonely? Why?

4.   'And still the hungry, angry heart | Hangs on and howls, biting at air.' Read these lines aloud, pausing at each comma. What do the alliteration of the 'h' sounds (repetition of the same letter or sound at the beginning of words) and the short phrases suggest to you about the man's emotional state as a result of his wife's death?

SECOND READING

5.

a   'But when my old woman died her soul | Went into that vacuum cleaner'. Explain why the man associates his dead wife with the vacuum cleaner.

b   How was the man's attitude to keeping the house clean different to that of his wife when she was alive?

c   Are there any indications in the poem

Howard Nemerov

433

that he now misses her cleaning the house? Use references from the poem to support your answers.

6. 'Its bag limp as a stopped lung', 'and I can't bear | To see the bag swell like a belly, eating the dust'.

a   Explain in your own words how these images suggest that the man associates the vacuum cleaner with death.

b   The poet also uses words connected to death about himself (line 5) and his wife (lines 7–8). Based on these images and lines, how would you sum up his feelings about death?

7. 'Because there is old filth everywhere', 'I know now how life is cheap as dirt'.

a   From these lines, would you describe the man's attitude to life as a positive or a negative one? Explain your answer with reference to these lines.

b   Do you think his attitude has been affected by his wife's death? Why?

THIRD READING

8. From the phrases below, choose the one which, in your opinion, best describes the poem:

- It is an amusing poem.

- It is a sad poem.

- It is a confusing poem.

  Explain your answer with reference to the poem.

9. 'The vacuum cleaner sulks in the corner closet'.
   Write a piece where the vacuum cleaner describes its feelings about

   the man and the death of the woman who used it so much.

10. The speaker in this poem links his wife to the vacuum cleaner because she spent so much time using it to clean the house. Describe the electrical or technological appliance that you would be linked to and explain what part it plays in your life.

Richard Wilbur
(1921–)

Richard Wilbur was born in New York and educated at Amherst College and Harvard University. He served in the American army during the Second World War and taught at Harvard and other universities. Among his collections of poetry are *The Beautiful Changes and Other Poems* (1947), *Ceremony* and *Other Poems* (1950), *Things of This World: Poems*, which won a Pulitzer Prize in 1956, and *New and Collected Poems* (1988). Wilbur believes that one of the main functions of poetry is to examine the inconsistencies and disharmony of modern life. He was made poet laureate of the United States of America in 1987.

A Summer Morning

Prescribed for the exam in 2016

Her young employers, having got in late
From seeing friends in town
And scraped the right front fender on the gate,
Will not, the cook expects, be coming down.

She makes a quiet breakfast for herself.   5
The coffee-pot is bright,
The jelly where it should be on the shelf.
She breaks an egg into the morning light,

Then, with the bread-knife lifted, stands and hears
The sweet efficient sounds   10
Of thrush and catbird, and the snip of shears
Where, in the terraced backward of the grounds,

A gardener works before the heat of day.
He straightens for a view
Of the big house ascending stony-gray   15
Out of his beds mosaic with the dew.

His young employers having got in late,
He and the cook alone
Receive the morning on their old estate,
Possessing what the owners can but own.   20

Notes

7	**jelly:**	jam
11	**catbird:**	a black and grey North American bird whose song often sounds like a cat mewing
16	**mosaic:**	a picture or pattern that is made up of small coloured pieces of stone or glass

Richard Wilbur

Explorations

1.

a   Why do the cook and the gardener not expect their 'young employers' to be 'coming down' on this summer morning?

b   What does the line 'And scraped the right front fender on the gate' suggest to you about the condition that the 'young employers' were in when they arrived back late?

c   What does this incident tell you about the attitude of the 'young employers' to the things they own?

2.

a   Lines 5–11 describe the scene inside the house where the cook is preparing her breakfast. Based on your reading of these lines, how do you picture the kitchen she is working in?

b   Do you think the cook looks after the kitchen well? What evidence can you find in the poem for your answer?

3.

a   Lines 12–20 move the poem outside to the garden of the house. Describe how you imagine the garden from the images the poet uses.

b   The gardener takes a moment to look at the garden and the house and 'his beds mosaic with the dew'. What do his action and the use of 'his' suggest about the gardener's attitude to this garden?

4.   Wilbur uses the senses of sight and hearing in the poem to help us appreciate how special this summer morning on the 'estate' is. Choose one image for each sense and explain why you particularly like it.

SECOND READING

5.

a 'He and the cook alone | Receive the morning on their old estate'. The word 'Receive' can be interpreted in two ways: to accept or take something that has been offered and to welcome and entertain a guest. Consider how each of these meanings can be applied in the lines above.

b Do you think these lines suggest that the cook and the gardener enjoy working on the 'estate'? Why?

c Is it significant that they think of it as 'their old estate'? Explain your answer.

6.

a 'Possessing what the owners can but own.'
Based on your reading of the poem, discuss how each of the people engages with (functions with, thinks and feels about) the 'estate'.

b Do you think that how you engage with something is part of the difference between 'possessing' and 'owning'? Why?

c Do you agree with the poet that there is a difference between possessing and owning? Use references from the poem to support your view.

7.

a Both the cook and the gardener use the term 'young employers' rather than the individual names of their employers. What does this tell you about the kind of relationship that the cook and the gardener have with these people?

b How do you think the cook and the gardener feel about the way the 'young employers' treat the estate? Refer to the poem in your answer.

THIRD READING

8.

a Based on Wilbur's descriptions of the kitchen and the gardens, how would you describe the mood of this summer morning?

b He uses a very regular rhyme scheme in each quatrain (group of four lines): line 1 rhymes with line 3; line 2 rhymes with line 4. This can be written as *abab*. Do you find that this scheme adds to the overall mood that is created in the poem? In what ways does it do this?

9. We have seen what the cook and the gardener are doing while the 'young employers' are still asleep. Write a piece describing what you think will happen in the kitchen and the garden when the 'young employers' do eventually come down.

10.

a Imagine that this estate is going to be sold. The auctioneer has asked the 'young employers', the cook and the gardener to write a short piece about the estate to be included in the information booklet. Do you think the three descriptions would be the same or different? Explain your answer.

b Try writing a paragraph for each of them in the way that you think they would write about the estate.

Richard Wilbur

Denise Levertov

(1923–97)

Denise Levertov was born in Essex in England. Her father had converted from Judaism to become an Anglican parson. She was educated completely at home and at five years old decided that she would become a writer. At the age of 12 she sent her poetry to T.S. Eliot, who responded very positively to her work. She published her first poem at 17 and her first collection in 1946. During the Second World War she worked as a civilian nurse during the bombing of London.

In 1947 she married an American and soon after moved to the USA with him. By 1956 she had become an American citizen. Her poetry became much less formal and she was heavily influenced by poets such as William Carlos Williams. Her second American volume, *With Eyes at the Back of Our Heads* (1959), established her as one of the great American poets, and her British roots were by now a thing of the past. During the 1960s she became very involved in activism and feminism. She was strongly opposed to the Vietnam War. *The Sorrow Dance*, which expresses her feelings about the Vietnam War and the death of her sister, is a passionate, angry collection. In all, she published more than 20 volumes of poetry. She died in December 1997.

An Arrival (North Wales, 1897)

Prescribed for exams in 2015 and 2016

The orphan arrived in outlandish hat,
proud pain of new button boots.
Her moss-agate eyes
photographed views of the noonday sleepy town
no one had noticed. Nostrils flaring,   5
she sniffed odors of hay and stone,
            absence of Glamorgan coaldust,
and pasted her observations quickly
into the huge album of her mind.
Cousins, ready to back off like heifers   10
were staring:
          amazed they received
the gold funeral sovereigns she dispensed
along with talk strange to them as a sailor's parrot.

Auntie confiscated the gold;   15
the mourning finery, agleam with jet,
was put by to be altered. It had been chosen
by the child herself and was thought
unsuitable. She was to be
the minister's niece, now,   20
not her father's daughter.
              Alone,
she would cut her way through a new world's
graystone chapels, the steep and sideways
rockface cottages climbing   25
mountain streets,

enquiring, turning things over
in her heart,
          weeping only in rage or when
the choirs in their great and dark and   30
golden glory broke forth and the hills
skipped like lambs.

Notes

1	**outlandish:**	unfamiliar, strange
3	**moss-agate:**	the colour of a semi-precious green gemstone
7	**Glamorgan:**	one of the most industrialised counties in Wales due to the rich coal deposits in the area
13	**sovereigns:**	a British gold coin
16	**jet:**	a black or dark-brown stone associated with funeral dress in the 19th century
20	**minister:**	member of the clergy

Explorations

BEFORE READING

1.

a   Moving or travelling to different places can be interesting but also challenging because of different customs and attitudes about dress, ways of living and language. Have you ever arrived in a place and noticed how different it was to your home? What were the differences that you experienced?

b   Did you find it easy or difficult to cope with these differences? As a class, share and discuss your experiences.

FIRST READING

2.

a   'she sniffed odors of hay and stone, | absence of Glamorgan coaldust'. What do the smells that the girl notices on her arrival suggest to you about the location of her new hometown?

b   What does the smell that she misses tell you about the locality of the town she has had to leave?

c   Do you think the girl might find it difficult to make such a change? Why?

3.

a   'The orphan', 'the mourning finery', 'not her father's daughter'. Based on your reading of these three phrases, can you suggest why the girl has had to move to a new town to live with unfamiliar relatives?

b   In your opinion, does this fact make the girl's situation more difficult for her to cope with? Why?

SECOND READING

4.

a   Lines 1–2 and line 16 make it clear that the 'orphan' tries to make a good impression on her unfamiliar relatives by wearing expensive mourning clothes. Based on these lines and the picture that accompanies this poem, describe the mourning outfit that the girl is wearing.

b   How does the 'Auntie' react to the girl's clothes in lines 16–17?

c   Do you think a difference in customs and attitudes has anything to do with her aunt's reaction? Why?

5.

a   The 'orphan' also tries to make a good impression on her relatives by giving them gifts of money ('gold funeral sovereigns'). In your own words, explain how her cousins react to her gift in lines 12–13.

b   How does the 'Auntie' react in line 15?

c   Again, do you think a difference in customs and attitudes caused these reactions? Why?

6.

a   'along with talk strange to them as a sailor's parrot'.
The third way that the 'orphan' tries to make a good impression on her unfamiliar relatives is by speaking to them. What does the line quoted above suggest to you about her relatives' reaction to the way that she spoke?

b   Can you suggest what causes them to react in this way?

7.   What impression do you get from lines 22–32 of the type of relationship that the girl develops with her relatives? Explain your answer with reference to this passage of the poem.

THIRD READING

8.

a   Differences in customs and attitudes can be caused not only by changes in geographical location, but also by historical time. This poem is set in the 19th century, when people lived in very different ways to those of the 21st century. What do lines 17–19 tell you about the 19th-century attitude to the amount of independence that young people ought to have?

b   What do you learn about the 19th-century custom regarding the social importance of men and women in lines 19–21?

c   Would you find it difficult to cope with this 19th-century attitude and custom? Why?

9. The difficulties that can be caused by differences in customs and attitudes are a theme (an important idea) in this poem. Working in pairs, can you suggest what (a) the orphaned girl (b) the 'Auntie' and (c) the cousins could have said or done to reduce their difficulties and to develop a happier relationship?

10.

a   In your opinion, is this a happy or a sad poem? Refer to the poem to support your view.

b   What do you think the poet is trying to tell us about how we should treat people who have different attitudes and customs to ours?

Patricia Beer
(1924–99)

Patricia Beer was born in Exmouth, Devon, into a Plymouth Brethren family. Her father was a railway clerk and her mother a teacher; Beer wrote a vivid account of her stern upbringing in *Mrs Beer's House* (1968). She won a scholarship to Exmouth Grammar School and achieved a first-class honours degree at Exeter University. She went on to St Hugh's College, Oxford, and lived in Italy teaching English from 1947 to 1953. After a succession of temporary jobs, Beer was appointed lecturer in English at Goldsmiths' College in London in 1962, where she remained for six years. In 1964 she married an architect, John Damien Parsons, with whom she refurbished a Tudor farmhouse in Up Ottery, Devon, where she lived for the rest of her life.

Patricia Beer left teaching to become a full-time writer in 1968. In all, Beer published nine volumes of poetry, one novel and an academic study, *Reader I Married Him*, an analysis of the major 19th-century women novelists and their female characters. Patricia Beer made her poems out of the ordinary events of daily life with a wry humour and a sharp eye for detail.

The Voice

Prescribed for the exam in 2018

When God took my aunt's baby boy, a merciful neighbour
Gave her a parrot. She could not have afforded one
But now bought a new cage as brilliant as the bird,
And turned her back on the idea of other babies.

He looked unlikely. In her house his scarlet feathers   5
Stuck out like a jungle, though his blue ones blended
With the local pottery which carried messages
Like 'Du ee help yerself to crame, me handsome.'

He said nothing when he arrived, not a quotation
From pet-shop gossip or a sailor's oath, no sound   10
From someone's home: the telephone or car-door slamming,
And none from his: tom-tom, war-cry or wild beast roaring.

He came from silence but was ready to become noise.
My aunt taught him nursery rhymes morning after morning.
He learnt Miss Muffett, Jack and Jill, Little Jack Horner,   15
Including her jokes; she used to say turds and whey.

A genuine Devon accent is not easy. Actors
Cannot do it. He could though. In his court clothes
He sounded like a farmer, as her son might have.
He sounded like our family. He fitted in.   20

Years went by. We came and went. A day or two
Before he died, he got confused, and muddled up
His rhymes. Jack Horner ate his pail of water.
The spider said what a good boy he was. I wept.

He had never seemed puzzled by the bizarre events   25
He spoke of. But that last day he turned his head towards us
With the bewilderment of death upon him. Said
'Broke his crown' and 'Christmas pie'. And tumbled after.

My aunt died the next winter, widowed, childless, pitied
And patronised. I cannot summon up her voice at all.   30
She would not have expected it to be remembered
After so long. But I can still hear his.

Patricia Beer

Explorations

1. What impression of the aunt do you get from the first stanza? How do you visualise her?

2. 'He looked unlikely.'
   What do you think the author means by this?

3. How do you imagine the aunt's home looked? Examine the detail in the two opening stanzas.

4. Why do you think the aunt taught the parrot nursery rhymes? Is there a connection with the loss of her baby son?

5. 'He fitted in.'
   How did the parrot fit in?

6. Why do you think the author 'wept'? How does she feel about the parrot?

7. What do you think the poet means by 'pitied | And patronised'? What does this tell us about how people perceived the aunt?

SECOND READING

8. Read the poem aloud. Jot down what you notice about its sounds and rhythms.

9. How do you react to the first sentence? Is it an effective opening?

10. Comment on the 'jungle' simile in the second stanza.

11. Do you get a sense of place from the references to Devon and the local pottery? Does this enrich the poem?

12.

a 'With the bewilderment of death upon him. Said | "Broke his crown" and "Christmas pie". And tumbled after.' Comment on these lines. Do you think the lines work well?

b   Can you detect some humour in the clever phrasing?

13. What evidence is there in the poem that the parrot was regarded more as a family member than a mere household pet?

14. How do you feel about the aunt's life? Can you suggest why we are not told her name?

THIRD READING

15. Briefly state what the theme of the poem is.

16. Would you agree that there is genuine warmth of feeling in this poem?

17. How do you react to the style in which the poem is written? Comment on any three features. You might consider the poet's conversational language, her wry humour, her eye for detail and her use of imagery.

18. What is the mood of this poem? What choice of words and images suggest the mood? Look closely at the final stanza.

19. What have you learned about the character of the author from reading the poem?

FOURTH READING

20. Write a paragraph giving your personal reaction to 'The Voice'. Would you recommend it?

Richard Murphy

(1927–)

Richard Murphy was born in County Mayo in 1927 and now lives in South Africa. He has published numerous collections of poetry, which have won many awards in Ireland, Britain and the US. His collected poems, *In the Heart of the Country*, was published by Gallery Press in 2000. He is a member of Aosdána.

Moonshine

Prescribed for the exam in 2015

To think
I must be alone:
To love
We must be together.

To think I love you   5
When I'm alone
More than I think of you
When we're together.

I cannot think
Without loving   10
Or love
Without thinking.

Alone I love
To think of us together:
Together I think   15
I'd love to be alone.

Notes

Moonshine:	either illicit whiskey or foolish ideas or plans, visionary talk

Explorations

BEFORE READING

1. What sort of ideas, feelings and images do you usually find in a love poem?

FIRST READING

2. What do you notice on first reading this?

3. What kind of person do you think the speaker is here?

4. The speaker is expressing a dilemma or conflict. Describe the dilemma in your own words.

SECOND READING

5. What do you find unusual about this love poem?

6. Which of the possible meanings of the title do you think best suits the poem or could they both apply? Explain your opinions.

7. Do you think the poet is taking this love stuff seriously? Explain.

Ted Hughes
(1930 –98)

Ted Hughes is well known as a poet and as the husband of Sylvia Plath, recognised in her own right as a poet. His work deals not just with nature, where he shows insight into the hidden cruelty of its existence, but he has also reworked a considerable number of writings from Greek and Latin writers. Chief among these are the *Metamorphoses* of Ovid and Seneca's *Oedipus* as well as some Greek plays. His range of poetry is impressive and its uncompromising depiction of the less pleasant aspects of creation remains in stark contrast to the more urbane poetry of many of his contemporaries.

The Stag

Prescribed for exams in 2015 and 2016

While the rain fell on the November woodland shoulder of Exmoor
While the traffic jam along the road honked and shouted
Because the farmers were parking wherever they could
And scrambling to the bank-top to stare through the tree-fringe
Which was leafless,   5
The stag ran through his private forest.

While the rain drummed on the roofs of the parked cars
And the kids inside cried and daubed their chocolate and fought
And mothers and aunts and grandmothers
Were a tangle of undoing sandwiches and screwed-round
    gossiping heads   10
Steaming up the windows,
The stag loped through his favourite valley.

While the blue horsemen down in the boggy meadow
Sodden nearly black, on sodden horses,
Spaced as at a military parade,   15
Moved a few paces to the right and a few to the left and felt
    rather foolish

Looking at the brown impassable river,
The stag came over the last hill of Exmoor.

While everybody high-kneed it to the bank-top all along the road
Where steady men in oilskins were stationed at binoculars,   20
And the horsemen by the river galloped anxiously this way
    and that
And the cry of hounds came tumbling invisibly with their echoes
    down through the draggle of trees,
Swinging across the wall of dark woodland,
The stag dropped into a strange country.

And turned at the river   25
Hearing the hound-pack smash the undergrowth, hearing the
    bell-note
Of the voice that carried all the others,
Then while his limbs all cried different directions to his lungs,
    which only wanted to rest,
The blue horsemen on the bank opposite
Pulled aside the camouflage of their terrible planet.   30

And the stag doubled back weeping and looking for home up a
    valley and down a valley
While the strange trees struck at him and the brambles lashed him,
And the strange earth came galloping after him carrying the
    loll-tongued hounds to fling all over him
And his heart became just a club beating his ribs and his own
    hooves shouted with hounds' voices,
And the crowd on the road got back into their cars   35
Wet-through and disappointed.

Notes

	Stag:	an adult male deer, usually with large antlers
1	**Exmoor:**	an area in south-west England of farmland and national park
8	**daubed:**	painted or plastered on roughly
12	**loped:**	ran with long jumping strides
20	**oilskins:**	waterproof clothing made of an oiled fabric
30	**camouflage:**	something that is used to hide or disguise
33	**loll-tongued:**	with hanging tongues
34	**club:**	thick, heavy stick with a wide end

Explorations

BEFORE READING

1.

a   Imagine that you want to post a tweet that sends a clear message about your feelings regarding people hunting animals for sport. Write your 140-character (25–30 words) tweet.

b   As a group, share your tweets. Perhaps you could write some of them on the board and discuss how clearly your tweets convey your message.

FIRST READING

2.

a   From your reading of stanzas 1–2 (lines 1–12), what impression do you get of the people who are following the hunt?

b   Which of the following words would you choose to describe the type of mood (feelings and atmosphere) that these people bring into the countryside: contented or discontented; aggressive or tranquil; chaotic or peaceful? Refer to stanzas 1–2 to support your answers.

3.   'The stag ran through his private forest', 'The stag loped through his favourite valley'.

a   Based on the two lines quoted above, which of the following words would you choose to describe the type of mood that the stag brings into the countryside: contented or discontented; aggressive or tranquil; chaotic or peaceful?

b   Using your work on the people following the hunt in Question 2 and

the stag in part (a), can you suggest how the people's relationship with the natural world is different to that of the stag?

SECOND READING

4.   In stanzas 3–4 (lines 13–24), the poet describes the two groups who are hunting the stag: 'the blue horsemen' and the 'hounds'. In your own words, explain what each group is doing as they are waiting for the stag. Use references to support your answers.

5.

a   How does the stag react to seeing the 'blue horsemen' and hearing the hounds in stanzas 5–6 (lines 25–36)?

b   What images (word-pictures) does the poet use to suggest that the stag is very frightened and is running away as fast as he can in lines 31–4? Refer to stanzas 5–6 to support your answers.

6.

a   Does the world of nature, to which the stag belongs, make the stag's escape easier or more difficult in lines 32–3? Explain your answer with reference to these lines.

b   What do you think Hughes is trying to tell us here about the way in which the natural world operates?

7.

a   'And the crowd on the road got back into their cars | Wet-through and disappointed.'
Why do you think the people are 'disappointed' at the end of the poem?

b   'Pulled aside the camouflage of their terrible planet.'
The meaning of this line could be

Ted Hughes

449

interpreted as (i) a screen hiding the hunters is pulled back so that they can shoot the stag or (ii) that all the people in the poem hide behind a camouflage of being civilised, but hunting the stag shows that they are really very brutal creatures who kill for sport. Do you think your work for Question 7(a) supports interpretation (i) or (ii) or both? Why?

THIRD READING

8.

a Hughes fills his poem with a lot of different sounds. Working in pairs, each of you draw two columns on a page. Put the heading 'Sound' at the top of one column and 'Made By' at the top of the second. Find and write down all the sounds that are mentioned in the poem in the 'Sound' column, then opposite each sound write down how it is made in the 'Made By' column. As a class, share and discuss your results.

b Do you think that these sounds help to make the poem more real and vivid? Why?

9.

a The poet uses personification when he writes about the stag, an animal, as if it were a person. Quote the lines in the poem where personification is used and explain why you chose them.

b Do you think that the poet's use of personification helps you to become involved in this poem? Why?

10.

a Based on your discussion about writing clear messages for Question 1, do you think Hughes has succeeded in conveying a clear message to you in this poem? Give reasons for your answer.

b Imagine that Hughes decided to tweet a friend summarising what happens in this poem. Write his 140-character (25–30 words) tweet.

Hawk Roosting

Prescribed for the exam in 2018

I sit in the top of the wood, my eyes closed.
Inaction, no falsifying dream
Between my hooked head and hooked feet:
Or in sleep rehearse perfect kills and eat.

The convenience of the high trees!   5
The air's buoyancy and the sun's ray
Are of advantage to me;
And the earth's face upward for my inspection.

My feet are locked upon the rough bark.
It took the whole of Creation   10

To produce my foot, my each feather:
Now I hold Creation in my foot

Or fly up, and revolve it all slowly –
I kill where I please because it is all mine.
There is no sophistry in my body: 15
My manners are tearing off heads –

The allotment of death.
For the one path of my flight is direct
Through the bones of the living.
No arguments assert my right: 20

The sun is behind me.
Nothing has changed since I began.
My eye has permitted no change.
I am going to keep things like this.

Notes

2	**falsifying:**	giving a false idea of something
6	**buoyancy:**	capacity to keep things afloat
10	**Creation:**	the universe, all that is created
15	**sophistry:**	using an argument that is false or meant to deceive
17	**allotment:**	distribution or dealing out
20	**assert:**	declare or justify

Ted Hughes

Explorations

FIRST READING

1.

a   Take a moment after reading this poem for the first time to think about it. Then, within a time limit of 60 seconds, quickly write down a list of words that you would use to describe the hawk in this poem.

b   Take it in turns to write one of your words on the board. Some words may be repeated – if so, just write the word once on the board. Take down all the words on the board.

2.

a   'I sit in the top of the wood, my eyes closed.'
What does the fact that the hawk has its 'eyes closed' tell you about its attitude to the other creatures in the wood?

b   'Between my hooked head and hooked feet'.
Can you suggest how a 'hooked head and hooked feet' might help the hawk to feel that it can safely close its eyes?

3.

a   In stanza 2 (lines 5–8), the hawk tells us that it finds 'the high trees', the 'air's buoyancy' and 'the earth's face upward' convenient and an 'advantage'. Explain in your own words why the hawk, a hunting bird, would find each of these convenient and advantageous.

b   Does the hawk regard these elements as being important in themselves or as being important only because they are helpful to it? Explain your choice.

4.

a   In lines 9–11, the hawk says that it took 'the whole of Creation' to 'produce' its 'foot' and 'each feather'. If someone said to you that it had taken 'the whole of Creation' to make him or her, what would your reaction be?

b   Based on your work for Questions 2, 3 and 4(a), sum up in two sentences the hawk's attitude to itself and to the world around it.

SECOND READING

5.

a   In lines 14–19, the hawk describes its attitude to killing other creatures. Do you think the hawk feels guilty about doing this? Refer to lines 14–19 to support your view.

b   Do you think it should feel guilty? Why?

6.

a   In line 21, the hawk says, 'The sun is behind me.' It also mentions 'the sun's ray' in line 6, so the sun and the direction of its light are obviously important to the hawk. Bearing in mind that the hawk is a hunting bird, can you suggest why these factors are important to him?

b   'The sun is behind me' could also be interpreted as suggesting that the sun supports the hawk in its killing. Do you think the hawk feels that this is true? Why? Refer to the poem in your answer.

7.

a   'I am going to keep things like this.' Are you surprised by this last statement from the hawk or do you think it matches its attitude in the rest of the poem? Explain your answer with reference to the poem.

b Some critics have suggested that this poem explores the world of the dictator. A dictator is a person who is in complete control in an area. Do you think the hawk is a dictator or is it just following its instincts? Explain your answer.

THIRD READING

8. Look at the words that were written on the board for Question 1.

Following your work on this poem, do you feel that any of the words should be crossed out or any new words added to the list? Give reasons for your suggestions.

9. Choose two images from the poem that you found to be striking and explain why you found them to be so.

10. Did the language used by the poet in this poem appeal to you? Explain your answer with reference to the poem.

Brendan Kennelly

(1936–)

Born in Ballylongford, County Kerry, in 1936, Brendan Kennelly was Professor of Modern Literature at Trinity College Dublin for more than 30 years until his retirement in 2005. He has published over 30 books of poetry, among them *My Dark Fathers* (1964), *Dream of a Black Fox* (1968), *Salvation the Stranger* (1972), *Cromwell* (1983), *The Book of Judas* (1991) and *Poetry Me Arse* (1995).

A prolific poet, he writes about everything: love, nature, history, Kerry and being alive. He communicates in direct, colloquial, down-to-earth language.

A Glimpse of Starlings

Prescribed for exams in 2015 and 2016

I expect him any minute now although
He's dead. I know he has been talking
All night to his own dead and now
In the first heart-breaking light of morning
He is struggling into his clothes,   5
Sipping a cup of tea, fingering a bit of bread,
Eating a small photograph with his eyes.
The questions bang and rattle in his head
Like doors and cannisters the night of a storm.
He doesn't know why his days finished like this   10
Daylight is as hard to swallow as food
Love is a crumb all of him hungers for.
I can hear the drag of his feet on the concrete path
The close explosion of his smoker's cough
The slow turn of the Yale key in the lock   15
The door opening to let him in
To what looks like release from what feels like pain
And over his shoulder a glimpse of starlings
Suddenly lifted over field, road and river
Like a fist of black dust pitched in the wind.   20

Explorations

FIRST READING

1. 'I expect him any minute now although | He's dead.'
    Judging by these first lines, what do you expect you might find in this poem? Discuss in pairs or groups.

SECOND READING

2. Write three sentences about what you think is happening in this poem. Discuss in pairs or groups.

3. Focus on the first 12 lines, where the poet imagines what his recently dead father is thinking and feeling.

a   What does he imagine the father doing on that morning?

b   How would you describe how the father feels – is he happy, sad or something else? What images make you think that? Explain.

c   'Eating a small photograph with his eyes'.
    Discuss in pairs or groups what you think this might mean. Do you think it is an effective expression?

d   'The questions bang and rattle in his head | like doors and cannisters the night of a storm.'
    Do you think this simile/comparison works well? Explain your thinking.

4. Do you think that, after death, our spirits may be like the father's – confused, disorientated, bewildered, needing the familiar, needing love? Discuss.

THIRD READING

5. Focus on 13–20 lines. The image of the father is realised through remembered familiar sounds. What are they?

6.

a   'The door opening to let him in | To what looks like release from what feels like pain'.
    In your own words, what might the father be thinking here?

b   What is the effect of the qualifying phrases 'what looks like' and 'what feels like'?

7.

a   In the final three lines the focus moves beyond the father to 'a glimpse of starlings'. What does the image suggest to you? Discuss in groups.

b   The image then develops into a simile/comparison: 'Like a fist of black dust pitched in the wind'. Is this out of place or might it be appropriate in the circumstances? Discuss.

FOURTH READING

8. Do you think the poet was close to his father? Explain your thinking with reference to words and phrases and to the emotions/tone of the poem.

9. The poem is written in the present tense. What is the effect of this?

10. What do you like about this poem? Discuss it in pairs or groups and then write up your opinions.

Brendan Kennelly

Night Drive

Prescribed for exams in 2017 and 2018

I

The rain hammered as we drove
Along the road to Limerick
'Jesus what a night' Alan breathed
And – 'I wonder how he is, the last account
Was poor.'   5
I couldn't speak.

The windscreen fumed and blurred, the rain's spit
Lashing the glass. Once or twice
The wind's fist seemed to lift the car
And pitch it hard against the ditch.   10
Alan straightened out in time,
Silent. Glimpses of the Shannon –
A boiling madhouse roaring for its life
Or any life too near its gaping maw,
White shreds flaring in the waste   15
Of insane murderous black;
Trees bending in grotesque humility,
Branches scattered on the road, smashed
Beneath the wheels.
Then, ghastly under headlights,   20
Frogs bellied everywhere, driven
From the swampy fields and meadows,
Bewildered refugees, gorged with terror.
We killed them because we had to,
Their fatness crunched and flattened in the dark.   25
'How is he now?' Alan whispered
To himself. Behind us,
Carnage of broken frogs.

II

His head
Sweated on the pillow of the white hospital bed.   30
He spoke a little, said
Outrageously, 'I think I'll make it.'
Another time, he'd rail against the weather,
(Such a night would make him eloquent)
But now, quiet, he gathered his fierce will   35
To live.

III

Coming home
Alan saw the frogs.
'Look at them, they're everywhere,
Dozens of the bastards dead.'   40

Minutes later –
'I think he might pull through now.'
Alan, thoughtful at the wheel, was picking out
The homeroad in the flailing rain
Nighthedges closed on either side.   45
In the suffocating darkness
I heard the heavy breathing
Of my father's pain.

Explorations

BEFORE READING

1. Have you ever been travelling in a
   car in severe weather conditions?
   If so, describe the weather as you
   remember it.

FIRST READING

2. How would you describe the weather
   in section I? What images, words or
   phrases convey this best?

3. Think about the description of the
   Shannon – 'A boiling madhouse
   roaring for its life | Or any life too
   near its gaping maw' – and also the
   image of 'Trees bending in grotesque
   humility'. Working in pairs, explore
   all possible suggestions from these
   lines. Use a dictionary for any difficult
   words.

4.

a What do you notice about the frogs?
   What words or images are most
   effective?

b How do you feel on reading these
   lines?

c How does the writer feel about
   them? Where is this suggested?

d What do the frogs add to the
   atmosphere of the section?

SECOND READING

5. What do you think is happening in
   this poem? Who is in the car?

6.

a How would you describe the
   atmosphere in the car? What words
   or phrases convey this best?

b What do you notice about the
   differences between the two men?

7.

a What do you notice about the sick
   man in the hospital bed?

b What similarities and differences do
   you notice between the journeys to
   and from the hospital?

c Do you think the sick man will pull
   through? Explain your thinking.

Brendan Kennelly

8. What does this poem say to you about death, love and families? These are the themes.

9. Consider the descriptive language of this poem. Discuss some examples that you think are particularly good.

10. Suggest a number of ways by which the poet conveys the tense, worried atmosphere.

Marge Piercy
(1936–)

Marge Piercy was born on 31 March 1936 in a Detroit shattered by the economic hardships caused by the American Depression. Her father Robert, like many men at the time, had struggled to find work until he finally got a job installing and repairing machinery. Piercy credits her mother and grandmother as major influences in her life, both in stimulating her imagination and love of reading and in encouraging her to develop a strong sense of her Jewish heritage. Piercy began to write at the age of 15. She has always written both poetry and fiction and frequently writes both at the same time. Often she finds herself developing themes from a novel that she is working on in her poetry: an approach that she claims, with some humour, helps her to avoid the dreaded writer's block. Piercy was very much a part of the feminist movement of the 1960s and still works to improve the position of women as well as that of society itself in her wider political activism. She lives and works with her husband, the writer Ira Wood, and a number of her beloved cats in Cape Cod. For Piercy, poetry is essential to the human condition because, as she explains, 'you have to know why, you have to know who you are, you have to know what you're doing and why you're doing it. You have to know what you believe in ... That's mostly poetry.'

Will we work together?

Prescribed for exams in 2017 and 2018

You wake in the early grey
morning in bed alone and curse
me, that I am only
sometimes there. But when
I am with you, I light   5
up the corners, I am bright
as a fireplace roaring
with love, every bone in my back
and my fingers is singing
like a tea kettle on the boil.   10
My heart wags me, a big dog
with a bigger tail. I am
a new coin printed with
your face. My body wears
sore before I can express   15
on yours the smallest part
of what moves me. Words
shred and splinter.
I want to make with you
some bold new thing   20
to stand in the marketplace,
the statue of a goddess
laughing, armed and wearing
flowers and feathers. Like sheep
of whose hair is made   25
blankets and coats, I want
to force from this fierce sturdy
rampant love some useful thing.

Notes

20	bold:	brave, daring, courageous
23	armed:	bearing weapons
27	sturdy:	strong, powerful
28	rampant:	occurring in an unrestrained way, growing wildly, out of control

Marge Piercy

Explorations

FIRST READING

1.

a   How does the poet imagine her lover reacting to her not being beside him when he wakes up?

b   Does she seem to be offended by the fact that he curses her?

c   Why do you think she feels this way about his cursing?

2.

a   How do you feel when you wake up to a 'grey' morning?

b   Can you suggest why Piercy decided to open this poem with the image of her lover waking in the 'grey' morning?

3.   Much of the poem (lines 4–18) is given over to the poet reminding her lover of how it is when she is there. Choose one image from this section that you feel really suggests the strength of her feelings and explain the reasons for your choice.

4.   Examine how the poet creates a strong sense of the physicality of her feelings in lines 4–18 by (a) references to parts of the body and (b) references to the senses of sight and touch.

5.   'I am bright | as a fireplace' (a simile), 'like a tea kettle on the boil' (a simile), 'My heart wags me, a big dog | with a bigger tail' (a metaphor), 'I am | a new coin printed with | your face' (a metaphor).
Take each of the similes and metaphors quoted above and explain

in your own words what she is trying to tell her lover about her feelings by using that simile or metaphor.

SECOND READING

6.

a   'I want to make with you | some bold new thing'.
What do these lines tell you about what the poet wants to happen with their love?

b   Are you surprised that she feels this way given what she has said in lines 4–18 or can you understand her feelings?

7.

a   'the statue of a goddess | laughing, armed and wearing | flowers and feathers.'
In ancient times a statue of a goddess was treated with great respect by the crowds in the marketplace and it would often survive for centuries, so the poet wants their relationship to involve respect and to be long term. Can you suggest what characteristics the other elements in the goddess's appearance stand for?

b   Do you think they are good characteristics to have in a relationship? Why?

8.

a   'I want | to force from this fierce sturdy | rampant love some useful thing.' How do these lines suggest the energy of their love?

b   Can you explain in your own words what the poet wants to do with this energy?

THIRD READING

9. Do you see this as a poem about love or passion or commitment, or perhaps all three? Use references from the poem to support your view.

10. Imagine that you want to persuade Marge Piercy to come to your school to talk about this poem. Write a letter to her explaining why you particularly like this poem and why you think it is relevant to you and your fellow pupils.

Tony Harrison
(1937–)

Tony Harrison comes from a working-class background in Leeds, where his father was a baker. He received a scholarship to Leeds Grammar School and then went to study at the University of Leeds, where he read Classics and Linguistics. He is a poet, playwright, filmmaker and often outspoken critic of world political issues. In his early poetry he explored aspects of his working-class background, in particular how education and educated language could estrange young people from their families and culture. This theme features prominently in one of his early collections of poetry, *Continuous: 50 Sonnets from the School of Eloquence and Other Poems* (1981), from which 'Book Ends' is taken.

Book Ends

Prescribed for the exam in 2018

I

Baked the day she suddenly dropped dead
we chew it slowly that last apple pie.

Shocked into sleeplessness you're scared of bed.
We never could talk much, and now don't try.

You're like book ends, the pair of you, she'd say,   **5**
Hog that grate, say nothing, sit, sleep, stare ...

The 'scholar' me, you, worn out on poor pay,
only our silence made us seem a pair.

Not as good for staring in, blue gas,
too regular each bud, each yellow spike.   **10**

A night you need my company to pass
and she not here to tell us we're alike!

Your life's all shattered into smithereens.

Back in our silences and sullen looks,
for all the Scotch we drink, what's still between's   **15**
not the thirty or so years, but books, books, books.

Note: This is only part one of the poem. Part two is not set for examination

Notes

6	**Hog that grate:**	position themselves so close to the fire that there's no room for anyone else
13	**smithereens:**	small fragments

Explorations

BEFORE READING

1. Do you have any experience of the death of a family member, relative, friend or someone who was well known to you? What did you feel, think and do when you first heard the news? And later? Perhaps you could share this in groups. Now read the poem.

FIRST READING

2.

a Concentrate on the first four lines. Who are the characters involved?

b What is the relationship between them?

c How would you describe the mood or atmosphere here?

3. Consider the same questions as in Question 2 with regard to lines 5–12.

4. Read all sixteen lines as a unit. What do you discover about the mother, the father and the son/speaker? Share your thoughts in a group discussion and make a note of all the ideas expressed.

5. The poet refers to 'sullen looks' in line 14. Can you think of any possible reasons for these? Share and discuss.

6.

a Despite this, do you think the son understands and sympathises with his father?

b What in the poem leads you to think this? What do you think really gets in the way of their talking?

SECOND READING

7. Write a letter that the speaker might later send to the father and keep it true to the events of the poem.

8. How do you think the poet felt about his mother? Does he miss her? Did he think she was wise, etc?

9. Write about the relationship between father and son.

THIRD READING

10. Do you think the poet deals well with elements of bereavement, such as sense of loss, memories, the difficulty of coping with what needs to be done, etc? Put your thoughts on paper.

11. What image of family life is contained in this poem?

12. 'Education can sometimes cause divisions in families.'
Debate this.

Tony Harrison

Les Murray

(1938–)

eslie Allan Murray was born in Nabiac on the north coast of New South Wales, Australia. He grew up in the neighbouring district of Bunyah, in poor circumstances on a small dairy farm which was rented from his grandfather. Even though life must have been difficult, particularly after his mother died when he was 12 and his father became ill, Bunyah has always been an important place in Murray's consciousness. He managed to buy back part of the land and returned to live there in 1985.

Murray was educated at the University of Sydney, where he developed an interest in ancient and modern languages. For some years he was a professional translator at the Australian National University.

Murray has produced many collections of prose writing and some verse novels, but he is most prolific as a poet, for which he has received many awards and prizes and recognition for his significant contribution to literature in Australia and internationally. Among his collections of poetry are *The Ilex Tree* (1965), *Poems against Economics* (1972), *The People's Other World* (1983), *The Daylight Moon* (1987), from which 'Joker as Told' is taken, *Dog Fox Field* (1990), *Subhuman Redneck Poems* (1996), *Poems the Size of Photographs* (2002) and *Taller When Prone* (2010).

Joker as Told

Prescribed for the exam in 2016

Not a latch or lock could hold
a little horse we had
not a gate or paddock.

He liked to get in the house.   5
Walk in, and you were liable
to find him in the kitchen
dribbling over the table
with a heap behind him

or you'd catch a hoof
right where it hurt bad 10
when you went in your bedroom.

He grew up with us kids,
played with us till he got rough.
Round then, they cut him,
but you couldn't ride him: 15
he'd bite your bum getting on,
kick your foot from the stirrup

and he could kick the spurs off
your boots. Almost hopped on with you,
and if he couldn't buck you 20
he'd lie down plop! and roll
in his temper, and he'd squeal.

He was from the Joker breed,
we called him Joker;
no joke much when he bit you 25
or ate the Monday washing.

They reckon he wanted to be
human, coming in the house.
I don't think so, I think he
wanted something people had. 30
He didn't do it from love of us.

He couldn't grow up to be a
full horse, and he wouldn't be a slave one.
I think he was looking for his childhood,
his foalhood and ours, when we played. 35

He was looking for the Kingdom of God.

Notes

14	**they cut him:**	neutered or gelded him
33	**full horse:**	able to breed and sire foals
36	**Kingdom of God:**	this may be a reference to St Matthew's Gospel, 18: 3, where Jesus said, 'unless you change and become like children, you will never enter the Kingdom of heaven'.

Les Murray

Explorations

BEFORE READING

1. Young children often have special pets, most often small animals, but on farms it could be a pet lamb or a calf that is hand reared and follows one around. What are your childhood memories of animals, the fun they brought and the trouble they caused?

2. If you had a pet, did you think of it and treat it almost as a human being? Discuss.

3. What do animals contribute to the lives and development of young people?

FIRST READING

4. Was Joker an uncomplicated pet? Explain your thinking.

5. This poem tells us as much about the way of life of people in the Australian countryside as it does about the horse. What insights into life on a farm do we discover?

6. 'They reckon he wanted to be | human'.
   Can you see their point of view? Explain.

7. But the writer doesn't agree. In your

groups, explore his views, which are outlined in lines 29–36. Read the Critical Commentary on the accompanying CD and discuss it. What do you think of the poet's explanation of Joker's behaviour?

SECOND READING

8. What would you like to ask the writer about this experience?

9. Overall, how would you describe the writer's attitude to Joker? Was he sympathetic to him, sorry for him, afraid of him, annoyed with him, etc.? Explain your thinking.

10. Do you think this childhood experience was significant for the writer? In what way?

11. Do you think childhood experiences help to form the person we later become? Discuss.

THIRD READING

12. What issues does this poem raise about the relationship between humans and animals?

13. Did you think this poem was worth reading? Outline your thoughts.

14. Did you find this a mainly humorous poem or a thought-provoking one?

Explain your thinking.

15. Murray has written about the prejudice he experienced against rural people:

'When I went to University in Sydney, I ran full-on into a prejudice I'd only vaguely heard of before; I was said to be a peasant, a provincial, a hick from the sticks ... I am one of those who managed to get home again. All of my books are full of a determination to bring sympathy and some truthful regard to those I had to leave in order to get an education and later a living ...' (*The Daylight Moon*, 1988)

Do you think he managed to 'bring sympathy and some truthful regard' to rural people in 'Joker as Told'?

Michael Coady
(1939–)

Michael Coady lives in Carrick-on-Suir in County Tipperary. He was born there in 1939 and although he has travelled outside Ireland, his life and his home have always been based in Carrick-on-Suir. He taught in a school in the town for 30 years until he retired, married his wife, Martina, and raised his three children there and much of his creative work focuses on exploring and celebrating the ways in which his hometown and the people who live there give him a sense of belonging. In his work, he also considers how, as a result of emigration to the US, many Irish people have had to cope with the loss of such connections.

Michael Coady did not begin to write poetry until he was in his late twenties. However, as he explained in an interview with Alice Vollmar (2004), he had always been interested in poetry, commenting, 'I grew up with poetry, and it enchanted me.' In spite of winning numerous prizes for his poetry and short stories, he does not limit his creativity to words alone and he enjoys exploring a variety of ways in which to express himself, including music and photography.

New World

Prescribed for the exam in 2018

Lovers are commonplace as day, so why
should I feel moved by this chance
glimpse of an uncaring starstruck
pair in a Chicago street, islanded
within their pristine pool of joy,   5
tasting with their hands and eyes
that fugitive and fabled spring
of shy collusion and surprise?

Why should a traveller feel so blessed
against the grimy street's cacophony   10
and frantic push of money-chasing,
among the flintfaced cops, the joggers
and pulsating roller skaters,
among the strip show touts and cool
receptionists, the loud construction   15
workers and the lost bag ladies?

Within this maelstrom I'm relearning
that ecstasy and innocence persist
like untouched havens, though everywhere
and always stormed by circumstance and   20
reefed about with dangers. Far from home
I'm blessed to find that lovers, though
forever falling out of love and into
everyday, are always there, that is

somewhere, and always gazing, gazing   25
deep into unmapped horizons, their
lifted hearts like ships full-sailing
as if they'd just descried a virgin
island or a dazzling El Dorado, as if
in their sweet turn and time   30
they hugged exclusively
some whispered secret out of Eden.

Notes

5	**pristine:**	unspoilt
7	**fugitive:**	passing
7	**fabled:**	legendary
8	**collusion:**	a shared secret understanding
10	**cacophony:**	a harsh combination of sounds
12	**flint:**	a hard grey stone
17	**maelstrom:**	a huge whirlpool
19	**havens:**	harbours or places of refuge
28	**descried:**	caught sight of
29	**El Dorado:**	the legendary 'Lost City of Gold' that attracted many European explorers to South America from the 16th century onwards in the hopes of finding it and making their fortune
32	**Eden:**	according to the Bible, God placed the first man and woman, Adam and Eve, in the beautiful and fertile Garden of Eden, where life was very happy. However, because they disobeyed God's command that they were not to eat any of the fruit from the Tree of Knowledge, God put them out of the Garden of Eden. As a result, they had to live in the harsher and unhappier world outside Eden.

Explorations

BEFORE READING

1. Have you ever visited a large, unfamiliar city in Ireland, or perhaps in Europe or the US? Take a moment to recall your first impressions of it (the sights, the sounds and the smells) and how it made you feel. You might like to write some short notes about your impressions and feelings. Then, as a class, share your experiences.

FIRST READING

2. Pick out any part of Coady's description of a street in the city of Chicago in stanza 2 that reminds you of your remembered experience from Question 1. What words and images

Michael Coady

469

(word-pictures) used in stanzas 2–3 convey the fact that this city is not the poet's home? Explain your answer.

3.

a   The poet begins stanza 1 with the comment, 'Lovers are commonplace as day'. What do you think he means by this phrase?

b   From the poet's description of the lovers in lines 3–8, can you suggest what made him notice this pair of lovers? Refer to the text in your answer.

4.   In stanza 3, the poet tells us that seeing the love shared by the couple reminds him of 'ecstasy and innocence'. Draw two columns on the board. Put the heading Ecstasy at the top of one and Innocence at the top of the other. Using your work for Question 3(b), work out which of the lovers' feelings in lines 3–8 can go into the Ecstasy column and which into the Innocence column.

5.

a   What two images does the poet use to convey the way that two people feel when they first fall in love in lines 25–32?

b   Based on these images, do you think the poet views love as a positive or negative experience for lovers? Use references from this stanza to support your opinion.

6.

a   From your reading of the poem, explain in your own words how the poet's mood (feelings) changes as a result of his 'glimpse' of the lovers.

b   Do you think he is happy or unhappy that he saw the lovers by chance? Why? Refer to the poem in your answer.

SECOND READING

7.

a   Images about the sea, ships and exploration are used to describe lovers falling in love in this poem. Using quotations from the poem, explain in your own words the ways in which Coady connects these images to the process of falling in love.

b   In your opinion, is this a good way to describe falling in love? Why?

8.

a   Coady chose 'New World' as the title for this poem. What are the different types of new worlds that the poet refers to in the course of this poem?

b   Do you think 'New World' is a good title for this poem or can you suggest an alternative title? Illustrate your answer with quotations from the poem.

THIRD READING

9.   Michael Coady likes to collect ideas from his everyday life to use in his poetry; he said, 'I carry a notebook and jot things down.' Based on your work on this poem, write out the short notes you think he might have made in his notebook on the day he briefly saw the two lovers in the Chicago street.

10.   Look at the picture that accompanies this poem. Do you think it is a suitable picture to illustrate this poem? Explain your answer.

Michael Longley

(1939–)

Michael Longley was born in Belfast on 27 July 1939, of English parents. His father fought in the trenches in the First World War and was gassed, wounded, decorated and promoted to the rank of captain. In *Tuppenny Stung*, a short collection of autobiographical chapters published in 1994, Longley describes his family, primary and secondary education and the forces of his early cultural formation: Protestant schoolboys' fears of the dark savageries supposedly practised by Catholics; an English education system dismissive of Irish culture and history; and Protestant Belfast's fear and resentment of the Republic. His early education and local socialisation made him aware of conflicting classes and religions and of the duality of Irish identity.

Later he was educated at the Royal Belfast Academical Institution and in 1958 he went to Trinity College Dublin, where he studied classics and wrote poetry but felt very under-read in English literature until taken in hand by his friend and young fellow poet, Derek Mahon.

Longley worked for the Arts Council of Northern Ireland from 1970 to 1991, when he took early retirement. His work for the arts was driven by a number of guiding principles, including nurturing indigenous talent and providing support for artists, not just the arts, allied to the need to transcend class barriers and bring the arts to the working class. He was a champion of cultural pluralism, fostering the artistic expression of both sides of the religious and political divide.

Among his collections of poetry are *The Ghost Orchid* (1995), *Broken Dishes* (1998), *The Weather in Japan* (2000), *Snow Water* (2004), *Collected Poems* (2006) and *A Hundred Doors* (2011).

Michael Longley is a fellow of the Royal Society of Literature and a member of Aosdána. In 2007 he was the Ireland Professor of Poetry. He is married to the critic and academic Edna Longley.

Prescribed for the exam in 2017

for Raymond Piper

I

Pushing the wedge of his body
Between cromlech and stone circle,
He excavates down mine shafts
And back into the depths of the hill.

His path straight and narrow   5
And not like the fox's zig-zags,
The arc of the hare who leaves
A silhouette on the sky line.

Night's silence around his shoulders,
His face lit by the moon, he   10
Manages the earth with his paws,
Returns underground to die.

II

An intestine taking in
patches of dog's-mercury,
brambles, the bluebell wood;   15
a heel revolving acorns;
a head with a price on it
brushing cuckoo-spit, goose-grass;
a name that parishes borrow.

III

For the digger, the earth-dog   20
It is a difficult delivery
Once the tongs take hold,

Vulnerable his pig's snout
That lifted cow-pats for beetles,
Hedgehogs for the soft meat,   25

His limbs dragging after them
So many stones turned over,
The trees they tilted.

Notes

2	**cromlech:**	a name formerly used for the remains of a portal tomb; here the poet uses it to mean the horizontal slab on top of the upright stones
14	**dog's-mercury:**	a herbaceous woodland plant, usually regarded as toxic
19	**a name that parishes borrow:**	the poet is referring to *broc*, the Irish for badger (in fact, the element Broc found in place names, for example *Domhnach Broc*, anglicised as Donnybrook, is the man's name Broc)

Explorations

FIRST READING

Section I

1. Think of section I as a picture or painting. What do you see? Consider the setting described, the background, the lighting and the main subject.

2.

a   What do you notice about the badger? How do you visualise the animal? Examine the connotations of descriptive words and phrases, such as 'the wedge of his body', 'Night's silence around his shoulders', 'he | Manages the earth'.

b   How do the badgers' paths differ from those of other animals and what might this suggest about the nature of the badger?

3. What is suggested here about the animal's relationship with the earth? Consider his association with 'cromlech and stone circle', how he

'Manages' the earth and how he 'Returns underground to die'.

4. Do you think the badger has particular significance for the poet? Explain.

5. How would you describe the atmosphere of section I? What words or phrases help to create it?

SECOND READING

Section II

6. What do you notice about the badger's diet?

7. What other aspects of the badger's environmental function are referred to in section II?

8. 'a head with a price on it ... a name that parishes borrow'.
What do these lines suggest about human attitudes to the badger?

THIRD READING

Section III

9. What do you think is happening in section III?

10. Contrast the humans' treatment of the environment in section III with the badger's management of the earth in sections I and II.

11. Do you think the poet has some sympathy for the animal in this section? Which phrases or images might suggest this?

12. Explore the ironies in lines 20–2.

FOURTH READING

13. What point is the poet making about humankind's interaction with the environment?

14. What other themes do you notice in the poem?

15. Would you agree that 'Longley displays the scientific assurance of a naturalist'?

16. 'Longley's view of the west of Ireland is a realistic rather than a romantic one.' On the evidence of the poem 'Badger', would you agree with this statement? Refer to the text to support your argument.

17. Summarise your thoughts and feelings on this poem.

Macdara Woods

(1942–)

Macdara Woods was born in Dublin in 1942. He is married to fellow poet Eiléan Ní Chuilleanáin and they have a son, Niall. Macdara Woods's commitment to the literary world was evident from an early age when he began to publish poetry as a teenager. He has been involved in the Irish poetry scene since the 1970s. In 1975, along with Eiléan Ní Chuilleanáin, Leland Bardwell and Pearse Hutchinson, Woods founded *Cyphers*, a title that was adapted from Cypher, the name of the family's black cat. Now one of Ireland's longest-established literary magazines, *Cyphers* does not limit itself to poetry alone and includes prose, graphics and reviews in its issues. Macdara Woods is similarly wide-ranging in his approach to his work and he has collaborated with a number of musicians in Ireland, Italy and the US to produce works that embrace both poetry and music. Although Woods lives in Ireland, he has a strong connection with Italy and tries to spend as much time as possible in the family house in Umbria because, as Eiléan Ní Chuilleanáin notes, 'Macdara likes being there to write'. Some of his works have even been translated into Italian.

Woods is particularly concerned with fighting against 'the process by which language becomes increasingly meaningless' because of 'so-called correctness, of dumbing down'. For him, the job of the poet is vital in today's world because it is the poet's task to use language to communicate how life is meaningful and special: 'That perspective, an illumination … Where the everyday now and the eternal now meet.'

Kavanagh in Umbria

● Track 30

Prescribed for the exam in 2016

I have seen him here in November
going home through the dark
on the tractor
a piece of sacking
thrown across his shoulders   5
against the winter fog
hunched up
between the unseeing olives
and the leafless sticks of vines
marvellously translated   10
but not translated at all
from where he is:
broken fields perishing calves
November haggard
and the mist where Genesis begins   15

August 2004

Notes

	Kavanagh:	Patrick Kavanagh, an Irish poet greatly admired by Macdara Woods
	Umbria:	a region in the centre of Italy where Woods spends some of his time
10	**translated:**	moved or changed from one place to another
14	**haggard:**	the enclosed area of farm buildings used for storing hay, grain and sometimes machinery
15	**Genesis:**	the first book of the Hebrew Bible and the Christian Old Testament. It includes the story of God creating all things. The word 'genesis' can also be used to refer to the origin or coming into being of a thing.

Explorations

BEFORE READING

1. The 'Kavanagh' mentioned in the title of this poem is Patrick Kavanagh, who was born in County Monaghan, the son of a small farmer. Images of the harsh conditions and barren landscape in which he lived and worked for a number of years fill many of Kavanagh's poems about his time there. In this way, his poetry was created out of the challenging conditions in which he lived. Before reading Woods's poem, you might like to read 'Shancoduff' in this anthology or 'A Christmas Childhood' by Patrick Kavanagh to form an impression of how he wrote about his environment.

FIRST READING

2.

a In lines 1–7, Macdara Woods describes a man driving his tractor home. What images in these lines might lead you to think that this poem is set in Ireland? Explain your answer with reference to lines 1–7.

b If the poem is set in Ireland, and bearing in mind the title of the poem, 'Kavanagh in Umbria', who do you think the man might be in line 1?

3.

a 'between the unseeing olives | and the leafless sticks of vines'.
   Were you surprised by these two lines coming after lines 1–7? Why?

b What effect did these lines have on your view of where the poem is set? Does the title of the poem, 'Kavanagh in Umbria', help you to decide where the poem is set? Explain your answer.

c Who do you think the 'him' in line 1 refers to now? Support your answer by reference to the poem.

4. Based on your work for Questions 2 and 3 about the way in which the setting of the poem seems to change from Ireland to Italy, what do you think the poet imagined happening to the 'him' referred to in line 1 when he uses the phrase 'marvellously translated' in line 10? You might find it helpful to look at the definition given for 'translated' in the Notes above.

SECOND READING

5. What images does the poet use in this poem to convey to us just how difficult and challenging the month of November is for farmers? Refer to the text in your answer.

6.

a 'and the mist where Genesis begins'. Explain what this line suggests about the part played by November in the cycle of growth in the world of nature. You might find it helpful to look at the definition given for 'Genesis' in the Notes above.

b How would an understanding of this keep the farmers working in spite of the difficult and challenging conditions that you considered in Question 5?

c Do you think the poet's decision to leave out the full stop at the end of the last line has anything to do with the meaning of this line? Why?

7. 'marvellously translated
but not translated at all
from where he is:'

Both Kavanagh and Woods realised that farmers know that it is important to keep working in harsh conditions because all their efforts will eventually result in growth: the production of crops and the feeding of livestock. Can you explain how the lines quoted above suggest that this important message, or truth about life, is true whether the 'him' and 'he' is Kavanagh farming with other farmers in Ireland or an Italian farmer being watched by the poet in Umbria?

THIRD READING

8.

a In your own words, describe the mood (the feelings and atmosphere) that is created in lines 1–14, referring to the images that you feel especially help to create this mood.

b How does the mood change in line 15? Refer to the poem to support your view.

c Do you think that the moods created in lines 1–14 and in line 15 contribute to your understanding of this poem? Why?

9. In this poem, Macdara Woods suggests that it is very important to keep working hard in difficult conditions because although it may not be obvious, 'Genesis', that is, the starting point for growth, begins in such conditions. Do you think that this important message, or truth about life, is any way relevant to you and your fellow students studying for the Leaving Certificate examination? Give reasons for your answer.

10. You decide to create a short video to capture the atmosphere of this poem. Describe how you might use location, lighting, soundtrack, music, etc. to communicate this.

Prescribed for the exam in 2018

In winter fire is beautiful
beautiful like music
it lights the cave –
outside the people going home
drive slowly up the road – the strains   5
of phone-in Verdi on the radio
three hours back a fall of snow
sprinkled the furthest hill
where clouds have hung all winter

The day gets dark uneasy   10
dark and darker still
and you little son come home
riding the tail of the wind
in triumph – tall and almost ten
with confetti in your hair   15
home successful from the carnevale
with your two black swords
and your gold-handled knife

I feel the chill and hear
the absent sound of snow   20
when you come in –
white fantastic scorpions spit
in the fiery centre of the grate
plague pictures cauterised –
In winter fire is beautiful   25
and generous as music – may you
always come this safely home
in fire and snow and carnevale

Notes

Carnevale:		an Italian winter festival celebrated before Ash Wednesday and the season of Lent. '*Carne vale*' translates literally as 'goodbye to meat'. This is an exuberant carnival involving music, entertainment and parades with carnival masks. Its origins go back through centuries of Italian history and even to pagan festivals.

Macdara Woods

| 6 | **Verdi:** | Giuseppe Verdi was one of the most important Italian Romantic composers of the 19th century, mostly of opera. Many of his musical themes are still found in modern popular culture. |
| 24 | **plague pictures cauterised:** | this may refer to one of the popular masks associated in particular with the Carnevale of Venice. It is the Plague Doctor mask (Medico Della Peste), a bizarre bird-like mask with a long beak in which herbs and spices could be stored to keep away the smell. The original is said to date from the 17th century. 'To cauterise' is to burn away flesh in order to stop bleeding; here it might mean to burn away memories of ancient horrors like the plagues. |

Explorations

BEFORE READING

1.

a   Have you had experience of an open fire in wintertime? Think of the last time you sat at an open fire. What atmosphere or mood does it create in a room?

b   How does it make you feel (other than warm)?

c   What do you think about as you look into the flames? (There are no 'right' answers to any of these questions.)

FIRST READING

2.   'In winter fire is beautiful | beautiful like music'.
Can you think of any comparisons between fire and music? Explain your thoughts.

3.   'it lights the cave'.
'Cave' is an unexpected word here. What does it suggest to you in this context?

4.   'the strains | of phone-in Verdi on the radio'.
Taken in conjunction with the Carnevale of the title, where do you think the poem is set?

5.   'and you little son come home'.
What do you notice about the boy's clothing and mood in the second stanza? What does it tell us about the celebration he has just come from?

6.

a   The fire is at the centre of the third stanza. What does the speaker see in the fire?

b   In what ways do you think the fire might be considered 'generous as music'?

c   Is there a connection between (a) and (b) here?

7.   The poem ends with a wish or a prayer. Do you find this a particularly good wish for anybody's life, be they a young person or adult? What are your thoughts on this?

SECOND READING

8.   The poem features both outside and inside the house. Examine all the references to outside – at the end of the first stanza, at the beginning of the second stanza and at the beginning of the third stanza. What is being suggested here about the world outside the home?

9.   Describe the atmosphere inside the home. How is this created in thoughts

and images? What is the poem saying about home?

10. How does the speaker feel towards his son – concerned, proud, protective? What do you think? Examine the detail and write about the relationship.

THIRD READING

11. The images of fire are rich and complex and add great depth to the poem. Examine each of them and write about the qualities of fire that are developed here.

12. This poem may remind Irish readers of Hallowe'en. What are the similarities and differences? Do you think it creates this atmosphere well? Explain your views on this.

13. This poem has a musical quality, not least in the rhythmic repetition of phrases and the Italian pronunciation of 'Carnevale'. In collaboration with songwriter/composer Brendan Graham, Macdara Woods has adapted the lyrics, which were recorded by Anuna in 1994. You might like to listen to the more recent version, released in 2007 under the Koch Records label, and discuss the song and the poem.

14. This poem is set in a particular place and time (Italy in winter). Do you think it has a universal quality? Could it be about people anywhere, in any era? Discuss this in your class.

Tess Gallagher
(1943–)

Tess Gallagher was born in 1943 in Port Angeles, Washington, the eldest of five children. Her father Leslie worked as a logger, a dockhand and on the small ranch owned by the family. Writing was very much a part of her life from an early age and she wrote both poetry and fiction; her first published work was a short story. It was when she joined a creative writing class conducted by the eminent poet Theodore Roethke at the University of Washington that, as Gallagher put it, 'poetry did rather kidnap me'. Her first, award-winning, book of poetry was published in 1976 and reflected Gallagher's roots 'in that generation of women writers who stepped forth out of the feminist revolution'. In later years, Gallagher has returned to short story writing, encouraged by her late husband, the writer Raymond Carver. In poetry, her exploration of what it is to be a woman has become an honest inquiry into the nature of being human. Since the late 1960s, in between writing, teaching and working on films, Gallagher has visited Ireland regularly and has embraced Irish culture, delighting in singing 'traditional Irish dirge', counting many Northern poets as her friends and collecting stories from the Irish storytelling tradition.

The Hug

Prescribed for the exam in 2017

A woman is reading a poem on the street
and another woman stops to listen. We stop too,
with our arms around each other. The poem
is being read and listened to out here
in the open. Behind us   5
no one is entering or leaving the houses.

Suddenly a hug comes over me and I'm
giving it to you, like a variable star shooting light
off to make itself comfortable, then
subsiding. I finish but keep on holding   10
you. A man walks up to us and we know he hasn't
come out of nowhere, but if he could, he
would have. He looks homeless because of how
he needs. 'Can I have one of those?' he asks you,
and I feel you nod. I'm surprised,   15
surprised you didn't tell him how
it is — that I'm yours, only
yours, etc., exclusive as a nose to
its face. Love — that's what we're talking about, love
that nabs you with 'for me   20
only' and holds on.

So I walk over to him and put my
arms around him and try to
hug him like I mean it. He's got an overcoat on
so thick I can't feel   25
him past it. I'm starting the hug
and thinking, 'How big a hug is this supposed to be?
How long shall I hold this hug?' Already
we could be eternal, his arms falling over my
shoulders, my hands not   30
meeting behind his back, he is so big!

I put my head into his chest and snuggle
in. I lean into him. I lean my blood and my wishes
into him. He stands for it. This is his
and he's starting to give it back so well I know he's   35
getting it. This hug. So truly, so tenderly,
we stop having arms and I don't know if

my lover has walked away or what, or
if the woman is still reading the poem, or the houses —
what about them? — the houses.   **40**

Clearly, a little permission is a dangerous thing.
But when you hug someone you want it
to be a masterpiece of connection, the way the button
on his coat will leave the imprint of
a planet in my cheek   **45**
when I walk away. When I try to find some place
to go back to.

Notes

8	**a variable star:**	a star that has fluctuations in its levels of brightness

Explorations

FIRST READING

1. For Gallagher, 'the image is still the important element' in her poetry. Choose one image from 'The Hug' that you find particularly striking and explain the reasons for your choice.

2.
a Describe in your own words the events that lead up to the poet giving her partner a hug in line 7.

b Can you suggest why these events made her feel like hugging?

3.
a What is her partner's reaction when the man asks, 'Can I have one of those?'

b How does the poet feel about this reaction?

c How would you feel if your partner said it was fine for you to hug a stranger?

4.
a Why do you think she decides to 'walk over' and hug the stranger?

b Which one of the following words best describes how she feels as she begins to hug the stranger: happy, shy, uncomfortable? Explain your answer.

c Would you feel the same if you were in her position? Why?

SECOND READING

5.
a 'Suddenly a hug comes over me and I'm | giving it to you', 'I finish but keep on holding | you'.

   Based on these lines, would you say that this is a one-person or a two-person hug? What clues lead you to this conclusion?

b 'I lean my blood and my wishes | into him. He stands for it. This is his | and he's starting to give it back'.

Tess Gallagher

From your reading of these lines, would you say that this is a one-person or a two-person hug? Explain your answer.

6. 'He's got an overcoat on | so thick I can't feel | him past it', 'This hug. So truly, so tenderly, | we stop having arms'.

a   How do these lines show that her hug with the stranger changes from a physical action to an emotional one?

b   Is there any sense of this change in the description of her first hug with her partner in lines 7–11? Support your answer by reference to the poem.

c   Which of the two hugs do you think is closest to being 'a masterpiece of connection'? Give reasons for your answer.

THIRD READING

7.

a   'He looks homeless because of how | he needs'.
    Can you suggest why the poet makes this link between being 'homeless' and having 'needs'?

b   Is the stranger the only person who 'needs' in this poem? Give reasons for your answer.

8.

a   'When I try to find some place | to go back to.'
    Do you think the poet is referring to a real physical place, an emotional place or both in these lines?

b   What 'place' was the poet in before she hugged the stranger?

c   How does her sense of this 'place' change as she hugs the stranger in lines 36–40?

d   Discuss whether the poet could also be seen as being 'homeless' at the end of the poem.

9.

a   Gallagher has related how some 'hardcore poetry people' wanted her to take 'The Hug' out of her book of poems because, as she explains, 'In the United States, if you have any jollity in a poem, it can't be a poem with a capital P.' Can you suggest what the differences might be between a poem with a capital P and a poem with a small p?

b   Where do you think the 'jollity', or fun, lies in this poem?

c   Do you think a poem can be fun and still be a poem with a capital P?

10. Imagine you have decided to read 'a poem on the street'. What poem from those that you have studied on the Leaving Certificate course would you choose to read? Explain the reasons for your choice.

Liz Lochhead
(1947–)

Liz Lochhead was born in Scotland, in a Lanarkshire mining village, on 26 December 1947. As a child, she spent much of her time drawing and painting. She attended Glasgow School of Art from 1965 to 1970 and then taught art until 1979, when she became a full-time writer.

Although her early writing was mainly poetry, in the 1980s Lochhead also began to write for the stage. Much of her poetry explores what it is to be Scottish and what it is to be a woman, often in a humorous way, while her work as a playwright, featuring a number of adaptations of ancient Greek plays, explores what it is to be human.

Liz Lochhead has won many prizes for her work and in 1998 was listed among Scotland's Fifty Most Influential Women in a Scottish Sunday newspaper. She now lives in Glasgow with her architect husband.

Revelation

Prescribed for exams in 2015 and 2017

I remember once being shown the black bull
when a child at the farm for eggs and milk.
They called him Bob – as though perhaps
you could reduce a monster
with the charm of a friendly name.   5
At the threshold of his outhouse, someone
held my hand and let me peer inside.
At first, only black
and the hot reek of him. Then he was immense,
his edges merging with the darkness, just   10
a big bulk and a roar to be really scared of,
a trampling, and a clanking tense with the chain's jerk.
His eyes swivelled in the great wedge of his tossed head.
He roared his rage. His nostrils gaped like wounds.

And in the yard outside,   15
oblivious hens picked their way about.
The faint and rather festive tinkling

behind the mellow stone and hasp was all they knew
of that Black Mass, straining at his chains.
I had always half-known he existed –   20
this antidote and Anti-Christ his anarchy
threatened the eggs, well rounded, self-contained –
and the placidity of milk.

I ran, my pigtails thumping on my back in fear,
past the big boys in the farm lane   25
who pulled the wings from butterflies and
blew up frogs with straws.
Past thorned hedge and harried nest,
scared of the eggs shattering –
only my small and shaking hand on the jug's rim   30
in case the milk should spill.

Notes

	Revelation:	to reveal or disclose information that was not known previously in a dramatic way. Often used about the revealing of knowledge to human beings by God or gods.
1	**bull:**	in mythology the bull is a symbol for masculinity and a brute strength that can slide over into violence. It can also represent the more primitive desires of human beings that civilisation does not always successfully control.
6	**threshold:**	a wooden or stone strip forming the bottom part of a doorway
9	**reek:**	a strong, unpleasant smell

16	**oblivious:**	unaware of something or someone
19	**Black Mass:**	a large black physical body; a quasi-religious ceremony that worships the devil
21	**Anti-Christ:**	the arch-enemy of Jesus Christ
21	**anarchy:**	disorder
23	**placidity:**	calmness
28	**harried nest:**	a nest from which the eggs have been stolen

Explorations

BEFORE READING

1.

a The title of this poem is 'Revelation'. Revelation can mean to reveal or disclose information that was not known previously in a dramatic way. Can you recall a television series, such as *Fair City*, or a film, such as *The Lord of the Rings* trilogy, or a book, such as the *Twilight* stories, where there was a memorable and dramatic revelation of some important information? As a class, share the revelations that you remember.

b Based on these revelations, discuss the reactions of the people who experienced the revelation – did they feel shock, anger, fear or another similarly strong emotion? Do you think that experiencing a revelation is an easy or a difficult process to go through? Why?

FIRST READING

2. From reading this poem, which one of the poet's memories did you find the most striking? Explain your answer with reference to the poem.

3.

a Lines 1–7 describe what life was like for the poet as a young girl before she saw the bull. Why does she go to the farm?

b Do you think she feels safe and cared for by the people at the farm? Why?

c What did she know about 'the black bull' before she is brought to see him?

4.

a In lines 8–14, the poet uses images (word-pictures) that appeal to the senses of smell, sight and hearing to convey just how dramatic it was for the girl to experience the size and strength of 'the black bull'. Discuss which sense is appealed to in each of the images in lines 8–14.

b Pick out two images from these lines that you feel vividly convey her impression of the bull's size and strength and explain why you chose them.

SECOND READING

5.

a 'He roared his rage. His nostrils gaped like wounds'.
What words in this line suggest that the girl understands that the bull's size and strength could easily turn to

Liz Lochhead

violent anger and the desire to injure? Give reasons for your choice of words.

b   In lines 19–21, the girl refers to the bull as 'that Black Mass' and the 'Anti-Christ his anarchy'. Explain how both of these references show that she also realises that the bull's violent anger and desire to injure are driven by evil.

c   The girl comments that she 'had always half-known he existed'. What do you think she means by this?

6.

a   Back outside the bull's 'outhouse', the girl realises that because of her revelation about the presence of evil in the world, her feelings and attitudes towards the bull have changed so that they are now very different to those of the hens. What do the hens know about the bull? How is this different to the girl's knowledge of the bull?

b   What is the hens' attitude to the bull? How is this different to the girl's feelings and attitude to the bull?

c   Do you think she might envy the hens' unchanged state? Why?

7.

a   Lines 24–31 describe how, because of her revelation about the presence of evil in the world, she no longer feels safe and cared for. What emotion drives her to run away from the farm?

b   How do the 'big boys' in lines 25–7 also make her feel afraid of her world? Explain how her fear is increased by nature in line 28.

8.   Think back to your work for Question 1. Do you think the girl finds her revelation an easy or a difficult

process to go through? Explain your answer with reference to the poem.

THIRD READING

9.

a   As a young girl, the poet went to the farm to collect 'eggs and milk'. Following her revelation, examine how her fear is suggested by her worries about the 'eggs and milk' in lines 22–3 and lines 29–31.

b   The eggs and milk are vulnerable because they can be easily broken and spilled. Do you think the girl now feels that she, too, is vulnerable in the world? Why?

10.   Would you include this poem in a collection of poetry for young people? Give reasons for your answer based on your reading of the poem.

Penelope Shuttle

(1947–)

Penelope Shuttle was born in Middlesex, England, in 1947. From an early age Shuttle was very aware of the natural world, feeling that she was 'part of a continuum with nature and weather'. As a teenager, she read, and was excited by, a wide range of poetry. In 1969 she met the poet and teacher Peter Redgrove, and in spite of a 16-year age difference, the two were drawn together by their 'affinity as poets'. Their marriage was immensely successful both personally and creatively, with Shuttle and Redgrove continuing to write poetry and prose as individuals and as a collaborative pair until Redgrove's death in 2003. Their move to Cornwall in 1970 was equally successful and Shuttle continues to live there today, because for her 'Cornwall is an artist itself ... with its glittering light and its granite shadows'.

Shuttle received the first of her many awards for writing in 1974 and she continues to participate actively in all aspects of the world of poetry, ranging from judging poetry competitions to giving readings of her work.

Jungian Cows

Prescribed for the exam in 2015

In Switzerland, the people call their cows
Venus, Eve, Salome, or Fraulein Alberta,
beautiful names
to yodel across the pasture at Bollingen.

If the woman is busy with child or book,   5
the farmer wears his wife's skirt
to milk the most sensitive cows.

When the electric milking-machine arrives,
the stalled cows rebel and sulk
for the woman's impatient skilful fingers   10
on their blowzy tough rosy udders,
will not give their milk;

so the man who works the machine
dons cotton skirt, all floral delicate flounces
to hide his denim overalls and big old muddy boots,   15
he fastens the cool soft folds carefully,
wraps his head in his sweetheart's sunday-best fringed scarf,
and walks smelling feminine and shy among the cows,

till the milk spurts, hot, slippery and steamy
into the churns,   20
Venus, Salome, Eve, and Fraulein Alberta,
lowing, half-asleep,
accepting the disguised man as an echo of the woman,
their breath smelling of green, of milk's sweet traditional climax.

Notes

	Jungian:	Carl Jung (1875–1961) was a Swiss psychiatrist whose work in psychology is still influential today. His ideas have also influenced a number of poets, including Penelope Shuttle and her husband, Peter Redgrove.
	Cows:	one of Jung's theories concerns the 'collective unconscious' (the feelings and thoughts about universal themes, or archetypes, that humans as a group inherit from earlier groups). Jung identified several key archetypes that recur, e.g. the mother. One of the symbols used to represent the mother archetype is the cow. For example, the ancient Egyptian goddess Hathor was often shown as a cow to emphasise her 'motherly' qualities. The cow has also been used to symbolise qualities traditionally held to be feminine, e.g. concern for the community or group or being instinctive. Jung believed that men have some feminine elements within them.
4	**Bollingen:**	a small village located on the north bank of Lake Zurich, Switzerland. Jung built a holiday home there and lived in it for several months each year.
9	**stalled:**	to stop; to be put in a compartment in a cowshed
11	**blowzy:**	rough looking
14	**flounces:**	a frill

Explorations

FIRST READING

1. Do you find this an amusing poem? Pick out the parts of the poem that amused you.

2. Using the clues in stanza 2, who do you think usually milks 'the most sensitive cows'? Can you suggest a reason why this is?

3.

a   What does stanza 3 tell you about how the cows reacted to the 'electric milking-machine'?

b   Are you surprised by their reaction? Why?

4.

a   What did 'the farmer' and 'the man who works the machine' do to persuade the cows to give the milk?

b   From your reading of the poem, would you say that the men were comfortable or uncomfortable about what they had to do?

5.

a   Do you think the cows were really fooled by what the men did? Refer to the poem to support your view.

b   Can you suggest why the cows decided to co-operate?

SECOND READING

6.

a   Divide a page into two columns. Put the heading Female over one column and Male over the other. Go through the poem and pick out all the words and phrases that are connected to females and write them in the Female column, then do the same for males in the Male column.

b   Using your lists, write a description in your own words of how being female is portrayed in the poem, then do the same with male.

c   Do you agree with the two portrayals? Explain your answer.

7.

a   Who would you say holds the most power in this poem, the male figures or the female figures? Support your view with quotations from the poem.

b   Given the lists that you made for Question 6, are you surprised by this distribution of power? Why?

8.

a   'till the milk spurts, hot, slippery and steamy', 'their breath smelling of green, of milk's sweet traditional climax'. How does the poet suggest in these lines that milk is a comforting and nourishing food that promotes life?

b   'Venus, Eve, Salome, or Fraulein Alberta', 'accepting the disguised man as an echo of the woman'.

c   What do you think the poet is suggesting here about the connection between female figures and the production and collection of milk, the promoter of life?

THIRD READING

9.

a   The poet uses the word 'traditional' in the final line of the poem. A tradition is a custom passed down through the generations. What traditions can you find in this poem?

b   Do you think we should always keep to the traditional way of doing things? Why?

10. Tell the story of this situation from the point of view of either 'the man who works the machine' or one of 'the stalled cows'.

Penelope Shuttle

Zoo Morning

Prescribed for the exam in 2018

Elephants prepare to look solemn and move slowly
though all night they drank and danced, partied
and gambled, didn't act their age.

Night-scholar monkeys take off their glasses,
pack away their tomes and theses,   5
sighing as they get ready for yet another long day
of gibbering and gesticulating, shocking
and scandalising the punters.

Bears stop shouting their political slogans
and adopt their cute-but-not-really teddies' stance   10
in the concrete bear-pit.

Big cats hide their flower presses, embroidery-frames
and watercolours;
grumbling, they try a few practice roars.
Their job is to rend the air, to devour carcasses,   15
to sleep-lounge at their vicious carnivorous ease.

What a life.
But none of them would give up show-business.

The snakes who are always changing,
skin after skin,   20
open their aged eyes and hinged jaws in welcome.

Between paddock and enclosure
we drag our unfurred young.
Our speech is over-complex, deceitful.
Our day is not all it should be.   25
The kids howl, baffled.

All the animals are very good at being animals.
As usual, we are not up to being us.
Our human smells prison us.

In the insect house   30
the red-kneed spider dances on her eight light fantastics;
on her shelf of silence she waltzes and twirls;
joy in her hairy joints, her ruby-red eyes.

Explorations

1. Think back to a visit you made to the zoo or to nature programmes you watched on television. How would you describe each of the following animals to a young child: elephants, monkeys, bears, big cats, snakes, spiders? Jot down words and phrases that capture how they move and behave.

FIRST READING

2. On first reading this poem, what do you notice?

3. Did you enjoy the descriptions of the dual life of elephants? Explain your reaction.

4.

a What do the monkeys in their night life personas remind you of?

b Do you think she describes the day life of the monkeys well? Explain.

5.

a How does she imagine the hidden life of bears?

b How does she feel about everyday bears?

c Do you think her description has caught an essential truth about the animals?

6. In pairs, explore:

a the contrast between the daytime and night-time lives of big cats. What do you notice?

b What words or phrases best catch their frightening fierceness?

c What patterns are emerging in this poem?

d Can you suggest what the poet might be up to?

Penelope Shuttle

7.

a When you saw the snakes opening their hinged jaws, did you feel welcomed?

b Does this description fit in with the tone of the poem?

8.

a 'Between paddock and enclosure'. Do you think this section accurately describes the experience of some family outings to the zoo? Develop your ideas.

b 'our unfurred young'. What do you think the poet is suggesting here?

c 'Our speech is over-complex, deceitful'. Discuss what this might mean and how it links to the rest of the poem.

9. Do you agree with what the poet is suggesting about human beings here?

10.

a Do you think the poet admires the spider? Explain your thinking.

b How does this stanza link with the previous one?

THIRD READING

11. The poet is turning the world as we see it on its head to make us view it afresh and really think about it. What does this poem make you think about? These are the themes.

12. Will your next visit to the zoo provoke new thoughts? Explain.

Kerry Hardie
(1951–)

Kerry Hardie was born in Singapore in 1951, grew up in County Down, studied English at York University and now lives in County Kilkenny. She has won many prizes for her poetry. Among her collections are *In Sickness* (1995), *A Furious Place* (1996), *Cry for the Hot Belly* (2000), *The Sky Didn't Fall* (2003), from which 'Daniel's Duck' is taken, and *The Silence Came Close* (2006).

Daniel's Duck

Prescribed for exams in 2015, 2016 and 2017

I held out the shot mallard, she took it from me,
looped its neck-string over a drawer of the dresser.
The children were looking on, half-caught.
Then the kitchen life – warm, lit, glowing –
moved forward, taking in the dead bird,   5
and its coldness, its wildness, were leaching away.
The children were sitting to their dinners.
Us too – drinking tea, hardly noticing
the child's quiet slide from his chair,
his small absorbed body before the duck's body,   10
the duck changing – feral, live –
arrowing up out of black sloblands
with the gleam of a river
falling away below.

Then the duck – dead again – hanging from the drawer-knob,   15
the green head, brown neck running into the breast,
the intricate silvery-greyness of the back;
the wings, their white bars and blue flashes,
the feet, their snakey, orange scaliness, small claws, piteous webbing,
the yellow beak, blooded,   20
the whole like a weighted sack –
all that downward-dragginess of death.

He hovered, took a step forward, a step back,
something appeared in his face, some knowledge
of a place where he stood, the world stilled,   25
the lit streaks of sunrise running off red
into the high bowl of morning.

She watched him, moving to touch, his hand out:
What is it Daniel, do you like the duck?
He turned as though caught in the act,   30
saw the gentleness in her face and his body loosened.
I thought there was water on it –
he was finding the words, one by one,
holding them out, to see would they do us –
but there isn't.   35
He added this on, going small with relief
that his wing-drag of sounds was enough.

Kerry Hardie

Notes

1	mallard:	a type of wild duck
6	leaching:	being drained away or sucked out
11	feral:	wild
12	sloblands:	muddy ground or land
19	piteous:	pitiful

Explorations

FIRST READING

1. Focus on the first two stanzas.

a Describe in sequence what happens.

b What do you notice about the kitchen, the reaction of the children and the reaction of the adults?

2. Focus on the description of the duck in the third stanza. Read it a number of times, then close your eyes and imagine it in detail. Now write a brief but detailed description of it.

3. What are your feelings on reading the description of the dead duck? Discuss them in groups.

4. Read the fourth stanza.

a Imagine you are Daniel. What do you see? What thoughts are going through your head?

b What thoughts might be going through the mother's head?

5. This incident provokes a moment of insight or new understanding (an epiphany) for each of the participants – the writer, the mother and Daniel. Describe each of these, using evidence from the text to support your ideas.

6. What do you think are the main issues or themes this poem deals with? Develop your ideas on this.

7. Do you think the poet has a good eye for observation? Support your ideas with evidence from the poem.

8. Imagine that you meet Daniel as an adult in later years and he remembers the incident. Write the dialogue as you think it might occur.

9. Write three paragraphs on what you liked about this poem and why.

10. How different from your own world is the world of this poem?

11. Do you think the mother should have brought the duck into the kitchen?

Paul Muldoon
(1951–)

Paul Muldoon was born in County Armagh and educated at Queen's University, Belfast. After leaving college he went to work as a producer for BBC Radio in Belfast. He also lived for a while in Dingle, County Kerry. Since then he has worked mainly as an academic; much of his teaching has been in the creative writing programme at Princeton University in the US. Recently, he was appointed to the prestigious position of Professor of Poetry at the University of Oxford.

Muldoon is a brilliant technical poet. He is equally at ease writing sonnets and long poems, lyric or narrative poetry. Some of his poetry is written about the North, but often only incidentally. He uses puns and word associations in a very deliberate way. His collections include *Mules, New Weather, Why Brownlee Left, Quoof, Meeting the British, Madoc: A Mystery, The Annals of Chile* and, most recently, *Hay*. His *Selected Poems* (1968-94) is probably the best introduction to his work.

Anseo

Prescribed for exams in 2015 and 2017

When the Master was calling the roll
At the primary school in Collegelands,
You were meant to call back *Anseo*
And raise your hand
As your name occurred.   5
Anseo, meaning here, here and now,
All present and correct,
Was the first word of Irish I spoke.
The last name on the ledger
Belonged to Joseph Mary Plunkett Ward   10
And was followed, as often as not,
By silence, knowing looks,
A nod and a wink, the Master's droll
'And where's our little Ward-of-court?'

I remember the first time he came back   15
The Master had sent him out
Along the hedges
To weigh up for himself and cut
A stick with which he would be beaten.
After a while, nothing was spoken;   20
He would arrive as a matter of course
With an ash-plant, a salley-rod.
Or, finally, the hazel-wand
He had whittled down to a whip-lash,
Its twist of red and yellow lacquers   25
Sanded and polished,
And altogether so delicately wrought
That he had engraved his initials on it.

I last met Joseph Mary Plunkett Ward
In a pub just over the Irish border.   30
He was living in the open,
In a secret camp
On the other side of the mountain.
He was fighting for Ireland,
Making things happen.   35
And he told me, Joe Ward,
Of how he had risen through the ranks
To Quartermaster, Commandant:

How every morning at parade
His volunteers would call back *Anseo*   40
And raise their hands
As their names occurred.

Explorations

BEFORE READING

1. What are your own memories of primary school – your teachers, friends and characters in your own class, especially the ones that got into a lot of trouble?

FIRST READING

2. What does the word '*anseo*' mean? When was it used in school?

3. Describe the 'Master'. What does his title say about him?

4. Why are Ward's forenames important?

5. What is Ward's life like at the end of the poem?

6. What do you imagine his soldiers' lives are like under his command?

SECOND READING

7. Why do you think Ward takes such care with the stick? Suggest reasons.

8. The narrator of the poem and the Master use puns. Isolate each pun and explain what they are referring to.

THIRD READING

9.
a The tone in the first verse is very unemotional. What effect does this have on your reading of the poem?

b Does the tone change later on? If so, how?

10. What contradictions are in the poem?

11.
a How do the first and last verses mirror each other?

b What point do you think the poet is making here?

FOURTH READING

12. 'What comes around, goes around.' Do you think this saying is relevant to the poem?

13. What is your own reaction to the life and experiences of Joseph Mary Plunkett Ward?

14. What do you think this poem is saying about life?

Paul Muldoon

Gary Soto
(1952–)

Gary Soto was born in Fresno, California, to poor working-class Mexican-American (Chicano) parents. As a young man he worked in the fields and the factories of San Joaquin and Fresno. He was educated at California State University, Fresno, and at the University of California, Irvine, where he earned a Masters in Fine Art. He taught at the University of California, Berkeley, for many years.

A prolific writer of novels, short stories, plays, memoirs, poetry and fiction for young people, much of his work deals with the experience of growing up and living in Mexican-American communities.

Among his collections of poetry are *The Elements of San Joaquin* (1997), *The Tale of Sunlight* (1978), *Black Hair* (1985), *Neighborhood Odes* (1992) and *Canto Familiar/Familiar Song* (1994). 'Oranges' is taken from *New and Selected Poems* (1995).

Oranges

Prescribed for the exam in 2017

The first time I walked
With a girl, I was twelve,
Cold, and weighted down
With two oranges in my jacket.
December. Frost cracking   5
Beneath my steps, my breath
Before me, then gone,
As I walked toward
Her house, the one whose
Porch light burned yellow   10
Night and day, in any weather.
A dog barked at me, until
She came out pulling
At her gloves, face bright
With rouge. I smiled,   15
Touched her shoulder, and led
Her down the street, across

A used car lot and a line
Of newly planted trees,
Until we were breathing   20
Before a drugstore. We
Entered, the tiny bell
Bringing a saleslady
Down a narrow aisle of goods.
I turned to the candies   25
Tiered like bleachers,
And asked what she wanted –
Light in her eyes, a smile
Starting at the corners
Of her mouth. I fingered   30
A nickel in my pocket,
And when she lifted a chocolate
That cost a dime,
I didn't say anything.
I took the nickel from   35
My pocket, then an orange,
And set them quietly on
The counter. When I looked up,
The lady's eyes met mine,
And held them, knowing   40
Very well what it was all
About.

        Outside,
A few cars hissing past,
Fog hanging like old   45
Coats between the trees.
I took my girl's hand
In mine for two blocks,
Then released it to let
Her unwrap the chocolate.   50
I peeled my orange
That was so bright against
The gray of December
That, from some distance,
Someone might have thought   55
I was making a fire in my hands.

Notes		
15	**rouge:**	a blusher powder used to give colour to the cheeks
18	**used car lot:**	an American term for the business where used cars are stored and sold
21	**drugstore:**	the American equivalent of a cornershop
25	**candies:**	American term used to refer to all kinds of sweets and chocolate
26	**bleachers:**	American term used to describe the raised, tiered rows of open-plank seating at sports fields
31	**a nickel:**	a 5 cent coin in American money
33	**a dime:**	a 10 cent coin, one-tenth of a dollar

Explorations

FIRST READING

For this first reading, think of the poem in four sections:

- Section 1 (lines 1–11): The journey to her house.

- Section 2 (lines 12–21): They greet and walk to the drugstore.

- Section 3 (lines 22–42): At the drugstore.

- Section 4 (lines 43–56): The finale.

Section 1 (lines 1–11)

1. If you filmed the boy's journey to the house, list all the details the film would pick up.

2. What do you think are the thoughts inside his head? Are there any indications as to how he feels?

Section 2 (lines 12–21)

3. If you happened to be passing on the street and you witnessed the girl emerging from her house, the greeting and their departure, what would you think was the relationship between them? Explain your thinking on this.

Section 3 (lines 22–42)

4. In the drugstore scene, what do you think would have been the thoughts inside the heads of (a) the girl (b) the boy and (c) the saleslady? Jot down what you imagine each was thinking and discuss these in groups.

5. In pairs, role play the conversation that might occur if they happened to meet later between (a) the girl and the saleslady and (b) the boy and the saleslady.

6. Role play the conversation about this incident between the boy and the girl one year later.

Section 4 (line 43–56)

7. Try to describe the boy's feelings here.

SECOND READING

8. What important insights into the lives of young adults does this poem reveal to us? List your thoughts and discuss the question in groups.

9. What do you like about this poem?

10. Do you think the title is a good one? Explain your thinking.

Julie O'Callaghan
(1954–)

Julie O'Callaghan was born in Chicago in 1954 and moved to Ireland in 1974. Her poetry for children is particularly popular and appears in a number of children's anthologies. Her poetry for adults is highly regarded and in 2001 she won the Michael Hartnett Poetry Award.

In April 2003, Julie O'Callaghan was made a member of Aosdána in recognition of the contribution she has made to the arts in Ireland. She was married to the poet Dennis O'Driscoll, who died in 2012

Problems

Prescribed for the exam in 2017

Take weeds for example.
Like how they will overrun
your garden and your life
if you don't obliterate them.
But forget about weeds   5
– what about leaves?
Snails use them as handy
bridges to your flowers
and hordes of thuggish slugs
will invade – ever thought about *that*?   10
We won't even go into
how leaves block up the gutters.
I sure hope you aren't neglecting
any puddles of water in your bathtub
– discoloration will set in.   15
There is the wasp problem,
the storms problem, the grass
growing-between-the-bricks-in-the-driveway problem.
Then there's the remembering to
lock-all-the-windows problem.   20
Hey, knuckleheads!
I guess you just don't appreciate
how many problems there are.

Notes

4	**obliterate:**	destroy completely
9	**thuggish:**	behaving in violent and lawless ways
21	**knuckleheads:**	stupid people

Explorations

FIRST READING

1.

a Count the number of problems mentioned in the 23 lines of this poem. Would you agree with the poet's decision to give this poem the title 'Problems'? Explain your answer.

b Some of the problems are vividly described. Choose the two descriptions you like the most and explain why you like them.

2.

a A lot of the lines in this poem are short, made up of only four or five words. What effect does this have on the pace, or speed, at which this poem is read?

b Experiment with reading it quickly and slowly and discuss which sounds better. Does the pace that you agreed on suggest anything to you about the speaker's feelings?

SECOND READING

3.

a ' – ever thought about *that?*', 'Hey, knuckleheads!', 'I guess you just don't appreciate | how many problems there are.'
How would you describe the speaker's tone of voice in these lines?

b What does this tone reveal about the speaker's attitude to the way in which other people view the problems that she is worried about?

c Do you think she is right to worry about these problems? Why?

4.

a ' – what about leaves?
Snails use them as handy
bridges to your flowers
and hordes of thuggish slugs
will invade'

Describe in your own words the picture that you see when you read these lines.

b How does the poet's use of rhyme in the phrase 'thuggish slugs' help to make the image of the slugs more memorable?

5. The speaker in the poem tends to exaggerate her problems. Do you think she does this because she is trying to be funny or because she is worried? Explain your answer.

6. In one sentence, sum up what you think the theme, or message, of this poem is.

THIRD READING

7. Examine how the poet creates the impression that the speaker in this poem is in conversation with someone else. You might like to look at the type of language used, the structure of the phrases and the use of questions.

8. A dramatic monologue is where a person speaks and through what is said reveals his/her character. From your readings of this poem, how would you describe the character of the speaker?

9. Imagine that you are a magazine agony aunt/uncle answering problems sent in to you by readers. You have received this poem in the post. Write your reply.

Julie O'Callaghan

10. The writer of this poem, Julie O'Callaghan, has said, 'I think it [poetry] should be a haven of quietness where you can hear yourself think.' What has this poem made you think about?

The Net

Prescribed for exams in 2015 and 2018

I am the Lost Classmate
being hunted down the superhighways
and byways of infinite cyber-space.
How long can I evade the class committee
searching for my lost self?   5

I watch the list
of Found Classmates
grow by the month.
Corralled into a hotel ballroom
Festooned with 70s paraphernalia,   10

bombarded with atmospheric
hit tunes, the Captured Classmates
from Sullivan High School
will celebrate thirty years
of freedom from each other.   15

I peek at the message board:
my locker partner,
out in California, looks forward
to being reunited with
her old school chums.   20

Wearing a disguise, I calculate
the number of months left
for me to do what I do best,
what I've always done:
slip through the net.   25

Notes

4	**evade:**	avoid
9	**Corralled:**	to be put into an enclosure, often used in connection with cattle or other animals
10	**paraphernalia:**	various objects
11	**bombarded:**	to attack with objects or to question a person constantly

Explorations

BEFORE READING

1.

a   The title of this poem is 'The Net'. How many different types of net can you think of? You might like to collect pictures to show the types of net that you have suggested.

b   Do the different types of net have anything in common?

FIRST READING

2.

a   What type of net is described in the first stanza of the poem? Pick out the words that lead you to this conclusion.

b   From your reading of lines 1–8, can you explain what is being organised using this net?

3.

a   Why do you think the poet describes herself as 'the Lost Classmate' in line 1?

b   Can you explain why she refers to the person that she was when she was at school as 'my lost self'?

c   Do you agree with the poet's view that as a person goes though life, he/she can have different 'selves'? Give reasons for your answer.

4.

a   In your own words, describe how the poet imagines the scene in the 'hotel ballroom' in lines 9–12.

b   Do the images she uses suggest that she considers it a pleasant or an unpleasant experience?

SECOND READING

5.   Using the clues in the first and last stanzas, do you get the impression that the poet does or does not want to be found by 'the class committee'?

6.

a   List all the different words that you would use to describe someone who is your friend.

b   Do the words 'locker partner' in line 17 suggest to you that this person was a friend of the poet's? Explain your answer.

7.   From your reading of the poem, what do you think happened during the poet's time at Sullivan High School to make her react in the way that she does to the reunion?

8.   Given the poet's reaction to the class reunion, are you surprised that she keeps checking the reunion website? Why?

Julie O'Callaghan

9.

a   'slip through the net'.
    How is the net that appears in the final
    line of the poem different from the net
    that was described in the first stanza?
    Explain your answer.

b   As far as the poet is concerned, what
    are the two nets trying to do to her?

10. Imagine that you are the poet when
    she was in her teens attending Sullivan
    High School. Write her diary entry in
    which she describes her experiences
    during a day at school.

Carol Ann Duffy

(1955–)

Carol Ann Duffy was born in Glasgow of Irish parents but grew up in Staffordshire, England. She attended university in Liverpool, where she studied philosophy. Her poetry often gives voice to the powerless or the mad. She is adept at putting herself in somebody else's head and then writing from their perspective, be they psychopaths, maids or tabloid editors. Her poetry has a wry humour and a lot of people who would not regularly read poetry are comfortable with her style.

She has won many awards for her collections, which include *Standing Female Nude* (1985), *Selling Manhattan* (1987), *The Other Country* (1990), *Mean Time* (1993) and *The World's Wife* (1999). This last collection featured a series of poems written from the perspective of the forgotten female: Mrs Midas, Queen Kong, Mrs Lazarus and others. Among her more recent collections are *Feminine Gospels* (2002), *Rapture* (2005) and *The Bees* (2011). She is also an accomplished playwright and has written picture books for children. In 2009 Carol Ann Duffy became the United Kingdom's twentieth poet lauteate.

Valentine

Prescribed for exams in 2015 and 2018

Not a red rose or a satin heart.

I give you an onion.
It is a moon wrapped in brown paper.
It promises light
like the careful undressing of love.   5

Here.
It will blind you with tears
like a lover.
It will make your reflection
a wobbling photo of grief.   10

I am trying to be truthful.

Not a cute card or a kissogram.

I give you an onion.
Its fierce kiss will stay on your lips,
possessive and faithful   15
as we are,
for as long as we are.

Take it.
Its platinum loops shrink to a wedding-ring,
if you like.   20
Lethal.
Its scent will cling to your fingers,
cling to your knife.

Carol Ann Duffy

Explorations

BEFORE READING

1. What do you associate with Valentine's Day?

FIRST READING

2. What is your first reaction on reading this poem? Discuss the various reactions.

3. The onion is given four times. What is it associated with each time?

4. Is there anything at all romantic about this poem?

SECOND READING

5. How long will the taste of onion stay on the lover's lips? How long will the couple last?

6. What type of relationship does the couple have? Have they been in love for long?

7. How does the onion promise light?

THIRD READING

8. How would you feel if you were given an onion for Valentine's Day?

9. The poet uses very short lines regularly in the poem. What effect do these short lines have?

10. Describe each metaphor that the speaker uses to describe the onion.

FOURTH READING

11. Read 'My mistress's eyes' by William Shakespeare and compare it with this poem.

12. This poem manages to be both 'cold and passionate'. How?

13. Do you think this is a good love poem? What makes it good or bad?

14. 'Love is particular to individuals and can't be represented by love hearts and teddy bears.'
    Does the poet agree? Do you?

Paula Meehan
(1955–)

Paula Meehan was born in the Gardiner Street area of Dublin. She was thrown out of school yet managed to study and attend Trinity College Dublin and Eastern Washington University. She made a huge impact with the publication of her third volume of poems, *The Man Who Was Marked by Winter*, and then with *Pillow Talk*. Meehan's poetry should be read out loud. She is a mesmerising reader of her own work. Her poetry has harrowing lyrical intensity. She uses regular language confidently yet without making it seem ostentatious or over the top. Many of her poems, such as 'The Pattern' or 'The Ghost of My Mother Comforts Me', celebrate women in adversity and give them a voice. She has also written a number of successful plays. One of these was *Cell* (1999), which was written after the poet had spent time giving poetry workshops in women's prisons.

The Russian Doll

Prescribed for the exam in 2016

Her colours caught my eye.
Mixed by the light of a far off sun:
carmine, turmeric, indigo, purple –
they promised to spell us dry weather.

I'd a fiver in my pocket; that's   5
all they asked for. And gift wrapped her.
It had been grey all month and damp.
We felt every year in our bones

and our dead had been too much with us.
January almost over. Bitter.   10
I carried her home like a Holy Fire
the seven miles from town,

my face to a wind from the north. Saw
the first primroses in the maw of a fallen oak.

There was smoke from the chimney   15
when I came through the woods

and, though I had spent the dinner,
I knew you'd love your gaudy doll,
you'd love what's in her
at the end of your seventh winter.   20

Notes		
	Russian Doll:	a hollow wooden figure that can be opened to reveal a series of similar figures, gradually decreasing in size, nesting inside each other
3	**carmine:**	a bright crimson or rich red colour
3	**turmeric:**	an Asian plant that can be used as a spice or a yellow dye
3	**indigo:**	a plant that produces blue dye
14	**maw:**	mouth or stomach
18	**gaudy:**	very bright

Explorations

BEFORE READING

1. Write a 140-character (25–30 words) tweet describing the month of January in Ireland. As a group, share your tweets – perhaps you could write some of them on the board and discuss the general feeling of the class about January.

FIRST READING

2.

a What impression do you get from the poem of the poet's attitude to January? Refer to the text of the poem in your answer.

b Pick out a line or phrase where you feel the poet expresses a similar view of January to the one that you expressed in your tweet for Question 1.

3.

a What characteristics of the Russian doll caught the poet's attention in lines 1–4? Refer to the poem to support your answer.

b Can you explain what the poet means when she says that the colours used to paint the doll are 'Mixed by the light of a far off sun'? You might find it helpful to read the Notes following the poem.

c What type of weather did the poet think of when she was looking at the Russian doll?

4.

a How did the poet feel about paying a 'fiver' for the doll in lines 5–6? Support your answer by reference to the poem.

b In line 17, we learn that the poet should have spent this 'fiver' on 'the dinner'.

Do you think she made the correct decision? Why?

SECOND READING

5. How do lines 11–13 suggest that carrying the Russian doll made the poet feel as if she was protected from the harsh January weather as she walked back home? Refer to lines 11–13 to support your answer.

6. 'the first primroses in the maw of a fallen oak',

   'There was smoke from the chimney | when I came through the woods'.
   The poet found that both of these sights make her feel more cheerful. Why do you think these sights affected her in this way?

7.

a What reaction to the doll did the poet expect to get from her daughter?

b What do you think the poet wanted to celebrate by giving her daughter this gift? Think about what is suggested by the phrase 'the end of your seventh winter'.

THIRD READING

8. Does the language used by the poet in this poem appeal to you? Explain your answer with reference to the poem.

9. In your opinion, is this mainly a happy poem or mainly a sad poem? Explain your answer by reference to the poem.

10. In this poem, the Russian doll cheered up the poet in spite of the January weather. Look back at your tweet about January in Ireland from Question 1, then write a piece describing what it would take to cheer you up in January.

Paula Meehan

William Wall

(1955–)

From Whitegate, County Cork, William Wall was educated at University College Cork, where he read Philosophy and English. He has taught English and Drama at Presentation Brothers College, Cork. He has published novels and short stories as well as poetry. Among his collections of poetry are *Mathematics and Other Poems* (1997), *Fahrenheit Says Nothing to Me* (2004) and *Ghost Estate* (2011), from which this poem is taken.

Ghost Estate

Prescribed for exams in 2015 and 2016

women inherit
the ghost estate
their unborn children
play invisible games
of hide & seek   5
in the scaffold frames
if you lived here
you'd be home by now

they fear winter
& the missing lights   10
on the unmade road
& who they will get
for neighbours
if anyone comes anymore
if you lived here   15
you'd be home by now

the saurian cranes
& concrete mixers
the rain greying into
the hard-core   20
& the wind
in the empty windows

if you lived here
you'd be home by now

the heart is open plan   25
wired for alarm
but we never thought
we'd end like this
the whole country
a builder's tip   30
if you lived here
you'd be home by now

it's all over now
but to fill the holes
nowhere to go   35
& out on the edge
where the boys drive
too fast for the road
that old sign says
first phase sold out   40

Notes

17	**saurian:**	belonging to a class of reptile; mostly used in reference to prehistoric reptiles

William Wall

Explorations

BEFORE READING

1. Examine a photograph of an unfinished estate. Imagine that you and your partner have bought a house in this estate, expecting that it would be completed in 18 months, as promised. What are your thoughts now?

FIRST READING

2. As you read, try to view the scene through the eyes of the speaker. What do you see?

3. What thoughts go through the speaker's mind? Discuss this in groups and make a list.

4. Prepare for a group reading of this poem. In your groups, discuss how you plan to read this poem aloud. For instance, each person could take a stanza, refrains could be read by everyone together or any combination of voices the group agrees on. In order to read it well, you first need to discuss what mood the speaker is in. Is he angry, afraid, sad, disappointed, hopeless, depressed, cynical, etc.? What is the evidence from the poem? Decide how each line or section should be read. Practise it.

SECOND READING

5. Listen to the poem as read aloud by each group. As you listened, did you notice anything you hadn't spotted before? Make notes.

6. Discuss the different tones of voice and mood conveyed in the readings. Which do you think reflect the poem on the page most accurately?

THIRD READING

7. What fears does the speaker have?

8. What does the speaker regret?

9. Do you think the speaker resents anything? Explain your thoughts.

10. Do you think the poem accurately captures people's feelings about the economic collapse? Discuss.

11. What do you think might be the poet's views on politics and the economy?

FOURTH READING

12. Is this a poem of the bleakest despair?

13. What would you like to ask the poet?

Greg Delanty

(1958–)

G reg Delanty was born in Cork and attended University College Cork, where he qualified as a teacher. He won the Patrick Kavanagh Award for his first collection of poetry, *Cast in the Fire*, and has won numerous awards and fellowships since. The Dowling

Fellowship enabled him to move to the US, where he became a Professor of English at St. Michael's College, Vermont.

Among the themes he writes about are family, exile, relationships and politics. The poem 'After Viewing...' is from his 1995 collection, *American Wake*. Many of the poems in that book deal with the experience of exile. Sometimes they introduce a feature of US life to an Irish audience, or sometimes, as in this poem, they introduce an aspect of Irish culture to a US audience.

After Viewing *The Bowling Match at Castlemary, Cloyne*, 1847

Prescribed for exams in 2015 and 2016

I promised to show you the bowlers
    out the Blarney Road after Sunday mass,
you were so taken with that painting
    of the snazzy, top-hatted peasant class
        all agog at the bowler in full swing,   5
        down to his open shirt, in trousers
as indecently tight as a baseballer's.

You would relish each fling's span
    along blackberry boreens, and delight
in a dinger of a curve throw   10
    as the bowl hurls out of sight,
        not to mention the earthy lingo
        & antics of gambling fans,
giving players thumbs-up or down the banks.

It's not just to witness such shenanigans   15
    for themselves, but to be relieved
from whatever lurks in our background,
    just as the picture's crowd is freed
    of famine & exile darkening the land,
    waiting to see where the bowl spins   20
off, a planet out of orbit, and who wins.

Greg Delanty

517

Background note on the painter

Daniel MacDonald (1821–53) was a well-known Irish artist of the 19th century, also born in Cork. Much of his work is a valuable social record of the times. He painted portraits and made drawings of local celebrities and characters such as the hedge school master, and he also painted many social and sporting events. His painting *The Dancing Master* shows the local community enjoying music and dance. The game of road bowling figured in a number of his works, of which *The Bowling Match at Castlemary, Cloyne* is best known. It was exhibited in London in 1847.

He was one of the few 19th-century Irish painters to focus attention on the Great Famine, particularly in the painting *The Irish Peasant Family Discovering the Blight in their Store*, which was exhibited in the British Institution, London, in 1847.

Notes

	The Bowling Match:	in modern times, road bowling usually involves two players in competition to see who can use the least number of throws of a 28 ounce metal ball to cover about 3 miles of winding country road. It was originally associated with the weaving trade and in the 19th century, at the time of the painting, a 6 pound lead ball was used.
	Castlemary, Cloyne:	Castlemary is a townland near Cloyne, County Cork, and about 18 miles from Cork city. It was also the site of a grand house and large estate, Castle Mary, that belonged to the Longfield family from the 17th century until 1978. It is suggested that MacDonald's painting shows Mountiford Longfield (1813–64) (the figure waiting his turn) in competition with another gentleman of the area, Abraham Morris (bowling). Perhaps the match took place on the Castle Mary estate.
4	**snazzy:**	slang for stylish or showy
5	**all agog:**	in eager expectation
10	**dinger:**	from the Old Norse 'dengja', meaning 'to hammer'. In modern usage it has many shades of meaning, mostly associated with speed. Here it suggests a throw of great power and speed.
12	**lingo:**	a slang term for 'language', from the Latin 'lingua' ('tongue')
13	**antics:**	foolish behaviour
14	**down the banks:**	colloquial phrase meaning to give out to or criticise
15	**shenanigans:**	tricks or mischief; could be derived from the Gaeilge 'sionnachaigh', meaning 'to play the fox'

Explorations

BEFORE READING

1. Look carefully at the painting. What
   do you notice about the competitors
   and the crowd? Discuss in groups
   and make a list of everything that
   people notice.

2. What aspects of the atmosphere of
   a sporting event does this painting
   manage to capture?

FIRST READING

3.

a In the first stanza, what elements in
   the painting attract the attention of
   the poet's companion?

b Are there elements you thought
   important that are not mentioned?
   What does this tell you about looking
   at pictures?

4. Who do you imagine the 'you'
   addressed by the poet in the opening
   line might be? Discuss.

5.

a With your eyes closed, listen to a
   reading of the second stanza. What
   do you see and what do you hear?

b Are all the words and phrases familiar
   to you? Where might you hear them?

6. How is the sense of excitement
   created in the second stanza?

SECOND READING

7. Were you surprised to find that this
   County Cork scene was painted in
   1847? What are the thoughts of the
   group on this?

Greg Delanty

8.

a   In the third stanza the poet puts forward a suggestion as to why the people in the picture might go to watch a bowling match at that particular time. What does he suggest?

b   Do you think this is a good insight into human nature?

9. In the third stanza the entire mood of the poem changes. What brings this about? Make a list of what contributes to the change and discuss these.

10. What note do you think the poem finishes on – is it sad, pessimistic, disappointed, frightened, uncertain or something else? Explain your thinking.

THIRD READING

11. In one paragraph, write what you think this poem is about.

12. What thoughts about people does it leave you with?

13. What thoughts about poetry does it leave you with?

14. How many songs or lyrics or poems about sport do you know? Share some of them.

Peter Sirr
(1960–)

Born in County Waterford in 1960, Peter Sirr went on to attend Trinity College Dublin before spending some years in the Netherlands and Italy. During this time, his poetic talent gained early recognition when he was awarded the Patrick Kavanagh Award in 1982, and the publication of his first collection of poetry, *Marginal Zones*, in 1984 excited considerable interest. On his return to Dublin, he became the first director of the Irish Writers' Centre, holding this post until 2003 when, as he puts it, he 'opted for the fruitful wilderness of freelance-dom'. Subsequently, while working as a freelance writer and translator, he also acted as the editor of *Poetry Ireland Review* for a number of editions, relishing the 'poetic adventure' of hunting for poems that 'cause the hair on the back of the neck to stand up'.

For Sirr, a poem is the result of a finely balanced interaction between emotion and words, as he explains: 'The poem which makes a successful emotional appeal must have a core of ice, must be built on formal attentiveness to language, line break, diction, syntax, technique.' Peter Sirr lives in Dublin with his wife, the poet and teacher Enda Wyley, and their daughter.

Madly Singing in the City

after Po Chü-i

Prescribed for the exam in 2017

And often, when I have finished a new poem,
I climb to the dark roof garden
and lean on a rail over an ocean of streets.
What news I have for the sleeping citizens
and these restless ones, still shouting their tune   5
in the small hours. Fumes rise from the chip-shop
and I am back at the counter, waiting my turn.
Cod, haddock, plaice, whiting.
The long queue moves closer;
men in white coats paint fish with batter,   10
chips leap in the drying tray.
There's a table reserved for salt and vinegar
where the hot package is unswaddled,
salted, drenched, wrapped again
and borne out into the darkness.   15
In darkness I lean out, the new words ready,
the spires attentive. St Werburgh's, St Patrick's, Nicholas
of Myra. Nearby the Myra Glass Company
from where we carried the glass table-top.
In a second I will sing, it will be as if   20
a god has leaned with me, having strolled over
from either of the two cathedrals, or from the green
and godly domes of Iveagh Buildings.
Ever since I was banished from the mountains
I have lived here in the roar of the streets.   25
Each year more of it enters me, I am grown
populous and tangled. The thousand ties of life
I thought I had escaped have multiplied.
I stand in the dark roof garden, my lungs swelling
with the new poem, my eyes filled with buildings   30
and people. I let them fill, then,
without saying a word, I go back down.

Peter Sirr

Notes

	Po Chü-i:	a poet who lived in China from 772 to 846 AD. He worked as a government official, but because of his determination to speak out against those in power and to highlight social problems, he was banished on a number of occasions. His poetry is characterised by its simplicity, clarity and flashes of sharp humour.
13	**unswaddled:**	unwrapped. Babies were once swaddled: cloth was wrapped closely around the baby's arms, body and legs to make a type of cocoon.
17	**St Werburgh's:**	a church in Dublin. The original was built in 1178 and was later rebuilt in 1715.
17	**St Patrick's:**	St Patrick's Cathedral, Dublin, Ireland's largest church, which dates from the 13th century. Said to have been founded beside a well used by St Patrick for baptisms in 450 AD.
17	**Nicholas of Myra:**	the Church of St Nicholas of Myra, Dublin, built in the 17th century. For a time it acted as a Pro-Cathedral.
22	**two cathedrals:**	St Patrick's and Christchurch Cathedrals
23	**Iveagh Buildings:**	buildings commissioned by the Earl of Iveagh to replace the slums that surrounded St Patrick's Cathedral in Edwardian Dublin
27	**populous:**	densely inhabited, full of people

Explorations

BEFORE READING

1.

a   Think back to a time when you were working really hard at something that took lot of effort but when you finished you were really pleased with the result. It could be when you had a summer job, doing your homework, fixing something, a sports training session, finishing an exam, etc. Describe what you were doing.

b   How did you feel as you were working on the task? Did you want to give up at any stage? If you did, what stopped you from giving up?

c   How did you feel when it was finished and you knew that you had done really well? Did you tell anyone about how good you felt? Did you do anything to celebrate? You might like to tell your story to the class and then write a short piece describing your experience.

FIRST READING

2.

a   Why does the poet feel like celebrating?

b   How does he want to celebrate successfully completing his task?

c   Are there any similarities between his feelings and the feelings that you remembered in Question 1?

3.   In your own words, describe how you picture the scene that the poet looks down on in lines 1–6.

4.

a   Do you find it easy to imagine the chip shop based on the poet's description in lines 7–15? Why?

b   Are you surprised to find a chip shop appearing in a poem? Can you suggest why the poet decided to include it in his description of Dublin?

c   How do you feel about the idea of a poet going into a chip shop?

5.

a   From your reading of the poem, can you work out how long the poet has been living in Dublin? Support your answer by reference to the poem.

b   Would you say that he has settled in well there? Why?

SECOND READING

6.   'What news I have for the sleeping citizens | and these restless ones, still shouting their tune' (lines 4–5)

'In darkness I lean out, the new words ready' (line 16)

'In a second I will sing, it will be as if | a god has leaned with me' (lines 20–1)

The lines above show how the poet is on the verge of 'singing' his poem out over the city on a number of occasions. However, each time he is distracted by something. For each of the quotations above, examine the poem to find out what it is that distracts him from singing.

7.   'I stand in the dark roof garden, my lungs swelling | with the new poem, my eyes filled with buildings | and

people. I let them fill, then, | without saying a word, I go back down.'

a   Given that the title of this poem is 'Madly Singing in the City', are you surprised that the poet goes 'back down' without making a sound? Why?

b   Can singing be an internal as well as an external experience?

c   'Singing' can mean celebrating something in verse. What do you think the poet celebrates in verse in this poem?

d   What does his use of the word 'madly' suggest about his feelings? You may find it helpful to look up 'madly' in the dictionary.

8.   Sirr uses everyday conversational language in this poem, but he arranges it in such a way that we really see and feel what he is writing about.

a   Examine how his use of the word 'ocean' in line 3 helps you to 'see' the view as he stands in the roof garden.

b   Why do you think Sirr uses the word 'unswaddled' to describe unwrapping the chips in line 13? What is he trying to tell us about how the chips were wrapped?

c   How do the commas and the rhythm of the words in line 14 suggest the feeling of people working quickly to keep the chips warm?

d   Choose another line where you think Sirr uses a word or phrase that really helps you to see or feel what he is writing about. Explain why you chose it.

Peter Sirr

9. In this poem, Sirr celebrates his space in the world, the centre of Dublin city, where he mixes with people and buildings, eats, makes memories, forms relationships and writes poetry: in short, the space where he lives. Write a paragraph or a poem entitled 'My Space' celebrating the space in the world where you live.

10. Peter Sirr has written, 'Poets can often seem to be working a narrow little seam of private experience. They don't seem to get out much.' Write a presentation, to be given to your class, entitled ' My Views on What Makes a Good Poet'. Use references or examples from your work on the Leaving Certificate Poetry course to illustrate your talk.

Joseph Woods
(1966–)

Born in Drogheda, Joseph Woods has worked as a chemist, teacher and director of a language school. He has also lived in Japan and Asia. His volumes of poetry include *Sailing to Hokkaido* (2001), which won the Patrick Kavanagh Award, *Bearings* (2005) and *Ocean Letter* (2011), from which 'Letting the Cat Out of the Bag' is taken.

Letting the Cat Out of the Bag

Prescribed for exams in 2016 and 2017

When my father stole
into the scullery

having faltered over fields
from the flooded quarry,

which naturally we were warned   5
against and was bottomless,

he announced he'd never
carry out an act like it again:

gathering the kittens
with their mother   10

and weighting the whole shebang
into a loose-stitched sack.

All the more strange,
even alarming,

when within a week   15
the mother arrived back

to sit on the windowsill
and observe for some years
my father's uneasy comings and goings.

Notes

2	**scullery:**	a small room attached to the kitchen where the washing up, etc. was done
11	**shebang:**	slang word that can mean 'the matter under discussion', 'thing' or 'this business'

Explorations

FIRST READING

1. What kind of person do you think the father is? Carefully examine his preparations for the deed, his reaction immediately after and his long-term reactions. What do these suggest?

2. Why do you think he did it? Discuss.

3. What was your initial reaction on reading this poem?

SECOND READING

4. Do you think this poem is just about cruelty to animals or is it more complicated than that? What issues are raised in this poem?

5. 'Despite the bleakness of the theme, there are flashes of humour.' Discuss this view.

6. Read Seamus Heaney's poem 'The Early Purges' and compare the two.

Joseph Woods

Enda Wyley

(1966–)

Born in Dublin in 1966, Enda Wyley's literary career began at the age of nine, when, boosted by her parents' encouragement, she entered a poetry competition and won first prize. At the time, she was living in Glenageary, County Dublin, and attending school in Dalkey. Indeed, Wyley looks back on her schooldays as 'the place where poems for me truly began'. A creative primary teacher helped to awaken Wyley to the wonders of the imagination. Some years later, it was in the school hall that the 13-year-old Wyley met the poet Brendan Kennelly, resulting in the two corresponding regularly about her poetry. Such support strengthened Wyley's determination to write and she 'soon owned several notebooks, filled with scribbles, quotes, half-lines – all the stuff of poetry being made'.

Although she has published three anthologies to date, it is this fascination with the making of poetry that drives Wyley, as she explains: 'it isn't the publishing of poetry, but the making of it that is most important'. As a primary school teacher she enthusiastically encourages her own pupils to set off on 'the adventure of writing', just as she was once encouraged. Enda Wyley lives with her husband, the poet Peter Sirr, and their daughter in Dublin.

Poems for Breakfast

Prescribed for the exam in 2018

Another morning shaking us.
The young potted willow
is creased with thirst,
the cat is its purring roots.
Under our chipped window   5
the frail orange flowers grow.
Now the garden gate clicks.
Now footsteps on the path.
Letters fall like weather reports.
Our dog barks, his collar clinks,   10
he scrambles, and we follow,
stumble over Catullus, *MacUser*,
Ancient Greek for Beginners,
cold half-finished mugs of tea,
last week's clothes at the bed's edge.   15
Then the old stairs begin to creak.

And there are the poems for breakfast –
favourites left out on the long glass table.
We take turns to place them there
bent open with the pepper pot,   20
marmalade jar, a sugar bowl –
the weight of kitchen things.
Secret gifts to wake up with,
rhythms to last the whole day long,
surprises that net the cat, the dog,   25
these days that we wake together in –
our door forever opening.

Enda Wyley

527

Notes		
12	**Catullus:**	a Roman poet who lived in the 1st century BC
12	*MacUser:*	a computer magazine

Explorations

BEFORE READING

1. Describe what you see and hear when you first wake up on a schoolday morning. How do you feel about getting up to go to school? Is there anything that makes you feel a bit happier about having to do this?

FIRST READING

2.

a Line 1 tells us that this poem happens in the 'morning'. What events in the first section of the poem reinforce the idea that it is morning?

b Do any of these events happen when you are getting up in the morning?

3.

a 'Another morning'.
What does this phrase suggest to you about the mood of the couple as they start to get up?

b Are there any images or sounds in the first section that you think reinforce this mood? Explain your choice.

4.

a Does the state of the room help to improve the poet's mood? Refer to the poem to support your view.

b How would you feel waking up in such a room?

SECOND READING

5.

a What is unusual about the breakfast table in the second section of the poem?

b How would you feel if you came down one morning to find the breakfast table set like this? Why?

6.

a Can you explain how the 'Secret gifts' got onto the table?

b How do these 'gifts' affect the mood of the couple as they face 'Another morning'?

c Do you think you might change the reaction you described in Question 5 if you knew that someone you really cared for had taken the time and effort to leave these 'Secret gifts' just for you? Why?

THIRD READING

7. 'rhythms to last the whole day long, surprises that net the cat, the dog, these days that we wake together in – our door forever opening.'

a How do these lines show a change in the poet's attitude towards her surroundings and the day?

b In what ways could reading the poems create 'rhythms to last the whole day' in the poet and her partner?

c   Consider what the image of the 'door forever opening' suggests to you. Could it refer to the type of relationship that they share? Does it tell you how their attitude to life is affected by sharing this relationship? Do you have another suggestion?

8.

a   Wyley creates a vivid image of the couple waking up in the morning, not only by using 'pictures' that we can see, but also by including sounds in her description. How do the sounds in the first section of the poem help to make this scene real for you?

b   Can you suggest why sound does not feature as much in the second section?

9. Wyley values clarity in her writing and often edits her work ruthlessly to cut out words or phrases that she feels interfere with the clarity of the piece. Clarity can be defined as clearness, simplicity and intelligibility. Would you agree that each of these characteristics is present in this poem? Refer to the poem to support your view.

10. Using the title 'Secret Gift', write a short story or a poem about the effects that a simple act of loving kindness can produce.

Colette Bryce

(1970–)

olette Bryce comes from Derry, Northern Ireland. She was Fellow in Creative Writing at the University of Dundee from 2003 to 2005 and Literary Fellow at the University of Newcastle upon Tyne from 2005 to 2007. Her first collection of poetry, *The Heel of Bernadette* (2000), won the Strong Award for new Irish poets. Her other collections are *The Full Indian Rope Trick* (2004) and *Self Portrait in the Dark* (2008). She has won many awards, including the National Poetry Competition in 2003. *Self Portrait in the Dark* was shortlisted for the Poetry Now Award in 2009.

Self-Portrait in the Dark (with Cigarette)

Prescribed for exams in 2015 and 2017

To sleep, perchance
to dream? No chance:
it's 4 a.m. and I'm wakeful
as an animal,
caught between your presence and the lack.   5
This is the realm insomniac.
On the street window seat, I light a cigarette
from a slim flame and monitor the street –
a stilled film, bathed in amber,
softened now in the wake of a downpour.   10

Beyond the daffodils
on Magdalen Green, there's one slow vehicle
pushing its beam along Riverside Drive,
a sign of life;
and two months on   15
from 'moving on'
your car, that you haven't yet picked up,
waits, spattered in raindrops like bubble wrap.
Here, I could easily go off
on a riff
          20
on how cars, like pets, look a little like their owners
but I won't 'go there',
as they say in America,
given it's a clapped-out Nissan Micra ...
And you don't need to know that   25
I've been driving it illegally at night
in the lamp-lit silence of this city
– you'd only worry –
or, worse, that Morrissey
is jammed in the tape deck now and for eternity;   30

no. It's fine, all gleaming hubcaps,
seats like an upright, silhouetted couple;
from the dashboard, the wink
of that small red light I think
is a built-in security system.   35
In a poem
it could represent a heartbeat or a pulse.

Or loneliness: it's vigilance.
Or simply the lighthouse-regular spark
of someone, somewhere, smoking in the dark.   40

Explorations

FIRST READING

1. Listen to the first section (lines 1–10). What do you see? List everything you notice and share the ideas in a group discussion.

2. How would you describe the mood of the speaker in the first section? What phrases or images suggest this?

3. Is there anything to suggest a reason for her sleeplessness?

SECOND READING

4. What do we find out about her life circumstances in the second section (lines 11–30)?

5. What do we discover about her as a person in this section? Do you like her?

6. In the final section (lines 31–40), her mood becomes more downbeat. In your own words, trace her thoughts here.

THIRD READING

7. Collect all the images of light you find in the poem. What do they suggest to you about the theme being developed in this poem?

8. This poem is described as a self-portrait. If you were actually painting her portrait, what are the characteristics of the speaker you think it should show if it was to represent her accurately?

Colette Bryce

9. As a love poem, do you find this
   depressing, hopeful, realistic or
   something else? Discuss.

10. Read 'Oranges' by Gary Soto (page
    505) and discuss the differences
    between the two poems.

David Wheatley

(1970–)

Born in Dublin in 1970, David Wheatley was educated at the Royal Irish Academy of Music and Trinity College Dublin. He now teaches English literature at the University of Hull. Among his published collections of poetry are *Thirst* (1997), *Misery Hill* (2000) and *Mocker* (2006).

Chronicle

Prescribed for the exam in 2018

My grandfather is chugging along the back roads
between Kilcoole and Newtown in his van,
the first wood-panelled Morris Minor in Wicklow.
Evening is draped lazily over the mountains;
one hapless midnight, mistaking the garage door   5
for open, he drove right through it, waking my father.

The old man never did get to farm like his father,
preferring to trundle his taxi along the back roads.
Visiting, I stand in his workshop door
and try to engage him in small talk, always in vain,   10
then climb the uncarpeted stairs to look at the mountains
hulking over soggy, up-and-down Wicklow.

Cattle, accents and muck: I don't have a clue,
I need everything explained to me by my father.
Clannish great-uncles somewhere nearer the mountains   15
are vaguer still, farming their few poor roods,
encountered at Christmas with wives who serve me oven-
baked bread and come to wave us off at the door.

My grandfather pacing the garden, benignly dour,
a whiskey or a woodbine stuck in his claw,   20
a compost of newsprint in the back of his van.
You're mad to go live in Bray, he told my father,
somewhere he'd visit on rare and timorous raids,
too close to 'town' to be properly *Cill Mhantáin*.

All this coming back to me in the mountains   25
early one morning, crossing the windy corridor
to the Glen of Imaal, where schoolchildren read
acrostics to me of 'wet and wonderful Wicklow',
and driving on down to Hacketstown with my father
we find grandfather's grandfather under an even   30

gravestone gone to his Church of Ireland heaven,
and his grandfather too, my father maintains,
all turned, long since turned to graveyard fodder
just over the county line from their dear old Wicklow,
the dirt tracks, twisting lanes and third-class roads   35
they would have hauled themselves round while they endured,

before my father and I ever followed the roads
or my mountainy cousins first picked up a loy
or my grandfather's van ever hit that garage door.

Notes

	Chronicle:	a detailed record of events in chronological order, i.e. in the order in which they happened
16	**roods:**	a measure of land, about 400 square metres
19	**benignly:**	gently or kindly
19	**dour:**	stern, obstinate; so 'benignly dour' is a contradiction
28	**acrostics:**	poems in which the first or last letters of lines when read vertically make a word or words
33	**fodder:**	food, used particularly to refer to food for cattle
38	**loy:**	a kind of spade

David Wheatley

Explorations

1. Explore your own genealogy. Try to trace your family tree, the record of your father's and your mother's family going back a few generations. Where did they live and what did they do for a living? Do you visit aunts and uncles and meet with cousins?

2. What is your attitude to these older generations? Do you feel proud of them, interested in their lives, sorry for them, couldn't care less? Jot down your thoughts or discuss in groups.

FIRST READING

3. What do you notice about the setting and about the people in this poem?

4. Can you see why the title is appropriate?

5. Do you find the poet's family interesting? Explain your views.

SECOND READING

6. Focus in particular on stanzas 1 and 4. Would you agree that the grandfather is a larger than life figure? What is the evidence for this?

7. The pace of life is slow. What words, phrases and images suggest this throughout the poem?

8.

a This poem draws heavily on the geography of County Wicklow. Would you agree? Explore the poem in detail for evidence.

b All the people mentioned have a particular love of County Wicklow. Write about this, referring to details from the poem to back up your views.

THIRD READING

9. Write two paragraphs on the main issue or theme dealt with in this poem.

10. Images of roads and of journeys taken or not taken form recurring patterns here. How do these tie in with the meaning?

11. How does the poet feel about his family and relations? Discuss this in pairs or groups and then write up your conclusions, using references to the poem as evidence.

12. Do you think this poem says something important about families and native place or áit dúchais? Discuss this and write up the conclusions.

Paul Perry

(1972–)

Paul Perry is a graduate of Brown University in the US and has been a Fellow of Creative Writing at the University of Miami and a Fellow of Poetry at the University of Houston. He has been Writer in Residence for County Longford and for the University of Ulster. He has won many prizes for his poetry. Among his collections of poetry are *The Drowning of the Saints* (2003), from which 'River of Light' is taken, *The Orchid Keeper* (2006) and *The Last Falcon and Small Ordinance* (2010).

River of Light

Prescribed for the exam in 2017

red, green and yellow neon
blur the highway
into a river of light

the intersection appears
like a mirage   5
smoke wafting from the policemen's flares

call them mourning candles
three a.m.
surrounding the scene

the intersection   10
like a small island of sorrow
the car should not

be cut in half
so easily, so simply
but it is, there   15
we watch, dumb spectators,
held back
by yellow tape

as the police measure
confer and agree   20
the yellow plastic

covering the unnamed dead
flaps in the wind
like an ignominious flag

a warning, a reminder   25
flapping absurdly in rhythm
with the smashed blinker

of the halved car,
again yellow
until the ambulance appears   30

and departs, easily, simply
the shattered glass swept away
the car removed

the tape taken
so that everything   35
looks as it did

an hour before
when we passed
on the other side

an unending kaleidoscope   40
a blurring, ever-moving
river of light

Notes

2	**highway:**	North American term for motorway
24	**ignominious:**	shameful, disgraceful

Explorations

FIRST READING

1.

a Read the poem a number of times. Listen to it read aloud. Close your eyes. What are the visual images that remain with you? List them.

b What in particular strikes you about each one you picked?

2. If you were one of the 'dumb spectators' at this scene, what are the factual things you would see?

3. Do you think the poet allows his emotions and feelings to engage with the scene? If so, where? What do you think this adds to the poem?

4. What feelings did this poem stir up in you? Write about this.

SECOND READING

5. What thoughts about our society did this poem provoke for you?

6. Do you think the poet is making a statement about how we live our lives today? Discuss this in groups and compile a list of the themes that you find.

7. What do you like or dislike about the language the poet uses and the form in which the poem is structured?

8. Do you think the title is a good one for this poem? Explain your view.

9. What questions would you like to ask the poet?

Paul Perry

Caitríona O'Reilly

(1973–)

Caitríona O'Reilly was born in Dublin in 1973 and grew up in County Wicklow. She attended Trinity College Dublin, where she was awarded a BA, followed by a PhD for her work on American literature. Indeed, the American poet Sylvia Plath has proven to be one of the key influences on O'Reilly's writing. In an article she wrote on Sylvia Plath, O'Reilly noted that 'the connections between a writer's life and her work are numerous, indirect, and mysterious'. This statement is equally true of O'Reilly's own writing, where she often explores the world of nature and the self. The 'connections' between O'Reilly's life and work are particularly evident in her first anthology, *The Nowhere Birds*, published in 2001, from which the poem 'Interlude' is taken. In this book, her poetry is concerned with childhood, adolescence and her student life, so that, as Jefferson Holdridge commented in his review of it, the anthology offers the opportunity of 'watching the maturation of a poet'.

Although her poetry has been very successfully received, O'Reilly does not limit her work with words to this area alone, as she also works as a freelance writer, critic, teacher and editor.

Interlude

Prescribed for exams in 2016 and 2017

With its *gelati* and bougainvillea-draped sculpture,
Italy hovered like a rumour five miles further.
Binn was worthy, litterless, Swiss;

where to breathe was like a sea-plunge, even in June.
Populated by six-foot clean-limbed blondes,   5
they bled pure gold, if they bled at all. Anaemic Knut

('like *Hamsun*') was an exception. He composed
electronically ('like *Kraftwerk*') and afterwards
dropped by for *Kräutertee*. I'd never even heard of *Hunger*.

Hector, who had a scar from nipple to navel, called me 'pure'   10
in nasty English. There was a failed seduction
by a man with a handlebar moustache and gold tooth,

a silly crush on a stout-legged father of five ...
The summer dragged to an end. Where the sun once fell
tremendously there was the noise of thunder.   15

I cracked the ice on the *bier-garten* tables, folded umbrellas,
bid a tender farewell to the urinals. A thousand pounds
in the heel of my shoe might have bought three months

in a Berlin flat. But in the airport a kitten wailed in a basket
dementedly and a jittery pilot sweated over his charts   20
and I was back, convincing them I'd ever been elsewhere.

Notes

	Interlude:	a time, space or event that is very different to what comes before and after it
1	*gelati*:	the Italian word for ice creams
1	**bougainvillea:**	a shrub with red or purple flowers that grows in warm climates
3	**Binn:**	a village in Switzerland that is located in the Swiss Alps
6	**Anaemic:**	pale and lacking in vitality

Caitríona O'Reilly

7	*Hamsun:*	Knut Hamsun (1859–1952), a Nobel Prize-winning Norwegian author whose novel *Hunger* describes how a young man is slowly driven mad by hunger and poverty
8	*Kraftwerk:*	a German group who were one of the first to play electronic music
9	*Kräutertee:*	a herbal tea
9	*Hunger:*	see note for *Hamsun* above
16	*bier-garten:*	the German for an open-air bar that serves beer and food

Explorations

BEFORE READING

1. Imagine that you have finished your second-level education and you want to take a gap year to go travelling. What reasons would you use to prove to your parents/guardians that you would learn a lot from your travels that would help you (i) as a person and (ii) with your future studies or career, and so persuade them to give you permission and funding?

a Working in pairs, write out your reasons in 5 minutes.

b As a class, write each reason that has been suggested once on the board, eliminating any that would not support your case.

c Referring to the reasons on the board, discuss the main areas of life that can be learned about from travelling.

FIRST READING

2.

a In lines 1–4, the poet describes her first impressions when she arrived in Binn, having come from the island of Ireland. Can you suggest why the closeness of one country, Italy, to another, Switzerland, made such an impression on her?

b She was also surprised that despite this closeness, Italy and Switzerland were very different. In your own words, explain how they were different. Refer to the poem in your answer.

3.

a List the people she remembers from her time in Binn, as described in lines 5–13.

b   Based on your reading of these lines, do you think the poet was travelling with her family, her friends or on her own? Explain the reason for your answer.

4.   What signs, described in lines 14–16, warned her that the summer was coming to an end and she would have to leave Binn? Support your answer with reference to these lines.

5.   What impression do you get from lines 17–21 of her feelings about returning home? Support your answer by reference to the poem.

SECOND READING

6.

a   In your own words, describe how you picture each of the four men that she encounters in lines 6–13.

b   What areas of life does she learn about through these experiences?

7.   In lines 19–21, the poet is in 'the airport' as she returns to her usual way of life. She seems to notice the kitten and the 'jittery pilot' because she has similar feelings to them. Discuss the feelings that you think she shares with the kitten and the 'jittery pilot'.

8.

a   There are three sections in this poem: the poet's time in Binn (lines 1–13), the ending of summer and her time in Binn (lines 14–19) and the airport (lines 19–21). Read each section, then describe the tone (the emotion in her voice) that is conveyed by her words in that section.

b   From your description of her tone in each section, which experience do you think she found the most difficult to cope with? Refer to the text in your answers.

THIRD READING

9.

a   Look back at the main areas of life that you decided travelling would help you to learn about for Question 1. Discuss which of these areas the poet learned about in her travels.

b   Do you think that the experiences she had in Binn would have helped her as a person and with her future studies or career? Why?

10.   Would you include this poem in a collection of poetry for young people? Give reasons for your answer based on your reading of the poem.

Caitríona O'Reilly

Sinéad Morrissey

(1972–)

Sinead Morrissey was born in Portadown, County Armagh, educated at Trinity College Dublin and lives in Belfast, where she lectures at Queen's University. She has won many prizes and awards for her poetry. Among her collections are *There Was a Fire in Vancouver* (1996), *Between Here and There* (2001), *The State of the Prisons* (2005), which 'Genetics' is taken from, and *Through a Square Window* (2009).

Genetics

Prescribed for the exam in 2018

My father's in my fingers, but my mother's in my palms.
I lift them up and look at them with pleasure –
I know my parents made me by my hands.

They may have been repelled to separate lands,
to separate hemispheres, may sleep with other lovers,   5
but in me they touch where fingers link to palms.

With nothing left of their togetherness but friends
who quarry for their image by a river,
at least I know their marriage by my hands.

I shape a chapel where a steeple stands.   10
And when I turn it over,
my father's by my fingers, my mother's by my palms

demure before a priest reciting psalms.
My body is their marriage register.
I re-enact their wedding with my hands.   15

So take me with you, take up the skin's demands
for mirroring in bodies of the future.
I'll bequeath my fingers, if you bequeath your palms.
We know our parents make us by our hands.

Explorations

BEFORE READING

1. What does the word 'genetics' mean? So what might you expect the poem to be about?

2. Have you ever heard expressions such as 'he has his father's hair' or 'she has her mother's eyes'? Do you resemble either of your parents or any other members of your family in any way? Jot down some thoughts on this and what it means to you.

FIRST READING

3. Do you think that the speaker feels happy and secure in her family in stanza 1? What makes you think that?

4.

a Do you find stanzas 2–3 unexpected coming after the first stanza?

b What details suggest that this was not an amicable separation?

5. Is there anything you find positive in stanzas 2–3? Explain.

THIRD READING

6. Replicate the hand shapes the poet makes in stanza 4. Does this remind you of any children's rhyme?

7. Do stanzas 4–5 provide yet another change of mood? Describe this mood and suggest how the poet creates it.

8. 'My body is their marriage register. | I re-enact their wedding with my hands.' Do you find the thought process here clever and creative, highly original or rather zany and fantastical? What is your reaction to these lines? Jot down your ideas and discuss them in groups.

9. Do you like how the poem ends? What are your thoughts on this?

Sinéad Morrissey

FOURTH READING

10. Is this poem anything like what you expected on first reading the title? What were you surprised by?

11. Explore the ways in which the images of hands carry a range of ideas throughout the poem. Trace the different ideas carried by the references to hands. Do you think these images tell quite a complex story about family?

12. ' "Genetics" provides an unusual and imaginative framework for thinking about the concept of family.' What do you think?

13. Do you find this a positive or a bleak poem? Discuss.

Unseen Poetry: Approaching the Question

Like any other work of art, such as a painting, sculpture, film or building, a poem needs many viewings or readings before we come to appreciate it fully. All the usual techniques we employ when viewing any new or unusual object can be of use here: first noticing the particularly striking or unusual features; then focusing in on a small area of it; drawing back and trying to see the whole structure; circling around it; finding words to describe it to ourselves; asking ourselves what we like about it; and so on. By circling the object and zooming in and out to examine interesting features, gradually we pick up more and more of the detail until the entire object makes sense for us. Many readings are the key to understanding. Here are some questions you might ask yourself as you read and reread.

What do I notice on a first reading?
List any and everything I notice on first reading the poem. This gives me the confidence to say something about it, even though I don't yet understand the full picture

What do I see?
- Where is it set? What scene or scenes are featured?
- What pictures strike me as interesting? Focus on a setting or an image. What are my thoughts on it?
- Follow the images through the poem. Is there a sequence or a pattern? Have the images anything in common?
- Do the images or settings suggest anything about the themes or issues the poem might be dealing with?
- What atmosphere or mood is suggested by the visual aspects? Which words or images are most powerful in creating this atmosphere?

What is the poem doing, and how is it structured?

1. **Does it tell a story?**
- Is there a narrative structure to this poem? If so, what is happening? What is the sequence of events? Am I clear about the storyline?
- What is my reaction to this story?
- Is there a main idea behind the narrative? What is the poet's central concern?
- What do I notice about the shape of the poem?
- If a narrative poem, is it in the genre of a ballad, epic, allegory, etc.?
- Is it serious, humorous, satirical or something else?

2. **Is it a descriptive piece, re-creating a scene?**
- Is its primary purpose to re-create the atmosphere of an event or the mood of a moment?
- Is it mainly decorative? Or has it a point to make, or a moral to transmit?
- How does the poet want me to feel? What mood is created in this poem? What words or phrases help to create this mood?
- If a lyric poem, is it in the form of a sonnet, ode, villanelle, sestina or something else?

- What is the poet's central concern (theme)?
- Leaving technical terms aside, how would I describe what the poem sets out to do?

The speaker

- Who is the speaker in the poem? What kind of person do I imagine him or her to be? What state of mind is the speaker in? What words or phrases reveal most about the attitude and state of mind of the speaker? Consider the tone of the poem and how it is created.
- What point of view is being put across in the poem? Am I in sympathy with it or not?
- Who is the speaker addressing in the poem?
- What do I notice about the poet's style?
- Does the poet rely heavily on images? If so, what do I notice about them?
- Does the poet use the musical sounds of words to create effects: alliteration, assonance, onomatopoeia, etc.? Does he or she use rhyme? What is the effect? What do the sounds of words contribute to the atmosphere of the poem?
- What do I notice about the type of words (diction) most frequently used – are they ordinary, everyday, learned and scholarly, technical, or something else?
- Does the poet use regular metre (rhythm or regular beat in the lines) or do the lines sound more like ordinary conversation or a piece of prose writing? What is the overall effect? Explore the rhythm of the language.
- Are any of these features particularly noticeable or effective? What do I like?

What is my reaction to it?

- Can I identify with the experience in this poem? Has there been any similar experience in my life?
- What are my feelings on reading this poem, and what words, phrases, images or ideas spark off these reactions in me?
- How do I react to it? Do I find it amusing, interesting, exciting, frightening, revolting, thought provoking, etc.?
- What seems to me most important about the piece?
- At a critical level, do I think it is a well-made poem? What in particular do I think is effective?

Some basic questions

A final line-by-line or stanza-by-stanza exploration should bring the poem into clearer focus and facilitate answers to the basic questions:

1. What is the poem about (theme)?
2. Is it an interesting treatment of this theme?
3. What is important about the poem?
4. How is the poem structured (form and genre: narrative or lyric, ballad, ode, sonnet, etc.)?
5. What are the poet's feelings and attitudes (tone)?
6. How would one describe the atmosphere or mood of the poem, and how is it created?
7. What features of poetic style are noticeable or effective?
8. What are my reactions to the poem?

Comparing a newly read poem with a prescribed poem

- Which ideas are similar?
- Which are different?
- Which poem made the greater impact on you, and why?
- What insights did you get from each poem?
- What is the attitude of the poet in each case?
- Are there similarities or differences in tone?
- How does each poet differ in use of language, imagery, etc.?
- Comment on the form and genre in each case.

Practice

To practise answering similar questions on unseen poems, use any of the poems in this anthology that are not on your prescribed course.

Past Examination Questions
Higher Level

John Donne

'Why read the poetry of John Donne?'
Write out the text of a talk that you would give, or an article that you would submit to a journal, in response to the above title. Support the points you make by reference to the poetry of John Donne on your course.

(Higher Level 2003)

John Keats

Often we love a poet because of the feelings his/her poems create in us. Write about the feelings John Keats's poetry creates in you and the aspects of the poems (their contents and/or style) that help to create those feelings. Support your points by reference to the poetry by Keats that you have studied.

(Higher Level 2001)

'John Keats presents abstract ideas in a style that is clear and direct.'
To what extent do you agree or disagree with this assessment of his poetry? Support your points with reference to the poetry on your course.

(Higher Level 2009)

Emily Dickinson

What impact did the poetry of Emily Dickinson make on you as a reader? Your answer should deal with the following:
- Your overall sense of the personality of the poet
- The poet's use of language/imagery

Refer to the poems by Emily Dickinson that you have studied.

(Higher Level 2005)

'Emily Dickinson's original approach to poetry results in startling and thought-provoking moments in her work.'
Give your response to the poetry of Emily Dickinson in the light of this statement. Support your points with suitable reference to the poems on your course.

(Higher Level 2011)

Gerard Manley Hopkins

'There are many reasons why the poetry of Gerard Manley Hopkins appeals to his readers.'
In response to the above statement, write an essay on the poetry of Hopkins. Your essay should focus clearly on the reasons why the poetry is appealing and should refer to the poetry on your course.

(Higher Level 2004)

W.B. Yeats

Write an article for a school magazine introducing the poetry of W. B. Yeats to Leaving Certificate students. Tell them what he wrote about and explain what you liked in his writing, suggesting some poems that you think they would enjoy reading. Support your points by reference to the poetry by W. B. Yeats that you have studied.

(Higher Level 2005)

'Yeats's poetry is driven by a tension between the real world in which he lives and an ideal world that he imagines.'
Write a response to the poetry of W.B. Yeats in the light of this statement, supporting your points with suitable reference to the poems on your course.

(Higher Level 2010)

'Yeats can be a challenging poet to read, both in terms of style and subject matter.'
To what extent do you agree with this statement? Support your answer with suitable reference to the poetry on your course.

(Higher Level 2011)

Robert Frost

'We enjoy poetry for its ideas and for its language.'
Using the above statement as your title, write an essay on the poetry of Robert Frost. Support your points by reference to the poetry by Robert Frost on your course.

(Higher Level 2003)

'Robert Frost – a poet of sadness?'
Write an introduction to the poetry of Robert Frost using the above title. Your introduction should address his themes and the impact of his poetry on you as a reader. Support your points with reference to the poems you have studied.

(Higher Level 2007)

'Frost's simple style is deceptive and a thoughtful reader will see layers of meaning in his poetry.'
Do you agree with this assessment of his poetry? Write a response, supporting your points with the aid of suitable reference to the poems on your course.

(Higher Level 2011)

T.S. Eliot

'The poetry of T.S. Eliot often presents us with troubled characters in a disturbing world.'
Write a response to this statement with reference to both the style and the subject matter of Eliot's poetry. Support your points with suitable reference to the poems on your course.

(Higher Level 2010)

Elizabeth Bishop

'Introducing Elizabeth Bishop.'
Write out the text of a short presentation you would make to your friends or class group under the above title. Support your point of view by reference to or quotation from the poetry of Elizabeth Bishop that you have studied.

(Higher Level 2001)

'The poetry of Elizabeth Bishop appeals to the modern reader for many reasons.'
Write an essay in which you outline the reasons why poems by Elizabeth Bishop have this appeal.

(Higher Level 2002)

'Reading the poetry of Elizabeth Bishop.'
Write out the text of a talk that you would give to your class in response to the above title. Your talk should include the following:
• Your reactions to her themes or subject matter.
• What you personally find interesting in her style of writing.
Refer to the poems by Elizabeth Bishop that you have studied.

(Higher Level 2006)

'Elizabeth Bishop poses interesting questions delivered by means of a unique style.'
Do you agree with this assessment of her poetry? Your answer should focus on both themes and stylistic features. Support your points with the aid of suitable reference to the poems you have studied.

(Higher Level 2009)

Philip Larkin

Write an essay in which you outline your reasons for liking and/or not liking the poetry of Philip Larkin. Support your points by reference to the poetry of Larkin that you have studied.

(Higher Level 2001)

'Writing about unhappiness is the source of my popularity.' (Philip Larkin)
In the light of Larkin's own assessment of his popularity, write an essay outlining your reasons for liking/not liking his poetry. Support your points with the aid of suitable reference to the poems you have studied.

(Higher Level 2008)

'Larkin's poems often reveal moments of sensitivity which lessen the disappointment and cynicism found in much of his work.'
To what extent do you agree with this statement? Support your answer with suitable reference to the poetry of Philip Larkin on your course.

(Higher Level 2012)

John Montague

'John Montague expresses his themes in a clear and precise fashion.'
You have been asked by your local radio station to give a talk on the poetry of John Montague. Write out the text of the talk you would deliver in response to the above title. You should refer to both style and subject matter. Support the points you make by reference to the poetry on your course.

(Higher Level 2009)

Sylvia Plath

If you were asked to give a public reading of a small selection of Sylvia Plath's poems, which ones would you choose to read? Give reasons for your choices, supporting them by reference to the poems on your course.

(Higher Level 2003)

'I like (or do not like) to read the poetry of Sylvia Plath.'
Respond to this statement, referring to the poetry by Sylvia Plath on your course.

(Higher Level 2004)

'The poetry of Sylvia Plath is intense, deeply personal, and quite disturbing.'
Do you agree with this assessment of her poetry? Write a response, supporting your points with the aid of suitable reference to the poems you have studied.

(Higher Level 2007)

Eavan Boland

Write a personal response to the poetry of Eavan Boland. Support the points you make by reference to the poetry of Boland that you have studied.

(Higher Level 2002)

'The appeal of Eavan Boland's poetry.'
Using the above title, write an essay outlining what you consider to be the appeal of Boland's poetry. Support your points by reference to the poetry of Eavan Boland on your course.

(Higher Level 2005)

'Boland's reflective insights are expressed through her precise use of language.'
Write your response to this statement, supporting your answer with suitable reference to the poetry on your course.

(Higher Level 2011)

Ordinary Level

W.B. Yeats

'An Irish Airman Foresees His Death'

1.

a   What, in your view, is the attitude of the airman to the war in which he is fighting? (10)

b   Write out the line or phrase from the poem that best shows his attitude. Give a reason for your choice. (10)

c   Write a short paragraph in which you outline your feelings towards the airman. Support your view by quotation from the poem. (10)

2.   Answer ONE of the following: [Each part carries 20 marks]

i   'I balanced all, brought all to mind'
What are the kinds of things the airman is referring to in this line from the poem?

OR

ii   Imagine the airman has to give a short speech to his fellow pilots as they prepare for battle. Write out the text of the speech he might give.

OR

iii   Suggest a different title for the above poem. Give reasons for your answer, supporting them by quotation from the poem.

(Ordinary Level 2002)

'The Wild Swans at Coole'

1.

a   According to Yeats, what qualities do the swans at Coole Park possess? Explain your answer. (10)

b   Which is your favourite stanza in this poem? Explain why you like it. (10)

c   This poem presents many pictures (images) to the reader. Choose two which appeal to you and explain why you find them appealing. [You may not choose images from the same stanza that you wrote about in 1(b) above] (10)

2.   Answer ONE of the following: [Each part carries 20 marks]

i   Based on this poem write an article for a travel magazine in which you encourage tourists to visit Coole Park.

OR

ii   'I have looked upon those brilliant creatures,
And now my heart is sore.'
From your reading of the poem explain why the poet feels like this.

OR

iii   There are two other poems by W.B. Yeats on your course, 'The Lake Isle of Innisfree' and 'An Irish Airman Foresees His Death'. Which of these two poems appeals to you more? Give reasons for your answer.

(Ordinary Level 2010)

Robert Frost

'Out, Out—'

1.

a   Which words and phrases in the first twelve lines (ending at '... when saved from work') help to give you a clear picture of the place where the poem is set? Explain your choice. (10)

b   Describe the boy's reaction when he realised that his hand had been badly damaged by the saw. (10)

c   Do you think the poet shows sympathy for the boy? Explain your answer. (10)

2.   Answer ONE of the following: [Each part carries 20 marks]

i   Write the diary entry of the boy's sister, in which she records her experiences and feelings on the day the accident happened.

OR

ii   People have said that this is a very dramatic poem. Do you agree? Explain your answer.

OR

iii   Which of the following statements best describes your response to the poem?
*   I found the poem cruel because . . .
*   I found the poem dramatic because . . .
*   I found the poem sad because . . .
   Give reasons for your answer.

(Ordinary Level 2007)

Gerard Manley Hopkins

'Spring'

1.

a   Choose the image from the first eight lines of the poem that, in your opinion, best captures the beauty of spring. Explain your answer. (10)

b   Do you think Hopkins creates a sense of prayer in the last six lines of the poem? Refer to the poem in support of your answer. (10)

c   From the phrases below, choose the one which, in your opinion, best describes this poem.
   – It is a joyful poem.
   – It is a personal poem.
   – It is a spiritual poem.
   Explain your answer with reference to the poem. (10)

2.   Answer ONE of the following: [Each part carries 20 marks]

i   Write about two differences you notice between the first eight lines (octet) and the final six lines (sestet) of this poem. You should refer to the poem in your answer.

OR

ii   In this poem Hopkins describes the beauty of spring. Write a piece in which you describe the beauty of a different season of the year.

OR

iii   Write a piece explaining why you did or did not enjoy studying the poetry of Hopkins on your course. (The other poem by Hopkins on the Ordinary Level Course is 'Inversnaid'.)

(Ordinary Level 2011)

T.S. Eliot
'Aunt Helen'

1.

a   From your reading of the poem, describe the sort of lifestyle you think Miss Helen Slingsby had. (10)

b   Of the three phrases below choose the one which, in your opinion, best describes the poet's reaction to his aunt's death.
– He is upset.
– He doesn't care.
– He is disappointed.
Explain your choice. (10)

c   Do you think this poem is serious or humorous or both? Explain your answer with reference to the poem. (10)

2.   Answer ONE of the following: [Each part carries 20 marks]

i   Imagine you are the footman in this poem. Write a letter to your friend in which you record your thoughts about having worked for Miss Slingsby and how you feel about her death.

OR

ii   Choose two words or phrases from the poem which you found especially appealing and explain why you found them to be so.

OR

iii   Having studied this poem your class has decided to make a video version for YouTube. Describe what your finished video would be like.

(Ordinary Level 2010)

Patrick Kavanagh
'Shancoduff'

1.

a   How does the poet show that he likes Shancoduff, his home place? Support your answer by reference to the poem. (10)

b   Where in the poem does he show that life in Shancoduff can be harsh? Support your answer by reference to the poem. (10)

c   On balance, do you think that Shancoduff would be a likeable or a harsh place to live in? Give a reason for your answer. (10)

2. Answer ONE of the following: [Each part carries 20 marks]

i Imagine Patrick Kavanagh puts his farm up for sale. Write the advertisement that might appear in the local newspaper. Base your advertisement on the poem.

OR

ii 'They are my Alps and I have climbed the Matterhorn . . .'
Why, in your opinion, does Kavanagh refer to the Alps and the Matterhorn in this poem?

OR

iii What do you think is the cattle-drovers' view of Kavanagh's way of life? Refer to the poem in your answer.

(Ordinary Level 2005)

W.H. Auden
'Funeral Blues'

1.
a How did this poem make you feel? (10)
b Do you think that the poet really loves the one who has died? Explain your answer. (10)
c Do you like the way the poet expresses sadness at the death of his friend? Give a reason. (10)

2. Answer ONE of the following: [Each part carries 20 marks]

i Imagine that the poet wanted to choose a line or two from the poem to be written on his lover's tombstone. Which line or lines would you advise him to choose? Write the lines and give reasons for your choice.

OR

ii Imagine you wanted to perform this poem to music with a group of musical friends. How would you perform it so that people would remember the experience?

OR

iii What things did you learn about the poet W. H. Auden from reading the poem? Refer to the poem in your answer.

(Ordinary Level 2003)

Elizabeth Bishop
'Filling Station'

1.
a What impression of the filling station and its inhabitants do you get from reading the first two stanzas of the poem? Refer to the text in support of your answer. (10)
b 'Somebody loves us all.' In your opinion, does this line provide a good ending to the poem? Explain your answer. (10)
c What impression of the poet, Elizabeth Bishop, do you get from reading this poem? (10)

2. Answer ONE of the following: [Each part carries 20 marks]
i 'Good poetry creates vivid pictures in our minds.' In your opinion, is this true of 'Filling Station'? Support your view by reference to the text of the poem.

OR

ii Imagine you are Elizabeth Bishop. Write a diary entry, based on your reading of the poem, in which you describe your experience of stopping at this filling station.

OR

iii Which of the following statements is closest to your own view of the poem?
– Life is full of surprises.
– Everyone needs love.
– We shouldn't judge by appearances.
Explain your choice, supporting your answer by reference to the text.

(Ordinary Level 2009)

Philip Larkin
'The Explosion'

1.
a What impression of the miners do you get from reading the opening four stanzas of the above poem? Support your view by reference to the text. (10)
b Stanza five ('At noon, there came a tremor . . .') describes the moment of the explosion. What effect does the poet achieve by describing the event in the manner in which he does? Give a reason in support of your view. (10)
c Why, in your opinion, does Larkin end the poem with the image of the 'eggs unbroken'? Support your answer by reference to the poem. (10)

2. Answer ONE of the following: [Each part carries 20 marks]
i Compare 'The Explosion' with any other poem by Philip Larkin that you have studied as part of your course.

OR

ii What, in your opinion, can we learn about Philip Larkin himself, the things he values or considers important from reading this poem? Support your view by brief reference to the poem.

OR

iii Imagine that the wife of one of the men killed in the explosion were to write an article describing the event for her local newspaper. Write out a paragraph that you think she might include in her article.

(Ordinary Level 2002)

Patricia Beer
'The Voice'

1.
a What picture of the poet's aunt emerges from this poem? Refer to the poem in your answer. (10)

b   In your opinion, what part did the parrot play in the aunt's life? Explain your answer by referring to the words and events in the poem. (10)

c   Which of the following statements best describes your response to the poem? Give a reason for your answer.
– I found the poem amusing.
– I found the poem sad.
– I found the poem both amusing and sad. (10)

2.   Answer ONE of the following: [Each part carries 20 marks]
i   Imagine that the poet was asked to make a speech at the 'funeral' of the parrot. Write out the speech that you imagine she might deliver.

OR

ii   'Nature's creatures should not be kept in cages for our amusement.'
Write a short piece outlining your views on this topic. You should refer to the poem to support the points you make.

OR

iii Imagine you were asked to make a short film or video using one moment or event from this poem. Describe the moment or event you would choose and explain the kind of film or video you would make.

(Ordinary Level 2006)

Sylvia Plath
'The Arrival of the Bee Box'

1.

a   What impression of the poet, Sylvia Plath, do you get from reading this poem? (10)

b   What words or phrases from the poem especially help to create that impression for you? (10)

c   The following list of phrases suggests some of the poet's attitudes to the bee box:
– She is fascinated by it
– She is annoyed by it
– She feels she has great power over it
Choose the phrase from the above list that is closest to your own reading of the poem. Explain your choice, supporting your view by reference to the words of the poem. (10)

2.   Answer ONE of the following: [Each part carries 20 marks]
i   Imagine you were asked to select music to accompany a public reading of this poem. Describe the kind of music you would choose and explain your choice clearly.

OR

ii   'The box is only temporary.'
What do you understand the last line of the poem to mean?

OR

iii   Write a paragraph in which you outline the similarities and/or differences between 'The Arrival of the Bee Box' and the other poem on your course by Sylvia Plath, 'Child'.

(Ordinary Level 2003)

Eavan Boland

'This Moment'

1.
a   Why in your opinion does the poet call the poem 'This Moment'? (10)
b   Write out two images from the poem that best help you to picture the neighbourhood at dusk. Give a reason for your choice in each case. (10)
c   Taken as a whole, does this poem give you a comforting or a threatening feeling about the neighbourhood? Explain your answer. (10)

2.   Answer ONE of the following: [Each part carries 20 marks]
i   Imagine you were asked to make a short film based on the poem 'This Moment'. Describe the sort of atmosphere you would try to create and say how you would use music, sound effects and images to create it.

OR

ii   'Stars rise.
Moths flutter.
Apples sweeten in the dark.'
Do you think these lines provide a good ending to the poem? Give reasons for your opinion.

OR

iii   Write a short letter to Eavan Boland in which you tell her what her poems on your course mean to you.

(Ordinary Level 2001)

Julie O'Callaghan

'The Net'

1.
a   Do you think the speaker in this poem is looking forward to her school reunion? Explain your answer with reference to the poem. (10)
b   In your opinion, what word or phrase best captures the speaker's feelings in this poem? Explain your choice with reference to the poem. (10)
c   From the three phrases below, choose the one which, in your opinion, best describes this poem.
    – This is mostly a humorous poem.
    – This is mostly an unhappy poem.
    – This is mostly a serious poem.
    Explain your choice with reference to the poem. (10)

2.   Answer ONE of the following: [Each part carries 20 marks]
i   Does the language used by the poet in this poem appeal to you? Explain your answer with reference to the poem.

ii   Think about the title of this poem ('The Net') and answer the following questions.
- What do you think the title means?
- Suggest a different title for this poem. Explain your choice.

OR

iii   Do you think 'The Net' is a poem that appeals to young people? Give reasons for your answer based on your reading of this poem.

(Ordinary Level 2011)

Acknowledgements

The authors and publisher are grateful to the following for permission to reproduce copyrighted material:

'Funeral Blues' by W.H. Auden is reproduced by kind permission of Faber and Faber Ltd. 'The Voice' by Patricia Beer from *Friends of Heraclitus* (Carcanet Press, 1993). Copyright © Patricia Beer. Reprinted by permission of the publisher, Carcanet Press Ltd; 'At the Fishhouses', 'In the Waiting Room', 'Filling Station', 'First Death in Nova Scotia', 'Questions of Travel', 'Sestina', 'The Armadillo', 'The Bight', 'The Fish', and 'The Prodigal', by Elizabeth Bishop from *The Complete Poems, 1927-1979*. Copyright © 1979, 1983 by Alice Helen Methfessel. Reprinted by permission of Farrar, Straus and Giroux, LLC; 'Child of our Time', 'Love', 'Outside History', 'The Black Lace Fan My Mother Gave Me', 'The Famine Road', 'The Pomegranate', 'The Shadow Doll', 'The War Horse', 'This Moment' and 'White Hawthorn in the West of Ireland' by Eavan Boland from *Collected Poems* (Carcanet Press, 2005). Copyright © Eavan Boland. Reprinted by permission of the publisher, Carcanet Press Ltd; 'New World' by Michael Coady, reprinted by kind permission of the author and The Gallery Press, Loughcrew, Oldcastle, County Meath, Ireland from *Oven Lane* (1987); 'Self-Portrait in the Dark (with Cigarette)' by Colette Bryce from *Self-Portrait in the Dark* (Picador, 2008). Copyright © Colette Bryce 2008. Reprinted by permission of Macmillan Publishers Ltd. on behalf of Colette Bryce; 'After Viewing *The Bowling Match at Castlemary, Cloyne, 1847*' by Greg Delanty from *Collected Poems 1986-2006* (Carcanet Press, 2006). Copyright © Greg Delanty. Reprinted by permission of the publisher, Carcanet Press Ltd; The poems by Emily Dickinson are reprinted by permission of the publishers and the Trustees of Amherst College from *The Poems of Emily Dickinson*, Thomas H. Johnson, ed., Cambridge, Mass: The Belknap Press of Harvard University Press, Copyright © 1951, 1955, 1979, 1983 by the President and Fellows of Harvard

College; 'Valentine' by Carol Ann Duffy from *Mean Time* (Anvil, 1993). Copyright © Carol Ann Duffy 1990. Reproduced by permission of the author c/o Rogers, Coleridge & White Ltd., 20 Powis Mews, London W11 1JN; 'En Famille, 1979', 'Father's Day, 21 June 1992', 'Ireland 2002', 'Madman', 'Nessa', 'Parents', 'Rosie Joyce', 'Six Nuns Die in Convent Inferno', 'Sport', 'The Arnolfini Marriage', 'The Difficulty That Is Marriage', 'The Girl with the Key's to Pearse's Cottage', 'The MacBride Dynasty', 'Wife Who Smashed Television Gets Jail', ' "Windfall", 8 Parnell Hill, Cork', by Paul Durcan from *Life is a Dream: 40 Years Reading Poems 1967–2007* (Harvill Secker, 2009). Copyright © Paul Durcan 2009. Reproduced by permission of the author c/o Rogers, Coleridge & White Ltd., 20 Powis Mews, London W11 1JN; 'A Game of Chess', 'Aunt Helen', 'East Coker IV', 'Journey of the Magi', 'Preludes', 'Rannoch by Glencoe' and 'Usk' by T.S. Eliot are reproduced by kind permission of Faber and Faber Ltd; The poems 'The Tuft of Flowers', 'Mending Wall', 'After Apple-Picking', 'The Road Not Taken', 'Birches', 'Out, Out—', 'Spring Pools', 'Acquainted with the Night', 'Design' and 'Provide, Provide' by Robert Frost are from *The Poetry of Robert Frost* edited by Edward Connery Lathem. Copyright 1916, 1928, 1930, 1934, 1939, 1969 by Henry Holt and Company, copyright 1936, 1944, 1951, 1956, 1958 by Robert Frost, copyright © 1964, 1967 by Lesley Frost Ballantine; 'The Hug' © 1988 Tess Gallagher, reprinted from *Amplitude: New and Selected Poems* with the permission of Graywolf Press, Saint Paul, Minnesota; 'Daniel's Duck' by Kerry Hardie, reprinted by kind permission of the author and The Gallery Press, Loughcrew, Oldcastle, County Meath, Ireland from *The Sky Didn't Fall* (2003); 'Bookends' by Tony Harrison is reproduced by kind permission of Faber and Faber Ltd; 'Hawk Roosting' and 'The Stag' by Ted Hughes are reproduced by kind permission of Faber and Faber Ltd; 'Shancoduff' by Patrick Kavanagh is reprinted from *Collected Poems*,